The past and the present revisited

THE AUTHOR

Since 1963 Lawrence Stone has been Dodge Professor of History at Princeton University. He was Chairman of the Department of History from 1967 to 1970, and in 1968 was appointed Director of the newly-established Shelby Cullom Davis Center for Historical Studies. Professor Stone is a member of the Editorial Board of *Past and Present*, and the author of numerous books, including *The Crisis of the Aristocracy 1558-1641* (Oxford University Press), *Family, Sex and Marriage in England 1500-1800* (Weidenfeld & Nicolson; Penguin) and *The Causes of the English Revolution 1529-1642* (Routledge & Kegan Paul; Ark paperbacks).

LAWRENCE STONE

The past and the present revisited

Routledge & Kegan Paul

LONDON AND NEW YORK

Parts of this book appeared as
The Past and the Present *in 1981*

This revised edition
first published in 1987 by
Routledge & Kegan Paul Ltd
11 New Fetter Lane, London EC4P 4EE

Published in the USA by
Routledge & Kegan Paul Inc.
in association with Methuen Inc.
29 West 35th Street, New York, NY 10001

Set in Linotron Garamond
by Input Typesetting Ltd, London
and printed in Great Britain
by Billing & Sons Ltd
Worcester

Library of Congress Cataloging in Publication Data

Stone, Lawrence.
    The past and the present revisited.
    1. History, Modern.   2. Historiography—History—
20th century.   3. Social sciences and history.
I.Title.
D210.S775   1987   907'.2   87–20480

British Library CIP Data also available
ISBN 0–7102–1253–4 (C)
ISBN 0–7102–1193–7 (P)

To

CONTENTS

Acknowledgments   ix

Introduction   xi

Part I · HISTORIOGRAPHY

1 History and the social sciences in the twentieth century   3

2 Prosopography   45

3 The revival of narrative: reflections on a new old history   74

Part II · THE EMERGENCE OF THE MODERN WORLD

4   The Reformation   99

5   Terrible times: the 1530s   121

6   Revolution and reaction   154

7   The crisis of the seventeenth century   166

8   Magic, religion and reason   178

9   Catholicism   199

10 Puritanism   206

11 Court and Country   215

12 The new eighteenth century   222

13 The Law   241

14 The university   252

15 Madness   268

16 Homicide and violence   295

17 Children and the family   311

18 Love   327

19 Sexuality   344

20 Old age   383

21 Death   393

    Notes   411

ACKNOWLEDGMENTS

Chapter 1 first appeared in a book entitled *The Future of History*, edited by C. Delzell, Vanderbilt University Press, 1976. Chapter 2 is reprinted by permission of Daedalus, Journal of the American Academy of Arts and Sciences, Boston, Massachusetts: Winter 1971, *Historical Studies Today*. Chapters 3 and 17, World Copyright: The Past and Present Society, Corpus Christi College, Oxford, England. These articles are reprinted with the permission of the Society from *Past and Present: A Journal of Historical Studies*, nos 85 (1979), 101 (1983) and 108 (1985). Almost all of the later essays were published in *The New York Review of Books* between 1965 and 1984, and are reprinted with permission from *The New York Review of Books*. Copyright © 1965/84, Nyrev, Inc. Parts of Chapters 4, 7 and 10 come from reviews in the *New Statesman* between 1962 and 1964, and part of Chapter 17 from a review in *The Times Literary Supplement* in 1966. Chapters 5 and 19 are reprinted by permission of *The New Republic* © 1982 and 1985. Chapter 18 is reprinted from *Passionate Attachments: The Essential but Fragile Nature of Love*, ed. E. S. Persons and W. Gaylin, The Free Press, New York, 1987. I am grateful to all these authorities for permission to republish. All the reviews have been abridged, expanded, and altered to focus attention upon broad historical problems and issues and away from the merits and defects of the particular books under review. Chapters 5, 12, 15, 16, 18 and 19 have been added to the essays included in *The Past and the Present*, 1981.

INTRODUCTION

The essays contained in this volume are of two kinds. The first consists of three surveys which try to describe and comment on some of the radical changes in the questions historians have been asking about the past, and some of the new data, tools and methodology which they have developed to answer them. I feel myself to have been peculiarly fortunate to have lived through, and taken some part in, so exciting a transformation of my profession. If, as seems likely, the flow of new recruits into academia is going to be very severely restricted over the next fifteen years for lack of job opportunities, it is probable that intellectual stagnation will set in, since it is from the young that innovation comes. If this happens the past twenty-five years will come to be seen as something of a heroic phase in the evolution of historical understanding, squeezed in between two periods of quiet consolidation of received wisdom.

The second group of essays were originally reflective book reviews, and are all, one way or another, concerned with a single theme. This is the problem which tormented both Marx and Weber: how and why did Western Europe change itself during the sixteenth, seventeenth and eighteenth centuries so as to lay the social, economic, scientific, political, ideological and ethical foundations for the rationalist, democratic, individualistic, technological industrialized society in which we now live. England was the first country to travel along this road, and it was indeed upon the English example that both Marx and Weber fastened.

All the essays in this book were written in the 1960s to 1980s, and they reflect a shift in interest from social, economic and political change to change in values, religious beliefs, customs and patterns of intimate behavior. In this shift the essays do not merely reflect changes in my own perspective upon the past, but rather a more general shift in the 1960s to 1980s from sociology to anthropology as the dominant source of new ideas in the historical profession in general. The books which I chose to review were those which I regarded at the time as making the greatest new advances, and the essays try to display something of the bubbling ferment of new ideas, new approaches and new facts which characterized that Golden Age of historiography. There are, therefore, few aspects of the 'new history' which are not touched upon somewhere in this volume, either generally in the three historiographical surveys or more specifically in the topical essays.

PART I

Historiography

THE EVOLUTION OF THE HISTORICAL PROFESSION

From the sixteenth to the mid-nineteenth century, history became increasingly popular as a field of research, writing, and education, and from Guicciardini through Ralegh and Clarendon to Gibbon, Voltaire, and Macaulay there appeared some of the most readable and enduring works of narrative history that have ever been written.[1] These books were essential elements in creating the high culture of their time, in the sense that all men of education and sophistication were expected to have read and to have absorbed their contents. At the same time, it was expected that an educated man would also be familiar, if only in translation, with the great classical historians such as Thucydides, Suetonius, Livy, Plutarch, and Tacitus.

History was widely accepted at this time as an essential part of a gentlemanly education for three main reasons. First, it was believed to be a source of moral instruction, a story which demonstrated how, thanks to the beneficent providence of God, virtue in the end triumphed over vice. This comforting theory was coolly ignored by Machiavelli in *The Prince* in the sixteenth century and savagely satirized by Voltaire in *Candide* in the eighteenth, but neither work seems to have had much effect on public consciousness. There is thus a great gulf between the attitude of past generations to the moral lessons of history and that of our own day, when it is assumed as almost axiomatic that the wicked will flourish and that most men in positions of political power are self-seeking and probably corrupt paranoiacs, and more interested in furthering their own careers than in serving the public good. This is an utterly different perception of the objectives, stature, and achievements of major political actors from that generally prevalent before the mid-nineteenth century.

Second, history was a prime source of entertainment, providing a

3

narrative story more gripping, more intriguing, and more meaningful than the long-winded and artificial romances and novels of the
day. Sober apparent truth, as elegantly told by historians, was
regarded as more interesting than the imaginative constructs of
creative writers. Third, history was thought to be an invaluable
source of instruction for adolescents, to teach them about the nature
of man and the nature of political power. As such, it was required
reading for the sons of the elite, who were being trained at home, in
academies, or at the universities for future positions of political
leadership.

It is possible to obtain an illuminating insight into the nature and
scope of history as it was regarded in 1850, just at the end of this
long amateur-status phase, and before it developed into a full-
fledged profession carried on almost exclusively by full-time experts
working in universities. The evidence comes from the inaugural
lecture in 1848 of the Regius Professor of History at the University
of Oxford, H. H. Vaughan. Vaughan had a tragic and ultimately
sterile career and produced little or nothing of permanent value, but
he had a vision of what history ought to be which is of considerable
historiographical signifícance today. The key issue every historian
should tackle, according to Vaughan, is 'a disclosure of the critical
changes in the condition of society.' It should be noted that the
emphasis here is on change, not on static description, and that the
nature of change in history is defined neither as recurrent nor
periodic, as in the social or natural sciences, but as critical and,
therefore, presumably unique. The subject matter of history
Vaughan described in the broadest of terms, ranging far into
popular, social, and cultural history in a way that would win the
approval of the newest of the 'new' historians of today: 'There are
institutions, laws, customs, tastes, traditions, beliefs, convictions,
magistracies, festivals, pastimes, and ceremonies, and other such
elements of social organization which are both in thought and in
fact distinguishable from the condition of a national unity.'
Vaughan's definition of the content of history thus went far beyond
the political evolution of the nation state, to embrace the widest
possible range of sociocultural phenomena. Indeed, he went out of
his way to express considerable skepticism about the writing of
history exclusively in institutional terms, on the ground that such
an approach provides a very misleading guide to change over time.
Institutions, he wrote, 'preserve their name, but they change their

qualities, or, maintaining the type of their original structure, they exercise new powers altogether. Under such conditions alone are they truly, actively and healthily permanent.'[2] This is the very same point made by Walter Bagehot in his classic study of the English constitution, published less than twenty years later.[3]

The qualities of a good historian, according to Vaughan, are three: the first is the 'principle of attraction to the facts' – in other words, a passionate curiosity about the past, and an infinite capacity for taking pains in delving into musty archives to find them. The second is 'instincts of expectations more or less definite' – in other words, a preconceived hunch to be tested against the factual record. This is a position normal enough for the social or natural scientist, but one which was for a century to follow to be anathema to the professional historian. The third is the 'habits of rapid recognition' – the intuitive gift of picking out the significant detail in a chaotic mass of documentation.

If Vaughan can be regarded as at all typical in his interpretation of the historian's function as seen in the middle of the nineteenth century, and there is some reason to think that he was, then the subject embraced a vast range of human experience – political, religious, intellectual, social, ritualistic and cultural – and was to be studied by a combination of prior theoretical formulations and the closest attention to the record evidence about the concrete and the particular circumstances. This is why the work of the nineteenth-century scholars like Burckhardt are still so extraordinarily fresh and exciting to students a century after they were written. Historians at that time were still inspired by endless curiosity, and the range of their interests was limitless. This is what makes them so immediately attractive to us today.

Between 1870 and 1930, history developed into an independent professional discipline in its own right. Separate history departments were created at the universities, Ph.D. programs for the training and accreditation of future professionals were instituted, professional associations were formed. Meanwhile, the prime subject matter of history, under the influence of the bourgeois liberal nationalism of the age, was defined as the administrative and constitutional evolution of the nation state and the diplomatic and military relationships between those states. National record offices were set up, and the basic documents relating to these issues were calendared and made available to scholars free of charge. The problems, the methods, and the sources were thus all well established by 1900, and the crowning monument to this great development of the profession was the massive volumes of the *Cambridge Modern History*.

From these volumes it is clear that the professional evolution of history and the definition of its purpose had made enormous strides, but that the gains had only been achieved at a considerable cost. That all-embracing sweep of subject matter, which had been so generously embraced by H. H. Vaughan and others in the middle of the century, had now been severely whittled down, partly because of deliberate choice by the historians, and partly as a result of professions organized within departmental structures, which now laid claims to their own share of the study of man in the past and the present. These included both the social sciences – anthropology, sociology, psychology, economics, human geography, and demography – and also specialized historical sub-disciplines such as the history of law, the history of art, the history of education, and economic history. Secondly, the theory of historicism was triumphant, and it was seriously believed that all that was needed to establish Truth was to cleave faithfully to the facts gleaned from the archives. History was value-free.

The results were both good and bad. The good included the development of narrative political history as a highly professional skill, firmly based on archival research, conforming to the highest standards of scholarly erudition and dependent on the formulation of special techniques in palaeography and diplomatics for testing the reliability and meaning of documentary sources. As a profession, history had come of age and had successfully mapped out the main outlines of the political, military, constitutional, and diplomatic evolution of the major Western powers over the last one thousand years.

On the other hand, as has been seen, the range of questions asked and of methods used had undeniably been severely narrowed. As a result the next generation, the historians of the early twentieth century, can be seen in retrospect to have fallen into two groups, the vast majority belonging to the first category. These were scholars content to elaborate on the problems and techniques established by 1900 and to describe in ever more minute detail discrete events, mainly political or administrative, without showing much desire to relate these events to anything else or to render them meaningful to more than a handful of fellow workers in that one highly specialized vineyard. The pages of the journals published by the official national organizations, and representing the views and interests of the professional elite, such as the *American Historical Review*, or the *English Historical Review*, or the *Revue Historique*, were from 1920 to the 1950s almost entirely devoted to such material, the scrapings and shavings of historical antiquarianism, the publication of documents merely because they had never been published before, and the rehashing over and over again of the same tired old questions. More specialized journals, such as the *Annales Historiques de la Révolution Française*, became even more myopic in their interests. Historians were no longer addressing the educated public: they were talking to a small handful of their professional colleagues.

Both social scientists and the general literate public, therefore, began rightly to accuse the historians of being narrowly devoted to the brute fact – especially to the unique fact – to the exclusion of all theory; of neglecting the irrational, as if Freud or Nietzsche had never lived, so that the men they wrote about were not only wholly rational, but also rational in certain very limited ways – *homo economicus* or *homo politicus* or *homo theologicus*, for example; of harboring very naive views about historical objectivity and value-free history; of underestimating the importance, if only as limiting possible options, of material economic conditions, as if Marx had never lived; of having little serious understanding of the significance or mechanisms of social structure and social mobility; of being content with a two-dimensional analysis of politics without probing the underlying forces; and of concentrating upon the activities of tiny elites and neglecting the masses below them.

The second, very small, group of historians, who were reacting somewhat extravagantly to the ever-narrower empiricism of their colleagues, went to the other extreme and became macrotheorists, either visionaries with global models of human evolution, like Spengler or Toynbee, or men working at a lower level of theoretical generalization, like Turner or Beard. What bound them together was a contempt for most of their professional colleagues, who were content to spend their lives on one tiny fragment of the vast mosaic which was supposed eventually to form the factual basis of defini-tive political history.

These two groups, the fact seekers and the macrotheorists, have been brilliantly described by Professor Emmanuel Le Roy Ladurie as the truffle hunters and the parachutists: the first grub about with their noses in the dirt, searching for some minute and precious fact; the second float down from the clouds, surveying the whole panorama of the countryside, but from too great a height to see anything in detail very clearly.

Meanwhile, the social scientists were also splitting up into two rather similar groups, the survey researchers and experimentalists, on the one hand, and the model builders, on the other. If one wished to be unkind, one could define the former as persons who say, 'We don't know whether what we find is particularly significant, but at least it is true,' and the latter as persons who say, 'We don't know whether what we allege is true, but at least it is significant.' It was the former who tended to predominate in the vast and spreading social science empires in American universities.

Unfortunately, neither group had – or has – much interest in or respect for historical evidence and methods. They did not recognize the relevance of history to their work, nor did they admit the possibility that every individual and every institution is profoundly influenced by its unique past. They despised the qualitative description of sets of unique events which characterized much of the old history, partly since such empirical particularism made impossible any comparative model-building, or even the development of medium-range general hypotheses, and partly since the methods employed failed to provide scientifically verifiable evidence. As a result, skepticism regarding the historical approach was common in political science, anthropology, psychology, and many of the other social sciences. Thus history was dismissed as irrelevant by most economists and sociologists, with a few very striking exceptions, like Joseph Schumpeter and Max Weber.[4] Many, especially the sociologists, cut themselves off still further from the historians by writing in an almost consciously antiliterary style, obscure, turgid, repetitive, flatulent, studded either with meaningless jargon and neologisms or with oversophisticated algebraic formulae and impenetrable statistical tables. As Liam Hudson has pointed out,[5]

> in the entrenched sciences, it is possible to transmit truth in prose that is as crabbed as it is evasive. But where foundations are

shakier, style not merely limits what we find it natural to express, it is, in important respects, the very essence of that expression.

This vice has been especially prevalent in American sociology, although there were and are some very distinguished exceptions like Robert K. Merton and C. Wright Mills, while many anthropologists wrote and write like angels. The prose of the most influential American sociologist, Talcott Parsons, is almost impenetrable to all but the *aficionados*, and it is a style that now shows signs of spreading to France and Italy.

Neither group of social scientists had much serious interest in either the facts of change or explanations of change. For the anthropologist, time was fixed at the moment his field notes were taken, and he probably had little interest in, and certainly no way of investigating, whether the phenomena he discovered were of ancient origin or merely of very recent development within the last generation. Psychology found itself trapped by unverifiable Freudian assumptions about the timeless centrality and universality of certain human experiences in childhood. Freud postulated an endlessly repetitive drama involving birth traumas, weaning traumas, toilet-training traumas, shame and guilt over infantile-childish sexuality, and Oedipal conflict with parents – an inevitable cycle which we now know to be historically, and probably also theoretically, untrue. These are culture-bound assumptions, which may have been correct for some sick members of European bourgeois society of the late nineteenth century, but which do not apply to most persons from most classes in most earlier and even later periods of time. Another flourishing school of psychologists were the experimental behaviorists, collecting ultimately trivial data about observable responses, and their modification under stress, in human beings or rats.

Sociology was also trapped in a wholly static vision of society, partly by its devotion to the survey research technique, and partly by its wholesale adoption of functionalist theory. Indeed, all social sciences were to some extent afflicted with the disease of functionalism. According to this theory, all behavior patterns and institutions must have some functional utility for the maintenance of the social system – and if this function is not apparent, there is promptly invented a 'latent function,' visible only to the expert eye. There are three reasons why the historian must reject functionalist theory if carried to its extreme limits (as it often is). First, all societies contain within them vestigial institutions, even less useful for system maintenance than an appendix in an individual, but which survive simply because they have taken on a quasi-independent institutional life of their own, which enables them to survive the overwhelming evidence of their social dysfunction. The early sixteenth-century church, or the early eighteenth-century university, or the late twentieth-century prison are cases in point. Similarly, the values of all individuals are moulded and fixed in their childhood and adolescence, and if they happen to be living in times of rapid change, the inherited baggage of values they carry over with them from their youth is no longer functional and conducive to system maintenance. Indeed, it is more likely to lead to acute intergenerational tension, protest, and even revolution. Any given society is thus saddled with dysfunctional institutions and dysfunctional values.

Second, many societies find themselves attacked by new and powerful ideologies which threaten to shatter their whole social, political, and cultural frameworks. Early Christianity in the late Roman Empire, Calvinism in the late sixteenth century, and Marxist-Leninism in the twentieth century are examples. Third, and most important of all, man is much more than a rational, system-maintaining being, and there are therefore many aspects of his society, his culture, and his institutions which lack functional utility. Man is among other things a playful animal – *homo ludens* – a seeker after pleasure, a lover of aesthetic enjoyment, a player of games, and for these purposes he devises a wide array of institutions and structures, like Las Vegas and Disneyland, football stadiums and ski slopes, bars and dance halls, gardens, art museums and theatres, which are basically for fun and not function – unless fun is to be defined as a system-maintaining, and therefore functional, criterion. He is also a creature whose life is ordered and given meaning by a series of symbols and rituals, by no means all of which have functional significance, as Victor Turner, Clifford Geertz, and other anthropologists are now busy telling us. They are profoundly illuminating about the deeper levels of meaning in the society, but do not necessarily display function.

Finally, both linguistic revolutionaries like Noam Chomsky and symbolic anthropologists like Claude Lévi-Strauss have suggested that vast areas of speech and ritual have no functional utility at all, but are indicators of underlying processes of thought which govern behavior, often in wholly irrational ways. Even if one discounts much of what is exaggerated in their hypotheses, they have none the less dealt functionalism a severe, perhaps a mortal, blow. If history, along with the social sciences, could at last rid itself of this perniciously simpleminded straitjacket of interpretation, they would all be freer to explore new and more sophisticated avenues of explanation of the vagaries of human behavior.

The result of these trends in both history and the social sciences in the period 1870 to 1930 was that the two moved further and further away from each other. History became more and more myopic and inward-turned, and social science became more and more ahistorical. The result was the breakup of the study of man in the past and the present into small fragments defined, and heavily defended, by professional departmental boundaries. The objection to such a fragmentation is the obvious one, that the solution to an important problem involving real people cannot normally be solved within any one, or even several, of these artificially constructed academic boundaries. The historians were increasingly cut off by the new disciplines from an ever-wider range of human experience, a situation despairingly described by Carl Bridenbaugh in 1965 as 'a mounting tendency to abandon history to the social scientists, who are even more culturally deprived than we are.'[6] The social scientists, on the other hand, were locked in by their total ignorance of, or interest in, the past; by their neglect of the effects of historical conditioning upon any existing situation, set of beliefs, or institutional arrangements; by their lack of interest in the processes of change and by their lack of any theoretical models to get at this problem of change; by their tendency to write crabbed and knotty prose; by their growing obsession either with experimental or survey quantification, often applied mindlessly to the most trivial problems, or with overarching macrotheory. Pleas by historically minded sociologists like R.K. Merton for mutual co-operation in the solution of middle-range problems went largely unheard, both by historians and by social scientists.

About 1930 the tide in the historical profession began to turn, and for the next thirty years or so, a civil war raged between the 'new' and the 'old' historians, especially fierce in France, but also spreading to England and America, which were the two other main centers of historical scholarship at the time. The war began with the launching in France in 1929 of the new historical review, *Annales d'Histoire: Économique et Sociale* (later to be retitled *Annales, Économies, Sociétés, Civilisations*), and the almost simultaneous launching of the *Economic History Review* in England (which in its early days embraced the whole range of social as well as economic history).[7] The battle was long and fierce, and some idea of its intensity can be gleaned from the title, style, and content of Lucien Febvre's book, *Combats pour l'histoire*.[8] By 1960 the 'new historians,' with their social science orientation, had captured the imagination and the passionate loyalty of the most talented of the young; and by 1976 in France, and to some extent in America, they had themselves become the power elite in control of academic patronage and were infiltrating at last into such bastions of orthodoxy as the Sorbonne and Harvard.

In England, *Past and Present*, a journal with similar ambitions and objectives as *Annales*, began a sudden upward trajectory of popular success in 1960, to become by the end of the decade its nearest rival in the world. It has exerted greater influence, perhaps, in America than in England, for although some members of its editorial board were well entrenched at Oxford, Cambridge, and London, and many now hold chairs, they were and are very far from capturing the critical levers of academic power and prestige in these major seats of English learning. It is not without significance that two members of the editorial board have since moved to the United States. In America, the flood of periodicals founded in the 1960s tells its own tale of the triumph of the new movement, while their titles indicate the way the wind has been blowing: *Comparative Studies in Society and History; Journal of Interdisciplinary History; Journal of Social History; Computers and the Humanities; Historical Methods Newsletter; The History of Childhood ᵥ Quarterly; Journal of Psycho-History;* and *Family History.*

Meanwhile, in the social sciences there were some slight, but in retrospect largely abortive, movements back towards history. In political science, Gabriel A. Almond in 1964 claimed that[9]

students of comparative politics, having turned away from history and towards sociological, anthropological and psychological theories and methods, may now be at the point of turning to history again. But if they do so, they will bring with them the questions, concepts and methods acquired in their prodigal sojourns.

In sociology there seemed to be signs of a similar turning back to history, the most notable evidence being the rush of translations into English in the 1950s and 1960s, for the first time, of perhaps the greatest of all historical sociologists, Max Weber. The translation of Weber probably did more to influence the writing of history in the 1960s than any other single influence from the social sciences, particularly since he offered an alternative to vulgar Marxist economic determinism, which was by then falling into historical disrepute; to Marxist theories of class, which were by then appearing to be largely inapplicable to premodern societies; and to vulgar Marxist theories of change in the means of production as the prime generating force for change in other aspects of society. From Weber historians learned that institutional, ideological, and cultural factors were not mere superstructures, a proposition whose validity had become more and more doubtful as research progressed. The translation of Weber, and also a renewed interest both in the early Marx and in Emile Durkheim, were immensely stimulating to historians who could neither understand the language of the acknowledged doyen of current American sociology, Talcott Parsons, nor fruitfully use for their own purposes what little they could grasp of his structuralist theories. They therefore turned back with relief to these classics of the nineteenth and early twentieth centuries.

Among the economists there was also a renewed interest in history, if only in order to gather more concrete data with which to test their theories. The result was an explosion of economic history, organized in very different ways, with significantly different results, in the different countries. In America, economic historians were mostly attached to economics departments rather than to history departments. This gave them a strong theoretical and statistical orientation with which to interpret and analyze their data. On the other hand, when American economics became concerned with macro-econometrics, the economic historians dutifully followed down this theoretically fascinating but historically rather sterile road, with somewhat mixed results. In France, economic historians were attached to history departments and were primarily concerned with data-gathering, with the assembly of long-run time series of quantitative information about prices, wages, money, rent, output *per capita*, capital investment, overseas trade, and other key economic variables. The most distinguished, like Henri See or Ernest Labrousse, used these data to reinterpret big historical problems, but others, like the traditional political historians they so much despised, were more concerned with the accumulation of concrete data rather than with the development of interpretative models. In England, by some mysterious quirk of administrative history, economic historians tended to belong neither to history departments nor to economics departments, but to set themselves up in wholly independent, and inevitably very small, economic history departments. Some members of these departments came out of economics, but most of them were trained as historians and followed the normal empirical methods of inquiry which seem to be deeply ingrained in English culture. Despite some brilliant early successes and a massive output of very high quality scholarly work, it seems likely that the administrative, and therefore ultimately the intellectual, isolation of English economic historians both from non-economic historians and from professional economists may in the long run lead to introversion and sterility. The pages of the *Economic History Review* today show clear signs of a growth of this inward-looking trend.

The most influential social science to turn to history to test its theories and expand its data base was demography, and the astonishing successes of historical demography over the last decades, the result of a fruitful intercourse between professional demographers and professional historians, will be discussed later. The social science which has most recently begun to show interest in both the past and in change over time is anthropology, where the static studies of men like Bronislaw Malinowski and Radcliffe Brown are being replaced by more sophisticated and more historically rooted work by men like Edward Evans-Pritchard, or more recently, the newest symbolic anthropology of scholars like Mary Douglas, Victor Turner, and Clifford Geertz. It is only in the last five years, beginning with Keith V. Thomas's *Religion and the Decline of Magic: Studies in Popular Beliefs in Sixteenth and Seventeenth-Century England* (London: Weidenfeld & Nicolson, 1971), that anthropology has begun to have a major impact upon the historical profession, particularly in the development of studies of popular religion (for example, coronation and funerary ceremonies, public festivities and group displays) or folklore and forms and meanings of popular culture. Whereas economics had most influence on history in the 1930s, sociology in the 1950s, and demography in the 1960s, it is these newer kinds of anthropology which are attracting most attention from some of the younger historians today.

The climactic years of the conversion of historians to an interest in the social sciences and of high hopes that the social scientists would themselves turn back to history came in the late 1960s. Evidence for this assertion is not hard to find. There is the admission at long last into the pages of at least two of the major official journals, the *American Historical Review* and the *Revue Historique*, of articles which clearly show evidence of the methods and problems of social science-influenced historians (the *English Historical Review* has so far maintained its traditional sectarian exclusiveness). The second piece of evidence is the invasion of American history departments by missionaries from the great French school of historians known loosely as the '*Annales* school' (from their in-house journal), or the 'VI^c Section School' (from their institutional affiliation with the VI^c Section of the École Pratique des Hautes Études in Paris).[10] Beginning with an exchange visitor program set up by the Princeton University History Department in 1968, the trickle has now grown to a flood, and the American historical profession is now becoming very familiar with the personalities and the works of this remarkably talented and innovative school of historical research. The third piece of evidence is the transformation of the subject matter of the sessions at the annual convention of the American Historical Association. Today a casual glance at the program gives the impression that hardly any work is in progress in America which is not concerned with the subject matter of the oppressed and inarticulate – slaves, the poor, or women – with problems such as social structure and mobility, the family and sex, crime and deviance, popular culture and witchcraft, and which is not using social science theories taken from psychology or sociology or anthropology and social science methodology like quantification. The first impression is on closer inspection not wholly an accurate one, but the change from 1965 to 1975 is startling.

Excluding sessions on teaching methods, there were 84 sessions at the American Historical Association convention in Atlanta in December 1975. No fewer than twelve of these 84 were concerned

with Women (8), the Family (3), and Sex (1), to say nothing of six
workshops on Women's History. The session on Sex included such
somewhat esoteric subjects as 'Buggery and the British Navy during
the Napoleonic Wars' – not, one would have thought, among the
more historically significant aspects of that period of European
crisis and upheaval. The dangers of fashionable faddishness were
very clear in the contents of the sessions at this convention.

The final accolade for the new movement was given in 1966 when
the *Times Literary Supplement* devoted three whole issues to 'New
Ways in History.' The articles were full of hope about the
prospective new historical millennium, which was, it seemed, just
around the corner, as soon as the old-fashioned historians could be
eased out of their chairs by retirement or death – or perhaps even by
a conversion experience to the New Light. For example, Edward
Shils, who spends half his life in Chicago and half in Cambridge,
England, wrote optimistically:[11]

> We are seeing in the United States the first signs of an amalgama-
> tion of history and the social sciences, at a time in which scholars
> have ceased to regard it as legitimate to confine themselves within
> the boundary of their own society, and historians are beginning
> to free themselves from the bonds of historicism. The outcome,
> which we can see at present only in a very incipient state, is a
> scholarly comparative social science and a comparative history.
> It is the beginning of a true 'science humaine.'

The ambition, so well described by Shils, is a noble one and not to
be dismissed with a sneer. It is to reunite history with all the social
sciences and the humanities, and to create once again a single field
for the study of all aspects of human experience in the past and the
present: to go back, in fact, to 1850, but with all the expertise
accumulated in the last 125 years in a wide variety of different
disciplines.

THE INFLUENCE OF THE SOCIAL SCIENCES

Having described the external evidence of the civil war and the
successful triumph of the revolutionaries within the profession of
history from 1930 to 1975, it is time to define more precisely what it
was that the social sciences contributed to the new movement. In
the first place, they forced historians to make their hitherto

unspoken and indeed unconscious assumptions and presuppositions more explicit and precise. The latter were told that the idea that they had no such assumptions was mere self-deceiving nonsense. Human thought, after all, 'before it is squeezed into its Sunday best, for purposes of publication, is a nebulous and intuitive affair: in place of logic there brews a stew of hunch and partial insight, half-submerged.'[12] The social scientists demanded that it be brought to the surface and exposed to view. Historians were now asked to explain just what set of assumptions and just what causal model of change they were using – things which most of them had tended to avoid like the plague. They were also prodded into defining their terms more carefully. Historians have always made use of general concepts of considerable vagueness, like 'feudalism' or 'capitalism' or 'middle class' or 'bureaucracy' or 'court' or 'power' or 'revolution,' without explaining very clearly just what it is they mean by them. This fuzziness has often led to confusion, and it is now clear, for example, that the two most ferocious and lengthy debates in English historiography since the Second World War, over the rise or decline of the gentry in the sixteenth and early seventeenth centuries, and its relation, if any, to the English Revolution, and the rising or falling standard of living of the working class in the late eighteenth and early nineteenth centuries, were caused, in large part at any rate, by the failure of all parties to define their terms with sufficient clarity. As a result, on many occasions the protagonists were talking past each other instead of confronting the issues directly. The same is also true of the great debate over the social origins of the French Revolution, which has raged for the last twenty years or more.

The third contribution of the social sciences has been to refine research strategies and to help define problems and issues. In particular, they have pointed to the need for systematic comparisons over time and space, so as to isolate the particular and the unique from the general; to the adoption of scientific sampling techniques; and to the use of another standard group with which to compare that under scrutiny, so as to avoid drawing fallacious conclusions from isolated examples. They have also pointed to some repetitive patterns of, and possible explanations for, such phenomena as witchcraft, millenarian movements, and 'great revolutions.'

Their fourth major contribution is in methodology, in the testing of common-sense assumptions and literary statements by quantitative data wherever this is possible to procure. Quantification, when used with discretion and common sense, has many advantages over the older methods of historical verification. In the first place, it uses as ammunition apparently precise testable data, which have to be either confirmed or rejected on logical and scientific grounds, instead of strings of selective quotations from favourable sources. As Dr Samuel Johnson remarked in 1783: 'That, Sir, is the good of counting. It brings everything to a certainty which before floated in the mind indefinitely.'[13] An argument over the reliability of the sources and the propriety of the statistical manipulation is necessarily conducted on a higher intellectual level than a mere battle of rhetorical wits or an exchange of contradictory quotations, and this in itself is a great historiographic advance. The result may make much duller reading, but it sheds more light while generating – usually – less heat.

Second, whatever its positive merits, quantification has even more powerful negative ones. It can often totally destroy unfounded hypotheses based on purely literary evidence and supported because of national or personal prejudice. To give but two examples, theories about the beneficent results of early Spanish colonization of Mexico collapsed utterly when it was discovered by the demographic quantifiers that the Indian population fell from about 25 million to about 2 million in less than fifty years after Hernando Cortes had first landed. Second, the theory that rapid geographical mobility was a special characteristic of the open frontier areas in late nineteenth-century America was destroyed by the discovery of similar patterns of constant movement in the eastern city of Boston.

Third, quantification brings out into the open assumptions that must, if words mean anything at all, be behind the traditional historians' use of such adjectives as 'more,' 'less,' 'greater,' 'smaller,' 'increasing,' 'decreasing,' etc. Such words cannot be used at all unless the author has some unstated quantitative figures to support them floating somewhere at the back of his mind. Quantification forces him to tell his reader what they are, and how they are arrived at. Fourth, quantification helps the historian to clarify his argument, for the simple reason that trying to express ideas in mathematical terms can be one of the most effective cures for muddled thinking that has yet been invented. But it can also be a means of evading thought, and it should also be noted that quantification in history has very great, and growing, dangers and drawbacks which will be examined in detail toward the end of this paper.

The fifth and last contribution of the social sciences to history has been to provide hypotheses to be tested against the evidence of the past. Today, therefore, we all make use, when it suits us, of such notions as the revolution of rising expectations, the disenchantment of the world, the role of charisma in politics, the value of 'thick description' as a way of interpreting culture, the critical importance of a shift from a patrimonial to a modern bureaucracy, the alienation of the intellectuals, the identity crisis of the adolescent, the differences between status and class, the stem and the nuclear family, etc, which are all theories borrowed from other social scientific disciplines.

One of the most notable examples of the consequences both of accepting social scientific determinants of human possibilities and of adopting a comparative perspective which transcends national boundaries is Fernand Braudel's *The Mediterranean and the Mediterranean World in the Age of Philip II*. First published in French in 1949, revised and enlarged in 1966, and finally published in English in 1972–3, this is without question one of the most influential single works of history to have appeared since the Second World War. It is significant for two reasons. First, it stresses very heavily geography, ecology, and demography as the constraining factors which set strict limits on all human action. Second, it frees itself entirely from any national perspective and ranges around the Mediterranean basin, seeing the great clash of Ottoman Islam and Latin Christianity that culminated in the battle of Lepanto in 1571 as a global whole, without any attempt to take sides. Compared with the vast inexorable tides of malaria, timber cutting, soil erosion, demographic growth and decline, bullion transfers, or price revolution, the actions of emperors like Philip II are made to seem of only marginal importance in the evolution of the societies that developed around the great inland sea. This is deterministic, fatalistic history which is alien to both liberal believers in free will and progress and Marxist believers in sociological evolution based on changes in the modes of production. Neither group is happy with this pragmatic pessimism based on the iron limitations of Malthusianism and ecology. Viewed from this perspective, that

dazzling urban phenomenon the Italian Renaissance looks like a
cultural luxury that the agricultural and technological resources of
the area simply could not sustain. This is not to argue that the
Braudel model is either true or false, but merely to point out the
radical shift of historical perspective involved in such borrowings
from the social sciences.

At this point some comment is necessary on how historians ought
to approach the mysterious and manifold disciplines of their social
scientific colleagues. For the historian to get what he wants for his
own purposes out of the social sciences, it is not necessary for him
to undertake a lengthy and intensive training in one or more of
them. The proper attitude of the historian to any social science
should not be one of awe at the arcane jargon, the high level of
theoretical generalization, and the complex algebraic formulae. He
should enter the field merely as a seeker after a specific idea or piece
of information. He cannot attempt to master the field, and he
should not be intimidated by that most idiotic of proverbs that a
little knowledge is a dangerous thing. After all, if the proverb were
true and we took it seriously, we should be obliged immediately to
abandon high school and undergraduate education altogether, since
it is all, by definition, superficial.

There is nothing wrong with poking about in a social science to
try to find some formula, some hypothesis, some model, some
method which has immediate relevance to one's own work, and
which seems to help one to understand one's data better and to
arrange and interpret them in a more meaningful way. Of course it
is of critical importance to choose the appropriate theory or method
rather than the wrong one, and this choice is not made easy by the
fact that no social science today has any one True Model, that all are
in a highly primitive and almost chaotic state. Indeed, at this
moment, some of them, notably economics, sociology, and
psychology, seem to be on the verge of intellectual disintegration
and collapse. On the other hand, this leaves the historian free to
pick and choose what suits him best. He can borrow from Marxist,
or Weberian, or Parsonian sociology; from social, or cultural, or
symbolic anthropology; from classical, or Keynsian, or neo-Marxist economics; from Freudian, or Eriksonian, or Jungian psychology. The best the historian can do is to select what seems to him to
be most immediately illuminating and helpful; to regard any
formula, model, hypothesis, paradigm, or method as a good deal

less than gospel truth; to stick to the firm conviction that *any* monocausal unilinear theory to explain a major historical event is bound to be untrue; and not to be overawed by methodological sophistication, especially in quantification: in fact, to use all the common sense he can muster to compensate for his technical ignorance.

This is, admittedly, a dangerous procedure. Every social science is a rapidly moving frontier, and it is only too easy for the hurried invader from another discipline to pick up a set of ideas or tools which are already outdated. To ignore the contributions of the social sciences is clearly fatal; to master them all, or even any one, is clearly impossible. The most the historian can usually hope to achieve is the somewhat superficial overview of the enthusiastic undergraduate interested in the field. This is usually enough, and indeed, because of the proliferation and the growing specialization of disciplines dealing with man, it is the most that can be hoped for. But the historian should advance gingerly in these areas and never forget the limitations imposed by his relative ignorance. It is an ignorance inescapably dictated by the enormous growth of knowledge, and its fragmentation into specialized watertight disciplines.

THE NEW HISTORY

The 'new history' that has emerged from this great upheaval in the profession over the last forty years has the following characteristics that distinguish it from what went before. First, it organizes its material in a new way; books are written in an analytical, not a narrative, arrangement, and it is no coincidence that almost all of what are regarded as the outstanding historical works of the last quarter of a century have been analytical rather than narrative. Second, it asks new questions; why did things happen the way they did and what were the consequences, rather than the old questions of what and how. It is to solve these new questions that the historian is obliged to adopt an analytical organization of his material. Third, it is concerned with new problems, primarily in three areas, all of them concerned with the relationship between man and society in the past. The first is the material basis of human existence, the limitations imposed by demography, human geography and ecology (a particular interest of the French), the levels of technology, the modes of economic production and distribution, capital accumulation, and economic growth. The second is the huge and still expanding field of social history. This covers the study of the functions, composition, and organization of a whole range of institutions below the level of those of the nation state, institutions for the unequal distribution of wealth, power, and status; institutions for socialization and education, such as the family, the school, and the university; institutions for social control, such as the family, the police, the prisons, and the asylums; institutions for work, such as business firms, monopolies, and trade unions; institutions for local government, such as town meetings, churchwardens, and urban political machines; and institutions for culture and leisure, such as museums, art galleries, publishing houses, the book trade, festivals, and organized sports.

Beyond social institutions, there is an intense interest in social processes: in social, geographic, and occupational mobility, both between groups and among individuals within groups, and changing patterns of distribution of the three key variables: wealth, power, and status. Efforts are being made to investigate such mobility – or lack of it – in terms of group conflict or co-operation. This leads on to a search for the social roots of political or ideological movements, both among the elite leaders and the mass following, for example of seventeenth-century Puritans, or eighteenth-century religious or political radicals, or nineteenth-century liberals, or twentieth-century fascists.[14]

The third main area of activity, and one that is rapidly growing in importance, is a new kind of cultural-social history. This takes the form of intensive studies of the effects on mass opinion of changing communications, through printing, literacy, and the smuggling of censored literature; of the links of high culture to its social and political matrix; of the two-way interaction between high and popular culture; and, last but by no means least, the culture of the semiliterate masses as an independent field of study in its own right, not merely as an important part of the growing field of labor history.

The fourth characteristic of the 'new history' is its new subject matter, namely the masses rather than the tiny elite of one, or at most two, per cent whose doings and writings have hitherto made up the stuff of history. There has been a deliberate attempt to break away from this ancient fascination with the hereditary holders of political and religious power, the monopolizers of the bulk of capital wealth, and the exclusive consumers of high culture. In his 'Elegy Written in a Country Churchyard,' Thomas Gray observed:

> Let not ... grandeur hear with a disdainful smile,
> The short and simple annals of the poor.

Until very recently historians have indeed looked upon the poor with a 'disdainful smile,' and concentrated most of their attention on kings and presidents, nobles and bishops, generals and politicians. In the last few decades this situation has changed dramatically, and some of the major works of history have been devoted to the inarticulate masses, whose annals have turned out, on inspection, to be certainly short but far from simple. The work of scholars like Eugene Genovese on American slaves; of E.P. Thompson and E. J. Hobsbawm on the English working class; of Marc Bloch, Georges Lefebvre, Georges Duby, Pierre Goubert, and Emmanuel Le Roy Ladurie on the French peasantry are generally acknowledged to be major classics of their generation. The challenge, which at any rate for the sixteenth century onward is being more or less successfully overcome, is how to find ways of reconstructing not only the economic and social experience, but also the mind set, the values, and the world view of people who have left behind them no written record of their personal thoughts and feelings: in other words, 99 percent of all the human race who ever lived before 1940. The impetus for this radical shift of subject matter undoubtedly came from anthropology and sociology, but the techniques for probing into such obscure areas of past experience have been and are still being developed on their own by a number of highly imaginative and dedicated historians who have been obliged to discover new source materials with which to work.

As a result of all these developments, there have been at least six major fields of historical inquiry which have been and still are in their heroic phase of primary exploration and rapid development, whose practitioners may enjoy the same excitement as the natural scientists in pushing back year by year the frontiers of factual knowledge and theoretical comprehension. They are fields in the first explosive stage of knowledge accumulation and hypothesis formation.

One of the six is the history of science, both as an internal self-contained story of the exchange of ideas between a hand-

ful of men of genius and as a reflection of the shifting culture
and society of the times. T. S. Kuhn's concept of the scientific
paradigm and how it changes and R. K. Merton's work on the
sociology of the scientific profession have together revolutionized
the field.

The second is demographic history, which has developed as a
result of a recognition by modern demographers of the critical role
of population size, growth, and age composition in determining so
many aspects of life in the twentieth century. The result has been a
massive attack on the demographic records of the past, mostly
census materials and parish registers of baptisms, marriages, and
burials, the full fruits of which are only just now beginning to be
gathered. But already it is clear that at least since the sixteenth
century north-western Europe and North America have experienced a unique pattern of very late marriage and relatively low
fertility. It is also apparent that there have been marked changes in
population size and trends in the past, and in both mortality and
fertility rates, which have combined to form a kind of homeostatic
pattern. This does not destroy the hypothesis of a fundamental
demographic transition in the nineteenth century from high birthrates and high deathrates to low birthrates and low deathrates, but it
significantly modifies its impact and undermines earlier assumptions about a uniform premodern demographic world.[15]

The third is the history of social change, the study of the
interaction of the individual and the society around him. This has
involved the identification of social status groups and social classes,
and the analyses of social institutions, structures, values, and
patterns of individual and group social mobility.

The fourth is the history of mass culture – of *mentalités* (that
untranslatable but invaluable French word). Drawing heavily on
anthropological ideas for inspiration, this new field has already for
the sixteenth and seventeenth centuries produced such striking
works as those of R. Mandrou on popular beliefs, N. Z. Davis on
rituals and festivals, K. V. Thomas on magic, E. Eisenstein on the
effects of the invention of printing and consequent literacy, and
whole shelves of books and articles on witchcraft; for the eighteenth
century it has produced studies of de-Christianization by Michel
Vovelle, and of the spread of the low culture of the Enlightenment
by Robert Darnton; and for the nineteenth century, the emerging
political culture of the working class has been explored by E. P.

Thompson for England and Maurice Agulhon and Charles Tilly for France.

The fifth is urban history, a field that still seems to be a subject in search of a problem, inasmuch as it is only vaguely defined by the fact that it includes everything that happens in cities. At present it is primarily quantitative in methodology and concerns itself with urban geography and ecology, urban religion and social values, urban sociology and demography, urban politics and administration.[16]

Finally, there is the history of the family, which is also currently in an explosive but still incoherent phase of development. This embraces not only the demographic limits which constrain family life but also kinship ties, family and household structures, marriage arrangements and conventions and their economic and social causes and consequences, changing sex roles and their differentiation over time, changing attitudes toward and practice of sexual relations, and changes in the affective ties binding husband and wife, and parents and children.

These six fields only cover what seem at present to be the most promising areas of new inquiry. But there are at least three other candidates for inclusion. New forms of political history, dependent on computerized studies both of legislative roll-call decision-making and the correlation of popular voting behavior with social and cultural variables, have so far made only rather tentative, although hopeful, starts. Both are enormously time-consuming, and the rewards are very slow in coming in. Moreover, the second, which depends on linking precinct or ward voting to ethnic, religious, economic, and other variables revealed in nineteenth-century census data, is open to the 'ecological fallacy,' which is by no means easy to solve. One cannot readily tie statistical information about the characteristics of a group living in a geographical area to the specific political behavior on a certain occasion of a particular, but unknown, set of individuals in that area.[17] The new political history has therefore only just gotten off the ground, despite the massive and expensive data bank now accumulated by the Inter-University Consortium for Political Research at Ann Arbor.

Psychohistory is now making increasingly insistent claims to be a legitimate field in its own right. This can take two forms, of which the first is the study of individuals, of the influence of infantile and childish experience on the psychological makeup, and therefore the behavior and actions, of adult intellectual or political leaders in the past. This involves probing into what is usually a highly obscure period in the life of even the best documented of men and women, as well as making certain theoretical assumptions about the linkage of childhood experience to adult behavior. It is a striking, and disheartening, fact that the most distinguished work in this area is still one of the oldest, Erik H. Erikson's *Young Man Luther: A Study in Psychoanalysis and History* (New York: W. W. Norton, 1958). The second form of psychohistory takes the form of a study of the psychology of particular groups, two of the most influential books of this type being Philippe Ariès, *Centuries of Childhood: A Social History of Family Life* (New York: Knopf, 1962), and Stanley M. Elkins, *Slavery: A Problem in American Institutional and Intellectual Life* (second edn, University of Chicago Press, 1968), dealing respectively with children and slaves.[18] As will be seen later in this essay, however, there are strong indications that psychohistory is developing along dogmatically ahistorical lines, based on unproven social science assumptions about human nature, which are wholly independent of the influence of historically based cultural conditioning.

Whether one should still include economic history as one of the fields still in the explosive stage of development is a very open question. Undoubtedly the heroic first phase took place between about 1910 and 1950, dominated by such scholars as Frederic C. Lane, Thomas C. Cochran, and John U. Nef in America; M. M. Postan, J. H. Clapham, and T. S. Ashton in England; and Marc Bloch and Henri Sée in France. These men, and others equally distinguished of their generation, are now all either retired or dead, and the professional journals and books give the impression that most of the current generation are concerned mainly with mopping-up operations, filling in factual gaps, modifying oversimplified hypotheses, and generally tidying up the field. The one new impetus is coming out of the American Middle West, the so-called 'new economic history,' heavily reliant upon the formal econo-metric models and the advanced mathematical sophistication of pure economics.[19]

The extent to which this 'new economic history' is likely to transform and revivify the subject is still very much an open question. There are grave doubts whether counterfactual history – described by one critic as 'if my grandmother had wheels she'd be a greyhound bus' history – is of much practical use to historians, who are concerned with what happened, not with what might have happened but didn't. It is, after all, a fact that America *did* build railroads instead of relying on water transport for bulk goods. Counterfactual history is a useful methodological aid to clear thinking about historical hypotheses, but nothing more.[20] There are even graver doubts whether the very shaky statistical data surviving even for periods as late as the nineteenth century are firm enough to form a solid foundation for the fragile and sophisticated superstructures which the 'cliometricians' – as they like to call themselves – delight in building. Dizzily impressive to look at, these edifices do not seem very securely built when subjected to detailed critical examination. One of the difficulties with applying economic theory to history is that it works best on problems where the variables are small and therefore manageable; but these problems are often so narrow as to be trivial. Another is that it deals with a world where choice is always free and always rational and is never distorted by personal prejudice, class bias, or monopoly power; but no such world has ever existed.[21]

It is noticeable that except for voting behavior and roll-call analysis, all of these areas fall under the broad rubric of either ecological, social, or mental history; that except for the history of science and individual psychohistory, they are all concerned with masses rather than elites; that they are mostly looking at change over long rather than short periods of time; and that their frame of reference tends to be either larger or smaller than the nation state.

To deal with the problems in these new areas, historians have adopted a variety of new techniques, all borrowed from the social sciences. One of them is prosopography, as the classical historians have called it for a long time, or career-line analysis, as the social scientists call it. This is a key tool for exploring any aspect of social history and involves an investigation of the common background characteristics of a sample group of actors in history by means of a collective study of a set of uniform variables about their lives – variables such as birth and death, marriage and family, social origins and inherited economic and status position, place of residence, education, amount and source of personal wealth and income, occupation, religion, experience of office, and so on. This tool is used mostly to tackle the two problems of the social roots of

political action, and social structure and social mobility. The studies
of elites, which were until recently the principal object of such
inquiries, borrowed relatively little from the social sciences, and the
work of scholars like Sir Ronald Syme and Sir Lewis Namier owed
little or nothing to Vilfredo Pareto, Gaetano Mosca, and other
theoreticians of elitism in politics. Students of the masses, on the
other hand, have been forced – or have deliberately opted – to
follow in the footsteps of the survey researchers, to ignore the rich
evocativeness of individual case studies, and to limit themselves to
statistical correlations of many variables for a sample of the
population, in the hope of coming up with some significant
findings. This technique has now spawned a number of new sub-
branches, such as psephology, or the study of voting behavior based
on a correlation of voting patterns of the electorate with census
data, and roll-call analysis, a study of the voting behavior of
legislators.[22]

The second significant method is local history, the in-depth study
of a locality, either a village or a province, in an attempt to write
'total history,' within a manageable geographical framework, and in
so doing to illuminate wider problems of change in history. The
greatest of these works have undoubtedly been produced by the
French, such as Pierre Goubert and Emmanuel Le Roy Ladurie for
whole provinces, Pierre Deyon for an individual city, and Martine
Segalen and Gerard Bouchard for a single village. But New England
colonial history has been revolutionized by similar studies by Philip
Greven, John Demos, Kenneth Lockridge, and others, while English history has been enormously enriched by the school of local
studies centered at Leicester, in particular the work of William G.
Hoskins and Joan Thirsk.[23]

The 'new' historians have also borrowed from the social scientists
a series of new techniques, most of which have already been
mentioned: quantification, conscious theoretical models, explicit
definition of terms, and a willingness to deal in abstract ideal types
as well as in particular realities. The one new tool they have
borrowed is the computer, which was first devised for the natural
scientists, was then adapted for and adopted by the social scientists,
and is now increasingly becoming a fairly common adjunct for the
working research historian in these new fields. About 1960 historians suddenly gained free access to this immensely powerful but
very obtuse machine, which can process enormous quantities of

data at fabulous speed but only if they are presented to it in limited, often rather artificial, categories, and if the questions are extremely clearly, precisely, and logically framed. Fifteen years of varied experience with the machine has led to a greater appreciation among historians both of its potential uses and its real defects. When dealing with large quantities of data, it can answer more questions and test more multiple correlations than any human mind could handle in a lifetime. But it cannot abide ambiguity and therefore demands that the data be processed in precise packaged form arranged in clearly defined categories, which may well distort the complexity and uncertainty of the reality. Secondly, the preparation of the material for the machine is immensely time-consuming, so that on the whole, while its use enormously increases the size of the sample and the complexity of the correlations of variables, it may slow down research rather than speed it up. Thirdly, its use precludes that feedback process by which the historian normally thinks, thanks to which hunches are tested by data, and the data in turn generate new hunches. When the historian uses the computer, this two-way process is impossible until the very end of the research, since it is only when the print-out is finally available that any clues are provided to possible solutions to the problems and therefore make possible the generation of new ideas and new questions. Unfortunately, it sometimes turns out that omissions or shortcuts in recording or coding the data preclude the possibility of obtaining the answers to these new questions generated at a later stage. Worst of all is the kind of atrophy of the critical faculties that the mere use of punch cards and computers seems to produce. As Dr Hudson remarks,[24]

Most social scientists who rely on punch-cards and computers seem in practice to abandon their powers of reasoning, and as a result, their data are almost invariably under-analyzed, or analyzed in a clumsy ham-fisted fashion. The research worker seems subtly to become the creature of the data-processing machinery, rather than vice-versa.

The historian, despite his largely humanistic training, is as liable to this insidiously corrupting mental deformation as are his colleagues in the social sciences.

The computer is a machine in the elementary use of which most professional research historians should henceforth be trained – a six-week course is ample for the purpose – but it is one which should only be employed as the choice of last resort. Wherever possible, quantitative historians are well advised to work with smaller samples and to use a hand calculator. Despite its undeniable and unique virtues, the computer is by no means the answer to the social historian's prayer that once it was hoped it might be.

THE FUTURE OF HISTORY AND THE SOCIAL SCIENCES

There can be little question that the 'new history' of the last forty years, which has owed so much to borrowings from the social sciences, has rejuvenated historical scholarship and has caused that time span to be, together with the forty years before the First World War, the most fruitful and creative period in the whole history of the profession. Anyone who has had the good fortune to have lived and worked throughout that time can have nothing but pride in what has been achieved in furthering the understanding of man in past society.

Today, however, the future looks rather less promising, partly because the very success of the movement is generating some signs of hubris. In the arrogance of victory, some of the more ebullient and aggressively self-confident supporters of some aspects of the new history are not only making exaggerated claims for their own achievements but are also treating the subject matter and the methodology of the more traditional historians with an undeserved contempt. This attitude is inevitably causing a backlash, so that there are signs of a renewed conflict of Ancients and Moderns – something that can only do harm to both sides. The lack of moderation in the new victors is best epitomized in the title and contents of some new handbooks by some of the most distinguished practitioners of the historical craft in America and in France. In 1971 David S. Landes and Charles Tilly published a collection of essays, *History as Social Science* (Englewood Cliffs, N.J.: Prentice-Hall), in which some very bold claims were made for the 'new history.' In 1974 Pierre Chaunu published *Histoire, science sociale: La durée, l'espace et l'homme à l'époque moderne* (Paris: Société d'édition d'enseignement supérieur), in which he asserted that history was neither more nor less than a social science. The basic assumption behind this attitude toward history as a discipline has been described by a hostile critic in the following terms: 'In some eyes the systematic indoctrination of historians in all the social sciences conjures up a scene of insemination, in which Clio lies inert and passionless (perhaps with rolling eyes) while anthropology or sociology thrust their seed into her womb.' The critic (E. P. Thompson) rightly pleads for a more active and energetic response from the Muse of History to this vigorous assault upon her person (and one more appropriate to the sexual revolution of our time).[25] The principal objection to the total integration of history into the social sciences, as advocated by Chaunu and others, is that 'the discipline of history is above all a discipline of context.' It deals with a *particular* problem and a *particular* set of actors at a *particular* time in a *particular* place. The historical context is all-important, and cannot be ignored or brushed aside in order to fit the data into some overarching social science model. Witchcraft in sixteenth-century England, for example, may be *illuminated* by examples of witch-craft in twentieth-century Africa, but it cannot so easily be *explained* by them, since the social and cultural contexts are so very different.

Looked at from the other side of the fence, in the eyes of some social scientists history apparently is now regarded as little more than a useful data source for the pursuit of their own theoretical investigations. History exists, it has been argued, in part 'for the explicit purpose of advancing social scientific inquiries,' an extreme position admittedly but one which is based on a fundamental misconception of the integrity and importance of history as a study of man in society in the past.[26]

Moreover, this seems in some ways an odd moment at which to choose to hitch the Muse of History to the chariot of the social sciences, almost all of which are currently in a state of severe crisis and in the process of an internal reassessment of their scientific validity. The notion of value-free anthropology has been blown up by the publication of Malinowski's diaries; value-free sociology has come under severe attack – to say nothing of its usefulness or wisdom; value-free psychology is clearly nonsense in the light of B. F. Skinner's self-evident ideological blinkers and the antithetical romantic ideas of R. D. Laing; while the hardest social science of them all – economics – has failed in its job of prediction and cure of the new problems of stagflation, the giant international corpora-tion, and the limits on natural resources. To change the metaphor, it might be time for the historical rats to leave rather than to scramble aboard the social scientific ship which seems to be leaking and undergoing major repair. History has always been social, and it was attracted by the siren songs of the social sciences because it thought – perhaps somewhat mistakenly, it now appears – that they were also scientific.

On the other hand, since every social science is in a process of upheaval and transition, no one can predict their future. At one time sociologists seemed most likely to be useful to historians, and indeed Max Weber and then R. K. Merton were, but they retreated into quantitative survey research or highly abstract functionalist theory, neither of which was of much service. Today the most powerful influence is coming from demography and from symbolic and social anthropology. Ten years from now some other discipline, perhaps social psychology, may have most to offer to the historian. In this perpetually moving frontier the most influential discipline changes from decade to decade, and the historian has to be perpetually watchful for new trends and new ideas. We may today be in no more than a temporary period of reappraisal before a new leap forward.

What can be said with some confidence, however, is that there are at least three ways in which the social-science-oriented historians seem at the moment to be in particular danger of allowing their enthusiasm to outrun their judgment. The first is through an intemperate and injudicious use of quantification as a solution to all problems.[27] It is only too easy to exaggerate the potentialities of the method and to allow the tool to become the end in itself. A classic case of the misapplication of this method is the revisionist work on American slavery of Robert W. Fogel and Stanley L. Engerman, *Time on the Cross: The Economics of American Negro Slavery* (Boston: Little, Brown, 1974). It now appears that the historical source materials were seriously misunderstood and misused, and that in the lust to quantify the authors came up with both false and meaningless results. It also seems that the statistical manipulations were themselves seriously defective. As a result, all the main conclusions of the book, about the relative mildness of slavery as a form of industrial discipline, about the rarity of the forced breakup of slave families, about the adoption by the slave workforce of the white Puritan ethic of hard work, and about the basic profitability and economic viability of the slave system are all certainly still unproved and perhaps untrue.[28] The claim to have successfully demolished a century of historical scholarship by the use of the most modern quantitative methods turns out to be a hollow boast.

There are several morals to be drawn from this example. The first is that no amount of quantitative methodology, however sophisticated, will compensate for misinterpreted or defective data. The only result is what computer experts call the 'GIGO effect': garbage in – garbage out. All statistical information before the mid-twentieth century is more or less inaccurate or incomplete or unhelpful (being normally intended for quite a different use from that to which the historian wishes to apply it), and as a result, it is not only futile but positively deceptive to deal in precise numbers and percentages down to one or two decimal points. A modest proposal for improving slightly the honesty of our profession would be to pass a self-denying ordinance against the publication of any book or article based on historical evidence before the twentieth century which prints percentages to even one decimal point, much less two.

Another serious defect of some of the more ambitious of the quantifiers is their failure to conform to those professional standards, designed to make possible a scientific evaluation of the evidence, which have been built up over a century of painstaking traditional scholarship. *Time on the Cross*, for example, was published in two volumes. The first, containing merely the conclusions, was made available in large numbers, and the second, dealing with sources and methods, in much smaller numbers and at a later date. Worse still, it is impossible to find the evidence in the second volume to support many of the conclusions in the first volume, nor is it possible even to find a list of the records which have been used. The reader is merely assured that unprecedented masses of data have been examined, the full publication of which is only now being prepared, long after the conclusions were published.

On the other hand, it is fair to explain that even when they are scrupulously anxious to describe their sources and methods, it is impossible for quantitative historians dealing with vast masses of information to print all the raw data upon which their study is based, and impossible for them to give more than the most summary account of how the raw material was manipulated. At most, they can do no more than give brief descriptions of sources and methods in a separate (very lengthy and boring) article or appendix, which still may conceal as much as it reveals in terms of how the nuances and ambiguities of the raw data were compressed into simplified machine-readable form, since the full code book is not available. Almost equally obscure is any subsequent statistical manipulation, so that, taking all three problems together, the reader is often obliged either to take on trust or to reject out of hand figures whose methods of verification are not fully revealed to him and would probably be beyond his comprehension if they were.

An excellent case in point is the stimulating new book by Charles, Louise, and Richard Tilly, *The Rebellious Century, 1830-1930* (Cambridge: Harvard University Press, 1975). In order to discover the sources and methods that lie behind graphs 5 to 8, on acts of collective violence in France over a century – the collection, coding and analysis of which took countless man-hours of many researchers over almost a decade – the reader is asked to track down descriptions of the methodology spread over no fewer than six different articles (p.314). Few readers will have the tenacity or curiosity to pursue the subject that far. The great majority will inevitably take the graphs at their face value, without probing any deeper. The major findings of the work stand or fall on the reliability of these graphs, and yet within the book itself there is no provision made for discovering how they were compiled, while the multivariate analyses used for explaining the ups and downs of the graphs are likely to baffle all but the most sophisticated of cliometricians. This is a book which lacks most of the basic scholarly apparatus, but which apparently conforms to the best standards of scholarship of which cliometric history is capable. It is the product of a decade of massive research, and yet the reader is left in a state of helpless uneasiness both about the reliability of the data and about the validity of the explanations put forward. It therefore poses in its starkest form the problem of verification in cliometric history. If the conscientious reader is baffled even by this work, it is certain that he will be baffled by all the other massive undertakings of a similar nature. The conclusion seems to be that for projects of this size there is no way of making all the raw data, the code books, and the statistical methodology readily available to the reader. As a result, the normal processes of verification by a checking of the footnote references is not possible. How historical revisionism can proceed under these circumstances is not at all clear. The only solution seems to be to deposit all the raw data – the code books, the programmes, and the print-out – in statistical data banks to which serious investigators can go to check through the whole process once again from start to finish. Such data banks are now beginning to spring up, as has already been noted, at Ann Arbor and elsewhere,[29] and they may eventually provide a partial solution to this problem, provided that scholars make available not only the end product – the computer tapes – but also the data sheets, code books, and other working materials.

It is only fair to add that the cliometricians are not the first to be guilty of this breach of scholarly standards. One of the most distinguished of all American intellectual historians of the past generation, Perry Miller, also failed to publish his footnotes, but merely deposited them in the Houghton Library at Harvard. When, thirty-five years later, a curious scholar took the trouble to examine them, the results were disquieting in the extreme. It became apparent that so far from relying on the widest possible range of sources, as he had claimed, Miller had drawn very heavily indeed on authors who were very limited in number and one-sided in viewpoint.[30] But an occasional lapse by one of the great traditionalist historians is no excuse for the wholesale adoption of such habits by the cliometricians.

It would be less than helpful to repeat the hackneyed reactionary cliché of the baffled humanist that 'one can prove anything with figures,' since it is very much easier to prove anything with words, which are always put together for rhetorical effect as a means of subjective persuasion as much as for logical argument. But it must be admitted that there is also a rhetoric of figures, and especially a rhetoric of graphs. The whole aspect of a graph can be radically altered by changing the vertical or the horizontal scales; by using semi-logarithmic rather than arithmetical graph paper; by the judicious selection of a base index number designed to highlight or downplay a trend; by using moving averages rather than raw figures. This manipulation of appearances is quite independent of the question of the reliability of the data and whether they have been compiled by extrapolation, adjusted by the application of an appropriate index error, or properly modified to take account of the rising or falling value of money. Percentages are equally open to manipulation, depending on the item which is selected as the base number. One of the major problems of quantification in history is that while the average historian has been trained to scrutinize words with the greatest care and suspicion, he tends to take a graph or table on trust and not to know how to evaluate its reliability or to examine how it has been arrived at. He is not trained to be a professional critic of numerical data.

Perhaps the most serious defect of some, but by no means all, of this new school of dedicated cliometricians, as they call themselves, is their tendency to ignore or neglect all evidence which cannot be quantified, whereas it is precisely from the combination of statistical evidence with literary and other materials of every possible variety that truth is most likely to emerge. Proof of an important historical argument is most convincing when it can be demonstrated from the widest possible range of sources, including statistical data, contemporary comments, legal enactments and enforcements, institutional arrangements, private diaries and correspondence, public speeches, moral theology and didactic writings, creative literature, artistic products, and symbolic acts and rituals.

A further danger arises from problems of scale. A peculiar combination of circumstances came together in the 1960s which made it possible for the first time to assemble and manipulate enormous quantities of data. The circumstances were the advent of the computer, whose use was *de facto* free, a growing interest in social mobility in the nineteenth century, the discovery by scholars of nineteenth-century census data, and a cornucopia of research funds suddenly made available for hiring large teams of helots to work on vast collective projects. The result was the emergence of the huge quantitative research project. Most of these gigantic enterprises, the grandest of which, the tyrannosaurus of the age, has already cost well over two and a half million dollars, grew up on the fertile American soil, but there are also examples in France and England. In a joint American and French project, David Herlihy and others have put on computer tape the Florentine *catasto* of 1427 which lists 60,000 families and 264,000 persons. In France a team working with Le Roy Ladurie has computerized 78 variables for 3,000 districts from the census of French conscripts between 1819 and 1930, while Louis Henry has for years been supervising a gigantic inquiry – much of it by hand-counting – into French historical demography, based both on aggregative data for hundreds of villages and towns and on family reconstitution of a small selection. In England an equally ambitious enterprise of the identical kind is under way under the direction of E. A. Wrigley at Cambridge, including aggregative data for over 400 villages and family reconstitution studies for up to a dozen. The French are also hard at work putting their own census data for the nineteenth century on computer tape, while the same thing is being done for selected sample areas of England by a team directed by D. V. Glass. In North America there are in progress the most gigantic enterprises of all, such as the academic factory directed by Theodore Hershberg which is analyzing by computer the 2½ million people covered by the Philadelphia censuses from 1850 to 1880, and another very similar factory, but operating on much more sophisticated lines, directed by Michael Katz, which is at work on the town of Hamilton, Ontario. These vast undertakings have more in common with the modern scientific laboratory, with its teams of researchers and its massive equipment operating under the direction of a single professor, than with the traditional lonely scholar sitting with his books in his study or turning over manuscripts in a record office.

There are many dangers inherent in such projects, the most serious of which is that to some extent the conclusions drawn from these highly costly and labour-intensive quantitative studies still depend on the utility and reliability of the variables selected for study by the director before the data collection begins. Thus if any variable is missed in setting up the code book – for example, the social distribution of literacy as evidenced by signatures in the 1427 Florentine *catasto* – it is too late to go back and do it again once the omission is discovered. Another drawback is that they depend entirely on the accuracy and completeness of the original records, and there are good reasons for thinking that some records, like parish registers, are seriously and inconsistently incomplete, sometimes for burials, sometimes for marriages, and usually for the births and deaths of infants who die in the first week of life; that tax records are hardly ever reliable; and that censuses, even today, are seriously inaccurate, especially in occupational categories and through omissions of the poor, women, children, and other subordinate groups. Moreover, even if the data are accurate, one still cannot be sure that all the research assistants are coding them the same way. There is nearly always some measure of personal judgment involved in the coding process. Worst of all is the fact that if the individual mentioned in one document is to be matched with that in another, record linkage problems become almost insuperable in the majority of cases, quite apart from the fact that those who move out of the area are lost to the sample altogether.

In view of all these problems, and in the light of the results which have hitherto been published, the question arises whether the concentration of such vast quantities of scarce resources of money and manpower on a few gigantic projects was altogether wise, and whether the funds might more usefully have been spread out to aid the researches of a large number of individual scholars. One can reasonably ask whether $7,000 each given to one hundred historians would have produced larger returns in terms of the advancement of knowledge than $700,000 spent on a single project. The evidence upon which to judge this issue is not yet in and will not be available for several years. In any case, even if some of these mammoth projects produce some really important conclusions in the next five years or so, it seems likely that they may die out altogether in the financial ice age of the 1980s. If so, some of them may leave nothing behind them but miles of computer tape and mountains of print-out, to be wondered at in years to come not so much for their potential value to scholarship as for their sheer size. Some may turn out to be rather like the project to put a man on the moon, more remarkable for the evidence they provide of man's vaunting ambition, vast financial resources, and technical virtuosity in the 1960s than for their scientific results in the advancement of knowledge.

Some of them do no more than prove the obvious, such as that the nineteenth-century labourer lived near his place of work, since he had to walk to get to it. Others provide information which seems to have no useful meaning and would not have been measured except for the fact that it was measurable – for example, the geographical distribution of hernias in early nineteenth-century France, or the average size of an English household from the sixteenth to the nineteenth century (4.75 persons).[31] Some threaten to get so bogged down in methodological problems, particularly those of record linkage – the struggle to prove that the John Smith or the Patrick O'Reilly in one record is the same John Smith or Patrick O'Reilly in another – that nothing of significance emerges for years or even decades. Indeed, the record linkage problem in tying one document to another is so serious that for projects looking at change over time it drastically reduces the number of usable items in the sample, often to those who happen to possess unusual names. The one book which deals with this problem is far from reassuring about the reliability of the results of quantitative methodology dependent on record linkage.[32]

It is likely that many of these excesses contain within them the seeds of their own destruction, but more dangerous for the profession is the growing belief among many graduate students that only a subject which is somehow quantifiable is worthy of investigation – an attitude which drastically reduces the subject matter of history and often leads to the same kind of scholastic triviality from which the early pioneers of the 'new history' were trying to liberate the profession. As a result, many students, lacking the resources needed for these giant projects, plunge single-handed into quantitative studies, many of which do no more than prove something which was already well known from literary sources, and many of which are hopelessly flawed by defects in the raw data. Many others are based on too small a sample to be meaningful – for example, a graph of medieval crime rates over centuries based on the records of a single manorial court of a village whose population was literally decimated by the Black Death. Indeed, the now popular study of crime through quantitative study of court records raises very serious methodological questions about the changing perception and meaning of crime among different classes in the same society – the lower-class criminals and the upper-class prosecutors and judges – at different times. It also raises the insoluble problem whether what is being quantified is the changing reality of the defined criminal activity or the changing zeal of police and prosecutors.[33]

This same conceptual difficulty applies to the work by the Tillys and others on changing levels of violence. Different societies take very different attitudes toward physical violence and draw different lines between the violent and the non-violent. For example, in early modern European regimes, the popular revolt was a semilegitimate means of protest by the inarticulate; it was the only means of protest they possessed, and in the means used there was a 'moral economy of the crowd' which had its own legitimacy.[34] Moreover, despite the terrible consequences of physical injury to individuals in an age when medical technology was either helpless or positively harmful, many societies took very calmly levels of interpersonal violence that would horrify us today. Until these difficult problems of relative historical perceptions are cleared up, quantitative studies of crime or of violence remain interesting but dubious ventures whose statistical results are open to a variety of interpretations.

Most disturbing of all are plans, now apparently in the developmental stage at Chicago, Harvard, and Rochester, by which graduate students in history will in future be trained in two significantly different ways.[35] The first group will be taught in the traditional manner, acquiring a mastery of the bibliographical literature in several major fields, a familiarity with broad interpretive historical concepts, and some experience in the handling of primary source materials. The second group will spend so much time acquiring highly sophisticated expertise in statistical methodology, model building, and knowledge of the social sciences as to make it impossible for them to obtain that broad historical knowledge and wisdom and that familiarity with the handling of sources which have hitherto been regarded as essential prerequisites for the professional historian. This is clearly the beginning of the development of two significantly different kinds of historian. The reason for such specialized training is clear enough, but on balance this is a methodological split which should be resisted if our discipline is to survive as a humane collective enterprise in which we can all participate.

The second area which now threatens to get out of hand is psychohistory. It is obvious that anyone making a serious study either of an individual or of a social group is obliged to make use of psychological explanations of human behavior. If the psychohistorians would stick to the simple proposition that the function of psychology is merely to improve the biography of the individual, all would be well. But nowadays many begin by postulating that there is a theory of human behavior which transcends history. This claim to possess a scientific system of explanation of human behavior based on proven clinical data, which is of universal validity irrespective of time and place, is wholly unacceptable to the historian since it ignores the critical importance of changing context – religious, moral, cultural, economic, social, and political. It is a claim, moreover, that has recently been rejected by many of the more perceptive members of the psychological profession itself. Thus Sigmund Koch has observed that 'modern psychology has projected an image of man which is as demeaning as it is simplistic.' Moreover, the whole notion of quantifying rationality, so dear to experimental psychology, is now looked on in some quarters as a 'disease in consciousness.'[36] Secondly, many of the psychohistorians show an attitude toward the normal rules of evidence so cavalier that it would cause a student adopting such methods to flunk the course. Even the most brilliant of all works in this genre –

Erik Erikson's *Young Man Luther* – depends for its data on a set of events many of which the author freely admits are mere posthumous legend and may never in fact have happened. 'We are obliged,' he says, 'to accept half legend as half history.' Finally, the historian finds it hard to swallow the act of faith by which the argument leaps from the trivial and the individual to the cosmic and the general – for example, from Luther's alleged constipation and his troubles with his father to his break with the Papacy and the emergence of the Lutheran Reformation. Most biographical studies using psychohistory have hitherto proved disappointingly unrewarding or unscholarly, and a more promising area seems to be the psychological study of well-defined social groups undergoing similar high-stress experiences, such as Ariès' dazzling *Centuries of Childhood* mentioned earlier. But this particular line of investigation is now also threatened by psychological reductionism of the most extreme type, as in Lloyd deMause's *History of Childhood* (New York: Psychohistory Press, 1974) and regularly displayed on some of the pages of the *History of Childhood Quarterly*. Perhaps the most promising line of inquiry of all is that which modifies the rigidity of Freudian psychological theory in the light of the influence of social and cultural history. The most successful example of this genre is Carl Schorske's exploration of changes in all aspects of bourgeois culture in late nineteenth-century Vienna.[37] But, so far, he has few imitators.

The third dangerous development is the habit of crunching historical explanation into a single one-way hierarchy of causation, which is now becoming the hallmark of much modern French scholarship. According to this dogma, there are three levels of explanation, of descending independence. First comes the infrastructure, the economic and demographic parameters which set the stage and are the prime movers of the historical process; then the structure, of political organization and political power; and lastly the superstructure, the mental and cultural system of beliefs. Treated too rigidly, this systematization threatens to strangle imaginative historical inquiry. It blocks off any possibility that historical explanation may, in fact, be a much messier and more loose-ended process. To borrow the language of the engineers, it may be a nonlinear, multiple-loop feedback system, with many semi-independent variables, each responsively reacting to the influence of some, or all, of the others.

The basic objection to these threats to the historical profession is that they all tend to reduce the study of man, and the explanation of change, to a simplistic, mechanistic determinism based on some preconceived theoretical notion of universal applicability, regardless of time and space, and allegedly verified by scientific laws and scientific methods. Both historians and social scientists must recognize at least three universal constraints on human cognition which affect all disciplines that are concerned with the nature of man. The sociologist Robert Nisbet has defined them as[38]

first, awareness of the element of *art* that lie in all efforts to grasp reality, no matter how undergirded by pretentious methodologies and computer systems these efforts may be; second, that however one proceeds, with whatever degree of objectivity and devotion to truth, he cannot escape the limitations imposed by the form of his inquiry; and third, that many words through which social scientists, humanists and others approach reality are unalterably metaphoric.

These are truths of which too many of the exponents of the 'new history' have today lost sight. The fundamental mistake, as Liam Hudson points out, is to think that[39]

people are reducible to the form of evidence about them that we find it easiest to collect. The first, statistical, tendency is a form of scholasticism to which we are all subject in greater or lesser degree. The second, reductive, is one of ideology, crude and brazen.

It would be misleading to end this paper on an unrelievedly pessimistic note. But it certainly looks as if the triumph of the 'new historians' has brought into being signs of a new illusion of value-free science, a new dogmatism, and a new scholasticism that threaten to become as stifling and sterile as those which first came under attack some forty years ago. It is impossible to pretend that the great journals of the 1930s, *Annales* and *The Economic History Review*, are still as exciting and stimulating today as they were in their heady youth. The latter is far more narrowly technical than it used to be, and the former, though still as adventurous and innovative as ever, is so large and diffuse as to be difficult to digest. Nor does their newer rival, *Past and Present*, now have quite the same path-breaking significance that it possessed only ten years ago. This decline in excitement is not because of any deterioration in the quality of the articles published, but because it is more stimulating and rewarding to be successfully converting the unbelievers than to be preaching to the already converted. On the other hand, the most recent addition to such journals, the American *Journal of Interdisciplinary History*, is still on a rising curve of intellectual success.

It may be that the time has come for the historian to reassert the importance of the concrete, the particular, and the circumstantial, as well as the general theoretical model and the procedural insight; to be more wary of quantification for the sake of quantification; to be suspicious of vast co-operative projects of staggering cost; to stress the critical importance of a strict scrutiny of the reliability of sources; to be passionately determined to combine both quantitative and qualitative data and methods as the only reliable way even to approach truth about so odd and unpredictable and irrational a creature as man; and to display a becoming modesty about the validity of his discoveries in this most difficult of disciplines.

If this can be done, it will arrest the possible threat of a split in the profession, especially in America. On the one hand, the 'new historians' are riding high on the crest of a wave of successful grantsmanship, laudatory articles in the popular press, the admiration of flocks of graduate students, and the capture at last of some of the key positions of power in the profession. On the other hand, some of the older humanists, like Jacques Barzun and Gertrude Himmelfarb, are now in full cry not only against the indefensible excesses of some of the 'new historians' but also against a latitudinarian toleration for a many-sided approach to history.[40]

There is a growing mood of skepticism abroad about the value to historians of much of the newest and most extreme social science methodology. This comes out well in the cautious tone of the series of articles on the 'new history' in *The Times Literary Supplement* of March 1975, as compared with the optimistic euphoria displayed in the three issues of the same journal nine years earlier, in 1966, whose publication is now cynically described as being the result of an editorial decision 'presumably in order to discharge avant-garde duties.' Warning signals are flying about threats of a new theoretical dogmatism and a new methodological scholasticism. No doubt the conservatives are unduly alarmist. But if the profession does indeed begin to narrow its viewpoint and closes off its intellectual options, as it certainly did in the early twentieth century, it runs the risk either of growing sterility or of factional fragmentation. Only if the two principles of methodological diversity and ideological pluralism are vigorously defended will the necessary intellectual interchange between the historian and the social scientist continue to be a fruitful one, and will the 'new history' continue to replicate its astonishing successes over the past forty years by helping to solve the fresh problems that will arise to preoccupy the next generation of professional historians.

CHAPTER 2 · Prosopography

In the last forty years collective biography (as the modern historians call it), multiple career-line analysis (as the social scientists call it), or prosopography (as the ancient historians call it) has developed into one of the most valuable and most familiar techniques of the research historian. Prosopography[1] is the investigation of the common background characteristics of a group of actors in history by means of a collective study of their lives. The method employed is to establish a universe to be studied, and then to ask a set of uniform questions – about birth and death, marriage and family, social origins and inherited economic position, place of residence, education, amount and source of personal wealth, occupation, religion, experience of office, and so on. The various types of information about the individuals in the universe are then juxtaposed and combined, and are examined for significant variables. They are tested both for internal correlations and for correlations with other forms of behavior or action.

Prosopography is used as a tool with which to attack two of the most basic problems in history. The first concerns the roots of political action: the uncovering of the deeper interests that are thought to lie beneath the rhetoric of politics: the analysis of the social and economic affiliations of political groupings, the exposure of the workings of a political machine and the identification of those who pull the levers. The second concerns social structure and social mobility: one set of problems involves analysis of the role in society, and especially the changes in that role over time, of specific (usually elite) status groups, holders of titles, members of professional associations, officeholders, occupational groups, or economic classes; another set is concerned with the determination of the degree of social mobility at certain levels by a study of the family origins, social and geographical, of recruits to a certain political status or occupational position, the significance of that position in a career, and the effect of holding that position upon the fortunes of the family; a third set struggles with the correlation of intellectual or religious movements with social, geographical, occupational, or other factors. Thus, in the eyes of its exponents, the purpose of prosopography is to make sense of political action, to help explain ideological or cultural change, to identify social reality, and to describe and analyze with precision the structure of society and the degree and the nature of the movements within it. Invented as a tool of political history, it is now being increasingly employed by the social historians.

The major contributors to the development of prosopography can be divided into two fairly distinct schools. Those of the elitist school have been concerned with small-group-dynamics, or the interaction, in terms of family, marriage, and economic ties, of a restricted number of individuals. The subjects of study have usually been power elites, such as Roman or United States senators or English MPs or cabinet members, but the same process and model can be and have been applied to revolutionary leaders as well.[2] The technique employed is to make a meticulously detailed investigation into the genealogy, business interests, and political activities of the group, the relationships being displayed by means of detailed case studies, supported to only a secondary and relatively minor degree by statistical underpinnings. The purpose of such research is to demonstrate the cohesive strength of the group in question, bound together by common blood, background, education, and economic interests, to say nothing of prejudices, ideals, and ideology. When the main problem is political, it is argued that it is this web of purely social and economic ties which gave the group its unity and therefore its political force, and to a considerable extent also its political motivation, inasmuch as politics is a matter of the ins against the outs. This school has owed little or nothing to the social sciences, despite the fact that it could have learned much from them, and has been largely innocent of conscious sociological or psychological theory. Its assumptions, however, are clearly that politics is a matter of the interplay of small ruling elites and their clients rather than mass movements, and that self-interest, meaning a fierce Hobbesian competition for power and wealth and security, is what makes the world go round.[3]

The second is the more statistically-minded mass school, which deliberately draws its inspiration from the social sciences. The members of this school have mostly, but by no means entirely concerned themselves with large numbers, about all – or indeed sometimes any – of whom in the nature of things nothing very detailed or very intimate can be known, since they are dead and therefore unavailable for an interview. The members of this school have a sense that history is determined by the movements of popular opinion rather than by the decisions of so-called 'great men,' or by elites, and they have been aware that human needs cannot usefully be defined exclusively in terms of power and wealth. They have necessarily been more concerned with social history than political history, and have therefore tried to ask a wider, if inevitably more superficial, set of questions than those usually posed by the members of the elitist school. They have also been far more concerned with testing the statistical correlations of the many variables than with conveying a sense of historical reality by a series of detailed case studies. In so far as they have tried to describe the past they have tended to do so more by the construction of Weberian ideal-types than by presenting a series of concrete examples. Much of their work has been concerned with social mobility, but some of it has looked for statistically meaningful relationships between environment and ideas, and between ideas and political or religious behavior. The two schools, therefore, differ significantly in their subjects of study, and somewhat in their presuppositions, means, and end, but they are similar in their common interest in the group rather than in the individual or the institution.

Both the elitist and the mass schools first became clearly identifiable in the profession in the 1920s and 1930s, when a number of works appeared that had a profound effect on all subsequent development. The raw materials from which these prosopographical studies were and are constructed are mostly of three broad kinds: bare lists of names of holders of certain offices or titles, or professional or educational qualifications; family genealogies; and full biographical dictionaries, which are usually built up in part from the first two categories and in part from an infinitely wider range of sources. The collection of biographical materials of this kind had been in progress for a very long time before the first professional prosopographers appeared on the scene. To take the case of English history (although Roman history would be an equally good example),[4] throughout the late eighteenth, nineteenth, and early twentieth centuries, diligent antiquaries, clergymen, and scholars had been producing biographical information of all kinds in quite astonishing quantities. From public and private presses there poured a flood of biographical collections of every description and every quality: MPs, peers, baronets, gentry, Archbishops of Canterbury, London clergy, Lords Chancellor, judges, sergeants at law, army officers, Catholic recusants, Huguenot refugees, Oxford and Cambridge alumni – the list is almost endless.[5]

The purpose of this outpouring – which was matched in the United States, Germany, and elsewhere – is not at all clear, since prosopography as a historical method had not been invented, and these publications were not used by professional historians except as quarries from which to dig out chunks of information about particular individuals. In terms of psychological motivation, these obsessive collectors of biographical information belong to the same category of anal-erotic males as the collectors of butterflies, postage stamps, or cigarette cards; all are by-products of the Protestant Ethic. But part of the stimulus came from local or institutional pride and affection, which took the form of a desire to record the past members of a corporation, college, profession, or sect. Part also derived from that inexhaustible passion for genealogy and ancestor-hunting which has gripped large sections of the English upper classes since the sixteenth century. With the huge expansion of the educated middle class in the nineteenth century, and with the growth of university and public libraries, there was at last a large enough market to justify the publication of these rather esoteric and unreadable volumes.

The supreme achievement of this century-long English movement for collective biography was the undertaking of the great *Dictionary of National Biography*, which is an enduring monument to the drive and dedication of the Victorians in the pursuit of information about the individual dead. When the first historical prosopographers got down to work after the First World War, they therefore found at hand a mass of biographical information already collected and in print, and merely waiting to be analyzed, collated, and used to construct an intelligible picture of society and politics.

The first historian to adopt the elitist method of prosopography to attack a major historical problem was Charles Beard, who as early as 1913 offered an explanation of the establishment of the

American Federal Constitution by a close analysis of the economic and class interests of the Founding Fathers.[6] In the key chapter, 'The Economic Interests of the Members of the Convention,' he asked himself whether they represented

> distinct groups whose economic interests they understood and felt in concrete, definite forms through their own personal experience with identical property rights, or were they working merely under the guidance of abstract principles of political science.

His conclusion was unambiguous: 'The first firm steps towards the formation of the Constitution were taken by a small and active group of men immediately interested through their personal possessions in the outcome of their labours,' a conclusion reached through an economic biography of all those connected with its framing. This remarkable and brilliant pioneering work seems to have had curiously little influence on post-war developments, perhaps because of the dogmatically rigid framework of economic determinism within which it was constructed. In his preface of 1935 Beard attempted to deny that his attitude to economic determinism was all-embracing, that he was deeply influenced by Marxist thought, or that he was attributing sordid and self-interested motives to the Founding Fathers. But his disclaimers are not altogether convincing.[7] What Beard contributed to elitist prosopography was a suspicious curiosity about the finances of a political actor and the hypothesis that they are important. What he missed was the role of social and kinship ties which were to bulk so large in the later studies of Sir Lewis Namier and others. On the other hand, Beard's work should have been familiar to Namier, who, however much he may have been repelled by the Marxist economic determinism, must surely have been impressed by the interpretive power of the method.

A year later another American scholar, A.P. Newton, published a less well known book which carried the method a little further.[8] He carefully tracked down kinship relationships and economic connections in order to demonstrate the formation of the Puritan opposition leadership to Charles I in the 1630s. His book was clearly a modest forerunner of Namier, but for some reason, perhaps because of the rather forbidding title, it never attracted much general attention.[9]

The real breakthrough into general acceptance by the profession did not come until the publication of Namier's *Structure of Politics*

at the Accession of George III (London, 1929), Sir Ronald Syme's
Roman Revolution (Oxford, 1939), and R. K. Merton's *Science,
Technology, and Puritanism in Seventeenth Century England
(Osiris,* IV, 1938). All three were able to draw on the store of
biographical information which had been accumulated and published over the previous century. Merton used the *Dictionary of
National Biography* for his work, Syme was indebted to two
German historians, M. Gelzer and F. Münzer,[10] and Namier could
exploit 130 years of data-collection about the lives of MPs. The
pioneer work of the pre-war German school of historiography was
of considerable importance for the later development of classical –
and possibly also of modern – prosopography, but its achievements
have been overshadowed by the more arresting and ambitious work
of Namier and Syme. Apart from Beard and Newton, the two latter
were the first historians of outstanding capacity to use this kind of
approach to attempt a major reinterpretation of a critical political
development which had been studied *ad nauseam* by more conventional historians over a very long period. Both worked impression-
istically through case studies and personal vignettes, which they
used to build up a picture of elitist personal interests, mainly
kinship groupings, business affiliations, and a complicated web of
favours given and received.

The third study, by R K. Merton, was rather different in both its
objectives and its method. As befitted an American sociologist
rather than a British historian, what he produced was a statistically
based group biography, rather than a group portrait pieced together
from a series of case studies. The problem he set himself was also
different, since he was not trying to account for specific political
actions but for a state of mind, and was explaining a mental set not
by family ties or economic interests but by ideological affiliations:
he was attempting to link a favourable attitude toward natural
science with allegiance to what he loosely described as Puritanism.
On the other hand, his work was similar to that of Namier and
Syme in that he was examining, although at a much shallower depth
of research, the behavior of an elite rather than a mass.

Both Syme and Namier, but particularly the latter, were to have
an enormous influence on the next generation of scholars in their
fields of specialty. Some years ago a reviewer surveyed the recent
and current work of historians of eighteenth-century British politics, and from the problems they set themselves and the methods

they used for resolving them, concluded that they were all members of a single corporation: 'Namier, Inc.'[11] Today both the case-study and the statistical methods – and especially the latter – have spread to other fields and time periods, and are being applied on an ever-widening scale to every aspect of the historical process, at every time and in every place. The mass school now has a flourishing political sub-branch called psephology, or the analysis of the voting behavior of the electorate; and the elitist school has spawned a more scientific sub-branch, roll-call analysis of the legislature. Both these new special fields are absorbing increasing amounts of time, money, and attention from historians and political scientists.[12]

INTELLECTUAL ROOTS

That these developments occurred at the same period in the writings of scholars working entirely independently (Sir Ronald Syme assures me that he had not read Namier) proves that there is more to them than mere serendipity. Prosopography would not have flourished the way it did in the 1920s and 1930s had it not been for a crisis in the historical profession, which was already discernible to the more perceptive young men of the coming generation.[13] This crisis stemmed from the near-exhaustion of the great tradition of Western historical scholarship established in the nineteenth century. Based on a very close study of the archives of the state, its glories had been institutional, administrative, constitutional, and diplomatic history. But the major advances in these areas had all been made by the race of giants of the late Victorian and Edwardian periods, the outstanding figures for English history being C. W. Stubbs, T. F. Tout, F. W. Maitland, and S. R. Gardiner. In their search for new and more fruitful ways to understand the working of the institutions, some young historians just before and after the First World War began to turn from the close textual study of political theories and constitutional documents or the elucidation of bureaucratic machinery to an examination of the individuals concerned and the experiences to which they had been subjected. Exasperated by the windy pieties of a generation of historical interpreters of the framing of the American Constitution, Beard introduced his own book with the acid remark that 'The Constitution was of human origin, immediately at least, and it is now discussed and applied by human beings who find themselves

engaged in certain callings, occupations, professions and interests.'
In his challenging introductory statement a quarter of a century
later, Syme also declared open war upon the older generation of
historians.[14] When dealing with the attitudes of Parliament toward
the American colonies before the Revolution, Namier did not
bother himself with the political theory of no taxation without
representation. Instead he asked:[15]

> What acquaintance with the American Colonies had the house in
> which the Stamp Act was passed and repealed, and in which the
> Townshend Duties were enacted? How many of its Members
> had been to the American Colonies, had connections with them,
> or had an intimate knowledge of American affairs? Were any of
> them American born?

Following this example, similar questions about who rather than
what have been asked about such diverse questions in English
historiography as Magna Carta, the House of Commons, riots, the
civil service and the Cabinet.[16] The unstated premise is that an
understanding of who the actors were will go far toward explaining
the workings of the institution to which they belonged, will reveal
the true objectives behind the flow of political rhetoric, and will
enable us better to understand their achievement, and more correctly to interpret the documents they produced.

The direction in which this attack on the conventional approach
to political institutions and policies would develop was powerfully
influenced by other important trends in the intellectual climate of
the period, of which the first and most important was cultural
relativism. Greater familiarity with foreign countries through travel
combined with the growing volume of anthropological studies to
reveal the extraordinary range of cultural patterns that have been
adopted by different societies around the world. The educated
public became uneasily aware that morals, laws, constitutions,
religious beliefs, political attitudes, class structures, and sexual
practices differ widely from one society to another, and this
awareness in time led to a recognition that there are few universal
norms of human behaviour or social organization. The stress on
environmental conditioning as the determining factor in creating
this variety was all the greater because the 1920s and 1930s was a
period when genetic explanations of cultural differences were not
treated with the seriousness it now begins to appear that they may
possibly deserve.[17] Social Darwinism, which was a powerful

influence around the turn of the century, laid far more stress on nature than nurture. However, the Freudian psychologists, who soon afterwards began to come into their own, laid greater stress upon the role of nurture, with particular emphasis on childhood and early sexual experience. It must be admitted, however, that Freudian psychology has not been much use to the historian, who is usually unable to penetrate the bedroom, the bathroom or the nursery. If Freud is right, and if these are the places where the action is, there is not much the historian can do about it. The subsequent modification of Freudian ideas by Erik Erikson, according to which character formation continues through childhood and adolescence, and crystallizes in an 'identity crisis' just before maturity, opens up new possibilities for the historian, who can sometimes discover a little about the thoughts and feelings of his subject in adolescence, even if he knows little or nothing about his infancy and early childhood. Up to now, however, Eriksonian psychology has been very little used by historians, and a far more important influence upon the profession has been behaviorist theories of challenge and response to environmental pressures.

The third influential element in the intellectual climate of the age was the decay of confidence in the integrity of politicians, and the decline of faith in the importance of constitutions. Much of this cynicism was generated by the political and moral disaster of the First World War, followed by the collapse of hopes of a better world order. Many people came to believe that this was the time when millions died and European civilization disintegrated, while politicians jockeyed for place and power by outbidding each other in the jingo rhetoric of hate. The result was the penetration into intellectual circles and into the upper classes of the ancient folklore of the poor, that all politicians are crooks. This was the muckraking era, in which the top was blown off the nineteenth century by books like Lytton Strachey's *Eminent Victorians* (1918) and Mathew Josephson's *The Robber Barons* (1934). Nor should it be forgotten that the events of the period did nothing to redress the balance; it was the era of Teapot Dome, Jimmy Thomas, and Stavisky. These popular assumptions and actual discoveries about the moral, and in particular the financial, laxity of politicians, led historians to think that if only one could get access to the private papers of past political actors, similar motives would be revealed as a driving force in history.

Apart from Fascism (which had little intellectual appeal), Marxism was the only powerful ideology of the period. Marxism gave many historians a somewhat naive belief in economic determinism, which strongly reinforced these dark suspicions about human motivation. Beard thus declared that 'the direct compelling motive' behind the framers of the American Constitution 'was the economic advantages which the beneficiaries expected would accrue to themselves first from their action.'[18] In its early stages, therefore, prosopography reflected a deeply pessimistic attitude toward human affairs, and was conducted either by radicals under Marxist influence, like Beard, or by men like Sir Lewis Namier and Sir Ronald Syme, who were openly of a conservative frame of mind. Syme frankly admitted of his own work that 'The design has imposed a pessimistic and truculent tone, to the almost complete exclusion of the gentler emotions and the domestic virtues,' while an early reviewer commentated with dismay of Namier's book that 'The political system which it describes is certainly not attractive, based as it was upon a possibly enlightened but a certainly sordid self-interest.'[19]

Nor was this cynicism confined to attitudes toward individual politicians; it also covered political systems. If revolutions mean no more than substitution of one grasping and self-centered ruling elite for another, if a handful of unscrupulous men steer the ship of state the way they want, whatever the constitutional flag under which they sail, then the difference between tyranny and democracy becomes blurred, to say the least. From this point of view the elitist school of historical prosopographers of the 1930s was deeply affected by the contemporary crisis of confidence in democracy. Namier deliberately set out to destroy theories about a tyrannical conspiracy by George III against the British constitution, and Syme appeared to remove any basis for moral judgments about the destruction of the Roman republic by Augustus. In 1939, A. Momigliano applied to Syme his own description of Tacitus: 'a monarchist from perspicacious despair of human nature.'[20] Robert Dahl has rightly observed, however, that 'for individuals with a strong strain of frustrated idealism, it [elite theory] has just the right touch of hard-boiled cynicism.'[21] The elite theorist and the elite historian tend to be disappointed egalitarians, whose misanthropy springs directly from outraged moral sentiment.

The attitude toward the workings of politics taken by the early prosopographers appears to owe little to the writings of political theorists. Marx himself stressed the role first of the feudal lords and then of the bourgeoisie, and directed attention to the self-interest that guided their actions. But the first fully-fledged elitist political theories came out of Europe in the early twentieth century, with the writings of R. Michels, G. Mosca, and V. Pareto. Although Michels was available in French, Pareto and Mosca were not translated into English before the 1930s, and there is no evidence that they had the slightest influence in historical circles in the Anglo-Saxon world until that time. Namier, Merton, and Syme were strongly anti-Marxist, and yet only Merton appears to have been familiar with these non-Marxist elitist models. What we have, therefore, is the development by political scientists of a full-blown theory of rule by elites a generation before the historians set to work. But apart from Merton, the historians carried out their empirical studies based on their own semiconscious assumptions about political behavior, without the benefit of the political theory which would have provided them with the framework they needed. It is one of the more bizarre episodes of intellectual history, a consequence of the slowness of the great European social scientists to be translated into English, and of the isolation of history from the other social sciences in the early twentieth century.

A key feature of the elitist interpretation of the historical process is the deliberate and systematic removal of both party programmes and ideological passions from the centre of the political stage, and their replacement by a complex web uniting patrons with their clients and dependants. For Roman history, this is expressly stated by Professors L. R. Taylor and E. Badian.[22] For English history Namier substituted the 'connection' for the party as the central organizing principle of mid-eighteenth-century politics, K. B. McFarlane invented the phrase 'Bastard Feudalism' to represent not dissimilar patron-client relationships which he believed could explain the fifteenth century, while Sir John Neale borrowed the word 'clientage' from the classical historians to make sense of the Elizabethan political system. In a key passage the latter wrote,[23]

> most of the gentry seem to have grouped themselves in close or
> loose relationships around one or other of the few great men of
> the country. ... The grouping and interdependence of the gentry,
> with its accompanying and constant struggle for prestige and
> supremacy, permeated English life. It assumed the part played

by politics in our modern society, and in the country, is the main clue to parliamentary elections.

For some scholars, prosopography was not merely a way of ignoring passions and ideas, it was adopted for the specific purpose of neutralizing these disturbing and intractable elements.

A fourth stimulus to elitist prosopography, which in turn reinforced the new awareness of the essential role played in politics by associations of dependants, was the almost obsessive concern of the anthropologist for the family and kinship, the full impact of which is only just beginning to make itself fully felt in the historical profession today. It was Namier's work on mid-eighteenth-century English politics which first drew the attention of historians to the potentialities of family arrangements and kinship links as political bonds.[24] It is perhaps not too farfetched to see a parallel between the preoccupation with such linkages of the elitist school of historians and similar preoccupations in contemporary fiction, notably Proust's *A la recherche du temps perdu* and Anthony Powell's more recent *A Dance to the Music of Time*.

These intellectual trends are sufficient in themselves to explain the rise of the elitist school between the wars. The more scientifically orientated mass school obviously owed something to all of them, but much more to the concurrent rise of the social sciences. From Weber to Merton the most intelligent and most successful of the social scientists have limited themselves to advancing middle-range hypotheses about such things as suicide or bureaucracy or receptivity to right-wing political views. Historical prosopography is obviously immensely valuable as a source of material for such investigations, and it is no coincidence that Marx and Weber and Merton have all had strong historical interests. The main inspiration for the type of questions asked and the methods employed to solve them by Merton and by a host of subsequent historical investigators of the mass school was the development of social survey techniques. From them comes the confidence in the sampling method and the habit of asking a very wide range of questions, many of which turn out to be wholly irrelevant, in the hope of picking out the significant variables by statistical manipulation later on.

Given these many converging trends in the intellectual life of the period between the two World Wars, it is hardly surprising that it was then that prosopography grew up. Indeed, in retrospect what is surprising is rather the slowness of its advance upon the historical stage, for it was not until the 1950s or even the 1960s that significant numbers of students began to use the method, and that a steady stream of useful findings began to be published.

LIMITATIONS AND DANGERS

Sufficient experience has now accumulated to make it possible to appreciate both the potentialities and the limitations of prosopographical studies. Some of the errors and deficiencies are inevitable consequences of pioneering in a new method, and can be avoided in the future by learning from the mistakes of the past. Others, however, go deeper, and arise from some political and psychological presuppositions which are embedded in the foundations upon which prosopography rests.

It is self-evident that biographical studies of substantial numbers of persons are possible only for fairly well-documented groups, and that prosopography is therefore severely limited by the quantity and quality of the data accumulated about the past. In any historical group, it is likely that almost everything will be known about some members of it, and almost nothing at all about others; certain items will be lacking for some, and different items will be lacking for others. If the unknowns bulk very large, and if, with the seriously incompletes, they form a substantial majority of the whole, generalizations based on statistical averages become very shaky indeed, if not altogether impossible. Studies which have to be confined to that tenth or twentieth part of the group about which enough is known depend for their reliability on the recorded minority being a genuinely random sample of the whole. But this is an unlikely assumption, since the very fact that more than usual has been recorded about the lives and careers of a tiny minority indicates that they were somehow atypical. To a degree which cannot measured, studies based on such fragmentary evidence will tend to exaggerate, and perhaps hopelessly to distort, the status, education, upward mobility, and so forth of the group under examination. For most social groups in most areas prosopography cannot usefully be employed before the explosion of record materials in the sixteenth century, caused by the invention of the printing press, the spread of literacy and the growth of the bureaucratic, record-keeping nation state.

The only exception to this generalization is when there exists a single detailed census-type survey, such as the Florentine *catasto* of 1427. These rare documents allow the historian to make a cross-section through a society at a given moment, but they cannot answer any questions about change over time, since there is usually nothing before or after with which to compare them. They also need to be handled with care, since they may silently omit certain classes of persons, such as beggars, their categories may be vague or erratic, and their financial statistics are likely to underestimate the affluence of the rich relative to the poor.

The second limitation imposed by the record evidence is that of status. At all times and in all places, the lower one goes in the social system the poorer becomes the documentation. As a result, most studies that have already been made or are in progress today have been devoted to elites. The most popular subject for prosopography has been and still is political elites, but other groups which lend themselves most readily to such treatment are members of certain high-status categories, such as civil servants, army officers, upper clergy, intellectuals and educators, lawyers, doctors, members of other professional bodies, and industrial and commercial entrepreneurs. The only elements of the lower classes about whom something can be done in anything more than a highly impressionistic way are persecuted minorities, since police reports and legal records often supply much of the necessary information, especially in societies with a long tradition of heavy bureaucratic and police control like France. The odd result is that the only groups of poor and humble about whom we can sometimes find out a good deal are minority groups, which are by definition exceptional since they are in revolt against the *mores* and beliefs of the majority.

The third limitation imposed by the evidence arises from the fact that it is abundant for some aspect of human life and almost nonexistent for others. The surviving records are concerned first and foremost with the amount, type, ownership, and transmission of property. It is this which is the prime concern of official and private legal records, official tax records, and public and private administrative records, which together form the vast bulk of the written material of the past. There is thus a strong bias toward treating the individual as *homo economicus*, and to study him primarily in the light of his financial interests and behavior, since this is what the records illuminate in the greatest clarity and detail. But economic interests may conflict, and even when the interest is clear, it is impossible to be sure that this is the overriding consideration. Moreover, the split between the compromisers and the last-ditchers is often more important politically than the split between clearly defined economic interest-groups.[25]

After economic interests, the second item of information that is relatively easy to discover about a person is his family background and connections. Among the upper classes marriage has been used in the past to provide young men with useful friends and contacts, as well as to merge properties and so create great territorial estates. Family ties have also played an important part in the construction of political groups and parties at all times from the Middle Ages to the eighteenth century and beyond. One has only to think of the Howards and Dudleys in sixteenth-century England, the Villiers in the early seventeenth century, the Pelhams in the eighteenth, and the Cecils and Cavendishes in the late nineteenth and early twentieth, to recognize the continuing importance of this factor. But this does not answer the question of how far it is safe to pursue this line of reasoning, for the cementing role of kinship clearly varies from place to place, from time to time, and from social level to social level. There are countless examples in history of members of the same family who have disagreed among themselves, often with extreme violence. Moreover, even when kinship ties were strong and can be shown to have been so, there are limits to the meaningful pursuit of genealogical links. Two diligent prosopographers working on the Long Parliament of 1640 tracked down genealogical connections which related the radical John Hampden to eighty fellow MPs, but unfortunately these kin turned out to be of widely varying political and religious opinions. When the authors found that by going back far enough they could find a kinship connection between Charles I and Oliver Cromwell, they realized that they had perhaps passed beyond the outer limits of utility of this particular line of inquiry. Similar doubts have been recently expressed about the role ascribed by the prosopographical school to kinship in classical Rome.[26]

ERRORS IN THE CLASSIFICATION OF THE DATA

Meaningful classification is essential to the success of any study, but unfortunately for the historian, every individual plays many roles, some of which are in conflict with others. He belongs to a civilization, a national culture, and a host of subcultures – ethnic, professional, religious, peer-group, political, social, occupational, economic, sexual, and so on. As a result, no one classification is of universal validity, and a perfect congruence of classifications is quite rare. Status categories may bear little relation to wealth, and also may vary in their importance over time. Class categories based on wealth may not reflect social realities, may be almost impossible to identify, and may be even more impossible to compare over time; professional categories may cut through both status and class lines and run vertically up and down the social system; power categories, such as political offices, may vary over time in the social status attached to them, in the power they wield, and in the income they produce.

The second danger which threatens every prosopographer is that he may fail to identify important subdivisions, and may thus be lumping together individuals who differ significantly from one another.[27] Good research depends on a constant interplay between the hypothesis and the evidence, the former undergoing repeated modification in the light of the latter. But if a subdivision which later turns out to be of critical importance has not been noted at the time, it is usually too late to go back and do the work all over again, a difficulty which is particularly acute in computer-aided studies, since the code book determines the questions that can later be asked.[28]

ERRORS IN THE INTERPRETATION OF THE DATA

Even if his documentation is adequate and his system of classification is properly designed, the unwary prosopographer is still liable to draw erroneous conclusions from his data. One common hazard which faces him is the possibility that that portion of the total population about which he can discover reliable information does not represent a random sample of the whole. If the unknowns mostly fall into a single slanted category, the figures taken from the sample of the known will give a distorted picture of reality. Thus Theodore Rabb himself provides reason to think that his sample of seventeenth-century English investors is biased, since it is quite likely that most of the unidentified 38 per cent of investors, both named and unnamed, were petty merchants.[29] This is a problem which affects all work which uses this methodology, and against which the only defense is the most careful assessment of the probabilities, and the application where necessary of an index error to correct the statistics. Another mistake which often occurs in prosopographical studies springs from a failure to relate the findings about the composition of the group under study to that of the population at large. A good example of the difficulties into which the historian may stumble if he neglects this point is the dispute about the social composition of the victims of the Terror in the French Revolution. Professor D. Greer discovered that the great majority of the victims were drawn from the lower or middle class rather than the nobility. It has since been pointed out that the proportion of noble victims may have been very small, but since the proportion of nobles in the population at large was even smaller, there is still a correlation of noble birth with execution. One can still say that a nobleman had 'X' times more chance of being killed in the Terror than a member of the bourgeoisie or a peasant.[30]

Another type of error which arises from neglecting the relationship between the part and the whole springs from the assumption that because a majority of members of a certain group come from a particular social class or occupation, that therefore they are representative, in the sense that a majority of members of their class or occupation belong to the group. Hugh R. Trevor-Roper pointed out that the men who seized power in England in the late 1640s and early 1650s were mostly drawn not from the old landed elite who had ruled England before the war, but from the poor gentry, mere gentry, or parish gentry, who had hitherto played no significant part in national and only a minor role in local affairs. Inspired by this discovery, he proceeded to generalize that the downwardly mobile mere gentry were the principal dissatisfied elements in the country and the main supporters of radicalism. In fact, however, it now seems fairly clear that a far larger number of the mere gentry – indeed the majority in the heartland of the class in the north and the west – were loyal church-and-king men who fought for King

Charles. The independent gentry who supported Cromwell were merely an untypical minority, goaded into taking a position so much at variance with that of most of their class by motives which at present we can only very dimly perceive, but one of which was certainly religious conviction.[31]

LIMITATIONS OF HISTORICAL UNDERSTANDING

So far, the errors which have been discovered have all been ones which can be avoided by learning the harsh lessons of experience, but there are others which will be more difficult to eradicate. In the first place, the concentration upon the study of elites has been part cause and part effect of a tendency to see history exclusively as a story of the ruling class, in which popular movements play little or no part. Syme claimed that 'In all ages, whatever the form and name of government, be it monarchy, republic, or democracy, an oligarchy lurks behind the facade.'[32] This is true enough as far as it goes, but one may reasonably question whether it goes far enough. Close study of the political maneuverings of the elite may conceal rather than illuminate the profounder workings of the social process. Major changes in class relationships, social mobility, religious opinions, and moral attitudes may be occurring among the lower strata, changes to which the elite will eventually be obliged to respond, it it is not to be swept away in violent revolution.[33]

If we look at the three most brilliant examples of prosopographical research on political elites, Syme's *Roman Revolution*, Namier's *Structure of Politics*, and Sir John Neale's great trilogy on the Elizabethan House of Commons, published in the 1950s, we can see the same narrowing of focus. Syme interpreted the transformations of the Roman republic into an empire as the consolidation of a new elite around Augustus, the result of complex factional infighting at the top. He proved his point, but he ignored the urgent demands of the nameless client masses upon their patrons which supported – and perhaps dictated – this shift of power. Political movements, and revolutions or counter-revolutions in particular, can hardly be satisfactorily explained by exclusive study of the leadership. Namier's picture of wheeling and dealing in the eighteenth-century House of Commons shattered conventional theories beyond repair, but his explanatory model could not include the springs of popular feeling generated by John Wilkes or the American War of Independence. Similarly, Sir John Neale's description of the relations between Queen Elizabeth and her parliaments needs modification through greater appreciation of the deep roots that Puritanism was sinking into the society. This was an ideology which both cut across and exploited the nexus of aristocratic clientage which Sir John so brilliantly and convincingly described.

The second great intellectual weakness of prosopographers has been their relative unwillingness to build into their perspective of history a role for ideas, prejudices, passions, ideologies, ideals, or principles. Intimate personal correspondence is a rarity among historical records. It usually got destroyed during life or at death, since, unlike genealogical, legal, or business records, nobody among the family or friends had any incentive to preserve it. Even in the rare cases when such material exists, it is often not very illuminating, since men rarely commit their deepest convictions to paper, even with their friends. Moreover, since in most periods in history it has been positively dangerous to express minority views about religion or politics, such written comments as survive about basic issues tend to be confined within the accepted norms of the society. The systematic bias in the historical record in favour of material interests and kinship ties and against ideas and principles fitted in well with the explicitly stated presupposition of the greatest of the early elitist scholars.[34] 'Spiritual interests of people are considered much less than their marriages,' complained Momigliano as soon as Syme's book appeared. Sir Herbert Butterfield protested with reference to Namier that 'human beings are the carriers of ideas, as well as the repositories of vested interest.'[35]

Despite some later disclaimers, there can be little doubt that in practice both Namier and Syme attached little importance to any ideal or prejudice which ran counter to the calculations of self-interest. The attention paid by these historians to the tactics rather than the strategy of politics presupposes a society without conviction in which manipulation and wire-pulling are more important than issues of principle or policy. It so happened that the mid-eighteenth century, upon which Namier first focused his attention, was a period in English history unusually devoid of major issues of controversy, and a period when the political actors formed an unusually homogeneous group: he thus chose, by accident or design, a period and a class which were especially susceptible to analysis by the methods he adopted. But some of his followers have found, to their cost, that it is not always safe to carry the same assumptions forwards and backwards in time. Robert Walcott tried to use the model for the reign of Queen Anne, with results that are now generally recognized to have been little short of disastrous.[36] One may also wonder whether Oliver Cromwell's failure successfully to manage his parliaments can really be explained by his lack of tactical skill, as Professor Trevor-Roper argues, or whether disagreement over fundamental constitutional and religious issues between the military and the civilians, and between Independents, Presbyterians, and Anglicans, put a settlement quite out of reach of even the most shrewd and assiduous manipulator of men.[37] One may therefore conclude that the explanatory power of the interest-group theory of politics, which has tended to be associated with the elitist prosopographical approach, is much greater at some periods and in some places than it is at and in others. The fewer the major political issues, the lower the ideological temperature, the more oligarchic the political organization, the more likely it is to provide a convincing historical interpretation.

Another limitation of the prosopographical school of historians is that its members sometimes unduly neglect the stuff of politics, the institutional framework within which the system functions, and the narrative of how political actors shape public policy. 'We are given a story that becomes silent or curiously neglectful as it touches the very things that government and Parliaments exist to do,' complained Sir Herbert Butterfield. He concluded harshly that:[38]

> There is little interest in the work of ministers within their
> departments; in the springs of policy and the origins of impor-
> tant decisions; in the actual content of the political controversies
> of the time; in the attitude of the public to measures and men;
> and in the thrust and counter-thrust of parliamentary debate . . .
> Such tendencies are calculated to raise the question whether the
> new form of structural analysis is not capable of producing in the
> practitioners of the craft its own kind of occupational disease.

The disease of which Sir Herbert complains is a form of colour-blindness which prevents its victims perceiving the political content of politics.

Many elitist prosopographers instinctively opt for a simplistic view of human motivation, according to which the springs of action are either one thing or another. We all of us ask our students to distinguish religious from political motives in the foreign policies of Gustavus Adolphus, or Oliver Cromwell, or whoever. In real life, human nature does not seem to function this way. The individual is moved by a convergence of constantly shifting forces, a cluster of influences such as kinship, friendship, economic interest, class prejudice, political principle, religious conviction, and so on, which all play their varying parts and which can usefully be disentangled only for analytical purposes. Moreover, there is reason to think that the relative importance of the various background characteristics will vary from culture to culture and nation to nation and time to time; that some attitudes can be more closely related to identifiable background characteristics than others; and that some background characteristics are moderately influential over a large range of attitudes while others are highly influential over a single attitude.[39]

In any case it is essential to distinguish sharply between relatively minor matters over which a politician is ready enough to favour a relative or client or to receive a bribe, and major issues of principle, over which he is likely to follow the dictates of his head and his heart rather than those of his blood or his pocketbook.

ACHIEVEMENTS

Nothing which has so far been said should be interpreted to mean that elitist prosopography is by its nature either useless or misleading. Red flags have been put up around the main danger spots where lie the bones of many pioneers in the method, and a case has been made for reducing the claims of prosopography generally as an explanatory tool. If past errors can be avoided, and if the limitations of the method are recognized, the potentialities are very great. Indeed, provided that it is accepted – as it surely must be – that values and behavior patterns are strongly influenced by past experience and upbringing, the power of the method can hardly be denied. All that is needed is more willingness to recognize the baffling complexity of human nature, the power of ideas, and the persistent influence of institutional structures. Prosopography does not have all the answers, but it is ideally fitted to reveal the web of sociopsychological ties that bind a group together. For example, to identify such ties among the leaders of the parliamentary opposition to Charles I in the late 1630s and 1640s does not help us to decide whether economic or constitutional or religious issues caused the Civil War. But it does most powerfully illuminate the process of radical party formation, and in the end makes any such question seem redundant, for the simple reason that men do not tear up their political institutions by the roots unless all these influences are working together to form an overwhelming incentive for change.

The best way to illustrate the full range of the contribution which prosopography has made to historical understanding in the last twenty years is to focus on some particular time and place, for which the religious, social and political history of England between 1500 and 1660 will serve as well as any. The first major problem which has been enormously enriched by these studies is the English Reformation. Although during the 1950s and 1960s the dominant textbook interpreted this event in primarily political terms, as an act of state carried out by a handful of determined men at the top, there was at the same time in train a whole series of monographs which were to shatter this simple picture. Examination of the educational, moral, and financial condition of the pre-Reformation clergy has shown up their many shortcomings, but has also indicated that what was happening was not so much a decline in the quality and zeal of the clergy as a rise in the demands made upon them by the laity.[40] Viewed in this light, the Reformation becomes yet another 'revolution of rising expectations.' The monks have also been studied prosopographically, with similar results, and it has been established that there was a decline in numbers in the pre-Reformation period, and a massive voluntary flight from monastic seclusion in the early 1530s. Monasteries and nunneries can be seen trying desperately to adapt themselves to the needs of the upper-class lay society by serving as old age homes for pensioned retainers and servants, as hotels for traveling gentlemen and noblemen, and as institutions for the deposit of unwanted children.[41] The fate of the monks after the Dissolution was early subjected to prosopographical analysis, which proved beyond doubt the fallacy of the hoary legend of the sufferings of the dispossessed.[42] The behavior of the bishops during the Reformation crisis has been elucidated and the divisions of opinion convincingly related to different education training – in theology or law – and to different career lines – in the church or the state bureaucracy.[43]

Even more important in its historical consequences than these valuable studies of members of the official hierarchies within the church has been the uncovering of the roots of religious radicalism in secular society. The great advance here came with the publication of Professor A. G. Dickens' pioneering work on *Lollards and Protestants in the Diocese of York* (1959), which used hitherto unexplored sources, and raised a whole range of new problems, which have since been further worked on by students and followers. Thanks to the patient tracking of Protestant heretics through secular and religious court records of prosecutions, the size, influence, social composition, occupational characteristics, and geographical spread of these persecuted minority groups have at last begun to emerge from the shadows. No serious scholar any longer dismisses the survival of Lollardy as of no consequence in the spread of radical religious ideas, and we can now see the dissemination of Protestant ideas not merely through the activities of a handful of scholars at Cambridge, but also through the penetration of imported Lutheran pamphlets, translated bibles, and other subversive literature from the seaports to the inland areas via traders, cloth workers, dissident friars, and the like.[44]

The subsequent religious history of England has also benefited enormously from prosopography. The Marian exiles, who fled abroad to escape Catholic persecution between 1553 and 1558, have been shown to be an intellectual and social elite for which there is hardly any parallel before the flight of the Jews from Hitlerite Germany in the 1930s, and their role in determining the shape of the Anglican Settlement of 1558-9 is now recognized to have been of the greatest importance.[45] Our understanding of why the Anglican church failed in its early years to win greater acceptance and to gain more converts has been illuminated through clerical prosopography, which has revealed the many shortcomings in numbers, education, zeal, and economic independence of the early Elizabethan parish clergy.[46] On one flank of the Established Church we are beginning to have a better picture of the growth of Puritanism through greater knowledge of who the Puritans were, though much work still remains to be done on Puritan merchants, dons, schoolmasters, clergy, and nobles.[47] On the other flank a very careful statistical and geographical comparison of Catholics in the 1560s and Catholics in the 1580s has proved conclusively, as no other method could, that the late Elizabethan development of Catholicism was a gentry-based revival, stimulated by the missionary activities of the seminary priests, and not a survival of popular pre-Reformation Catholicism.[48]

Social history, which is concerned with groups rather than individuals, ideas, or institutions, is a field to which prosopography probably has most to contribute. Attempts to generalize about social change in advance of either detailed local studies or global statistics based on serious archival research lead to the kind of impasse into which the famous 'gentry controversy' got itself stuck twenty years ago, during which rival hypotheses about broad social movements between 1540 and 1640 and their relationship to the revolution were bandied about on the basis of craftily selected examples whose typicality was altogether unknown. Since that time there have appeared several local studies of groups of gentry, and one general study on the aristocracy, which together go some way to eliminate certain hypotheses and to put statistical weight behind some others.[49]

For example, as a result of many years of very careful work upon the gentry of Yorkshire, it has been shown that of those gentry of the country who were in economic decline before the war and who took sides, three quarters joined the royalists and only one quarter the parliamentarians.[50] If this is true across the country, it disproves Professor Trevor-Roper's hypothesis that the radicals on the parliamentary side represented the declining 'mere gentry.' The same study also brings out the importance of Puritanism among so many parliamentarians and of Catholicism among a significant number of royalists. It adds one more nail to the coffin of the old Marxist theory, tentatively supported by R. H. Tawney and J. E. C. Hill, that the civil war was a conflict between capitalist entrepreneurial landlords and old-fashioned *rentiers*. In this case, detailed prosopographical analysis has put to the test – as nothing else could – the many theories of the social causes of the revolution, and has begun to sift truth from falsehood among them.[51]

As one might expect, the greatest concentration of prosopographical energy has been directed toward the political elite, and in particular toward the MPs. The late nineteenth- and early twentieth-century historians had established the key role played in English political history by the increasingly independent and powerful House of Commons, and it had long been known that it was here that the basic issues were fought out. But it was not until after the Second World War that scholars began to ask what sort of people it was who made this history. Today we have studies of the MPs of almost every parliament between 1559 and 1660, and a much richer and more convincing picture has emerged as a result.[52] Through comparative statistics and a series of detailed case studies, we can watch the expansion in the numbers of MPs and trace its cause in a desire by Elizabethan magnates to extend the range of their patronage, and in the willingness of Elizabeth to make concessions, however politically unwise in the long run, which did not cost her money in the short run. Statistical inquiries have revealed the striking growth in the educational training and administrative experience of MPs and the persistent rise in the proportion of gentry. We know now how the members were elected and how electoral contests were fought and won, and we are beginning to learn a little about the changing relationship between the electors and their representatives. We can trace the decline in the electoral influence of the great court magnates before 1640, as it gave way to that of local gentlemen, and even of townsmen themselves for borough seats.

Prosopographical studies of local elites outside parliament in the counties and the cities are just beginning to be even more helpful in illuminating the social and economic factors behind the party line-ups in the Civil War. They have already revealed that in some counties and towns – but not in all – there was a withdrawal from positions of authority in the late 1640s of members of the greater gentry and the old urban oligarchies, and their replacement by men drawn from the lesser gentry and small merchants, as more radical policies were adopted for the prosecution of the war and achievement of a political settlement.[53]

The principal conclusion which emerges from this survey of the literature is that the method works best when it is applied to easily defined and fairly small groups over a limited period of not much more than a hundred years, when the data are drawn from a very wide variety of sources which complement and enrich each other, and when the study is directed to solving a specific problem. Lollards and Protestants in the early sixteenth century, Captain Swing rioters in the early nineteenth, make ideal subjects. Ambitious surveys of many thousands of individuals over very long time spans, using only the most easily accessible printed source materials, and applying a shotgun scatter approach to the problems which may be answered, are far less likely to produce worthwhile results.

CONCLUSION

Prosopography is today in the process of coming of age. It has passed through the follies and excesses of adolescence and is now settling down to the humdrum routine of responsible early middle age. If the elitist school had its origins in Germany and the United States, it was first developed in England, both in classical and in modern history, and a good deal of the best work still comes from there. But this early pioneering is now being overtaken, both in quantity and quality, by the scholarly outpourings from America. The latter has always been the main center of the mass school, the scale of whose output and the sophistication of whose methods is now increasing fast.[54] The principal causes of this proliferation of scientific historical prosopography in the United States has been the great influence of sociology and political science and the advanced training in the use of, and easy access to, the computer. The most impressive institutional achievement of this school has been the creation of the Inter-University Consortium for Political Research at the University of Michigan. Here there is being collected and put into machine-readable form information about the voting behavior, as recorded in congressional roll-calls, of every congressman since 1789. In addition, the psephologists are being supplied with data about popular voting at the county level in every election since 1824, correlated with information from the census returns since 1790 about income, race, religion, and other key variables for each county and state.[55] A beginning is now being made in collecting machine-readable statistical data for earlier periods of American history and also for other countries.

It is indicative of the parting of the ways between British and American scholarship in the 1960s that the parallel monument to prosopography on the eastern side of the Atlantic takes the rather different form of the post-war History of Parliament project. Initiated and planned by Sir Lewis Namier, this began in 1951 and will result in a multi-volume biographical dictionary of all MPs linked by introductory volumes which use this personal information to provide illuminating case studies, to put together statistical comparisons, and to draw political conclusions. It is characteristic of the British approach that this project is paid for by the government and not by universities or foundations, that the biographical information it assembles is not being prepared in machine-readable form (except for one period under the editorship of an American), and that more emphasis is placed on the biographies and case studies than on the statistics.[56]

France is the third major center of historical research in the world, but for the last thirty years the best French historians have been preoccupied with some dazzlingly successful explorations of other new techniques of research. They have pioneered some brilliant environmental studies of local societies seen as a totality and examined in great depth, they have produced some massive statistical time-series about prices, foreign trade, and industrial output, and they have pioneered the scientific study of historical demography. Only in the last few years have French historians begun to take to prosopography, and in conformity with their long-standing emphasis upon quantification they are now embarked upon some very large-scale projects of the mass school, using the most sophisticated computer gadgetry.[57] These are being supported by the VI Section of the Ecole Pratique des Hautes Etudes in Paris, which for decades has been the center of statistical historical inquiry in France.

One of the reasons – although a poor and irrelevant one – why prosopography will continue to develop on both sides of the Atlantic is because it is so ideally suited to the requirements of research papers and doctoral dissertations. It introduces the novice student to a very wide range of sources, it teaches him to evaluate his evidence and to apply his judgment to resolve contradictions, it demands meticulous accuracy and the arrangement of information on a methodical basis, and it offers a topic which can readily be expanded or cut down by modifying the size of the sample in order to meet the requirements of available time and resources. Some of this research undoubtedly contributes to the New Antiquarianism – data collection for data collection's sake – but under skilled and organized leadership the projects can be fitted together by the director to produce a useful contribution to the sum of historical knowledge.

A second powerful – but equally irrelevant – reason for a further expansion of prosopography is the arrival of the computer, the full significance of which is only just becoming apparent. As historians slowly and timidly began to explore the potentialities of this new technological tool, they began to realize its almost limitless capacity for handling just the sort of material that prosopography throws up. The correlation of numerous variables affecting large masses of data, assembled on a uniform basis, is precisely what the computer can do best; it is also what is most laborious, and in many cases virtually impossible, for even the most mathematically-minded of historians working without electronic aids. It is painful to admit that the advent of a technical gadget should dictate the type of historical questions asked and the methods used for solving them, but it would be adopting the posture of the ostrich to pretend that this is not happening now, and will not happen on an even greater scale in the years to come.

It must be admitted that there are some serious dangers inherent in the very success and popularity of prosopography. The first is that the really large undertakings, like Sir John Neale's work on Elizabethan parliaments, Professor W. K. Jordan's on charitable giving, or Sir Lewis Namier's even grander History of Parliament project, must be carried out by teams of researchers, assembling data on the lines laid down by the director. This material is then studied, collated, and eventually published by the director, to whom alone the credit goes.[58] Collective research is already fully accepted by the physical scientists as a familiar and necessary process, but it involves a degree of intellectual peonage by students and junior faculty to the professor, which many scholars bred in the older individualistic and independent tradition of historiography find disturbing. The second danger is that instead of coming together, the mass and elitist schools will specialize more and more on their different approaches, the one becoming more scientific and quantitative and the other more impressionistic and devoted to individual examples inadequately controlled by random sampling. This would be a disaster for the profession, since it would spell the end of fruitful cross-fertilization. The danger has been greatly increased by the advent of the computer, which has been embraced by the more statistically-minded with all the undiscriminating enthusiasm of the nymphomaniac, and rejected by the less scientific partly from intellectual prudery, and partly from complacent ignorance of what pleasures they are missing. The availability of the computer will increasingly tempt some historians to concentrate their energies on problems that can be solved by quantification, problems which are sometimes – but by no means always – the most important or interesting ones. It will also tempt them to abandon sampling techniques, which are frequently perfectly adequate for their purposes, and to embark on very time-consuming statistical investigations of total populations, which in many cases is a wholly unnecessary procedure. Other historians may increasingly come to regard the computer as a threat to their intellectual predominance, and may retreat still further into the dark recesses of impressionistic methodology. To make matters worse, there are strong national overtones to the split, since the American and the French have far greater access to and confidence in the computer than their English colleagues; strong cultural overtones, with threats of a new war between the Ancients and the Moderns, the Humanities and the Sciences; and even philosophical overtones, with a clash between Fact and Fancy, Mr. Gradgrind and Sissy Jupe. As a result, it may be a long while before there is a full meeting of minds.

Prosopography nevertheless contains within it the potentiality to help in the re-creation of a unified field out of the loose confederation of jealously independent topics and techniques which at present constitutes the historian's empire. It could be a means to bind together constitutional and institutional history on the one hand and personal biography on the other, which are the two oldest and best developed of the historian's crafts, but which have hitherto run along more or less parallel lines. It could combine the humane skill in historical reconstruction through meticulous concentration on the significant detail and the particular example, with the statistical and theoretical preoccupations of the social scientists; it could form the missing connection between political history and social history, which at present are all too often treated in largely watertight compartments, either in different monographs or in different chapters of a single volume. It could help reconcile history to sociology and psychology. And it could form one string among many to tie the exciting developments in intellectual and cultural history down to the social, economic, and political bedrock. Whether or not prosopography will seize all or any of these opportunities will depend on the expertise, sophistication, modesty, and common sense of the next generation of historians.

I

Historians have always told stories. From Thucydides and Tacitus to Gibbon and Macaulay, the composition of narrative in lively and elegant prose was always accounted their highest ambition. History was regarded as a branch of rhetoric. For the last fifty years, however, this story-telling function has fallen into ill-repute among those who have regarded themselves as in the vanguard of the profession, the practitioners of the so-called 'new history' of the post-Second-World-War era.[1] In France, story-telling was dismissed as 'l'histoire événementielle.' Now, however, I detect evidence of an undercurrent which is sucking many prominent 'new historians' back again into some form of narrative.

Before embarking upon an examination of the evidence for such a shift and upon some speculations about what may have caused it, a number of things had better be made clear. The first is what is meant here by 'narrative.'[2] Narrative is taken to mean the organization of material in a chronologically sequential order, and the focusing of the content into a. single coherent story, albeit with subplots. The two essential ways in which narrative history differs from structural history is that its arrangement is descriptive rather than analytical and that its central focus is on man not circumstances. It therefore deals with the particular and specific rather than the collective and statistical. Narrative is a mode of historical writing, but it is a mode which also affects and is affected by the content and the method.

The kind of narrative which I have in mind is not that of the simple antiquarian reporter or annalist. It is narrative directed by some 'pregnant principle,' and which possesses a theme and an argument. Thucydides' theme was the Peloponnesian Wars and their disastrous effects upon Greek society and politics; Gibbon's was exactly what his title suggests; Macaulay's was the rise of a liberal participatory constitution in the stresses of revolutionary politics. Biographers tell the story of a life, from birth to death. No narrative historians, as I have defined them, avoid analysis altogether, but this is not the skeletal framework around which their work is constructed. And finally, they are deeply concerned with the rhetorical aspects of their presentation. Whether successful or not in the attempt, they certainly aspire to stylistic elegance, wit and aphorism. They are not content to throw words down on a page and let them lie there, like cow-flops in a field, on the grounds that since history is a science, it needs no art to help it along.

The trends here identified should not be taken to apply to the great mass of historians. All that is being attempted is to point to a noticeable shift of content, method and style among a very tiny, but disproportionately prominent, section of the historical profession as a whole. History has always had many mansions, and must continue to do so if it is to flourish in the future. The triumph of any one *genre* or school eventually always leads to narrow sectarianism, narcissism and self-adulation, contempt or tyranny towards outsiders, and other disagreeable and self-defeating characteristics. We can all think of cases where this has happened. In some countries and institutions it has been unhealthy that the 'new historians' have had things so much their own way in the last thirty years; and it will be equally unhealthy if the new trend, if trend it be, achieves similar domination here and there.

It is also essential to establish once and for all that this essay is trying to chart observed changes in historical fashion, not to make value judgments about what are good, and what are less good, modes of historical writing. Value judgments are hard to avoid in any historiographical study, but this essay is not trying to raise a banner or start a revolution. No one is being urged to throw away his calculator and tell a story.

II

Before looking at the recent trends, one has first to back-track in order to explain the abandonment by many historians, about fifty years ago, of a 2,000-year-old tradition of narrative as the ideal mode. In the first place, in spite of impassioned assertions to the contrary, it was widely recognized, with some justice, that answer-

ing the *what* and the *how* questions in a chronological fashion, even
if directed by a central argument, does not in fact go very far
towards answering the *why* questions. Moreover, historians were at
that time strongly under the influence of both Marxist ideology and
social science methodology. As a result they were interested in
societies not individuals, and were confident that a 'scientific
history' could be achieved which would in time produce generalized
laws to explain historical change.

Here, we must pause again to define what is meant by 'scientific
history.' The first 'scientific history' was formulated by Ranke in
the nineteenth century, and was based on the study of new source
materials. It was assumed that close textual criticism of the hitherto
undisclosed records buried in state archives would once and for all
establish the facts of political history. In the last thirty years, there
have been three very different kinds of scientific history current in
the profession, all based not on new data, but on new models or
new methods: they are the Marxist economic model, the French
ecological–demographic model, and the American 'cliometric'
methodology. According to the old Marxist model, history moves
in a dialectical process of thesis and antithesis, through a clash of
classes which are themselves created by changes in control over the
means of production. In the 1930s this idea resulted in a fairly
simplistic economic/social determinism which affected many young
scholars of the time. It was a notion of scientific history which was
strongly defended by Marxists up to the late 1950s, as can be
demonstrated by the fact that the change of the subtitle of *Past and
Present* from 'A Journal of Scientific History' to 'A Journal of
Historical Studies' did not take place until 1959. It should be noted
that the current generation of 'neo-Marxists' seems to have abandoned most of the basic tenets of traditional Marxist historians of
the 1930s. They are now as concerned with the state, politics,
religion and ideology as their non-Marxist colleagues, and in the
process appear to have dropped the claim to be pursuing 'scientific
history.'

The second meaning of 'scientific history' is that used since 1945
by the *Annales* school of French historians, of whom Professor E.
Le Roy Ladurie may stand as a spokesman, albeit a rather extreme
one. According to them the key variable in history is shifts in the
ecological balance between food supplies and population, a balance
necessarily to be determined by long-term quantitative studies of

agricultural productivity, demographic changes and food prices. This kind of 'scientific history' emerged from a combination of long-standing French interests in historical geography and historical demography, coupled with the methodology of quantification. Le Roy Ladurie told us bluntly that 'history that is not quantifiable cannot claim to be scientific.'[3]

The third meaning of 'scientific history' is primarily American, and is based on the claim, loudly and clearly expressed by the 'cliometricians,' that only their own very special quantitative methodology has any claim to be scientific.[4] According to them the historical community can be divided into two. There are 'the traditionalists,' who include both the old-style narrative historians, dealing mainly with state politics and constitutional history, and the 'new' economic, demographic and social historians of the *Annales* and *Past and Present* schools - despite the fact that the latter use quantification and that for several decades the two groups were bitter enemies, especially in France. Quite separate are the scientific historians, the cliometricians, who are defined by a methodology rather than by any particular subject matter or interpretation of the nature of historical change. They are historians who build paradigmatic models, sometimes counter-factual ones about worlds which never existed in real life, and who test the validity of the models by the most sophisticated mathematical and algebraical formulae applied to very large quantities of electronically processed data. Their special field is economic history, which they have virtually conquered in the United States, and they have made large inroads into the history of recent democratic politics by applying their methods to voting behavior, both of the electorate and the elected. These great enterprises are necessarily the result of team work, rather like the building of the pyramids: squads of diligent assistants assemble data, encode them, program them, and pass them through the maw of the computer, all under the autocratic direction of a team leader. The results cannot be tested by any of the traditional methods, since the evidence is buried in private computer tapes, not exposed in published footnotes. In any case, the data are often expressed in so mathematically recondite a form that they are unintelligible to the majority of the historical profession. The only reassurance to the bemused laity is that the members of this priestly order disagree fiercely and publicly about the validity of each other's findings.

These three types of 'scientific history' overlap to some degree, but they are sufficiently distinct, certainly in the eyes of their practitioners, to justify the creation of this tripartite typology.

Other 'scientific' explanations of historical change have risen to favor for a while and then gone out of fashion. French structuralism produced some brilliant theorizing, but no single major work of history – unless one considers Michel Foucault's writings as primarily works of history, rather than of moral philosophy with examples drawn from history. Parsonian functionalism, which itself was preceded by Malinowski's *Scientific Theory of Culture*, had a long run, despite its failure to offer an explanation of change over time and the obvious fact that the fit between the material and biological needs of a society and the institutions and values by which it lives has always been less than perfect, and often very poor indeed. Both structuralism and functionalism have provided valuable insights, but neither has come even near to supplying historians with an all-embracing scientific explanation of historical change.

All the three main groups of scientific historians, which flourished respectively from the 1930s till the 1950s, the 1950s to mid-1970s, and the 1960s and early 1970s, were supremely confident that the major problems of historical explanation were soluble, and that they would, given time, succeed in solving them. Cast-iron solutions would, they assumed, eventually be provided for such hitherto baffling questions as the causes of 'great revolutions' or the shifts from feudalism to capitalism, and from traditional to modern societies. This heady optimism, which was so apparent from the 1930s to the 1960s, was buttressed amongst the first two groups of 'scientific historians' by the belief that material conditions such as changes in the relationship between population and food supply, changes in the means of production and class conflict, were the driving forces in history. Many, but not all, regarded intellectual, cultural, religious, psychological, legal, even political developments as mere epiphenomena. Since economic and /or demographic determinism largely dictated the content of the new *genre* of historical research, the analytical rather than the narrative mode was best suited to organize and present the data, and the data themselves had so far as possible to be quantitative in nature.

The French historians, who in the 1950s and 1960s were in the lead in this brave enterprise, developed a standard hierarchical arrangement: first, both in place and in order of importance, came the economic and demographic facts; then the social structure; and lastly intellectual, religious, cultural and political development. These three tiers were thought of like the storeys of a house: each rests on the foundation of the one below, but those above can have little or no reciprocal effect on those underneath. In some hands, the new methodology and new questions produced results which were little short of sensational. The first books of Fernand Braudel, Pierre Goubert and Emmanuel Le Roy Ladurie will rank among the greatest historical writings of any time and place.[5] They alone fully justify the adoption for a generation of the analytical and structural approach.

The conclusion, however, was historical revisionism with a vengeance. Since only the first tier really mattered, and since the subject matter was the material conditions of the masses, not the culture of the elite, it became possible to talk about the history of continental Europe from the fourteenth to the eighteenth centuries as 'l'histoire immobile.' Professor Le Roy Ladurie argued that nothing, absolutely nothing, changed over those five centuries, since the society remained obstinately imprisoned in its traditional and unaltered 'éco-démographie.'[6] In this new model of history, such movements as the Renaissance, the Reformation, the Enlightenment and the rise of the modern state simply disappeared. Ignored were the massive transformations of culture, art, architecture, literature, religion, education, science, law, constitution, state-building, bureaucracy, military organization, fiscal arrangements, etc. which took place among the higher echelons of society in those five centuries. This curious blindness was the result of a firm belief that these matters were all parts of the third tier, a mere superficial superstructure. When, recently, some scholars from this school began to use their well-tried statistical methods on such problems as literacy, the contents of libraries and the rise and fall of Christian piety, they described their activities as the application of quantification to 'le troisième niveau.'

III

The first cause of the current revival of narrative is widespread disillusionment with the economic determinist model of historical explanation and this three-tiered hierarchical arrangement to which it gave rise. The split between social history, on the one hand, and intellectual history, on the other, has had the most unfortunate consequences. Both have become isolated, inward-looking, and narrow. In America, intellectual history, which had once been the flagship of the profession, fell upon hard times and for a while lost confidence in itself;[7] social history has flourished as never before, but its pride in its isolated achievements was but the harbinger of an eventual decline in vitality, when faith in purely economic and social explanations began to ebb. The historical record has now obliged many of us to admit that there is an extraordinarily complex two-way flow of interactions between facts of population, food supply, climate, bullion supply, prices, etc., on the one hand, and values, ideas and customs, on the other. Along with social relationships of status or class, they form together a single web of meaning.

Many historians now believe that the culture of the group, and even the will of the individual, are potentially at least as important causal agents of change as the impersonal forces of material output and demographic growth. There is no theoretical reason why the latter should always dictate the former, rather than vice versa, and indeed evidence is piling up of examples to the contrary.[8] Contraception, for example, is clearly as much a product of a state of mind as it is of economic circumstances or technological inventions. The proof of this contention can be found in the wide diffusion of this practice throughout France, long before industrialization, without much population pressure except on small farms, and nearly a century before any other Western country. We also now know that the nuclear family antedated industrial society, and that concepts of privacy, love and individualism similarly emerged among some of the most traditional sectors of a traditional society in late seventeenth- and early eighteenth-century England, rather than as a result of later modernizing economic and social processes. The Puritan ethic was a by-product of an unworldly religious movement which took root in the Anglo-Saxon societies of England and New England centuries before routine work-patterns were necessary or the first factory was built. On the other hand there is an inverse correlation, at any rate in nineteenth-century France, between literacy and urbanization on the one hand, and industrialization on the other. Levels of literacy turn out to be a poor guide to 'modern' attitudes of mind or 'modern' occupations.[9] Thus the linkages between culture and society are clearly very complex indeed, and seem to vary from time to time and from place to place.

It is hard not to suspect that the decline of ideological commitment among Western intellectuals has also played its part. If one looks at three of the most passionate and hard-fought historical battles of the 1950s and 1960s – about the rise or decline of the gentry in seventeenth-century England, about the rise or fall of working-class real income in the early stages of industrialization, and about the causes, nature and consequences of American slavery, all were at bottom debates fired by current ideological concerns. It seemed desperately important at the time to know whether or not the Marxist interpretation was right, and therefore these historical questions mattered and were exciting. The muting of ideological controversy caused by the intellectual decline of Marxism and the adoption of mixed economies in the West has coincided with a decline in the thrust of historical research to ask the big *why* questions, and it is plausible to suggest that there is some relation between the two trends.

Economic and demographic determinism has not only been undermined by a recognition of ideas, culture and even individual will as independent variables. It has also been sapped by a revived recognition that political and military power, the use of brute force, has very frequently dictated the structure of the society, the distribution of wealth, the agrarian system, and even the culture of the elite. Classic examples are the Norman conquest of England in 1066, and probably also the divergent economic and social paths taken by Eastern Europe, North-Western Europe and England in the sixteenth and seventeenth centuries.[10] The 'new historians' of the 1950s and 1960s will undoubtedly be severely criticized for their obsession with social, economic and demographic forces in history, and their failure to take sufficient account of political organization and decision-making and the vagaries of military battle and siege, destruction and conquest. Civilizations have risen and fallen due to fluctuations in political authority and shifts in the fortunes of war. It is extraordinary that these matters should have been neglected for so long by those who regarded themselves as in the forefront of the historical profession. In practice, the bulk of the profession continued to concern itself with political history, just as it had always done, but this is not where the cutting edge of innovation was generally thought to be. A belated recognition of the importance of power, of personal political decisions by individuals, of the chances of battle, has forced some historians back to the narrative mode, whether they like it or not. To use Machiavelli's terms, neither *virtu* nor *fortuna* can be dealt with except by a narrative, or even an anecdote, since the first is an individual attribute and the second a happy or unhappy accident.

The third development which has dealt a serious blow to structural and analytical history is the mixed record to date in the use of what has been its most characteristic methodology – namely quantification. Quantification has undoubtedly matured and has now established itself as an essential methodology in many areas of historical inquiry, especially demographic history, the history of social structure and social mobility, economic history, and the history of voting patterns and voting behavior in democratic political systems. Its use has greatly improved the general quality of historical discourse, by demanding the citation of precise numbers instead of the previous loose use of words. Historians can no longer get away with saying 'more', 'less', 'growing', 'declining', etc., all of which logically imply numerical comparisons, without ever stating explicitly the statistical basis for their assertions. It has also made argument exclusively by example seem somewhat disreputable. Critics now demand supporting statistical evidence to show that the examples are typical and not exceptions to the rule. These procedures have undoubtedly improved the logical power and persuasiveness of historical argument. There is no disagreement that whenever it is appropriate, fruitful and possible from the surviving records, the historian should count.

There is, however, a difference in kind between the artisan quantification done by a single researcher totting up figures on a hand-calculator and producing simple tables and percentages, and the work of the cliometricians. The latter specialize in the assemblage of vast quantities of data by teams of assistants, the use of the electronic computer to process it all, and the application of highly sophisticated mathematical procedures to the results. Doubts have been cast on all stages of this procedure. Many question whether historical data are ever sufficiently reliable to warrant such procedures; whether teams of assistants can be trusted to apply uniform coding procedures to large quantities of often widely diverse and even ambiguous documents; whether much crucial detail is not lost in the coding procedure; if it is ever possible to be confident that all coding and programming errors have been eliminated; and whether the sophistication of the mathematical and algebraic formulae are not ultimately self-defeating, since they baffle most historians. Finally, many are disturbed by the virtual impossibility of checking up on the reliability of the final results, since they must depend not on published footnotes but on privately owned computer tapes, in turn the result of thousands of privately owned code sheets, in turn abstracted from the raw data.

These questions are real and will not go away. We all know of doctoral dissertations or printed papers or monographs which have used the most sophisticated techniques either to prove the obvious or to claim to prove the implausible, using formulae and language which render the methodology unverifiable to the ordinary historian. The results sometimes combine the vices of unreadability and triviality. We all know of the doctoral dissertations which languish unfinished since the researcher has been unable to keep under intellectual control the sheer volume of print-out spewed out by the computer, or has spent so much effort preparing the data for the machine that his time, patience and money have run out. One clear conclusion is surely that, whenever possible, sampling by hand is preferable to, and quicker than, and just as reliable as, running the whole universe through a machine. We all know of projects in which a logical flaw in the argument or a failure to use plain common sense has vitiated or cast in doubt many of the conclusions. We all know of other projects in which the failure to record one piece of information at the coding stage has led to the loss of an important result. We all know of others where the sources of information are themselves so unreliable that we can be sure that little confidence can be placed in the conclusions based on their quantitative manipulation. Parish registers are a classic example, upon which a gigantic amount of effort is currently being spent in many countries, only some of which is likely to produce worthwhile results.

Despite its unquestionable achievements, it cannot be denied that quantification has not fulfilled the high hopes of twenty years ago. Most of the great problems of history remain as insoluble as ever, if not more so. Consensus on the causes of the English, French or American Revolutions is as far away as ever, despite the enormous effort put into elucidating their social and economic origins. Thirty years of intensive research on demographic history has left us more rather than less bewildered. We do not know why the population ceased to grow in most areas of Europe between 1640 and 1740; we do not know why it began to grow again in 1740; or even whether the cause was rising fertility or declining mortality. Quantification has told us a lot about the *what* questions of historical demography, but relatively little so far about the *why*. The major questions about American slavery remain as elusive as ever, despite the application to them of one of the most massive and sophisticated quantitative studies ever mounted. Its publication, so far from solving most problems, merely raised the temperature of the debate.[11] It had the beneficial effect of focusing attention on important issues such as the diet, hygiene, health and family structure of American blacks under slavery, but it also diverted attention from the equally or even more important psychological effects of slavery upon both masters and slaves, simply because these matters could not be measured by a computer. Urban histories are cluttered with statistics, but mobility trends still remain obscure. Today no one is quite sure whether English society was more open and mobile than the French in the seventeenth and eighteenth centuries, or even whether the gentry or aristocracy were rising or falling in England before the Civil War. We are no better off now in these respects than were James Harrington in the seventeenth century or de Tocqueville in the nineteenth.

It is just those projects that have been the most lavishly funded, the most ambitious in the assembly of vast quantities of data by armies of paid researchers, the most scientifically processed by the very latest in computer technology, the most mathematically sophisticated in presentation, which have so far turned out to be the most disappointing. Today, two decades and millions of dollars, pounds and francs later, there are only rather modest results to show for the expenditure of so much time, effort and money. There are huge piles of greenish print-out gathering dust in scholars' offices; there are many turgid and excruciatingly dull tomes full of tables of figures, abstruse algebraic equations and percentages given to two decimal points. There are also many valuable new findings and a few major contributions to the relatively small corpus of historical works of permanent value. But in general the sophistication of the methodology has tended to exceed the reliability of the data, while the usefulness of the results seems – up to a point – to be

in inverse correlation to the mathematical complexity of the
methodology and the grandiose scale of data-collection.

On any cost-benefit analysis the rewards of large-scale computerized history have so far only very occasionally justified the
input of time and money, and this has led historians to cast around
for other methods of investigating the past, which will shed more
light with less trouble. In 1968, Le Roy Ladurie prophesied that by
the 1980s 'the historian will be a programmer or he will be
nothing.'[12] The prophecy has not been fulfilled, least of all by the
prophet himself.

Historians are, therefore, forced back upon the principle of
indeterminacy, a recognition that the variables are so numerous that
at best only middle-range generalizations are possible in history, as
Robert Merton long ago suggested. The macro-economic model is a
pipe-dream, and 'scientific history' a myth. Monocausal explanations simply do not work. The use of feed-back models of
explanation built around Weberian 'elective affinities' seems to
provide better tools for revealing something of the elusive truth
about historical causation, especially if we abandon any claim that
this methodology is in any sense scientific.

Disillusionment with economic or demographic monocausal
determinism and with quantification has led historians to start
asking a quite new set of questions, many of which were previously
blocked from view by the preoccupation with a specific methodology, structural, collective, and statistical. More and more of the
'new historians' are now trying to discover what was going on
inside people's heads in the past, and what it was like to live in the
past, questions which inevitably lead back to the use of narrative.

A significant subgroup of the great French school of historians,
led by Lucien Febvre, have always regarded intellectual,
psychological and cultural changes as independent variables of
central importance. But for a long time they were in a minority, left
behind in a remote backwater as the flood tide of scientific history,
economic and social in content, structural in organization and
quantitative in methodology, swept past them. Now, however, the
topics they were interested in have quite suddenly become fashionable. The questions asked, however, are not quite the same as they
used to be, since they are now often drawn from anthropology. In
practice, if not in theory, anthropology has tended to be one of the

most ahistorical of disciplines in its lack of interest in change over time. None the less, it has taught us how a whole social system and set of values can be brilliantly illuminated by the searchlight method of recording in elaborate detail a single event, provided that it is very carefully set in its total context and very carefully analyzed for its cultural meaning. The archetypal model of this 'thick description' is Clifford Geertz's classic account of a Balinese cock-fight.[13] We historians cannot, alas, actually be present, with notebooks, tape-recorders and cameras, at the events we describe, but here and there we can find a cloud of witnesses to tell us what it was like to be there.

One of the most striking recent changes in the content of history has been a quite sudden growth of interest in feelings, emotions, behavior patterns, values, and states of mind. In this respect, the influence of anthropologists like Evans-Pritchard, Clifford Geertz, Mary Douglas and Victor Turner has been very great indeed. The first cause for the revival of narrative among some of the 'new historians' has therefore been the replacement of sociology and economics by anthropology as the most influential of the social sciences. Although psychohistory is so far largely a disaster area – a desert strewn with the wreckage of elaborate, chromium-plated vehicles which broke down soon after departure – psychology itself has also had its effect on a generation now turning its attention to sexual desire, family relations and emotional bonding as they affect the individual, and to ideas, beliefs and customs as they affect the group. This change in questions being asked is also probably related to the contemporary scene in the 1970s. This has been a decade in which more personalized ideals and interests have taken priority over public issues, as a result of widespread disillusionment with the prospects of change by political action. It is therefore plausible to connect the sudden upsurge in interest in these matters in the past with similar preoccupations in the present.

This new interest in mental structures has been stimulated by the collapse of traditional intellectual history treated as a kind of paper-chase of ideas back through the ages (which usually ends up with either Aristotle or Plato). 'Great books' were studied in an historical vacuum, with little or no attempt to set the authors themselves or their linguistic vocabulary in their true historical setting. The history of political thought in the West is now being rewritten, primarily by Professors J. G. A. Pocock, Quentin Skinner and

Bernard Bailyn, by painfully reconstructing the precise context and meaning of words and ideas in the past, and showing how they have changed their shape and color over time, like chameleons, so as to adapt to new circumstances and new needs.

The traditional history of ideas is concurrently being directed into a study of the changing audience and means of communication. There has sprung up a new and flourishing discipline of the history of the printing press, the book and literacy, and of their effects upon the diffusion of ideas and the transformation of values.

One further reason why a number of 'new historians' are turning back to narrative seems to be a desire to make their findings accessible once more to an intelligent, but not expert, reading public, which is eager to learn what these innovative new questions, methods and data have revealed, but cannot stomach indigestible statistical tables, dry analytical argument, and jargon-ridden prose. Increasingly, structural, analytical, quantitative historians have found themselves talking to each other and to no one else. Their findings have appeared in professional journals or in monographs so expensive and with such small press runs (under 1,000) that they have been in practice almost entirely bought by libraries. And yet the success of popular historical periodicals like *History Today* and *L'Histoire* proves that there is a large audience ready to listen, and the new historians are now anxious to speak to that audience, rather than leaving it to be fed on the pabulum of popular biographies and textbooks. The questions asked by the new historians are, after all, those which preoccupy us all today: the nature of power, authority and charismatic leadership; the relation of political institutions to underlying social patterns and value systems; attitudes to youth, old age, disease, and death; sex, marriage and concubinage; birth, contraception and abortion; work, leisure and conspicuous consumption; the relationship of religion, science and magic as explanatory models of reality; the strength and direction of the emotions of love, fear, lust and hate; the impact upon people's lives and ways of looking at the world of literacy and education; the relative importance attached to different social groupings, such as the family, kin, community, nation, class and race; the strength and meaning of ritual, symbol and custom as ways of binding a community together; moral and philosophical approaches to crime and punishment; patterns of deference and outbursts of egalitarianism; structural conflicts between status groups or classes; the means, possibilities and limitations of social mobility; the nature and significance of popular protest and millenarian hopes; the shifting ecological balance between man and nature; the causes and effects of disease. All these are burning issues at the moment and are concerned with the masses rather than the elite. They are more 'relevant' to our own lives than the doings of dead kings, presidents and generals.

IV

As a result of these convergent trends, a significant number of the best-known exponents of the 'new history' are now turning back to the once despised narrative mode. And yet historians – and even publishers – still seem a little embarrassed when they do so. In 1979, the *Publishers' Weekly* – itself an organ of the trade – promoted the merits of a new book, a story of the trial of Louis XVI, with these peculiar words: 'Jordan's choice of *narrative rather than scholarly treatment* [my italics] ... is a model of clarity and synthesis.'[14] The critic obviously liked the book, but thought that narrative is by definition not scholarly. When a distinguished member of the school of 'new history' writes a narrative, his friends tend to apologize for him, saying: 'Of course, he only did it for the money.' Despite these rather shamefaced excuses, the trends in historiography, in content, method and mode, are evident wherever one looks.

After languishing unread for forty years, Norbert Elias's path-breaking book about manners, *The Civilising Process*, has suddenly been translated into English and French.[15] Dr Zeldin has written a brilliant two-volume history of modern France, in a standard textbook series, which ignores almost every aspect of traditional history, and concentrates on little other than emotions and states of mind.[16] Professor Philippe Ariès has studied responses over a huge time span to the universal trauma of death.[17] The history of witchcraft has suddenly become a growth industry in every country, as has the history of the family, including that of childhood, youth, old age, women and sexuality (the last two being topics in serious danger of suffering from intellectual overkill). An excellent example of the trajectory which historical studies have tended to take over the last twenty years is provided by the research interests of Professor Jean Delumeau. He began in 1962 with a study of an

economic product (alum); followed in 1969 by that of a society
(Rome); in 1971, of a religion (Catholicism); in 1976, of a collective
behavior (*Les Pays de Cocagne*); finally, in 1979, of an emotion
(fear).[18]

The French have a word to describe the new topic – *mentalité* –
but unfortunately it is neither very well defined nor very easily
translatable into English. In any case, story-telling, the circumstantial narration in great detail of one or more 'happenings' based
on the testimony of eye-witnesses and participants, is clearly one
way to recapture something of the outward manifestations of the
mentalité of the past. Analysis certainly remains the essential part of
the enterprise, which is based on an anthropological interpretation
of culture that claims to be both systematic and scientific. But this
cannot conceal the role of the study of *mentalité* in the revival of
non-analytical modes of writing history, of which story-telling is
one.

Of course, narrative is not the only manner of writing the history
of *mentalité* which has been made possible by disillusionment with
structural analysis. Take, for example, that most brilliant reconstruction of a vanished mind set, Peter Brown's evocation of the
world of late antiquity.[19] It ignores the usual clear analytical
categories – population, economics, social structure, political system, culture, etc. Instead, Brown builds up a portrait of an age
rather in the manner of a post-impressionist artist, dabbing in rough
blotches of color here and there which, if one stands far enough
back, create a stunning vision of reality, but which, if examined up
close, dissolve into a meaningless blur. The deliberate vagueness,
the pictorial approach, the intimate juxtaposition of history, literature, religion and art, the concern for what was going on inside
people's heads, are all characteristic of a fresh way of looking at
history. The method is not narrative but rather a '*pointilliste*' way of
writing history. But it too has been stimulated by the new interest
in *mentalité* and made possible by the decline of the analytical and
structural approach which has been so dominant for the last thirty
years.

There has even been a revival of the narration of a single event.
Professor Georges Duby has dared to do what a few years ago
would have been unthinkable. He has devoted a book to an account
of a single battle – Bouvines – and through it has illuminated
the main characteristics of early thirteenth-century French feudal

society.[20] Carlo Ginzburg has given us a minute account of the cosmology of an obscure and humble early sixteenth-century north Italian miller, and by it has sought to demonstrate the intellectual and psychological disturbance at the popular level caused by the seepage downward of Reformation ideas.[21] Professor Emmanuel Le Roy Ladurie has painted a unique and unforgettable picture of life and death, work and sex, religion and custom in an early four-teenth-century village in the Pyrenees. *Montaillou* is significant in two respects: first because it has become one of the greatest historical bestsellers of the twentieth century in France; and second because it does not tell a straightforward story – there is no story – but rambles around inside people's heads. It is no accident that this is one of the ways in which the modern novel differs from those of earlier times. More recently, Le Roy Ladurie has told the story of a single bloody episode in a small town in southern France in 1580, using it to reveal the cross-currents of hatred that were tearing apart the social fabric of the town.[22] Professor Carlo M. Cipolla, who has hitherto been one of the hardest of hard-nosed economic and demographic structuralists, has just published a book which is more concerned with an evocative reconstruction of personal reactions to the terrible crisis of a pandemic than with establishing statistics of morbidity and mortality. For the first time, he tells a story.[23] Professor Eric Hobsbawm has described the nasty, brutish and short lives of rebels and bandits around the world, so as to define the nature and objectives of his 'primitive rebels' and 'social bandits.'[24] Mr Edward Thompson has told the story of the struggle in early eighteenth-century England between the poachers and the authorities in Windsor Forest, in order to support his argument about the clash of plebeians and patricians at that time.[25] Professor Robert Darnton's latest book tells how the great French *Encyclo-pédie* came to be published, and in so doing has cast a flood of new light on the process of diffusion of Enlightenment thought in the eighteenth century, and the problems of catering to a national – and international – market for ideas.[26] Professor Natalie Davis has presented a narrative of four *charivaris* or ritual public shame procedures in seventeenth-century Lyons and Geneva, in order to illustrate community efforts to enforce public standards of honor and propriety.[27]

The new interest in *mentalité* has itself stimulated a return to old ways of writing history. Keith Thomas's account of the conflict of magic and religion is constructed around a 'pregnant principle' along which are strung a mass of stories and examples.[28] My own recent book on changes in the emotional life in the English family is very similar in intent and method, if not in achievement.[29]

All the historians mentioned so far are mature scholars who have long been associated with the 'new history', asking new questions, trying out new methods, and searching for new sources. Now they are turning back to the telling of stories. There are, however, five differences between their stories and those of the traditional narrative historians. First, they are almost without exception concerned with the lives and feelings and behavior of the poor and obscure rather than the great and powerful. Second, analysis remains as essential to their methodology as description, so that their books tend to switch, a little awkwardly, from one mode to the other. Third, they are opening up new sources, often records of criminal courts which used Roman law procedures, since these contain written transcripts of the full testimony of witnesses under interrogation and examination. (The other fashionable use of criminal records, to chart the quantitative rise and fall of various types of deviance, seems to me to be an almost wholly futile endeavor, since what is being counted is not perpetrated crimes, but criminals who have been arrested and prosecuted, which is an entirely different matter. There is no reason to suppose that the one bears any constant relation over time to the other.) Fourth, they often tell their stories in a different way from that of Homer, or Dickens, or Balzac. Under the influence of the modern novel and of Freudian ideas, they gingerly explore the subconscious rather than sticking to the plain facts, and under the influence of the anthropologists, they try to use behavior to reveal symbolic meaning. Fifth, they tell the story of a person, a trial, or a dramatic episode, not for its own sake, but in order to throw light upon the internal workings of a past culture and society.

V

If I am right in my diagnosis, the movement to narrative by the 'new historians' marks the end of an era: the end of the attempt to produce a coherent and scientific explanation of change in the past. Models of historical determinism based on economics, demography or sociology have collapsed in the face of the evidence, but no full-blown deterministic model based on any other social science – politics, psychology or anthropology – has emerged to take its place. Structuralism and functionalism have not turned out much better. Quantitative methodology has proved a fairly weak reed which can only answer a limited set of problems. Forced into a choice between *a priori* statistical models of human behavior, and understanding based on observation, experience, judgment and intuition, some of the 'new historians' are now tending to drift back towards the latter mode of interpreting the past.

Although the revival by the 'new historians' of the narrative mode is a very recent phenomenon, it is merely a thin trickle in comparison with the constant, large and equally distinguished output of descriptive political narrative by more traditional historians. A recent example which has met with considerable scholarly acclaim is Simon Schama's book about Dutch politics in the eighteenth century.[30] Works such as these have for decades been treated with indifference or barely concealed disdain by the new social historians. This attitude did not have very much justification, but in recent years it has stimulated some of the traditional historians to adapt their descriptive mode to ask new questions. Some of them are no longer so preoccupied with issues of power and, therefore, with kings and prime ministers, wars and diplomacy, but are, like the 'new historians,' turning their attention to the private lives of quite obscure people. The cause of this trend, if trend it be, is not clear, but the inspiration seems to be the desire to tell a good story, and in so doing to reveal the quirks of personality and the inwardness of things in a different time and culture. Some traditional historians have been doing this for some time. In 1958, Professor G. R. Elton published a book composed of stories of riot and mayhem in sixteenth-century England, taken from the records of Star Chamber.[31] In 1946, Professor Hugh Trevor-Roper brilliantly reconstructed the last days of Hitler.[32] Just recently, he has investigated the extraordinary career of a relatively obscure English manuscript collector, conman, and secret pornographer, who lived in China in the early years of this century. The purpose of writing this entertaining yarn seems to have been sheer pleasure in storytelling for its own sake, in the pursuit and capture of a bizarre historical specimen. The technique is almost identical to that used years ago by A. J. A. Symons in his classic *Quest for Corvo*,[33] while the motivation appears very similar to that which inspires Richard Cobb to record in gruesome detail the squalid lives and deaths of criminals, prostitutes, and other social misfits in the underworld of Revolutionary France.[34]

Quite different in content, method and objective are the writings of the new British school of young antiquarian empiricists. They write detailed political narratives which implicitly deny that there is any deep-seated meaning to history except the accidental whim of fortune and personality. Led by Professor Conrad Russell and John Kenyon, and urged on by Professor Geoffrey Elton, they are now busy trying to remove any sense of ideology or idealism from the two English revolutions of the seventeenth century.[35] No doubt they, or others like them, will soon turn their attention elsewhere. Although their premise is never explicitly stated, their approach is pure neo-Namierism, just at a time when Namierism is dying as a way of looking at eighteenth-century English politics. One wonders whether their attitude to political history may not subconsciously stem from a sense of disillusionment with the capacity of the contemporary parliamentary system to grapple with the inexorable economic and power decline of Britain. Be that as it may, they are very erudite and intelligent chroniclers of the petty event, of *l'histoire événementielle*, and thus form one of the many streams which feed the revival of narrative.

The fundamental reason for the shift among the 'new historians' from the analytic to the descriptive mode is a major change in attitude about what is the central subject matter of history. And this in turn depends on prior philosophical assumptions about the role of human free will in its interaction with the forces of nature. The contrasting poles of thought are best revealed by quotations, one on one side and two on the other. In 1973, Emmanuel Le Roy Ladurie entitled a section of a volume of his essays 'History Without People.' By contrast, half a century ago Lucien Febvre announced 'Ma proie, c'est l'homme,' and a quarter of a century ago Hugh Trevor-Roper, in his inaugural lecture, urged upon historians 'the study not of circumstances but of man in circumstances.'[36] Today, Febvre's ideal of history is catching on in many circles, at the same time as analytic structural studies of impersonal forces continue to pour out from the presses. Historians therefore, are now dividing into four groups: the old narrative historians, primarily political historians and biographers; the cliometricians who continue to act like statistical junkies; the hard-nosed social historians still busy analyzing impersonal structures; and the historians of *mentalité*, now using narrative to chase ideals, values, mind sets, and patterns of intimate personal behavior – the more intimate the better.

The adoption by the last group of minute descriptive narrative or individual biography is not, however, without its problems. The trouble is the old one, that argument by selective example is philosophically unpersuasive, a rhetorical device not a scientific proof. The basic historiographic trap in which we are ensnared has recently been well set out by Carlo Ginzburg:[37]

> The quantitative and anti-anthropocentric approach of the sciences of nature from Galileo on has placed human sciences in an unpleasant dilemma: they must either adopt a weak scientific standard so as to be able to attain significant results, or adopt a strong scientific standard to attain results of no great importance.

Disappointment with the second approach is causing a drift back to the first. As a result, what is now taking place is an expansion of the selective example – not often a detailed unique example – into one of the fashionable modes of historical writing. In one sense, this is only a logical extension of the enormous success of local history studies, which have taken as their subject not a whole society but only a segment – a province, a town, even a village. Total history only seems possible if one takes a microcosm, and the results have often done more to illuminate and explain the past than all the earlier or concurrent studies based on the archives of the central government. In another sense, however, the new trend is the antithesis of local history studies, since it abandons total history of a society, however small, as an impossibility, and settles for the story of a single cell.

The second problem which arises from the use of the detailed example to illustrate *mentalité* is how to distinguish the normal from the eccentric. Since man is now our quarry, the narration of a very detailed story of a single incident or personality can make both good reading and good sense. But this will be so only if the stories do not merely tell a striking but fundamentally irrelevant tale of some dramatic episode of riot or rape, or the life of some eccentric rogue or villain or mystic, but are selected for the light they can throw upon certain aspects of a past culture. This means that they must be typical, and yet the wide use of records of litigation makes this question of typicality very difficult to resolve. People hauled into court are almost by definition atypical, but the world that is so nakedly exposed in the testimony of witnesses need not be so. Safety, therefore, lies in examining the documents not so much for their evidence about the eccentric behavior of the accused as for the light they shed on the life and opinions of those who happened to get involved in the incident in question.

The third problem concerns interpretation, and is even harder to resolve. Provided the historian remains aware of the hazards involved, story-telling is perhaps as good a way as any to obtain an intimate glimpse of man in the past, to try to get inside his head. The trouble is that if he succeeds in getting there, the narrator will need all the skill and experience and knowledge acquired in the practice of analytical history of society, economy and culture, if he is to provide a plausible explanation of some of the very strange things he is liable to find. He may also need a little amateur psychology to help him along, but amateur psychology is extremely tricky material to handle successfully – and some would argue that it is impossible.

Another obvious danger is that the revival of narrative may lead to a return to pure antiquarianism, to story-telling for its own sake. Yet another is that it will focus attention upon the sensational and so obscure the dullness and drabness of the lives of the vast majority. Both Trevor-Roper and Richard Cobb are enormous fun to read, but they are wide open to criticism on both counts. Many practitioners of the new mode, including Cobb, Hobsbawm, Thompson, Le Roy Ladurie and Trevor-Roper (and myself) are clearly fascinated by stories of violence and sex, which appeal to the voyeuristic instincts in us all. On the other hand it can be argued that sex and violence are integral parts of all human experience, and that it is therefore as reasonable and defensible to explore their impact on individuals in the past as it is to expect to see such material in contemporary films, television, and novels.

The trend to narrative raises unsolved problems about how we are to train our graduate students in the future – assuming that there are any to train. In the ancient arts of rhetoric? In textual criticism? In semiotics? In symbolic anthropology? In psychology? Or in the techniques of analysis of social and economic structures which we have been practising for a generation. It therefore remains an open question whether this unexpected resurrection of the narrative mode by so many leading practitioners of the 'new history' will turn out to be a good or a bad thing for the future of the profession.

In 1972, Le Roy Ladurie wrote confidently:[38]

Present-day historiography, with its preference for the quantifiable, the statistical and the structural, has been obliged to
suppress in order to survive. In the last decades it has virtually
condemned to death the narrative history of events and the
individual biography.

But in this, the third decade, narrative history and individual
biography are showing evident signs of rising again from the dead.
Neither look quite the same as they used to do before their alleged
demise, but they are easily identifiable as variants of the same genus.
Despite this resurrection, it is far too early to pronounce a funeral
oration over the decaying corpse of analytical, structural, quantitative history; it continues to flourish and even to grow if the trend in
American doctoral dissertations is any guide.[39]

It is clear that a single word like 'narrative,' especially one with
such a complicated history behind it, is inadequate to describe what
is in fact a broad cluster of changes in the nature of historical
discourse. There are signs of change in the central issue in history
from the circumstances surrounding man to man in circumstances;
in the problems studied from the economic and demographic to the
cultural and emotional; in the prime sources of influence from
sociology, economics and demography to anthropology and
psychology; in the subject matter from the group to the individual;
in the explanatory models of historical change from the stratified
and monocausal to the interconnected and multicausal; in the
methodology from group quantification to individual example; in
the organization from the analytical to the descriptive; and in the
conceptualization of the historian's function from the scientific to
the literary. These many-faceted changes in content, objective
method, and style of historical writing, which are all happening at
once, have clear elective affinities with one another: they all fit
neatly together. No single word is adequate to sum them all up, and
so, for the time being, 'narrative' will have to serve as a shorthand
code-word for all that is going on.

My hope is that, by drawing attention to the revival of narrative,
this article will stimulate further thought about its significance for
the future of history, and about the changing – and now increasingly tenuous – relationship of history to its sister social sciences,
assuming that history belongs with the social sciences in the first
place.

PART II

The emergence of the modern world

CHAPTER 4 · The Reformation

One of the more striking features of Christianity has been its perennial tendency to fission. With difficulty held together during the Middle Ages, it suddenly split asunder in the early sixteenth century. Not only did a series of new and independently organized churches emerge after the earthquake – Calvinist, Lutheran and Anglican – which together form what has usefully been described as the 'Magisterial Reformation'; in addition there oozed through the cracks in the fabric of medieval Christendom a host of strange new sects with alarmingly revolutionary beliefs and aspirations – collectively known as the 'Radical Reformation'.[1]

There are two ways of looking at this crisis of European civilization. The one lays principal stress on popular undercurrents of religious emotion and faith, and sees the Reformation as a series of responses by men in authority and by institutions to pressures and demands from below.[2] Its strength lies in sympathy for and understanding of the ideological tensions and conflicts which were at work in late medieval Europe, and its appreciation of the deep undercurrents of history which were sweeping along even the most powerful princes, like Charles V, and the most charismatic prophets, like Luther.

The other interpretation places the main emphasis on the outstanding personalities and their use of power, particularly the power of the sword.[3] There is a good deal of sense in this approach, for again and again we see a determined minority imposing its doctrinal views on an indifferent or reluctant majority by the use of force. The first half-century of Calvinist rule in the Netherlands and of Anglican rule in England, are striking examples. On the other hand, it exaggerates the degree to which state power was effective in the sixteenth century, and underestimates the role of popular feeling.

When setting out to analyze the causes of the Reformation, one must clearly begin with a description of the social scene in early sixteenth-century Germany. One theory, which goes back at least to Henri Hauser half a century ago, is that the area was a victim of violent economic and social dislocation. The result of rapid population growth was rising food prices, drift to the towns, unemployment, fragmented rural holdings, high rents and low wages, and a widening gulf between rich and poor. Artisans and peasants were particularly affected by the low wage-high price system, and were further squeezed by rising taxation to feed the developing state machines of Europe and by landlord exploitation of a surplus of labor. The result, so the theory runs, was poverty, disorientation, and resentment, which early found expression in millenarian religious revival and also in receptiveness to the more disciplined and rational appeals of Luther or Calvin.

The difficulty, however, about this theory is that there is very little evidence that population pressures had become really serious by 1520; very little evidence that the plight of peasants and artisans was much worse than it was later on; no evidence at all that such misery as existed was particularly severe in Germany. In Luther's day this was the most prosperous area in Europe, and the crushing of peasants and artisans by the weight of taxation and high rents had hardly begun. In the towns, the economic and political deprivation of the artisan class was only just beginning, and was to get much worse later.

The second hypothesis, which was first put forward by Engels and Marx, is that the Reformation is related to the rise of the bourgeoisie. But in the first place, it is not at all clear that the bourgeoisie was rising at this time. The growing commercial activity of Europe was probably increasing the wealth and the numbers of the merchant community, and the numbers, if not the wealth, of the artisans. But it is very doubtful indeed whether this increase was as great as the growth of aristocratic and princely wealth which was to result from the seizure of church property, the rise in rents, and the increase in state revenues from taxes. In terms of power, moreover, the town authorities were everywhere losing their sovereignty in the face of encroachments from princes and nobles. Second, not all bourgeois were Protestant. It is true that the early reformers – Luther, Calvin, and Zwingli – made an immediate appeal to influential groups in the free cities of central Europe, especially, it seems, to the younger generation in the new trades who were anxious to seize power from the older, more conservative

patriciate. On the other hand, the patricians of the greatest European cities, Antwerp, Paris, Amsterdam, and London, seem to have
been either hostile or indifferent, while some of the most fanatically
Protestant areas, like Scotland, had virtually no bourgeoisie at all.
All that can reasonably be said at this stage is that when the dust
settled in the late sixteenth century, it appeared that the growth
points in the European economy – the cities of the western seaboard
– were predominantly Protestant, while the stagnating cities of the
central land-mass were largely Catholic once more. But whether
anything can be made of this association so far as causation is
concerned is at present very doubtful.

A third, perhaps more plausible, sociological explanation of the
Reformation is that it reflects the rise of an educated elite of laymen,
ready and anxious to take over the spiritual and administrative
functions of a now superfluous and discredited clergy. In broad
terms, this is indeed what happened, and the growing control of the
laity over the clergy is a phenomenon common to all stages of the
Reformation. Perhaps the most important theological change was
the reduction in the role of salvation played by the sacrament. This
in turn involved a sharp reduction in the authority and prestige of
the clergy as controllers of this ritual; and a consequent increase in
the independence and self-confidence of the laity. Anti-clericalism
has long been recognized as one of the principal forces behind
the Reformation, but only recently has it been appreciated that this
feeling is the product less of a change for the worse in the character
of the priesthood than of a change for the better in the demands of
the laity. This sense of the superiority of the laity over the clergy
was greatly strengthened by the work of the Humanists. Their
educational reforms adapted the medieval grammar school and
university to the needs of amateur gentlemen rather than of
professional clerics, their study of antiquity demonstrated the moral
worth even of a non-Christian laity, and the translations of the New
Testament destroyed the historical foundation of priestly authority.
This new mood of aggressive Erasmianism was soon reflected in a
shift of political power. Princes took on the congenial role of priest-
kings, uniting in one person the headship of church and state.
Nobles seized church property and the power to appoint the local
clergy; city corporations, as at Zurich or Geneva, were associated
with the clergy in a tight control of economics and morals. In any
case, one of the key aspects of the Reformation was the destruction

of the hierarchy of intercessors between God and the individual. Christianity ceased to be a tolerant polytheism with prayers directed to saints and angels and the Virgin Mary rather than to Christ; the role of the sacrament and therefore of its agent the priest, were minimized, and salvation was shifted to the individual act of faith rather than the routine performance of certain rituals.

To sum up then, there is general agreement that the Reformation appealed to certain specific groups within sixteenth-century society. To princes, who found Lutheranism an ideal tool for state-building; to the more progressive urban oligarchs, who found the moralizing energy of Zwingli or Calvin a convenient instrument for the social control of their cities; to artisans and merchants in the newer trades who sought ideological support against an entrenched patriciate; to nobles seeking moral and religious justification for the transfer of church property to themselves and for taking over the administrative and ideological function of the clergy; to aristocratic wives, tormented by the futility of their idle and neglected lives, for whom the new doctrines at last seemed to offer some explanation for their existence; and lastly to the intellectuals, often minor clergy, monks, friars, or academics, who had lost all confidence in their role in the Catholic church and saw in the Reformed religion a more inspiring approach to the problem of salvation, and a faith with which they could make over the corrupt and worldly society in which they lived.

The main distinguishing doctrines of the Reformation were salvation by faith alone and the priesthood of all believers, both of which had as a result the down-grading of the priesthood and the creation of a new hierarchy and a new elite. The key factor in the dissemination of these ideas was the printing press, without which it is probable that there would have been no Reformation at all. The development of moveable type some centuries before the development of an efficient police force gravely weakened the power of the state to control ideas within its own borders (once police powers increased, of course, the balance shifted back again, and today there is overwhelming ideological power in the hands of the state). It was the printing press which disseminated at such speed the ideas of Luther, and the printing press which made that revolutionary document, the bible, available to an unsophisticated but semi-literate laity. The result was the most massive missionary drive in history, a combined assault on indifference, cynicism, paganism, and ignorance conducted by the Reformers, on the one hand, and the Counter-Reformers, on the other. So far as it conveyed to the ordinary man and woman the true meaning of Christianity, the sixteenth century was far more effective than all the long centuries of the Middle Ages and it is no wild paradox to speak of the sixteenth century as the era of the rise of Christian Europe – and of the decline of the bourgeoisie.

The Reformation would not have achieved such immediate success if it had not been able to harness the powerful feelings of separatism and nationalism. Not only did independent state churches spring up to satisfy princely demands for total sovereignty, but the translation of the bible into the vernacular and the substitution of a vernacular for a Latin ritual in church enormously increased the homogeneity of the national cultures. (It would be interesting to speculate about the consequent superiority in internal coherence of Protestant over Catholic states during the last four hundred years.)

Lastly the Reformation era was one in which an attempt was made to restructure the ideal personality of the West. This ambitious program of social engineering was at first widely diffused across Europe. What was adumbrated in theory by the Catholic Thomas More in the *Utopia*, was put into practice in Calvinist Geneva and Boston. On both sides of the ideological gap, Jesuit, Jansenist, and Calvinist preachers taught austerity, discipline, and self-control, and shifted the main thrust of moral instruction from issues of property and violence to those of pride and sex. Morality was personalized and internalized, as confidence in the priestly capacity for the remission of sins declined. Guilt and the Devil replaced atonement and the Virgin.

If these are the main underlying forces behind the Reformation, they still only add up to a sufficient rather than a necessary assemblage of causes. To them must be added the spiritual condition of the Catholic church and the political configuration of Europe. The trouble with the church was not, as the Humanists thought, that it was full of abuses which cried out to be cleaned up, but rather that it had lost its sense of spiritual purpose which allowed such abuses to flourish. For several hundred years it had successfully absorbed radical reform movements, up to and including the Franciscans, and so had maintained its spiritual vitality. But from the late fourteenth century it had crushed such movements as heretical – like the Lollards and Hussites – and so, in consequence, had gone into slow ideological decay. Obsessed with administrative issues of law and finance, it had lost sight of its essential purpose.

That the Reformation could begin and spread rapidly in Germany can be explained by the fact that in this politically fragmented area there were princes who were ready to offer protection and support. That it could survive and take root can partly be explained by its popular appeal, but partly also by the fact that important political interests felt themselves threatened by the efforts of the Emperor Charles V to crush it.

The princes – even the Catholic princes – were afraid, since they thought that the suppression of Protestantism might be the first step towards the suppression of princely liberties. France – Catholic, persecuting France – was afraid that if the Habsburgs crushed the Protestants, they would obtain overwhelming strength and so upset the balance of power in Europe. Even the pope was afraid, since a militarily triumphant emperor in Germany might threaten his own consolidation of territorial power in Italy. Because of this opposition, together with the need to repel the Turks, Charles V was never able to crush the Reformation heresy. For the same reasons, the triumphant march of the Counter-Reformation back into Northern Europe during the Thirty Years War a hundred years later was blocked by the active intervention on the side of the Protestants of Catholic France, and by the ambivalent attitudes of the Catholic princes of the empire. Again and again, the balance of power took precedence over religious solidarity. The blood of national self-interest was thicker than the water of ideology.

In the first half of the sixteenth century Europe was faced with a variety of religious alternatives. There was the old, unreformed, polytheistic Catholicism of relics, indulgences and all the rest of the degenerate paraphernalia of salvation at the bargain basement, whose survival was now virtually impossible in view of the rising demand in Europe for spiritual nourishment. There was the possibility of a Catholic church reformed along the lines of the Christian Humanists; that is, purged of its administrative and financial abuses, made tolerant, humane, and easy-going. The suggestion that had it not been for Luther the church might have evolved on these lines has been toyed with by one or two historians, and the idea is superficially an attractive one. But, as Dr Elton points out, it involves a transfer of twentieth-century values to the sixteenth century and ignores the fact that Erasmian Humanism was essentially moralistic and elitist. It neither desired nor was able to satisfy the theological needs of the intellectuals or the spiritual needs of the poor, but it was precisely their needs which were tearing Christendom apart.

The third possibility was the abortive Radical Reformation, the full significance of which is only just becoming apparent partly because of the publication of Professor Williams's book and partly because so many of the ideas it embraced find a direct resonance in the 'counter-culture' of our contemporary society. Few historians have had much time or sympathy for the radicals, and fewer still have admitted that they have had any influence on future thinking. But some of their ideas cropped up again among the English Levellers and the wilder sects of the Interregnum. Some of the more moderate of these ideas passed into English reformist thought in the late seventeenth and eighteenth centuries, even if mainstream Whig political ideology owed most to James Harrington.

And so the unreformed late medieval church was incapable of defending itself, the Christian Humanist Erasmians never had a chance, and the radical sects were persecuted almost to extinction. The spiritual needs of Europe were met first by the Magisterial Reformation, as Professor Williams calls it, and later by the Catholic Counter-Reformation. Of the three main branches of the Magisterial Reformation, two, the Lutheran and Anglican, almost immediately adapted to the existing political authority and lost all capacity for expansion: they became local, particularist, and conservative. Calvinism, however, was made of sterner stuff, for it had all the ingredients for dynamic growth. It had a sacred book, the Bible, the militant Old Testament being more often read than the pacific Gospels; it had a cellular organization and rigid discipline; and it had a mystical faith in the future triumph of the cause. The doctrine of predestination of the elect, by its very determinism, screwed men up to ever greater feats of activity, just as the similarly deterministic faith of Marxism does today.

Opposed to this expansionist religion was a revitalized Catholic church. Faced with siege conditions, Rome reacted in a predictable way: it became more centralized, more dogmatic, more rigid, more persecuting, and more fanatical; it also became more spiritually and intellectually alive, more fertile in institutional innovation, more active in the battle for souls than it had been for centuries. The combination of the administrative centralization of the papacy, the repressive activities of the Inquisition, the educational drive of the Jesuits, the spiritual and aesthetic regeneration of baroque Catholicism, and the military conquests of the Habsburg armies succeeded in the seventeenth century in rolling the tide of heresy back into Northern Germany, and in recovering the whole of Eastern Europe.

In the face of these antagonistic forces, sensible politicians did what they could to avoid disaster by settling for a division of Europe on geographical lines. The *cuius regio eius religio* formula of the Peace of Augsburg of 1555 was a cynical but practical device to prevent the total destruction of Europe in ideological conflict. In practice, if not in theory, it gave secular powers the freedom to exterminate dissenters within their own borders without running much risk of external intervention. Within a generation ideology had consequently ceased to be analyzable in terms of class or group feelings, and had become a mere matter of geography. Europe was fragmented, areas like the Netherlands were artificially split in two, but peace was preserved in Germany for seventy years.

In the end, therefore, it was the boundaries of nation states which dictated the religious faith to which the great majority of the population in fact subscribed. This should not surprise us too much, because by and large the same generalization of *cuius regio eius religio* applies even more to the twentieth century, the second era in which Western civilization has been split ideologically down the middle. In Bolshevik Russia, fifty years of political pressure have largely destroyed the Orthodox faith; and another thirty years of political pressure in Eastern Europe may perhaps suffice to reduce Roman Catholicism east of the Iron Curtain to negligible proportions. In America, on the other hand, members of the Communist party are as rare as bald eagles, and for much the same reasons.

It is a curious fact that the problem of Protestant thought control during the Reformation is one that has hitherto been badly neglected by historians. Volumes have been written about how the Catholics suppressed Protestantism in Spain or Italy, but very little about how the Protestants suppressed Catholicism in England or Holland. The sixteenth-century states were very much weaker than those of today, and yet after seventy years of Protestant rule, Roman Catholicism in England was reduced from virtually the only religion to that of a tiny, ostracized minority. There are three possible explanations of how this came about. Either nobody cared very much one way or the other, so that the state did not need to exert itself; or there was an active and growing minority which was sympathetic to reform anyway, so that state policy was merely following the tide of influential opinion; or the state exerted strong and effective police powers to destroy overt opposition, stamp out vocal dissent, and convert the population, or at any rate the younger generation, to the new orthodoxy.

Dr Elton is an administrative and constitutional historian who, by his own clearly expressed statements, has no time for historical pluralism. He is strongly opposed to such novelties as social history or quantitative methods, and he regards the study of state policy and state power as the highest and truest function of the historian. Not for him the thought that the community of historians might profitably live in many mansions and learn something from each other's lifestyles. He is also a most distinguished Tudor historian, his reputation depending mainly on a major study of the administrative innovations of Henry the Eighth's chief minister in the 1530s, Thomas Cromwell.[4] He has failed to persuade more than a small minority of his colleagues in the profession that the changes that took place at that time can reasonably be described as a 'revolution in government', but it is an idea with which every serious student of the period must henceforth grapple.

He has now made a detailed study of the repressive aspects of the bureaucratic machinery described in the earlier volume, its use as an instrument for social control at a time when religious orthodoxy was being altered for the first time since the initial conversion of the English to Christianity nine hundred years before, when the hereditary succession to the throne was being changed arbitrarily from year to year according to the marital whims of King Henry, and when the state was in the process of seizing for itself between a quarter and a third of the landed property of the kingdom.[5] As the preface makes clear, the chief motive behind this book is to vindicate Thomas Cromwell from the charge of the Victorian scholar R.B. Merriman that he practiced a 'reign of terror.' This is why Dr Elton confines himself to the period of Cromwell's rule, and this is the theme to which he continually returns. This is, therefore, a book with a prime didactic purpose, to return a verdict of not guilty upon an individual with whom over the years Dr Elton has formed a close attachment – almost an identification – as well as a broader aim to 'reveal the realities of government.'

The argument runs as follows. (1) 'If there was terror, it existed in the mind only' (i.e. it was a mild regime since only about 350 persons at most were executed for political reasons in nine years). (2) 'His control involved the enforcement of the law as it stood, by the age's lawful methods of trial and investigation' (i.e. he kept within the letter of the law, and that is what matters). (3) 'Great care was taken to establish the truth before the power of the law was brought into action' (i.e. casual punishment of innocent victims of malicious denunciation was not a part of official policy). (4) 'No attempt was made to organize ... anything resembling a network of spies; no rewards or inducements were offered' (i.e. he merely relied on a daily post-bag of poison-pen letters). (5) 'Cromwell did what he thought he had to do; the hatred and vindictiveness belonged to the King' (i.e. Cromwell was the coldly efficient bureaucrat, Henry was the man of passion). (6) 'Without such activities society collapses ... the revolution which he guided had major constructive ends in view.' 'The King and his ministers were not men of gentle kindness. They were riding a revolution and needed drastic instruments of repression' (i.e. you can't make an omelet without breaking eggs, and it was a good omelet anyway).

In order to judge the validity of this set of propositions, it is necessary to look closely at the methods employed to arrive at them. The book is composed of an endless series of denunciations of unknown individuals by other unknown individuals, and of reports of official investigations into the accused. Not only are the stories themselves disconnected and often trivial, and only rarely amusing, but in a great many cases Dr Elton has no idea what happened to the accused in the end. As he himself says, 'I am uneasily aware of the barriers to enjoyment set by so many stories of often petty events, too many of them, moreover, devoid of that satisfaction which knowledge of the final outcome would bring.' This ignorance of the final outcome is partly because the records of Quarter Sessions and Assizes are either non-existent or incomplete or poorly indexed; partly also it is because Dr Elton has largely restricted himself to a meticulous examination of that body of data he knows better than anyone else in the world, Cromwell's personal files. Again and again, therefore, his stories peter out inconclusively: 'whatever steps were taken have left no evidence behind'; 'no more is known'; 'she looks to have got off'; etc. When in doubt, he tends to assume that the accused was spared, without much hard evidence to support the conclusion. Some at least of the 109 capital cases he labels 'Probably dropped' may in fact have to be added to the list of sufferers of the terrible penalties for treason, namely death by torture. As a result, it is hard to avoid the conclusion that Dr Elton's statistics about victims are not entirely trustworthy.

A more serious defect is that the list of executions is in any case only the moraine thrown up and drifting on a great invisible glacier of repression and punitive actions, of floggings, tortures, imprisonments, public humiliations, harassments, etc., carried out by lesser authorities all over the country. Dr Elton himself admits that under ceaseless goading from Cromwell to suppress loose talk, rumors, false news, etc., the local JPs often 'acted summarily, using public disclaimers, the pillory, and the whip as fancy took them or the seriousness of the offence seemed to warrant.' Thus a zealous – or sycophantic – Cornish justice reported to Cromwell that he was freely using the pillory and the stocks 'according to the contents of your former letters to me directed.' Because Dr Elton has confined himself to a close reading of the contents of the in-tray on the desk of the leading minister in London, his evidence offers no more than one or two of these faint suggestions about the true weight of non-capital punishment as it bore down in real life on the villages and towns of England; it is therefore impossible from this book accurately to assess its severity.

The second methodological flaw is that, on the grounds that they are 'a highly special case,' Dr Elton omits all discussion of the suppression of the series of major armed rebellions which broke out in the north of England in 1536-7, and which for a time threatened the stability of the regime itself. But this was the supreme challenge to Cromwell's system of repression, the outbreak of which gives a measure of the pent-up resentments of the population, and the defeat of which marks the turning point in the long battle for social control with which this book is concerned.

Another set of objections to Dr Elton's approach to his problem is concerned with questions of historical imagination. These are delicate issues of moral sensibility rather than historical method, and it may be that they are too subjective to be relevant. But they are bothersome. Dr Elton is personally an amiable man, but there is a chillingly heartless tone to these endless descriptions of persecution, and sometimes torture and execution, of little people caught up by a loose word or a slip of the tongue in a moment of anger or drink in the cogs of a great revolution and ground to dust by the Moloch of the state. He tells us cheerily that one victim 'succeeded in getting himself executed' as if the wretched man had perversely insisted on thrusting himself upon the executioner. Another's 'loose tongue got him a month in prison awaiting Cromwell's pleasure, but no more.' Has Dr Elton ever stopped to consider what life was like for a poor man in a sixteenth-century prison, certainly half-starved, and possibly chained up in a dark cellar to wallow in his own filth? Or how his family survived while the bread-winner could earn no money? To Cromwell such gossips were merely tiresome nuisances who had to be silenced, and Dr Elton agrees with him: 'Fish was asking for trouble. People's credulity was a burden to King and Government. Cromwell said so often enough … ' Equally disturbing is another failure of the historical imagina-tion. Dr Elton seems to be totally unaware of the damage done to the fabric of a society when governments positively encourage denunciations of neighbors by neighbors, thus opening up a Pandora's box of local malice and slander. No one who has read a little about life in occupied Europe under the Nazis, or has seen the movie *Le Chagrin et La Pitié* could share the satisfaction of Dr Elton as he triumphantly concludes that his hero encouraged private delation rather than relying on a system of paid informers. (Inciden-tally, it is on this issue that a serious case of *suppressio veri* occurs. In his discussion of whether or not Cromwell was planning or operating a police state, Dr Elton omits altogether to mention that sinister little sentence in one of his memoranda to himself in 1534: 'to have substantial persons in every good town to discover who speaks or preaches thus' (i.e. 'in favor of the Pope's authority').[6]

Finally, there is the question of Dr Elton's curiously respectful attitude towards the enacted law. For him it seems that there can be no meaningful difference between a statute and natural justice. He speaks of 'the purposes of government, purposes which, as the law stood, must be called the ends of justice too.' In 1536 Cromwell managed, after a struggle, to get a statute passed in Parliament which extended the meaning – and penalties – of treason to cover the spoken word, or even a refusal to take the Oath of Supremacy, or, as judicially interpreted, the mere dissemination of rumor, while at the same time preserving the medieval tradition that a single

witness is adequate for conviction. Executions by torture inflicted
as a result of this atrocious statute were lawful, and in Dr. Elton's
eyes were apparently therefore just. Dr Elton's paragraph on this
statute (pp. 287-8) is worth reading as a masterpiece of sophistical
casuistry.

Where, then, does this leave Dr Elton's main thesis? Defective
though his evidence clearly is, limited though he is in his empathy
with the victims, confused though he is about the difference
between legality and natural justice, blind though he is to every
consideration save that of *raison d'état*, he has proved one point
without much doubt: there was no blood-bath, nothing like the
Terror under Robespierre, or the Great Purges under Stalin.
Annual executions did not exceed fifty, which is small stuff by
modern standards. Compared with what happened during the
French Revolution, whose endless bloody horrors have recently
been displayed, perhaps in excessively loving detail, by Professor
Cobb, the instruments of social control exercised by Cromwell
during the first stage of the English Reformation were both weak
and poorly organized. For one thing, Cromwell had neither a paid
local bureaucracy nor a standing army to enforce his will. It also
seems that Cromwell was not an erratic and arbitrary sadist,
although he was certainly a cold and heartless brute. He did mostly
act within the limits established by the law, however tyrannical it
may have been, and he did make some effort to sift truth from
falsehood in the stream of denunciations, in so far as he could spare
the time from more urgent business. How far he succeeded is
another matter, on which the records are unhelpful.

On the other hand, compared with the Middle Ages, or modern
open societies, the degree of thought control and the loss of
personal liberty are startling indeed. It was the crisis of the
Reformation that first drove the politicians and bureaucrats of
Europe to strive for a domination over the hearts and minds of their
subjects far more total than any that had been seen before.

Whether the orchestrated repression directed and supervised by
Cromwell and reaching down to the lowest levels of civic administration added up to a 'reign of terror' must remain an open question.
But it should be noted that repression works best through the fear
inspired by example. The well-chosen and well-publicized executions of key figures like More and Fisher and the Abbot of Reading,
the frequent spectacles of the public punishments of the spreaders of

rumors by putting them in the pillory, cutting off their ears, and flogging them half-naked about the town on market days until they were drenched in blood were enough to cow all but the most dedicated or the most foolish. The regime was certainly not as murderous as some other regimes of later ages, but it was the most repressive that the primitive administrative machinery of the age could manage. My reading of the evidence offered in this book is that it reinforces the belief that Cromwell was driving England steadily towards a legalized Renaissance despotism with the overlay of more modern forms of thought-control, and that its further development was only arrested by his premature death – appropriately enough on the scaffold – and by subsequent major errors in state policy, such as selling off most of the seized church property to pay for a supremely futile war.

The fundamental methodological argument that is here being made is that the history of repression cannot be written merely by telling stories out of the leading repressor's post-bag. In the first place, some hard analysis is necessary to assess the capacity of the king's chief minister to bend local officials to his will. This involves a careful study of the distribution of local power, and of the desire and capacity of the magnates and local gentry to obstruct orders from London. The four-way relationship between the central government, great nobles, gentry, and articulate yeomanry and peasantry, was changing at this period, as the Pilgrimage of Grace showed, but Dr Elton does not deal with such matters. We are told nothing, for example, about the way in which Henry and Cromwell enhanced the power of the dependable gentry of the north, so as to undermine that of the unreliable magnates of that area, and thus to extend the area under control of the central government. Although Cromwell's files offer ample evidence, we are told nothing whatever about his methods and success in developing a chain of local agents and dependents and clients upon which political effectiveness depended in this age of patronage. We need to see how Cromwell's clientage system related to those of his enemies, like the Duke of Norfolk, many of whom were also important power-brokers and as anxious to protect Roman Catholics as Cromwell was to silence them. Only by such a study, which Dr Elton has not undertaken, will it be possible to 'reveal the realities of government.'

In the second place, the story of repression has to be told, not only from the point of view of the policeman, as Dr Elton tells it,

but also from that of the victims, as Professor Cobb has tried to tell
it.[7] It is significant that ideology, passionate religious dedication to
either Protestantism or Catholicism, plays only a minor part in Dr
Elton's innumerable stories. But that it did play a major part, along
with cruelty, slander, greed, envy, malice and all uncharitableness,
can hardly be doubted. In the end the opinions of people from
weavers to nobles, formed through the reading of the bible or a
desire for church land or a dislike of priestly authority, were at least
as important as the Reformation crisis. But this is a story which can
only be told, as Professor Dickens has told it, from local and legal
records.[8] What really happened to the English in the 1530s – indeed,
what really happens to any people at any time – cannot be
discovered merely by examining the correspondence of the leading
minister.

If we turn from the causes and methods to the consequences of
this gigantic upheaval in the life of Europe, we are at once faced
with a grave semantic difficulty. Many forces, like literacy, nationalism, or anti-clericalism, are both a cause and a consequence: their
presence helped the Reformation to take root, but the Reformation
in its turn enormously stimulated their subsequent growth. In the
short run the results are clear enough. There was a gigantic increase
in man's inhumanity to man, in violence and cruelty; there was a
sharp decline in freedom of thought, in rational ideas of toleration
and moderation, as the Humanists were displaced by the extremists;
there was much redistribution of property from the clergy to the
laity in both Catholic and Protestant areas; and lastly there was a
striking rise in religious enthusiasm penetrating all classes in the
social structure: Europe was Christianized at last.

The long-term consequences, however, were both unintended
and quite different. In politics, the stalemate between Protestants
and Catholics confirmed the particularist fragmentation of Germany by the stimulus given to the princes; and confirmed the
national fragmentation of Europe by the stimulus given to state
churches. The challenge of the radicals forced the Lutherans further
into an alliance with the lay authorities than they would otherwise
have wished to go; and the challenge of Protestantism forced Rome
to adopt a rigid and reactionary posture of centralized authoritarianism from which it is only emerging today, some four hundred
years later.

One of the great organizing hypotheses of modern times was

advanced by Max Weber, who argued that the teachings of the Reformers created the necessary ethical conditions without which modern capitalism could not flourish. The hypothesis was reinterpreted by R. H. Tawney, who argued that the ideas of the Reformers were adjusted over time in order to fit the needs of the capitalist, bourgeois society in which they had to take root. Neither Professor Dickens nor Dr Elton thinks much of these propositions, and the latter, relying heavily on the work of a Swedish historian, Dr Samuelsson,[9] launches into a ferocious onslaught on the whole idea, pouring particular scorn on Tawney's great book, *Religion and the Rise of Capitalism*. He writes:

> His book has had an extraordinary influence. Especially in England and America, it has greatly assisted in the decline of Protestant self-confidence and the consequent revival of Roman Catholicism, in the reaction against capitalism as an economic system, and even perhaps in the West's increasing inclination to relinquish world leadership.

The most charitable thing one can say about this extraordinary outburst is that the explanation it offers for the decline of the West at least has the virtue of novelty. (One of the more puzzling phenomena of our time is the way conservative intellectuals, like Dr Elton or Professor Trevor-Roper, who are capable of taking a cool and dispassionate view of Karl Marx, are driven to frenzies of hatred by the writings of that mild Christian socialist, R. H. Tawney.)

The criticisms of Weber and Tawney formulated by Dr Samuelsson and repeated by Dr Elton are based on a failure to understand what they were talking about, or indeed to read them with care. Weber was not concerned with human greed and acquisitiveness, which he realized perfectly well to be a persistent psychological trait, nor with the emergence of 'booty capitalists' battening on government, finance, monopolies, war, piracy, or usury. So to trot out the Fuggers, or Calvin's hostility to usury, is entirely beside the point.

Weber believed that this ethic arose from the abandonment of the Catholic cycle of sin and atonement according to which salvation can be assured by priests and aided by good works, and its replacement by the creed of salvation by faith alone and the doctrine of the elect. The only way a man could prove to his own satisfaction that he was saved was by continuous godliness, achieved by unremitting self-discipline in which diligent application to one's calling played a vital part, if only as a means of distraction from the manifold temptations of the Devil. The result was the creation of a disciplined workforce well adapted to the continuous production lines of modern industry, self-imposed saving through thrift which provided the necessary capital for investment, and canny but honest entrepreneurs concerned with long-term output rather than quick, speculative profit.

This 'Protestant ethic', if widely dispersed among a whole population, must inevitably lead, thought Weber, to that routine application to business which is the essence of modern capitalism – 'the rational capitalist organization of (formally) free labor.' If one is to criticize this thesis, it must at least be in terms of what it says. Now it is certainly true that 'middle-class morality' towards sex and work and punctuality has been a prime characteristic of the industrial societies of the West, and that this morality seems to derive its origin from Calvinist theology. The fact that by the eighteenth century it had become divorced from its religious foundation and had become the purely secular value system of Benjamin Franklin merely proves that it had taken sufficient root to survive the waning of religious enthusiasm.

There are, on the other hand, three objections to the Weber – Tawney thesis, which have yet to be answered. The first is the evidence that up to the early seventeenth century at least, much of Calvinist thinking was strongly hostile to capitalist acquisitiveness and the rule of the market-place. *Laissez-faire* and the doctrine of the maximization of profit regardless of the public welfare had no place in Calvin's Geneva. The dilemma of the pious Calvinist merchant seeking both to conform to the Calvinist ethic code about the just price and to pursue his calling to the best of his endeavor, is revealingly portrayed in the agonized autobiography of the seventeenth-century Boston merchant, Robert Keayne.[10] The Puritan ethic drove him to maximize his profits, but the economic morality of his church condemned him publicly when he did it. In the end, as we know, the growth of capitalism eroded the moral restraints, even in Boston, but this psychic tension, this precarious balance, is something overlooked by Weber and denied by Tawney. Second, we are beginning to be aware of the existence of a 'Catholic Puritanism,' particularly marked in French Jansenism, which throws doubt on the unique role of Protestantism in developing

these ethical characteristics. Third, study of early modern entre-
preneurship shows a recklessness in risk-taking and a very high
failure rate, which look more like the characteristics of medieval
'booty capitalism' than of modern, cost-benefit conscious corporate
endeavors. Moreover, the really large profiteers usually depended
heavily on bribing and blackmailing governments into granting
monopolies and concessions that amounted to licences to print
money. All this seems a far cry from the Protestant ethic.

The most important contribution of the Reformation to capitalism, science, and the spirit of toleration was in fact not intended at
all. The religious fragmentation of Christian Europe undermined
confidence in the existence of a single road to truth. The red-hot
enthusiasm of the seventeenth century led directly to the cool deism
of the eighteenth. The appalling bloodshed and destruction of the
religious wars finally stimulated recognition of the economic and
political advantages of toleration. The failure of persecution to
extirpate other creeds in many Protestant areas forced several
countries, and in particular England, to accept, willynilly, a plural
society where many beliefs and opinions could flourish. Once this
happened, some of the discredited ideas of the Radical Reformers
about liberty, equality, and fraternity could once more emerge into
the open and even achieve, here and there, some measure of
respectability. The shift of authority from clergy to laity led in the
end to a shift of values from the next world to this, as the book
production and the library holdings of the late seventeenth century
plainly show. In the last resort, therefore, the Reformation, like all
other great movements in history, had consequences quite other
than those which were intended by its leaders and their followers.

So far in this discussion, attention has been focused on the
'Magisterial Reformation' as it affected the ruling elites and state
authorities. But meanwhile more disturbing things were happening,
for between 1520 and 1580 cracks appeared in the hard crust of
European society. For a period of about half a century, princes and
magistrates, landlords and patricians, priests and presbyters felt a
threat to their authority and their sense of values. Fissures in the
social, political and intellectual fabric appeared all over Europe
from Poland to England, and through them there oozed a host of
new social and religious revolutionaries: Adamites, Amosites,
Anabaptists, Blandratists, Budnyites, Davidjorists, Farnovians,
Familists, Gabrielites, Gonesians, Hoferites, Hutterites, Loists,

Melchiorites, Mennonites, Münsterites, Obbenites, Pinczovians, Quintinists, Schwenchfeldians, Servetians, Socinians, Unitarians, Utraquists and Valdesians. Primarily, of course, these sectaries were religious fanatics, obsessed with strange theological doctrines. But they were also men and women who gathered together to preach and practice pacifism, community of goods and of production, equality of the sexes, the abolition of class distinctions, the exaltation of sexual activity in marriage as a quasi-religious sacrament, divorce on the grounds of adultery, the abolition of usury, tithes and taxes, and the withdrawal of Christians from all offices in secular government.

Naturally enough, the life of these people was nasty, brutish and short. Society turned on them with that passionate ferocity which it reserves for those who challenge the assumptions, standards and structure of authority by which it lives and is governed. All established churches, both Catholic and Protestant, were united in their hatred of these 'libertines, revolutionaries, fanatics, visionaries, blasphemers and communists.' One of them, Michael Servetus, escaped from the Catholics at Lyons, who burnt him in effigy, only to fall into the hands of the Calvinists at Geneva, who burnt him in the flesh. They were massacred swiftly in hot blood, tortured lingeringly in cold blood with the rack, the boot and the thumbscrews, they were burnt at the stake, broken on the wheel, drowned, beheaded, hanged, flogged, torn with red hot pincers, eviscerated and dismembered. By 1580 their day was mostly done. They survived in Poland and Transylvania, but it was in seventeenth-century England that they were to make their mark on history by establishing the non-conformist conscience that is still a leaven in English society today.

Hitherto these sectaries have been casually treated as no more than the lunatic fringe of the Reformation proper. In a massive and revolutionary survey of the whole field, Dr Williams now suggests that this traditional view is a false one. He argues that the Reformation took two distinct forms: the Magisterial Reformation of Luther, Zwingli, Calvin and Cranmer, carried through in support of secular authority, enforced by its power of coercion, and developing comfortably within the established framework of cities, principalities and nation states; and the Radical Reformation, which was international, revolutionary, and anti-social. It was characterized by its apocalyptic expectancy of the millennium, its indifference or hostility to the authority of the state, its rejection of the institutions, practices and discipline of the medieval church, and its association of all the believing fellowship into a new lay apostolate.

Like all models, this division of the Reformation into two distinct halves is admittedly an over-simplification of a complex situation. It was 'Magisterial' Zwingli who once wrote 'Never will the world be a friend to Christ. He sent his own as sheep among wolves,' and Calvinism was widely regarded, for example by Queen Elizabeth, as subversive to the doctrines of hierarchy and lay authority upon which all civil institutions rest. It is none the less a useful classification, which serves to bring into proper perspective the more radical element in the Reformation. The beginnings of radicalism are to be found in the Catholic reformers of the early decades of the century, notably Erasmus, with his emphasis on moral virtue rather than theological bickering, on pacifism, and on the freedom of the individual will. Thereafter the movement gathered impetus, devoloping more extremist and diversified theological and social doctrines. Before long there emerged true revolutionaries like Thomas Muntzer who declared that 'in the face of usury, taxes and rents no one can have faith.' Some held that it was wrong for a Christian to hold office, or own property; others expressed contempt for the clerical office, and ignored class distinctions in seating communicants and in correspondence. In Eastern Europe there were landlords who freed their serfs and practiced total pacifism.

The mass of ephemeral sects which sprang up in the next half-century may be divided into three main groups. There were the spiritualists, the radical flank of Lutheranism, often millenarian in character and led by charismatic leaders. They tended to believe in 'direct revelation to the elect of the imminence of the Kingdom of God, and the disparagement of the external word and sacrament in preference to direct leadings from the Holy Spirit.' There were the Evangelical Radicals, especially prevalent in Italy, usually aristocratic or clerical in background, whose creed was based on Italian humanism and a sober study of the bible. Primarily ethical theists, they were pacifist, tolerant and philanthropic, dispensed with sacraments and doubted the divinity of Christ. Lastly there were the Anabaptists on the radical flank of Zwinglianism who denied the virtue of infant baptism, gathered in detached associations of the Elect and would have little truck with the masses outside the ban.

These Anabaptists divide into three basic psychological types: the
pacifists, the violent missionaries, and the mystics.

Dr Williams is primarily an historian of religion and only
secondarily a sociologist. Not for him the wider speculations about
the social causes of these bizarre manifestations of the human spirit
that engaged the attention of Mr Norman Cohen in his book *The
Pursuit of the Millennium*. There is no place in Dr Williams's
enormous index for Dukhabors or Cargo Cults. The background
was clearly that combination of material, social and ideological
alienation which has already been described. Into this fertile soil
was injected the bible, now at last gathered together, translated, and
made accessible to the uneducated. Almost any view about God or
society can be, and has been, deduced from this work, but to the
sixteenth-century peasant and artisan, the prime and astonishing
discovery was of Christ's hostility to priests and princes, to the rich
and the powerful, and his affection for the poor, the humble and the
ignorant. It is hardly surprising that so startling a revelation should
have unhinged the wits of some frustrated self-educated intellectuals
drawn from the laboring classes.

Dr Williams has shown that the ideas first put about by these
religious fanatics of the sixteenth century lie at the root of many of
the most fundamental beliefs of Western democracy today. These
despised and persecuted visionaries were among the first to raise the
voice of protest against the breaking of children's wills by physical
brutality. It was they who first denounced religious persecution as
an anti-Christian act.

> Who would wish to be a Christian, when he saw that those who
> confessed the name of Christ were destroyed by Christians
> themselves with fire, water, and the sword without mercy. ...
> Imagine Christ, the judge of all, present. Imagine him pronounc-
> ing the sentence and applying the torch. Who would not hold
> Christ for a Satan? What more could Satan do than call upon the
> name of Satan?

It is in part thanks to them that a Christian historian of religion
from America and an agnostic reviewer from England can share the
same ideals of the brotherhood of men of all classes, the equality
of opportunity for men and women, and the solidarity of all races –
ideals which run directly counter to observed historical evidence,
but which have in fact succeeded here and there in softening the
harsh asperities of social, sexual and racial exploitation. For all their

follies and excesses, their fanaticism and hysteria, their obsession with obscure points of theological doctrine, their rigidity and literal-mindedness in the interpretation of biblical texts, the sectaries established the principle that the individual has a right to his own beliefs, and that in extreme cases he has the duty to defy the physical power of authority and the moral conformism of society. If we are unlikely to see Mr A. J. P. Taylor being burnt at the stake in the Broad at Oxford, Canon Collins broken on the wheel before St Paul's Cathedral, or the late Lord Russell's head adorning a spike on London Bridge, it is in some small part because of the struggles and sufferings of these bigoted, anti-social, impossible outsiders of the sixteenth century.

CHAPTER 5 · Terrible times: the 1530s

By and large, historians do three things. They try to establish *why* things happened the way they did: why the fall of Rome; why the modernization of the West; why the French Revolution; and so on. These are not easy questions, and indeed they may in the deepest sense be unanswerable. History resembles a natural science in that its explanations are hypothetical and tentative: Newton can always be modified by Einstein. But history is very unlike a natural science in that its hypotheses cannot definitely be proved by repeated testing of the experiment. One cannot rerun the American Revolution to check that it always turns out the same way, given the same conditions. Nor can one modify one or more of these conditions to see what would have happened if George III had been less intransigent, or George Washington less able. Finally, only a very few, rather modest problems can be conclusively solved by the method of quantification which is basic to scientific proof.

Second, historians try to establish *how* things happened, a much easier task and one which is the bread and butter of the profession. The surviving data can usually provide adequate evidence for a fairly accurate factual narrative of the what and the how.

Third, historians are increasingly attempting to uncover what it was like to have lived at certain times in certain places. They painfully reconstruct the character formation, the thought processes, the values, the lifestyle, and the behavior of the dead – that is, they attempt to re-create the very texture of human life as it was lived by organisms which have long since turned to dust. For this task they depend upon the chance survival of some very rare and special kinds of evidence, of which the Lisle letters are one.

Why today in 1982 should we care about the intimate doings of one English aristocratic family over a seven-year period from 1533 to 1540?[1] The first reason is that immersion in their lives enlarges our understanding of human experience in the past, and thus helps us better to understand ourselves and our society, and to locate ourselves in time. There are plenty of collections of papers which tell us how ordinary people in the past lived their ordinary drab lives. But there are only a handful that display the struggles of a family to survive amid a great national crisis, and reveal how the private and the public inexorably intersect, often with diastrous consequences. There are the tough resilient patriarchs and stubborn children of the Paston family fighting tooth and claw to survive amid the lawless chaos of fifteenth-century Norfolk. There are fussy, dictatorial Sir Ralph Verney and his kin trying to preserve estates and family during the English Civil War and its aftermath. There are the Adamses, supporting each other through the trials of political crisis and war leading up to and during the American Revolution. There are the Joneses, whose vast correspondence reveals their tormented responses to the problems of the South before and during the American Civil War. Of course there are others, but they are few and far between. With the Lisles, one more family can be added to the slim list of historical witnesses.

The correspondence covers exactly seven of the most tormented years in English history: the period during which Henry VIII decisively broke with Rome and established himself as Supreme Head of the English Church; in which he seized for the state church property which may have amounted to between one-fourth and one-third of all the real estate in the country; and in which he half-heartedly opened the floodgates for Protestant propaganda by ordering a translated version of the Bible to be placed in every church, and by tentatively allowing, and then trying to repress, the flowering of Protestant religious ideas. At the same time there was a massive concentration of government at the center, with the final incorporation of the North, the West, Wales, and Ireland under London-based national control. It was also a fearful period of blood-soaked, arbitrary tyranny, changes of royal policy or wives being signaled by the drum beat of confessions extracted by torture, and of vengeful executions. For the Lisles, public and domestic affairs were at all times closely intertwined, and at the end they came together in a shattering climax in 1540.

Some historians have called these years the age of the Tudor Revolution in Government, and of the establishment of the sovereignty

of the King in Parliament. Others have called it the apogee of
Tudor despotism and the Age of Plunder. The Lisle letters throw
decisive new light upon all these interpretations. That these letters
have survived at all is largely fortuitous, caused by two accidents.
The first is that the leading actors, Lord and Lady Lisle, were in
Calais for these seven years, and were obliged to keep up their ties
to the court and to their patrons, clients, agents, friends, and
tenants in England by letter rather than word of mouth; and the
second accident is that in 1540 all Lisle's papers were seized by
state officials to be sifted through for evidence to support a charge
of treason. The resultant haul is neither complete nor uncensored.
Large numbers of letters from the leading minister of the crown,
Thomas Cromwell, are missing, presumably skillfully extracted
from the file during the course of examination lest they might
incriminate their author. Others, by Lord Lisle himself, are also
missing, presumably set aside to be shown to the King, and never
replaced in the files. Moreover, the surviving letters are less than
illuminating upon the great events of the day. In a stifling and
fearful atmosphere of conspiracy, sudden arrest, torture, and
execution for a mere word or sentence out of place, prudence
dictated that little or nothing of importance should be committed
to paper.

From 1535, as the clouds darkened and Sir Thomas More and
Bishop John Fisher were sent to the scaffold, Lisle's agent in
London became more and more cautious, often refusing to put any
news at all in his letters. 'The matter I send your Lordship word
of by mouth,' he wrote. He explained that if he passed on news,
'I thereby might put myself in danger of my life, and also put your
Lordship to displeasure,' for several men had found themselves in
the Tower of London 'for publishing abroad of news.' Viscount
Lisle, by nature the most open of men, was warned by an influential
well-wisher that 'you must keep all things secreter than you have
used,' if he wished to keep out of trouble. He took the hint, and
many letters were probably burned upon receipt.
    In her editorial capacity, Miss St Clare Byrne has exercised
consistently sound judgment. She has selected some seventeen
hundred letters out of three thousand to keep the edition to an
even barely manageable proportion, and she has printed them in
modernized spelling and punctuation, with occasional examples of

what the originals look like. Without this treatment they would have been utterly impenetrable to the average reader. Dictionaries had not yet established even the rudiments of standardized spelling, and phonetic transliteration was very common. How many modern readers would immediately identify 'the Pop' as the Pope, or deduce that 'for agges' means 'for a guess' and 'vthe' means 'youth,' or could patiently endure to read Calais spelled in nineteen different ways? Another correct decision was to keep to a chronological order, but to group together whole sections of correspondence which deal exclusively with the education and careers of the children.

The most important decision of all was to include as much commentary as text – a million words of text and a million words of introductory remarks, appendices, footnotes, and miscellaneous illustrative and explicatory material. We read as much of Miss St Clare Byrne as we do of the Lisles and their correspondents. But for this we should be grateful, for she draws upon her fifty-year familiarity with the archives and the period. She plugs the gaps, describes the previous and future careers of the actors, offers her interpretation of their characters, investigates the background of the lawsuits, explicates the quarrels, and generally makes intelligible even to a reader ignorant of the period the whole complex story with its cast of hundreds and its dozens of plots and subplots. The letter-writers range from an Exeter merchant who spent all seven years trying, in the face of an unbelievable chain of disasters by shipwreck, false imprisonment, and the hazards of war, to recover some cannon abandoned in Italy, to a poor spinster daughter trying vainly to establish herself in peace in one room of the old family manor house, to the infinitely complicated legal chicanery of Sir Edward Seymour (later Lord Protector Somerset) to defraud the Lisles of their Basset inheritance, to bureaucratic infighting within the council at Calais and within the court at London over personal claims for position, money, or power. Like an old and reliable sheepdog, Miss St Clare Byrne steers her readers through the thickets and over the hills. Without her at our elbow at every turn we should all soon be lost, even if we cannot help occasionally being irritated by her nannying ways. Her commentaries are as important as the letters themselves in rounding out the picture.

Ignoring for the moment the dozens of often eccentric and bizarre individuals who flit briefly across the stage, who are the main characters in the play? Although overshadowed by several more powerful personalities, the central figure is Arthur Plantagenet, Viscount Lisle, Lord Deputy of the town of Calais, England's last fortress outpost on the coast of continental Europe. The illegitimate son of Edward IV by a gentlewoman, Lisle was uncle of Henry VIII, and the last man alive to bear the Plantagenet name, that of the royal dynasty previous to the Tudors. As such he must surely have been a source of some suspicion to the Tudors. Miss St Clare Byrne brushes aside any possibility that he might have had claims to the throne, but the idea is not altogether far-fetched. Henry VII himself derived his claim from an illegitimate grandson of Edward III, and in the 1520s Henry VIII was apparently contemplating the possibility of making his illegitimate son Henry, Duke of Richmond, his heir. This was a sufficiently credible option to cause it to be rumored that the young man's death in 1536 was a result of poisoning by Anne Boleyn to clear the way for her baby Elizabeth. If illegitimacy was no bar to the throne for the Tudors, then a Plantagenet might also one day be tempted to stake out a claim. Small wonder that both Henry VII and Henry VIII chose to keep Arthur Plantagenet close to their side at court.

In fact, however, he was entirely harmless – a genial, affable, feckless, hospitable, insecure worrier of a fellow, who was no danger to anybody and was loyal to the core of his being. His simple-minded loyalty, his open hospitality, his life-long friendship with Henry VIII, his relative indifference to religious change, and his wife's connection with Anne Boleyn made him an ideal choice as Lord Deputy of Calais in 1533, even if he did lack the desirable strength of character, administrative ability, and financial resources of his own. The first two made him a rather feeble commander of so vital a military outpost, while his relative poverty forced him into corruption. If we can believe the local chronicler, he set a bad example by selling all offices under his command, and secretly pocketing the salaries of men who died. His open-handed hospitality to important travelers to the castle town, like the French ambassador or Anne of Cleves, was highly appreciated at home, but only plunged him further into financial troubles. As a result, he was hopelessly in debt to the King for taxes and rents which were decades in arrears, and he never paid a tradesman for goods or services supplied unless he absolutely had to.

He lacked self-assurance, and tended to panic when he got a sharp letter from Cromwell or the King. He had constantly to be reassured by his plain-spoken agent, John Husee, who feared he had 'some motions of melancholy.' When Cromwell told him brutally that the King and Council thought 'your practices and doings very ill, and not well nor circumspectly considered,' he had to turn to Husee to draft a reply for him. The latter kept urging him not to take setbacks 'so heavily and after a desperate sort,' and lamented that he 'in any adversity, extremity or need, should now fall into this sudden agony.' 'Howbeit I know your nature is such that you cannot forbear it.' This tendency to panic was compounded by a natural diffidence in lobbying for his own interests, and a foolish tendency to 'trust promises and fair words.' His wife and Husee ordered him to 'be earnest in his own affairs' and hoped 'he will be plain with the King,' but on the few occasions he had a royal audience he always fumbled the ball. He made his pitch, but was too easily put off by a purely verbal promise, and was later astonished to find that it did not result in action. Sometimes Husee was so exasperated by his employer's timidity and incompetence that he could barely contain himself. When Lisle failed to press his suit for money in a crucial audience with the King, Husee burst out, 'Your Lordship is in the blame of all this matter, for had you been in earnest with the King, . . . you might as well have had a thousand marks as a hundred pounds.' All in all he well deserved his reputation as 'my gentle Lord Lisle' and Cromwell's testimonial that 'I have ever thought you to be of a good and gentle nature.' Even Henry VIII admitted that he 'had the gentlest heart living.' This amiable old gentleman was no match for predatory sharks like Cromwell and the bright young men on the make around him in London. He relied entirely upon the promptings of his faithful agent Husee and the support and advice of his tough-minded wife Honor, to whom he was absolutely devoted. He described her as one 'for whom I do as much long for as doth the child for his nurse, and that God knoweth,' an analogy which accurately sums up the marital relationship (the nurse in the sixteenth century being normally, closer to the child than the mother – witness Juliet).

When Lisle married her as his second wife in 1529, Honor Basset
was already a widow aged about forty with seven children by a
first marriage.

For Honor, marriage to so exalted a nobleman so close to the
King was clearly a big step up, even if he was some fifteen years
older than herself. For Lisle it was socially a step down, but she
had useful political connections with the rising Boleyn family, and
in view of her age the marriage was unlikely to result in children.
Since he had no son of his own, the Plantagenets would die out in
the male line, which was perhaps just as well. Although this was
probably a marriage of convenience on both sides, by 1538 the
couple were clearly deeply devoted to each other. He relied upon
her for advice, love, and encouragement, and for all her difficult
character she seems to have been equally devoted to him. When he
was away in London on a visit, she wrote to him, 'I think there is
no woman living have thought the time of her husband's absence
longer than I have done yours'; or again, 'I shall think every hour
ten till I be with you again.' He addressed her as 'mine own
sweetheart,' and signed himself 'your own loving husband forever.'
She addressed him as 'good sweetheart' and signed herself 'your
loving and true wife.' This verbal display of mutual tenderness
appears to represent genuine emotion, and the Lisles provide a
welcome exception to the rule of at best distant and businesslike
marital relationships, especially in this class. These affectionate
letters between an elderly married couple are some of the very first
to have survived in Western Europe. That the feelings expressed
were genuine on his side is certainly beyond dispute. She too
appears to have been sincere enough, and the only hint of other
emotions at work within her is the way she manipulated him for
her own ends, and also the ugly rumors flying about Calais that
she was in love with one of his chaplains.

This affection is all the more remarkable since the Lisles themselves in their treatment of their children, and all their correspondents, viewed marriage as a business transaction. As a relative
remarked of one of Lisle's own daughters, without a good dowry
'ye may be sure there is but few would harken unto her.' A patron
asked Lisle for a job for a client in the Calais garrison, arguing that
'it should be a great help and his advancement for his preferment to
a good marriage.' When the surveyor of Calais made an imprudent
marriage, Cromwell remarked that if he had known he was contem-

plating matrimony, 'he would have gotten him a wife . . . worth a thousand pounds.' Katherine Basset, left by her father with a dowry of only £66, asked Lisle to make it up to £200 or more, for with that 'she shall have an heir which shall spend a thousand marks.' Thus everyone, including the children themselves, thought of marriage in terms of money.

There can be no doubt that Lisle's new wife Honor was a woman of strong passions, hasty temper, and iron will. She was a shrewd, scheming, and meddling termagant. So 'very sharp and hasty' was she that she had trouble recruiting gentlewomen attendants to wait upon her, and there are many proofs in her correspondence of her quick and fiery temper. Her life rotated around three or four prime concerns. The first was to promote the careers of her seven Basset children by her first husband, all of whom she provided with a typically medieval education. These letters provide vivid detail about the upbringing of elite children in the early sixteenth century, such as can be obtained from nowhere else. It is thus a pity that none of the children were subjected to even a trace of that new scholarly neoclassical education that was beginning to make itself felt in England under the inspiration of Erasmus and the patronage of More. But the Bassets and Lisles were not among that minority of families learned in the new humanist style. Honor could read English, but not French or Latin, and she could write nothing beyond her own name. Lisle could write, but nearly always found it easier to dictate his letters. Indeed the vast bulk of the correspondence is dictated to scribes and secretaries. This has the advantage of giving so much of it the vivid immediacy of the spoken word, because that is exactly what it is. Here in these letters we meet the brisk, inventive, playful language of Shakespeare already fully formed.

Honor's eldest son, John, was a dull, shy fellow, but that did not stop her intriguing actively to push him into Thomas Cromwell's service. The younger son, James, was a bright, self-willed, calculating boy. She intended him for the Church, but he preferred a secular career, eventually winding up under the patronage of the Catholic Bishop Gardiner, and husband to the pious and learned Catholic granddaughter of Sir Thomas More. Not a very likable young man, he had the saving grace of a genuine and passionate devotion to the Catholic faith – devotion which later gained him admission to Queen Mary's Privy Chamber. During the 1530s, between the ages of ten and seventeen, he was already successfully manipulating the grownups to suit himself, and obtaining precisely the education he wanted, whether in Paris or in London. All the daughters were educated in the traditional way to catch a husband, and were barely literate. Some were placed in the safekeeping of abbots and abbesses and priors in England – which was cheap but turned out to be a mistake when the monasteries were dissolved. Others were sent to learn French and social graces in French aristocratic households, and two, along with their Plantagenet stepsister, were kept under their mother's eye in Calais. Two of them were then pushed into the court at London to compete for jobs as maids of honour to Henry's rapid succession of queens. Henry chose the pretty one, Anne, but repeatedly rejected the plain one, much to her mother's disappointment. Honor seems never to have concerned herself with the possible risk to Anne's virtue, if Henry's lustful eye should fall upon her. Indeed, despite her high ambitions for her brood, there are few signs of love between mother and children, except with her favorite, Mary. It was in general a relationship manipulative on the one side and deferential on the other. It is hardly surprising, therefore, that Honor did not hesitate to plan purely mercenary marriages for her children without even bothering to consult them. She succeeded in marrying her Basset son and heir to her eldest Plantagenet stepdaughter – a social coup that raised some eyebrows. But it was a policy which, as we shall see, could lead to disaster, when a love affair induced her favorite daughter to kick over the traces.

Honor's ambitions were not confined to the promotion of the careers of her children. Despite her age, she had high hopes of becoming the mother of a boy by Lisle, and thus of giving birth to the last of the Plantagenets. So fixed was her ambition and so strong her will to succeed that for nine months she convinced herself and the world that she was pregnant. Her belly duly swelled (by swallowing air) and she boasted about her condition to everyone, including the King. She pestered all her noble friends to lend her a bed and hangings suitable for the occasion, and even the royal wardrobe was pressed for a loan to help decorate her bedroom suitably for the delivery of a semiroyal child. She hired herself a midwife, laid herself down upon the state bed in the opulently fitted room – and nothing happened. Letters fall discreetly silent over what must have been a traumatically disappointing experience for the Lisles. Husee heard with dismay that 'your Ladyship weepeth and sorroweth without comparison,' and urged her to cheer up.

As for Honor's relations with her noble and elderly husband, they were at once close and bossy. Everyone knew that she was as tough and grasping as he was weak and easygoing, and those who wanted to get anything out of Lisle took care to work through her. This soon got back to London, and she received a stinging rebuke that reports were circulating that 'ye do intermeddle much in my lord's business concerning the King's causes.' Men openly remarked that they could twist Lisle round their little finger 'so that my lady were not in the way.' Cromwell, who was no sympathizer with feminist aspirations, flatly told Lisle that 'although my lady be right honorable and wise, yet in such causes as belongeth to your authority her advice and discretion can little prevail.' Later he angrily told Lisle that 'it is thought against reason that the prayers of women and their fond flickerings should move any of you.'

Apart from promoting her Basset children, defending their estate, trying to produce a Plantagenet boy, and dabbling actively in the political affairs of her husband the Lord Deputy, Honor's main preoccupation was a passionate and deeply felt defense of the Roman Catholic religion. It was widely known that 'Your Ladyship was given to be a little papish,' and that she was an active protector of papists and supporter of the persecution of Protestants in the deeply divided Council of Calais. Her devotion was intense and sincere, but it was rash to exhibit such qualities at a time when the official theological and liturgical lines were changing year by year at the whim of the King, and the penalties for disobedience were brutally severe. Prudence dictated silence, but prudence was not one of Honor's strong points.

According to the Calais chronicler, Honor was wildly extravagant in her taste for rich clothes, food, and drink, which helped to aggravate her husband's increasingly precarious financial condition. There is indeed hard evidence for her extravagance in clothes, for the inventory taken of her goods in 1540 included items like a pair of crimson satin sleeves with 800 pearls, and a black velvet pair with 573 pearls and 84 'paired stones' of gold.

The third key figure, and clearly the hero of the story, is John Husee, the loyal, devoted, shrewd, cheerful, and indefatigable London agent and lobbyist of the Lisles. His job was to keep the lines of communication open between the King, Cromwell, and the leading courtiers in England, and his master and mistress across the English Channel. Without him, it is plain that the Lisle family would have come to grief long before it did. Again and again it was only heroic exertions by Husee that kept them out of trouble. Was Lord Daubigny scheming to pull off a piece of legal duplicity that would deprive the Bassets of much of their estate? It was Husee who came to the rescue by planting a spy in Daubigny's household to report his every move, who tirelessly lobbied Cromwell, the Lord Chancellor, and the judges, and who finally sketched out the deal by which Cromwell intervened with Henry to save the situation, in return for a slice of the pie. Did the Lord Admiral need buttering up? It was Husee who had to keep a live porpoise for weeks in a netted enclosure in the Thames at Wapping, feeding it daily at his own considerable expense until he could make the gift. (Unfortunately, the porpoise was not appreciated by the Lord Admiral and so Husee's pains and money were wasted.) Did Lisle want a grant of one of the dissolved monasteries to save his tottering finances? It was Husee who sought out a suitable one, and spent hours, days, and months, even years, in dogged pursuit of it, haunting the antechambers of the powerful until they caved in. Did officials need to be bribed to get things done? It was Husee who recognized the need, assessed the amount, and arranged the payoff. Was Cromwell's intervention in some suit essential? It was Husee who waylaid the great man as he walked briskly from his house to the court, trotting along beside him and bending his ear.

It was Husee who personally carried to Henry VIII Lisle's New Year's gift on the first of January every year, and duly reported every word of gratitude that passed the King's lips. Husee presents us with an unforgettable picture of the King, watchful and piggy-eyed as usual, leaning against a cupboard and chatting and joking with Cromwell as nobles and courtiers came forward with their ritual presents, and a clerk wrote them all down in a book behind him. Once when Husee gave a handful of golden coins, Henry simply grabbed them and stuffed them in his pocket. It was Husee also who had to chase to and fro across London to track down items on Honor Lisle's detailed and specialized shopping lists, who paid the tradesmen's bills when he had to, and let the others run up as long as he could without irreparably damaging the honor of his master and mistress. His judgment of men and things seems to have been impeccable, and his capacity for work limitless.

Husee was properly discreet about his religious opinions, but now and then his feelings show through. Like most others, he did not much mind about the dissolution of the monasteries, and was as eager as the next man to help his master to some of the plunder. But he was truly shocked at the wanton destruction of the sacred images and relics of the saints, and the looting of the precious metals and jewels of the shrines. When Cromwell's agent Pollard was busy dismantling and packing up the shrine of St Thomas à Becket at Canterbury, Husee could not restrain his sarcasms. Mr Pollard, he reported to Honor, 'hath been so busied, night and day, in prayer with offering unto St Thomas' shrine and head' that he had no time to deal with her affairs. He will try again when Pollard's 'spiritual devotion is past.'

One of the more disagreeable aspects of the story is how few thanks Husee received from either Lisle or Honor, both of whom mostly complained fretfully that he had not performed the impossible. After one such nagging letter, Husee told Lisle that 'your Lordship hath almost made me weary of my wife.' He was paid a mere pittance, which was often in arrears. It was typical of the age that the money came not out of Lisle's own pocket, but by having arranged for him to be put on the payroll as one of the garrison at Calais – in flat defiance of all the rules of residence, since he was hardly ever there.

At the far end of the line of communications which ran from Calais to London there were the two towering figures of Henry VIII and Thomas Cromwell. The latter was the King's chief minister: the supreme bureaucrat who threw up a welter of new agencies – all run by his stable of ambitious young men – to digest the largest transfer of power from the provinces to the center ever to take place in England. What sort of a man do these letters reveal him to be? He emerges as intelligent, patient, and resourceful, but also cynical, cunning, and corrupt. He was above all supremely self-confident and ambitious, and jealous of all competition. To stay in power he was prepared to put up with anything and to sacrifice anyone. He had climbed to the top by trampling men and women underfoot on his way up, and he intended to stay there. If the King chose to abuse him and clout him about the head in anger, as he did, so be it: he would suffer in silence. This was the man with whom Husee had to deal, and we can see him more clearly through these letters than we have ever seen him before. It is some comfort to discover that this cold and calculating careerist had his weaker side. Women did not interest him, but good French cheese and quails, and above all good French wine, certainly did. It is also surprising to find that he regularly took a summer holiday of six weeks or so.

Over all loomed the huge, brooding, suspicious, erratic personality of the King, already prematurely ageing and running to fat, and with a sore upon his leg which would not heal. He has aptly been described by Professor J. H. Hexter as 'splendid, magnificent, spendthrift, lustful, idle, envious, treacherous, rapacious, jealous, and stupidly and stupefyingly vain-glorious.' Apart from himself, his attention seems to have been focused upon only three things. One was military affairs, especially the technology of gunnery, armor, and fortifications, in all the details of which he took a close personal interest. Thus it was he who personally chose the suit of armor for Lisle, he who decided which guns should be set up on which towers in the fortifications of Calais, and he who wanted immediately to view in person a newly invented double cannon.

His second concern was theology, upon his skill in which he took great pride. Did he not after all bear the proud title of *Fidei Defensor*, conferred upon him by the Pope? He personally supervised the drawing up of the various official theological positions, as he twisted and turned in his opinions throughout the 1530s. Although he broke from Rome, he never wavered in his position about the Mass, and he personally engaged in formal public disputation about the Real Presence with a heretic Protestant – whom he duly burned alive after defeating him in argument to his own satisfaction.

His third passion was for women, whom he pursued with a relentless and indiscriminate lust which seemed insatiable. Despite his sexual adventurism, Anne Boleyn as early as 1535 complained to a friend that Henry was often unable to satisfy a woman, and it may well have been this growing impotence which drove Catherine Howard to adultery some six or seven years later. In his quest for female flesh he was utterly shameless, and he deeply shocked the French Ambassador in 1538 by suggesting to him that there be sent from Paris to Calais a sample of royal or noble French young ladies for his personal inspection as a potential wife. The Ambassador retorted sarcastically: 'Ne voudriez vous point, Sire, encore monter sur toutes, une après l'autre, et après retenir pour votre personne celle qui irait la plus douce?'

Of his ruthless treachery and cruelty, there can be no doubt. He had begun his reign by sacrificing the two leading ministers of his father, later added More and Cromwell, and would have killed his last minister, Norfolk, if he had lived a few days longer. He liked to play cat and mouse with his victims, leaving them for days or months in the Tower of London awaiting execution and then suddenly ordering their death; or he would bring them on to the scaffold, delay the execution for a few hours, then let it proceed; or whimsically issue a pardon at the last moment.

The greatest hatred of his life was directed toward Cardinal Reginald Pole, once his bosom companion, who had fled abroad because of his refusal to accept Henry's assumption of Supreme Headship of the Church. From there, he wrote a blistering letter, accusing Henry of being a brutal and teacherous tyrant. Anyone who had the remotest contact with Pole or his servants was immediately suspect and usually killed – a fact that in the end was to affect the fate of Lisle himself. Such was the man, 'as vicious and dangerous as a rogue elephant,' as Miss St Clare Byrne describes him, who presided over English affairs, and the lives of the Lisles, during these seven years.

If the Lisles, Husee, Cromwell, and Henry are the main actors, their relationships with one another and with hundreds of other actors in the play cannot be understood without reference to certain fundamental features of the society in which they lived. At the risk of drastically oversimplifying the changing social structure of Europe, one can propose that there have been three, and only three, ideal types which have roughly followed one upon another in chronological order. The first was the feudal society, in which each man posessed an ascribed status based upon his tenurial relationship to the land. Each man owed fealty for his land to someone above him, and was in turn owed fealty by those below him. This was replaced in the early modern period by a new social order based on personal ties of patronage – known to English historians as bastard feudalism in the fifteenth century, clientage in the sixteenth and seventeenth centuries, and connection in the eighteenth century. In the nineteenth century, modernization brought about another shift to the principle of meritocracy, whereby each man stands upon his own feet, and rises or falls by reason of his education, talents, and exertions. Obviously no such societies have ever existed in a pure form, and most have contained elements of all three. Concepts of merit and efficiency played some part in power relations in the early modern period, just as patronage unrelated to merit still does in large areas today.

What the Lisle letters reveal more clearly than any other source is the mechanism of patronage at its peak. 'A man without a patron is like a hop without a pole,' remarked Elizabeth's leading minister, Lord Burghley. In the world of the 1530s in which the Lisles moved, everyone was seeking a 'good lord' of rising power and influence to whom to attach themselves, and as eagerly seeking to disassociate themselves from a 'good lord' whose star was on the wane. The more obsequious correspondents of Lisle, like his auditor John Smith or the ill-starred merchant John Cheriton, did not hesitate to lay it on with a trowel. 'Right honorable and my singular good lord,' begins a letter from the latter, 'pleaseth your good lordship to know that I have received your lordship's letter, wherein your good lordship has written your gracious pleasure unto me, more than ever that I am able for to make your good lordship any recompense.' There followed his latest tale of woe – 'I am undone forever' – and the conclusion, 'wherefore, good my lord, to be so gracious lord unto me as to send me in all haste your gracious letter for to restrain again all my enemies.' Others were less verbose in their promises: 'I will be your servant, and the King's, God willing, during my life.' In a similar vein, Lisle himself wrote to his superior, Thomas Cromwell, 'beseeching you to continue my good lord,' while he assured Husee that Cromwell 'hath always been my good lord and friend.' In many cases the concept of good lordship was linked to kinship and became a form of nepotism, at that time considered a moral duty for any man of honor. One lobbied Lord Lisle's help for a client of his 'to whom I heartily beseech you to be good lord, and the better for his old mistress's sake, your kinswoman.' Another recommended a man to Honor on the grounds that he 'must needs be at my lord's commandment and your ladyship's, considering that he married your niece.'

It was this power of patronage, or 'good lordship' as it was called, sometimes linked to the claims of kinship, which made the wheels of both government and society go round. All promotion, all reward, all aid, all safety, depended on the protection and lobbying of the patron, and the greater the patron the more the clients and the more powerful the influence. This is why Thomas Cromwell was daily mobbed by such throngs of suitors that he hardly dared set foot outside his door. 'Your lordship will not believe the importunate suit that Mr. Cromwell daily hath, which continually increaseth,' wrote Husee as early as 1534. If the great man fell sick and kept to his chamber, the suitors piled up in frustrated droves for weeks outside the door. But constant waiting was the essence of the matter. 'One hour missing attention upon my Lord Privy Seal [Cromwell] may hinder a month's suit,' remarked Husee with his usual acuity. Others were not so philosophical about the waste of time, and Lisle's other agent in London, Thomas Warley, complained bitterly of his sufferings:

> The search from auditor to auditor, from clerk to clerk of [the
> Court of] Augmentations, and daily attendance, passeth the
> Bishop of Rome's feigned purgatory, for it lighteth the purse,
> wearyeth the legs, distempereth the body.

The language is not only vivid, but displays an acute appreciation of the latest change in theological doctrine – purgatory was now nonoperative.

If 'good lordship' was the key relationship in political and social life, the oil that lubricated the system was the exchange of gifts. Many primitive societies exchange gifts, but few on the scale of early sixteenth-century England. Gifts, of course, can come in many kinds. In the sixteenth century, they began with the mere 'token,' like the flowers or pot of homemade jam which we still exchange with friends to this day. These tokens often took the form of rings, frequently 'cramp-rings' which had been blessed by the King and were believed to ward off the pains of rheumatism and arthritis. Honor was an avid collector of 'cramp-rings' by the dozen.

One stage above these tokens of mere friendship were gifts on a
somewhat more generous scale, made with the expectation of the
grant of a favor or an equivalent gift in return. Others, more
expensive still, were douceurs, that is, bribes more or less trans-
parently disguised as gifts. And finally there were outright bribes,
although it was not considered altogether gentlemanly in the best
of circles to ask or receive such things. When the avaricious Thomas
Pope (the future pious founder of Trinity College, Oxford) made
it clear that he had 'rather have ready money than wine, yea and
doth look for the same,' he was regarded by Husee as a cad.

Naturally enough, the token, the gift, the douceur, and the bribe
in practice all tended to run smoothly into one another, and it is
often difficult to tell them apart. For those who had everything,
like the King or the Queen, the trick was to find some 'novelty'
to whet their jaded appetites. There was a great to-do in 1534,
when Anne Boleyn heard about Honor's favorite puppy dog
Purquoy, and let it be known she wanted it. Husee wrote firmly:
'Madam, there is no remedy, your ladyship must needs depart
with your little Purquoy, the which I know well shall grieve your
ladyship not a little.' Honor procrastinated, but finally had to
give it up. Rare food was a favorite gift – dotterells, quails, early
peasecods, cherries and grapes, sturgeons, and boars' heads for the
royal table. Anne Boleyn had a particular liking for fat quails during
her pregnancy, and Lisle hastened to oblige.

What is so remarkable is that even the simplest request or exchange
of politeness had to be accompanied by a physical gift. How they
poured to and fro across the Channel by their hundreds! To the
Lisles from England came stags and does and pies of venison from
English noblemen, Cornish conger eels from a West Country
parson, 'a dish of puffins against Lent,' twenty gulls, eleven egrets,
a hundred quinces, a barrel of honey, two cheeses, and endless
cramp-rings. Richer presents, usually in expectation of or return
for a favor, tended to be the animals of the chase, like horses,
greyhounds, and hawks. From the Lisles an even larger number of
gifts flooded back across the Channel to their superiors or equals.
The two great weapons to get things done were wine and quails.
They seem to have had a monopoly of the best French burgundy
for England, and of the fattest quails. At times when they were

lobbying hard for something from the court, whether a favor over a job or lawsuit, or the grant of a monastery or an annuity, the Channel was thick with ships carrying the precious cargo. Men of influence were literally bombarded with tuns of fine French wine and hundreds of plump quails, often more than the recipients knew what to do with. Sometimes things went terribly wrong, as when Lisle tried to curry favor with the Earl of Hertford by sending him a singing linnet in a cage, but the ship was wrecked at sea. Husee reported to Honor the end of the story: 'Madam, to write the misfortunes of this poor man Sparke had, it were too much!' For when he had with difficulty saved the bird from the shipwreck and brought it home to Billingsgate, it was eaten by his cat, 'which my Lord of Hertford took right grievously.' Honor had to send along instead 'mine own bird, the best in all this town,' of which the Earl was 'not a little proud.'

Some gifts were very odd, since they conformed to the concept of 'novelty,' that passionate urge of men of the Renaissance to see and handle something new and strange. Contemporaries were extraordinarily attached to pets – witness Anne Boleyn's fixation on Honor's pet dog Purquoy. She also enjoyed a linnet in a cage, but hated monkeys. Lisle's daughter Mary sent her father a parakeet 'because he maketh much of a bird.' Exotica were always in demand. The French Lord Admiral, as he passed through Calais, gave the Lisles as a thank-you present two marmosets and a monkey from Brazil, along with instructions about their care and feeding. Bishop Bonner sent Lisle as a 'novelty' a couple of prints of the human anatomy. 'The anatomy of the man is judged here to be done exquisitely,' he commented, but 'the anatomy of the woman pleaseth me not so much,' though as a clerical bachelor he admitted ignorance on the subject.

What was the meaning of this incessant transfer of gifts, ranging from the insignificant token to the expensive present? Many had merely symbolic significance, physical tokens of friendship or loyalty. But this was important to contemporaries, and Lisle's stepdaughter Mary was genuinely upset that her father 'hath not sent me anything,' not even a token. Many other gifts were not expensive, but were hard to get in the days before the advent of sophisticated consumer market arrangements. Living as they did on the French coast at Calais, the Lisles were very well placed to provide 'novelties' which were designed to be of real use and pleasure to the recipients, and thus to reinforce their reciprocal sense of obligation and goodwill. Gifts were the sixteenth-century means to achieve what President Nixon, in his ineffable way, used to call 'stroking.' What is interesting about this flood of gifts is that the custom seems to have been so strictly time bound. It is far less prominent in the Paston letters of the fifteenth century and far less prominent in the Salisbury letters of the early seventeenth century or the Walpole correspondence of the early eighteenth century. The incessant habit of gift exchange displayed in the Lisle letters is an anthropological curiosity at its apogee, at a time when patronage itself had also reached its apogee. The two went together.

When it comes to douceurs or bribes, we move into a more familiar world, even if today we would hardly think of bombarding the influential politicians from whom we want a favor with tuns of wine or hundreds of quails. Although the type of douceur or bribe has changed, the principle and the practice remain the same: the sixteenth century, like ours, was an age of corrupt politicians. One feature, however, marks the century as drastically different from our own. All early modern states were run by an unreformed 'patrimonial bureaucracy' – to use Max Weber's terminology – in which officials were appointed and promoted by patronage and/ or corruption rather than merit; in which offices were bought and sold by the incumbents to their successors, with the corrupt consent of their superiors; in which, since salaries were relatively insignificant, officials made a living by taking fees or tips from clients to perform the services the state employed them to carry out; and in which absenteeism and sinecure offices performed by deputies were an accepted norm. In his capacity as Lord Deputy of Calais, Lisle was inevitably deeply enmeshed in such a system, and much of his correspondence is concerned with the struggle for appointments, the purchase and sale of jobs, the use of patronage in securing jobs – all competing with the rival need of the state for a high level of military readiness in a key fortress perched precariously on the coast of France.

There can be no doubt that here and there the efficiency principle had taken fragile root in the interstices of the system, although in the main it was overridden by the pressure to conduct business as usual, that is by patronage or purchase. For example, Cromwell got Parliament to pass a law to improve internal navigation by destroying fish weirs on all navigable rivers in England. Honor owned one, and fought desperately but unavailingly to keep it. She tried lobbying the King, but he sent all such petitions on to Cromwell, who rejected them outright. She tried going through Anne Boleyn, but fared no better. The plain fact was that 'Mr. Secretary is very earnest in the same, and will show no favour.' In this case, Cromwell successfully defended the public interest of free river transportation against all private interests, including his own and the King's. More typical was the prolonged struggle to reflood a marsh outside the walls of Calais, which in a thoughtless moment Henry had granted to a former Deputy at Calais, Sir Robert Wingfield. The drainage of the marsh by Wingfield greatly increased his profits, but dangerously impaired the defenses of the town and castle, and Henry told Sir Robert to 'put it down.' But years went by and absolutely nothing happened. It took a full year after Lisle and the Calais Council had urgently asked for firm instructions on reflooding the marsh for Cromwell to write the necessary clear ten-line letter. Even then, Wingfield did not give up, and kept lobbying for fair compensation for his financial losses for another two years. For at least a year Lisle and the Council of Calais could think of little else but this petty struggle between the warring principles of private interest and the public good.

A critical case that bulks large in the Lisle letters, in which the public interest in national security fought – largely unsuccessfully – against the private interest in the purchase and sale of offices, is that of appointments to the military garrison of Calais, nominally at the disposal of Lisle as Lord Deputy. In practice his freedom was constantly restricted by interference from Henry, Cromwell, and other influential patrons. Intermittently, Henry worried about the situation. He ordered two commissions to investigate conditions at Calais, and also passed an Act of Parliament, but none of them did much good.

One key question was whether an incumbent member of the garrison should be allowed to sell his office to whoever offered him the most money, regardless of competence. Thus Lisle was offered twenty marks to get a man's nephew the job of 'an archer on horseback' – no hint being given as to whether he could shoot a bow or ride a horse. In 1533 Sir John Russell declared flatly that 'this thing I am and have always been against . . .; for such shall buy it for money that shall not be able to serve the King when they have it.' But a few weeks later a man was offering Lisle twenty marks and Honor a skirt for permission for a friend to buy 'a room of a spear of Calais.' The Lisles were clearly up to their necks in all this buying and selling. Cromwell protested that they 'put all things to sale' in order to finance their 'excess of living,' despite Honor's implausible claim that she 'would not for a hundred pounds take one penny, nor never did of no man.' Henry also took a strong line from time to time, but never followed it up. One minute he insisted that 'there should be no rooms bought nor sold hereafter this in Calais'; the next he said that 'if rooms may be sold, he will have the advantage himself.' He forced through the Act of Parliament forbidding all sales, and then actively connived at the continuation of the practice. There were 'new letters daily for rooms, all clean contrary to the Act.' In one striking case he allowed Sir Richard Grenville to buy the important office of Marshal at Calais from the incumbent for £400 'with the King's good will and favor.' In gratitude for his help with Henry, Grenville sent Cromwell the large douceur of 18,000 Cornish slates to roof his new buildings.

Even worse was the problem of grants of reversions of offices at Calais. It was the habit of Henry to issue warrants for reversions as favors to patrons in such numbers that candidates were stacked up in droves, waiting for a vacancy and jockeying for priority in the line. As Henry signed letter after letter in favor of aspirants to reversions of offices still held by others, Husee remarked acidly, 'your Lordship may see what stableness in promises and writings.' As a result of the activities of the King, Cromwell, and the court-iers, in 1540 most of the garrison in Calais was revealed to be either incapable of bearing arms or absentee, or both. Lisle, who had to decide among these competing claims to offices nominally at his disposal, was obliged to spend much of his time adjudicating bitter disputes. But this was not the least of the problems created by the malfunctioning of the administrative system. Henry and Cromwell compounded Lisle's difficulties by permitting the salaries of the garrison to go unpaid for months, and by denying Lisle the money to repair the crumbling fortifications, or even licenses to import food to build up a stockpile to withstand a siege. So sluggish and obstructive was the bureaucracy that even Cromwell's direct intervention could not get the garrison paid on time, with the result

that some of them had no money for their own dinners. It would
be hard to devise a system better calculated to undermine morale
and weaken the defenses of the most important military outpost in
the kingdom.

This disorder at Calais was merely symptomatic of the general
administrative situation. For one thing, the whole system was
corroded by the ubiquity of the douceur and the bribe. Nothing
could be done without large gifts, usually in kind, but sometimes
in hard cash. Take, for example, the payoffs made by Bruton
Abbey in 1532 in order to obtain, with the support of the Lisles,
a grant of two fairs a year in the town. A servant of Sir Richard
Weston got ten shillings for lobbying his master; Mr Sulyard got
£10 for mentioning the matter twice to the King; Cromwell got £5
for reading the bill to the King; and Sir Richard Weston got £20
for obtaining the King's signature to the bill. All of them 'look for
thanks of your Ladyship,' for they did it as a result of patronage
pressure from Honor as well as bribes.

Writing or speaking to one another, high officials made no bones
about their financial interests. Cromwell wrote that Henry agreed
to a nomination of an abbot by the Lord Chief Justice and backed
by Lisle, 'so that his Highness may have me remembered somewhat.' Here the King was personally insisting that his minister be
paid off. Indeed, almost everything, including judicial favor, was
up for sale. When Honor was fighting Lord Daubigny in the courts
to protect her Basset lands, Husee advised her to send a letter to
the Lord Chief Justice, along with a firkin of sturgeon. When, in
an unprecedented coup, the Lisles got the case forcibly transferred
from the Common Law Courts to the personal arbitration of the
King, Husee advised lavish rewards to everyone involved, including
the Lord Chancellor.

The atmosphere of corruption was all-pervasive, the more so the
closer one approached the higher levels of officialdom. 'Friendship
taketh small place, where money fails,' lamented Husee. 'Here
nothing is done without it.' He learned the hard way the prevalence
at court of 'a fair face and a false dissimulating heart.'

The irresponsible corruption of Lord Sandys, bosom friend of
the King, Lord Chamberlain of the household, and absentee captain
of the castle of Guînes, close by Calais, is scarcely credible. He
was accused, with some plausibility, of drawing £1,000 a year to

pay a garrison of a hundred soldiers at sixpence and eightpence a day. Instead, he paid a mere sixpence a day to fifty at a cost of £300, and pocketed the remaining £700 for himself. It is hardly surprising that Calais fell so easily to the French less than twenty years later.

If Sandys was on the take, so was everybody else, including that paragon of efficiency, Thomas Cromwell himself, who took bribes like everyone else but on a much larger scale. The story of how he squeezed a piece of property out of the Lisles in return for obtaining the official grant of an annuity and a friary, already promised to Lisle verbally by the King, is a long and illuminating affair in itself. The most amazing evidence of the scale of Cromwell's corruption, however, comes from the account book of his receiver. Cromwell was arrested, totally unexpectedly, at three in the afternoon on 10 June 1540. Royal agents rushed to his house to remove all the cash, jewels, and valuables before nightfall. The last items in the receiver's notebook record what they found 'under a cushion in the middle window in the gallery' where Cromwell was accustomed to receive his clients. Tucked away there they discovered two white purses containing, respectively, £100 and £120 in gold, another with £50 in gold, and £20 in gold inside a glove – surely the original golden handshake, as Miss St Clare Byrne observes. What were all these huge sums doing under a cushion? They must have been the bribes that Cromwell had accepted during the day before his arrest, which he had not had time to hand over to his accountant.

We would make a great mistake, however, to apply our own standards to the sixteenth century, and to recoil in horror and virtuous disgust. Even today most governments in the world operate in much the same way, which is why it is so short-sighted to expect American businesses to prosper in Third World countries without passing on the accustomed douceurs or bribes. Corruption, Lord Keynes once remarked, is the only practical alternative for a state too weak to assess and raise taxes on wealth and income.

What does all this tell us about the so-called Tudor Revolution in Government? What is revealed in the Lisle letters is an administration struggling to manage its affairs in the face of ingrained habits and popular customs, deeply entrenched sale and patronage practices of a patrimonial bureaucracy, widely diffused corruption reaching right up to the King himself, a social order based on

personal clientage to a 'good lord,' a general atmosphere of every
man for himself, and an almost total lack of zeal for the broader
interest of the nation at large. Henry and Cromwell and Parliament
could huff and puff, but as often as not nothing would ever happen.
It was considered morally legitimate to lobby and bribe everyone
for everything, even the Lord Chief Justice for favor in the suit 'to
be good to you and your son,' as Honor was advised. The gap
between legal enactment and actual practice was vast. Henry and
Cromwell could pass an Act of Parliament forbidding the Welsh
to speak their native tongue, in order to break their cultural
autonomy. But today Welsh is still spoken in homes and pubs,
broadcast on television, and even displayed on signposts to
the utter confusion of English tourists. They could pass an
Act of Parliament to prohibit diversity of opinion in religion –
only to start a century of the most vigorous, widespread, and
passionate debate on religious matters in English history. In
financial matters the confusion was rapidly getting worse, with
no central control whatever over the growing multiplicity of
agencies that both received and disbursed income. Thus the
problem for Lisle, when he finally got his £200 annuity, was to
discover the most financially secure agency upon which to have
it drawn:

> They say that the Treasurer of the Chamber is often without
> money, and the Jewel House; Augmentations and First
> Fruits is as ill, and the Exchequer worse; and to be paid at
> Calais by the Treasurer or the Receiver is worst of all, unless
> your Lordship would first compound with them [i.e. bribe
> them].

Looked at from the worm's eye view of Lisle, the man on the
spot, the Tudor Revolution in Government, allegedly engineered
by Thomas Cromwell, is nothing more than a mirage. Cromwell
did indeed vastly expand the scope of the authority of the state,
but bureaucratic efficiency was only very intermittently attempted,
and the main result was a transfer of clientage from a diffused mass
of little local patrons to the King, his leading ministers at the court,
and the great aristocratic families in the countryside now tied in to
court politics. This was indeed centralization, but no revolution
in government. The Lisle letters effectively lay the myth to rest.
Particularly after the monastic lands began to be granted and sold

after 1542 – a period which Lisle unfortunately did not live to see –
it looks more like an Age of Plunder.

The second great question is whether this was a period of the
reinforcement of the rule of law and the establishment of the sovereignty of the King in Parliament – that is, a constitutional
monarchy. Or was it rather the most ferocious period of arbitrary
and bloody tyranny in English history? The evidence in the Lisle
letters points strongly to the latter. The law was normally subser-
vient to the royal will, the last gasp of independence coming in
1534, when Lord Dacre of the North successfully defended himself
against a charge of treason for collusion with the Scots, and was
acquitted by his peers. The acquittal gave rise to 'the greatest shout
and cry of joy that the like no man living may remember that ever
heard it.' No other treason trial was ever so bungled again. Those
whom the King accused were henceforth duly convicted and killed
if that was his pleasure. When the Carthusiasn friars were to be
tried a year later for denying the royal supremacy over the Church,
Cromwell closeted himself with both judges and sergeants in
advance to avoid any chance of a slip-up. Husee knew before the
trial that 'they were like to die this week.'

It was from that moment that the blood began to flow, as Henry
grew increasingly paranoid, increasingly obsessed with his own
egomaniacal self-importance as ruler of the 'Empire' of England
and Supreme Head of the Church, and increasingly whimsical and
arbitrary in his disposal of his opponents, real or imaginary. The
French Ambassador regarded him as 'the most dangerous and cruel
man in the world,' and there was truth in the charge. Because of
the need for caution, the Lisle letters give only hints of the reign
of terror. In 1534 Husee reported laconically that 'two carts full of
friars' were sent to the Tower one day, 'and more coming after';
that the Earl of Kildare was in the Tower, and 'methinketh he shall
there rest his bones'; that 'Sir Adrian Fortescue shall lose his head.'
In 1536 Mark Smeaton, a musician, was 'grievously wracked' to
force him to confess to the (wholly false) charge of adultery with
Anne Boleyn, and to implicate four gentlemen of the court,
including Anne's own brother, since Henry fancied that fratricidal
incest would be a good way to discredit his now hated Queen.
Unfortunately for Lisle, one of the innocent victims was Sir Henry
Norris, the Keeper of the Privy Purse, who had been his best and

most influential contact with the King. Lisle did not miss a beat, however, and promptly joined the vultures in lobbying for a grant of some of Norris's property even before the execution. He had got the message: it was every man for himself now.

When the major peasant revolt in the North, the Pilgrimage of Grace, broke out, Henry lulled the rebels into dispersing with promises of pardon and reform, and then when he had assembled his forces, crushed them with unparalleled ferocity. He ordered 'such dreadful execution to be done upon a good number of the inhabitants of every town, village and hamlet' by hanging, drawing, and quartering them and scattering the pieces of the bodies in every locality 'as they may be a fearful spectacle to all others hereafter.' His commander, Norfolk, reported proudly that 'I think the like number have not been heard of put to execution at one time.' Husee told Lisle that Norfolk 'hung them up and put them to death upon every bush.' Many hundreds, perhaps thousands, of English peasants died to satisfy the royal vengeance. Two years before, Henry had told the French Ambassador that he intended to exterminate the whole families of Montagu and Pole – Lisle's cousins who might have some possible claim to the throne – and that is exactly what he later proceeded to do, down to the last man, woman, and child. He was furious at missing Cardinal Reginald Pole, who had escaped to France, and so he planned to get him: 'we would be very glad to have the said Pole by some means trussed up and conveyed to Calais,' he wrote. This plot failing, he offered a reward for Pole's assassination, but hit men were less competent in the sixteenth century than they are today, and Pole escaped to the relative safety of Rome.

In 1535 Henry had three Carthusians put in the Tower for refusing to acknowledge his supremacy over the Church. They were fixed upright to posts with iron bands around their necks, legs, and arms, and left there to starve amid their own excrement. After seventeen days they were taken down, hanged, drawn and quartered. Two years later Henry did exactly the same to ten more obdurate Carthusians in Newgate Prison. Unfortunately More's heroic daughter bribed her way in, and for some time fed them and cleaned the filth off them, which merely prolonged their agony. After six weeks, eight of the ten were dead, still hanging from the posts by their iron collars. Nothing in English law authorized such death by slow torture.

Three years later, in 1540, the torture and execution of those who refused to acknowledge the royal supremacy of the Church was still occurring, to the terror of England's population. In April of that year a ghastly scene, probably witnessed by Honor, was enacted in Calais itself, when two recalcitrant priests were publicly executed.

> After they were hanged and cut down, they arose and stood on their feet, and helped the hangman to put off their clothes, and so living were laid on a board, fast bound, and then dismembered, their bowels burned afore them, and spake always till their hearts were pulled out of their bodies; which was a piteous death.

When a ship put in to the shore of England and a sailor asked what news, he was told 'ill news, for they kill and hang up men in this country.'

The age of humanitarianism had not yet dawned in the West, but even by the standards of the day, the 1530s were regarded by all as a peculiarly brutal period. Miss St Clare Byrne rightly has nothing but contempt for the generations of English historians who have somehow found excuses for Henry, Cromwell, and the rest of the gang around them. She concedes the point of Henry's seventeenth-century biographer that 'I do not find him bloody but where the law, or at least pretexts drawn from the law, did countenance his actions.' But we are sufficiently familiar with similar legal camouflage today not to be taken in. As Miss St Clare Byrne says flatly, 'Henry was a killer,' and many of his victims, including Anne Boleyn, were deliberately framed.

As for the role of Parliament in all this, it was kept busy passing statute after statute extending and altering legislation concerning treason to embrace more and more crimes of opinion rather than of action, and evidenced by speech rather than writing or deeds. In 1539 Husee was again denied access to Cromwell, who was busy fixing the parliamentary election so that he could assure his master that 'Your Majesty never had more tractable Parliament.' Cromwell was in fact over-optimistic, but this is clearly what Henry understood by the sovereignty of 'the King in Parliament.'

It remains to tell the story of the downfall of Lisle himself, that affable, spendthrift, neurotic old man who for twenty-five years had been the friend and companion of the King. His troubles arose from his inability to steer his way through the thickets of court intrigue over the mounting conflict between Catholicism and Protestantism. Lisle himself was a moderate conservative Catholic, but one who was willing to go along with whatever the King should determine (even though his wife Honor was a zealous Catholic supporter). Lisle did not hesitate to lobby actively for a piece of the loot of the monasteries, asking Cromwell, in an unforgettable phrase, for 'some old abbey in mine old age.' He did quite well, and picked up a priory in England and a friary in Calais. But Calais was at the crossroads of all the currents of religious controversy, surrounded by Catholic France but with Protestant men and ideas pouring in from Germany. Moreover, both Cromwell and the Archbishop of Canterbury, Cranmer, were active supporters of the advanced Protestant position, and during the 1530s they were more or less successfully pushing the reluctant King in their direction. Behind the King's back they were also jobbing Protestants into chaplaincies and clerical posts in Calais, and protecting them when they got into trouble. As Lord Deputy, Lisle was caught between Cromwell and Cranmer on the one hand, and the official royal instructions and his wife's nagging on the other.

In 1539 the internal politics in London changed dramatically. The fear of a Franco-imperial alliance against him, which had driven Henry into a Lutheran alliance, now faded. One look at his Lutheran fourth wife, Anne of Cleves, had nauseated the King, who was in any case swinging back to a conservative Catholic position. Henry was now head over heels in love with a beautiful young Catholic nymphomaniac, Catherine Howard, who held the old man in total sexual thrall. As a Howard, she was a pawn of her uncle Norfolk, the leading Catholic nobleman at court. If Cromwell did the King's bidding and engineered a divorce from Anne of Cleves, Henry would marry Catherine, and Norfolk would automatically replace him as the leading minister. But if he refused he was done for anyway. It was a Catch-22 situation, and Cromwell at last was trapped.

Norfolk's plan to spring the trap was to set up a commission to expose the way Cromwell had for years illegally favored Protestants at Calais. And this is where Lisle and his wife Honor came in. Honor, as we have seen, was a devout, indeed perhaps fanatical, Catholic, and no doubt because of her zeal she had very poor judgment when it came to choosing clergymen for Calais and chaplains for the Lord Deputy's household. In the early 1530s, when official policy had been moving steadily in the Protestant direction, the main complaints from London were that the Lord Deputy, under Honor's influence, was dragging his feet, neglecting to administer the Oath of Supremacy to the population, and persecuting the more advanced Protestants. It was reported to Cromwell that Lisle tolerated 'papish dregs,' and Cranmer complained that he 'nothing favoreth the word of God.' Lisle himself, 'always indifferent' according to Husee, was willing enough to destroy the relics of the saints, but Honor had to be advised by Husee to abandon prayers for the dead and other popish ceremonies, to avoid getting a bad name at court.

Lisle's real trouble began with the arrival in Calais of one Adam Damplip. He was an intelligent but slightly deranged young man who had started life as a zealous chaplain to the Catholic martyr Bishop Fisher. After the execution of his master, he had gone off to Rome in the naive expectation of finding there 'all godliness and sincere religion.' Shortly before, the unfortunate merchant John Cheriton had been there and reported cynically that 'our holy father the Pope, he has two the fairest women to his wives that ever I saw out of England.' Damplip, by contrast, was shattered to find 'blasphemy of God, contempt of Christ's true religion, looseness of life, and abundance of all abominations and filthiness.'

The scales fell from his eyes and he became an instant Protestant, and an extreme one at that. Refusing friendly overtures from Cardinal Pole at Rome, he rushed back north to spread the word. He was a charismatic young man, and in 1538 he took the town of Calais by storm, preaching to packed audiences including Lisle and even Honor. By now Calais was full of heretics whose revulsion at Catholicism took the form of an extreme rejection of all the more mystical elements of that creed. In particular they rejected the capacity of priests to pardon sins or to turn bread and wine into the Real Presence in the ceremony of the Mass. It was, they said, 'not in a knave priest to make God.' Anyway, 'a mouse would as soon eat the body of God as another cake.' As for prayers for the dead, the Mass was 'ordained to sing for dogs' souls or hogs' souls, or some say for ducks' souls.' Damplip was thus preaching to a receptive audience, and in the excitement of the moment he publicly denied the Real Presence in the Sacrament. Even Honor was temporarily carried away, and in her enthusiasm gave him money and clothes to take him to London for examination by Cranmer.

This spread of heresy in a key garrison town was all very well so long as it did not run too far ahead of official policy, but by 1539 Henry had seen the dangers of religious anarchy and was swinging back to conservative Catholicism. To make the point, he had 'one hanged for eating flesh on Friday,' and himself crept on his knees from the chapel door to the altar. As orders came from London to enforce the new conservative policy, Lisle was in a quandary. The Calais Council was split, the town itself evenly divided, and Cromwell was quietly sabotaging any efforts he might make to enforce the royal will. In May of 1539, therefore, he secretly sought other patrons around the King who were known to be reliable conservative Catholics, thus going behind the back of his former principal patron, Cromwell, who had so long been his 'good lord.' Young James Basset was quietly removed from Cromwell's household to that of his deadly enemy, Bishop Gardiner, although his elder brother John remained with Cromwell.

At this point Honor fell for a glib, ambitious, and more than a little crack-brained young Catholic priest named Gregory Botolf, familiarly known as Gregory Sweetlips. She was fascinated by his pious conversation, and got him a job as one of Lisle's three private chaplains. Unfortunately he secretly fled to Rome, got in touch – if he is to be believed – with the Pope and Cardinal Pole, and returned to Calais full of a crazy scheme to seize a tower of Calais and betray the city to the Catholic French. Meanwhile the conservative faction at the court led by Norfolk was moving in on Cromwell by instigating the setting up of a commission to investigate Protestant heresy at Calais and in particular to expose Cromwell's role in protecting the accused. Lisle was a member of the commission and an active witness; Honor entertained the members lavishly and urged them on.

Although still hedging their bets, the Lisles now clearly pinned their hopes for the future on shifting their allegiance from Cromwell to Norfolk, the rising Howard clan, and the Catholic reaction. Had it not been for the antics of Gregory Sweetlips, the plan would probably have worked. But Cromwell soon got to hear of the Botolf conspiracy, as it was called, laid hands on the conspirators, and then used the presence of Sweetlips and the others in the Lisle household among the conspirators to persuade the King that Lisle himself was involved. By now half-crazed with suspicion, Henry swallowed the unlikely story that his Lord Deputy and uncle was mixed up in a plot to betray Calais to the French. Lisle had returned to England in expectation of an earldom and promotion to a higher position, but instead, on 19 May 1540, he found himself suddenly clapped in the Tower on a charge of treason. Cromwell had earned himself a temporary reprieve by a preemptive strike which discredited the chief witness against him.

Back in Calais, Honor was the next day separated from her children and put under house arrest, and a thorough search for documents took place, to which we owe the survival of these letters. The investigators turned up yet another suspicious circumstance that could be twisted to cast doubt on Lisle's loyalty. It was found that Honor's daughter Mary Basset had fallen in love with a young French nobleman, exchanged love letters with him, and had foolishly contracted herself secretly in marriage to him. Honor had known about the secret contract for a month, but had not told her husband. Presumably consumed with ambition for so grand a match for her daughter, she had kept the news to herself until the arrival of a formal offer of marriage over four weeks later. She had done this despite the fact that it was treason for one in Lisle's position to contemplate a marriage of one so near to the royal blood to a nobleman of a foreign and potentially enemy country. To make matters worse, Mary Basset had thrown her fiancé's love letters into the privy just before the official searchers arrived – which naturally aroused the worst suspicions. Rumors – certainly untrue – spread through the town that the letters were in fact love letters to Honor from Gregory Sweetlips, and Mary and her mother had a hard time explaining away their actions. Mary was made to reconstruct the contents of the destroyed letters from memory.

Without a moment's notice, on 19 May 1540, all the plans and hopes and dreams of Honor and Lisle came crashing to the ground. Lisle himself remained in the Tower of London, under immediate threat of trial and execution at any moment, if the King should so decide. As for Honor, she was confined to a private house in Calais, where remorse, guilt, and despair brought about a complete nervous breakdown. Indeed, she had much to feel guilty about. It was she who had patronized Gregory Sweetlips in the first place; she who had concealed the secret engagement of her daughter; quite probably she who had pushed her husband into swinging back to the Catholic party in London behind Cromwell's back, for it seems too Machiavellian a maneuver for Lisle to have thought of by himself. If anyone was to blame for the collapse of the house of Lisle, it was Honor. She was, as the French Ambassador cruelly remarked, 'the mother of the evil.' No wonder she 'fell distraught of mind' and never recovered.

The end of the story is soon told. Lisle languished in the Tower on the verge of death by execution for nearly two years while the ghastly history of Henry's latter days unfolded. In 1540 Henry had all the heads of executed traitors removed from the spikes on London Bridge – to make way for others from his projected blood-bath. Soon after, Cromwell was arrested for supporting heresy, joined Lisle briefly in the Tower, and was duly executed. The last of the Lisle cousins, the Poles and the Courtenays, were one by one taken from the Tower and executed in a general housecleaning. Two years later, Catherine Howard, the last great love of the old King, was found to be a fornicator and adulteress, and went to the block along with her lovers. Of the two Calais priests who had caused all the trouble at Calais, the Protestant Adam Damplip was arrested and executed for accepting some money from the hated Cardinal Pole at Rome way back in 1537. The Catholic conspirator Sweetlips also died the horrible death of a lower-class traitor. Only Lisle remained, apparently because Henry could not quite bring himself to believe in his guilt. He was, he told his associates, probably more a fool than a conspirator, and his misdeeds 'proceeded rather by ignorance than otherwise.'

The end was sudden and unexpected. On 17 February 1542, four days after the execution of Catherine Howard, the dejected and moody King traveled down river by barge to Greenwich, passing close beside the Tower of London. According to the contemporary Calais chronicler, in January Lisle had been given greater freedom of the Tower, and was taking his exercise on the leads. He saw the barge going by, and 'raised his hands high and shouted hoarsely for mercy and release from prison.' The words traveled on the cold winter air, the King heard him, and sent him a diamond ring from his finger by his secretary to say that he would be pardoned and his estates restored within a few days. For twenty months Lisle, who was naturally inclined to depression if things went wrong, had been confined to the Tower and in daily expectation of a warrant for his execution. Almost monthly some fellow prisoner had been led out to the block or dragged off to Tyburn for death by torture. If he also knew that his beloved Honor had gone mad, the psychological strain must have been enormous. Now suddenly the clouds lifted, and his heart was full of joy – so full that that night he died of a fatal coronary seizure. As an eighteenth-century historian remarked, 'the King's mercy was as fatal as his judgments.'

As for Honor, she was released and returned from Calais to her home on the Basset estates, where she lived on for another twenty-four years until 1566. But the Calais chronicler records that 'I never heard that God gave her back her senses.' If true, the shock of the arrest had permanently unhinged her brain.

Like Mother Courage and Dr Zhivago, Honor and Arthur Lisle lived in terrible times. But it is precisely the interplay between ordinary human lives and horrible public events that makes this record so utterly absorbing. As Miss St Clare Byrne rightly says of the Lisles, 'for these seven years they were humanity itself, clinging to its moment of time.'

CHAPTER 6 · Revolution and reaction

In the last decade a huge, although not very readable, body of literature has sprung up on the subject of modernization, the process by which so many societies have reached the stage of advanced urbanization, industrialization and bureaucratization. One of the most intriguing questions which this body of work raises is the way in which the interaction of the different social classes and the weight of different intellectual traditions have resulted in very different patterns of political evolution. The problem of explaining why some states have taken the authoritarian path and others the democratic is clearly of no little importance, even if no satisfactory solution is yet in sight.

Professor Barrington Moore set himself the task first, of examining the role of two social groups, the landed elite and the peasantry, over the last 300 years or so; and second, of using the comparative method to try to isolate the factors which are likely to result in political systems of either an authoritarian or a democratic character.[1] It is self-evident, however, that it is impossible to deal adequately with landlords and peasants without studying what was happening to society as a whole. A social history of the modern world without the haute bourgeoisie is as meaningless as *Hamlet* without the Prince of Denmark. It is essential to study the interaction of the monied and industrial elite on the one hand, and the agrarian elite on the other. As Moore finally admits: 'no bourgeois, no democracy.' Nor do the elements in the equation end with these three, lord, peasant and bourgeois, for any examination of the French Revolution obliges the historian to take account of the role of the petty bourgeois, the *sans-culottes*, while the study of Russia and China involves some analysis of an agrarian bureaucracy. Thus it is necessary to examine the social structure in all its operative parts, rather than to focus exclusively on landlord and peasant. Indeed, one society, the USA, has never had a peasantry anyway, unless one counts the post-bellum Southern share-croppers (as Moore does rather tentatively).

Authoritarianism or democracy are not easy to define, unless one classifies societies in accordance with a formalistic, institutional and legal frame of reference. The sort of constitutional history which used to be taught at Harvard or Oxford forty years ago took it for granted that the institutions of Anglo-Saxon societies are the last word in political equity and wisdom, and that the degree of liberty and democracy in a society can be tested by a close analysis of the formal rules of the constitutional game, that is according to their nominal approximation to the Anglo-Saxon model. Today, however, bitter experience of the total failure to export Anglo-Saxon democratic constitutions to emergent Africa has taught us to know better. In the first place, we have been forced to recognize that liberty has many faces, not all of which are embodied in Magna Carta, the Bill of Rights or an elective assembly, and that (as Stalin and Verwoerd have proved) tyranny can flourish behind a facade of constitutionalism. We are also now aware that what really matters is the state of mind according to which the rules are operated: whether or not there exists a consensus about the desirability of equality of opportunity for all, a spirit of toleration and compromise, and above all, a recognition of the moral limitations placed on the exercise of sovereign power, whether imposed by a majority on a minority, or vice versa. The belief that not all means are justified by the ends, and that even unpopular minorities have certain inalienable rights is central to the ideology.

Even if the terms are defined in the less legalistic and more anthropological manner, the problem looks rather different in the early 1970s from a quarter of a century ago. Scholars then wanted to know why in the twentieth century great modernizing, industrializing societies like Germany, Italy, Japan, China and Russia had taken an authoritarian path, whether communist or fascist, as opposed to the democratic way adopted by England, France and the USA. This question seemed real enough in the days when smoke was still rising from Hitler's funeral pyre in Berlin, when Stalin was exercising one of the most relentless and gigantic tyrannies the world has ever seen, when George Orwell was writing *Nineteen Eighty-four*. Today, however, these questions of authoritarianism *versus* democratic ways seem rather less fundamental, not because we care less about liberty in the 1970s than in the 1950s, but because the constitutional forms seem both superficial and temporary. Anthropological studies of primitive and traditional societies have revealed ways of achieving consultation and consent unknown to Anglo-Saxon constitutional lawyers, and Marx's criticism of legal institutions as epiphenomena dependent on social structure and economic relationships has merely been strengthened by the test of time. Fascism and Stalinism both now look like a short-term transition phase rather than some permanent and deep-seated structural phenomenon. In the light of the short-term fluctuations in the degree of liberty and democracy in different societies, one may reasonably ask whether the question should not be rephrased. It might be better to ask under what conditions a given society is likely to (or needs to, as some theorists of modernization assert) pass through a relatively brief authoritarian phase as it enters the modern world. This is a significant question, but on a long view not a terribly important one, if one accepts the hypothesis that the phase is not likely to be prolonged much beyond the period of industrial take-off.

There are, however, two related and far more interesting and fundamental questions than this. The first is what are the social roots and social consequences of Great Revolutions, English, French, Russian and Chinese, which in these cases seem to have been the prelude to modernization, and in particular what part is played in them by landlords and tenants? Second, what are the pre-requisites for entry into the modern, industrialized, urban world, what changes need to be effected in the countryside to make such an evolution possible, and what is the necessary social cost of such a process?

If these are the questions, what are the answers? Moore suggests that there are three alternative roads to modernization. The first, and in his view, the most desirable, is the road followed by England, France and the USA, in which democracy and capitalism are achieved after revolution. The second road, followed by Germany and Japan, achieves capitalism without revolution, by way of a fascist dictatorship of landlords and industrialists. The third road, followed by Russia and China, runs first through a peasant revolution which destroys landlords, then through a communist dictatorship which destroys peasants, to end up also with a capitalist, but not a democratic, society. In all the countries which have followed the first road, Moore sees an era of violence as a necessary pre-requisite of the subsequent evolution of political liberty and economic progress. In the English case, this violence took two forms, first, the Civil War and execution of Charles I in 1649, symbolic of the humbling of the crown and the reduction of state power; and second, the destruction of the peasantry by enclosures in the eighteenth century. The latter Moore regards as a cruel but historically necessary process, partly since it demonstrates the shift of the landlord class to commercial agriculture, and partly since it eliminated from the scene a potentially reactionary class, the small peasant proprietor, and so opened the way to a more democratic society in the future. According to this theory, England's peculiar political evolution has depended on four things: the early rise to great power and wealth of a formidable bourgeoisie with aristocratic aspirations; the early shift (thanks mainly to an interest in wool export) of the landed aristocracy to a commercial rather than feudal attitude to land ownership; the extremely important fact that the alliance of these two groups developed independent of, and indeed antagonistic to, the state in the seventeenth and eighteenth centuries; and the elimination of the peasantry from English society in the eighteenth century.

This interpretation of the evolution of English society fits in well with the ideas of C. B. McPherson, who explains English political thought from Hobbes to Locke in similar terms of the rise of a competitive, individualistic, market-oriented attitude to social and economic relationships.[2] The basic objections to this view are two-fold. First, it greatly exaggerates the degree to which English society, especially rural society, had gone over to a competitive, individualistic, commercialized value-system. The tenantry (whether small peasants or tenant farmers is irrelevant) remained deferential to their betters until the late nineteenth century, while the landlord remained paternalistic in his attitude toward his subordinates. In a traditional society there are severe restraints upon the maximization of profits that are usually successfully internalized through the socialization process and are monitored by the pressure of public opinion. Let us agree at once that the farm laborer is likely to get a far larger share of the cake under a system of collective bargaining by trade unions than by reliance on the generosity or sense of obligation of a paternalist employer. That goes without saying. But to ignore the role of the latter is to miss the significance of a set of social norms that were of supreme importance in regulating social relationships in the past. Nor is it either willful romanticism or black reaction to argue that they served a morally defensible purpose that was often advantageous to both parties. It is important to remember that the English peasantry remained passive and quiescent even during the upheavals of revolution. The constant, desperate, ferocious peasant revolts of seventeenth-century France simply did not happen in England after 1549, one reason for which was the relative restraint of the landlord class and the deference to their superiors instilled into the laborers. Thus it is impossible in the light of modern research any longer to maintain that the enclosure movement of the eighteenth century was a brutal act of violence, a cruel process of dispossession and depopulation. Enclosure in England was a slow and continuous process that lasted some three centuries, many of the enclosures were relatively equitable in intent and effect, and the eighteenth-century ones in particular involved very little mass eviction of peasants. The population of the English village, after enclosure, was normally greater in the 1830s than it had been in the 1730s. The main result of enclosure was to provide sufficient food to sustain a massive burst of demographic expansion. Finally, in what sense the tenant farmer of the nineteenth century, who had moral and practical, if not legal, claims to security from generation to generation, differed fundamentally from the small independent proprietors of the seventeenth century in terms of status, security or income is a question which has yet to be answered.

In conclusion, then, let us admit that, with these important provisos, Moore's model for England is roughly correct, so far as we know, and makes tolerable good sense. The most important contribution he has to make to our rethinking of the English experience is the emphasis he places on the fact that the alliance of landlord and bourgeoisie took place in antagonism to, rather than in partnership with, the state.

What of France? Here the problem is why a very different social background has led to a not dissimilar political system. In eighteenth-century France the aristocracy took part of their profit from the land in the form of seigneurial dues, so that commercialization actually strengthened feudalism, rather than weakening it. The bourgeoisie was feudalized, rather than the aristocracy embourgeoised, and both were linked together by mutual dependence upon the state for defense of their hereditary privileges and offices. For the state operated a large agrarian bureaucracy manned by bourgeois and nobles, which also served to strengthen rather than to weaken tenurial relationships, privilege and dependency. As a result, the Revolution, when it came, contained within it significant anti-capitalist elements, notably the *sans-culottes* and the peasantry, as well as the entrenched official class. The successive revolutionary lurches to the left proceeded normally until the interests of rural peasantry and urban *sans-culottes* split apart over the issue of price control. At that point the French Revolution came to an end, with results very different from the English.

One of the many virtues of Moore's analysis is its sophisticated awareness of the complexities of social change. Not for him the straw man of the rise of a homogeneous French bourgeoisie on the ruins of feudalism, such as Professor Alfred Cobban has recently taken such perverse pleasure in setting up and then knocking down. He sees the results of the revolution, like its causes, as a mixed alliance of disparate groups, one of which, the industrial and commercial bourgeoisie, was particularly favored by the new politico-legal system of opportunity and private property which the revolution had erected. This was the long-run effect, but in the short run what mattered was the dislocation of aristocratic privilege and the consolidation of a property-owning peasantry. The importance of the former was to eliminate the aristocracy from French life, which in Moore's view saved France from a fascist alliance of landed and monied elites, with the support of the military, such as occurred in Prussia and Japan. The importance of the latter was that the peasantry, satisfied in its ideological aspirations by the granting of citizenship, and in its material aspirations by the acquisition of freehold, henceforward became a solidly conservative force, holding back the modernization of France from that day to this. On the whole this analysis of French developments seems acceptable. One could quarrel over details. One could argue that the political overthrow of the aristocracy did not happen until 1830, that a proto-fascist alliance of landlords and haute bourgeoisie can be detected in the France of both Napoleon III and Marshal Pétain. One could point out that the aristocracy were not purely feudal and that they played an important part in the development of heavy industry in the eighteenth and nineteenth centuries. And yet it seems clear that this activity and the purchase of hereditary offices in the state were ultimately dead-ends up which both the German and the French aristocracy marched to their destruction. The fact that French society was modernized in association with, rather than in antagonism to, the state, the destruction both politically and in terms of ideology of aristocratic and official privilege, and the entrenchment of peasant proprietorship are all important keys to an understanding of French history.

Fitting American history into the model raises almost insuperable difficulties, especially since the American Civil War is supposed to play the same role as the English and French Revolutions in paving the way for future liberty, democracy, and economic progress. According to modern revisionist theory, the Southern plantation economy was an economic threat to Northern industrial, interests, while opinions sharply differ about its relative efficiency in terms of agricultural output. But Moore sees not economic rivalry, but a clash of deep-seated cultural values. The South was anti-urban, aristocratic, elitist, hierarchical, anti-industrial, even if a plantation operated with slave labor was as fully capitalistic and entrepreneurial in its management as any Northern factory. The Northern industrialists wanted to preserve the Union as a unified market, and to prevent the authority of the Federal Government being used to protect and extend the institution of slavery, which offended its beliefs in equality of opportunity, individualism, and democracy. The free Western farmers were also afraid of the extension of slavery as a threat both to their values and their interests, and the result was a coalition of Northern industrialists and Western farmers against Southern planters over issues so deeply embedded in cultural values that they were not negotiable. Moore suggests that the only alternative to war was a reactionary alliance of Northern industrialists and Southern planters against slaves, urban workers and free farmers; an alternative to which he regards the war as infinitely preferable, despite its cost. Had the war been avoided and the reactionary coalition consolidated in the 1850s, instead of in the 1880s after the failure of Reconstruction, the ideological and political trend towards equality and democracy would have been arrested, and the values officially held up to admiration in America (for all the inevitable failure fully to implement them in practice) would not have been those that are prevalent today. Putting the Federal Government permanently out of the business of enforcing slavery was worth all the blood of the Civil War.

This is a highly moralistic interpretation, which contrasts sharply with the more dispassionate examination of other societies. Moore concludes this section with an eulogy of Pericles' Funeral Oration and Lincoln's Gettysburg Address, which, however moving, none the less suggests that we have moved a long way from an objective survey of landlords and peasants and the formation of a modern society. Moreover, if the reactionary alliance of industrialists and planters came about anyway, after the failure of Reconstruction, one may reasonably ask whether the Civil War was in fact not negotiable after all, and whether its results were truly decisive. Moore's analysis of American history contains serious inconsistencies, moral and factual, his socio-economic classifications are much cruder than elsewhere, and his optimistic conclusion is at variance with the plight of the black in contemporary society and with the persistence in the South, until the 1900s, of a backward-looking cultural pattern. He seems, in this chapter, to be a victim of his theory about the necessity for violence as a prelude to democracy and to the intensity of his passion for liberty, equality and democracy.

How can we sum up Moore's thesis? Basically it is that for modernization to proceed it is necessary to get rid of agriculture as the major economic activity; this involves the destruction of the political hegemony of the landed elite, and the conversion of the peasantry into substantial farmers producing for the market (or possibly into an agricultural proletariat in collectivized agrovilles). If these two groups, landlords and peasants, are not successfully eliminated, two pernicious ideologies are likely to develop. The first is the aristocratic disease, amateurism. This leads to balanced judgment on non-scientific matters, and to a devotion to culture and the arts, but it also has its drawbacks, as England knows only too well: aesthetic snobbery, incompetence, and anti-intellectualism. The second is the peasant disease, Catonism, the backward-looking ideal of the organic beauty and harmony of the rural life, lived close to Mother Nature and away from the sinful cities and the satanic mills of industry. This is a rearguard action to protect a decaying landlord–peasant society, and soon spills over into paeans of praise for patriotism, war and death in battle. It is not merely fiercely anti-intellectual, it is also opposed to all the trends of the modern world, including democracy.

Like most other writers on the subject, therefore, Moore believes that it is essential to transform rural society, and he believes that in nearly all societies, the elimination of landlord and peasant has involved the use of violence at some stage or another. The communist way is likely to occur when there is a weak bourgeoisie and a reactionary aristocracy, and involves a maximum use of force in order to cram the destruction of both landlords and peasants into a single, violent upheaval. The fascist way is likely to occur if landlord and industrialist unite to use the state power in order to force modernization on their own terms and at the expense of the lower orders. The democratic way is most likely to occur if the peculiar conditions are fulfilled of a very slow political evolution, the slow elimination of the peasantry, and a union of commercially minded noble and bourgeois in opposition to, rather than in co-operation with, the power of the state. England is the ideal type of such an historical evolution.

In his treatment of the evolution of Western liberal societies, Moore repeatedly stresses his belief that violence, and in particular the violent destruction of the peasantry, is a necessary pre-requisite of a democratic society in the future. The one case where it might seem to fit is England, but here modern scholarship has shown that the process was very slow, very long-drawn-out, and largely free from violence. In France, violence was used during the Revolution, not to destroy the peasantry but to reinforce it. Democracy and an independent peasantry have not been incompatible bedfellows in France, rather it is modernization and peasantry which seem to be necessarily incompatible. Similarly, General MacArthur and his advisers used force in Japan after the Second World War to redistribute property to the peasantry, a process which so far has not proved incompatible with democracy. The point is not merely a technical one of interpretation, for it involves a basic judgment about the moral and practical justification for the use of violence on a large scale for the purpose of social engineering . In almost all historical cases such violence has proved self-defeating, in the sense that the long-term objectives have hardly ever been achieved, if only because the very use of violence creates a new situation demanding a new solution. Violence generates bitter cleavages within the society which, as the French, English and American examples suggest, may take between 70 and 150 years to work themselves out. The cost of these cleavages in holding back the society and in preventing its purposeful economic and political development usually far outweigh any temporary gain from the rapid elimination from power of a backward-looking group.

There are admittedly some societies where extreme inequalities of income and status are carefully preserved and protected by the state, and in which the ruling elite is wholly intransigent and opposes all attempts to modernize or to reform. In these relatively rare cases it may be that nothing short of a brief but fierce blood-letting will open the way to social progress. But this is not the only, or indeed the most important, role of violence as seen by Moore, who lays far more stress on its function in the destruction of the peasantry.

In his methodology, Moore is both old-fashioned and insular in his insistence on the legal formation of Anglo-Saxon constitutionalism and his definition of political liberty. He is also old-fashioned in two other ways, of which the first is his suspicious attitude toward the use of quantitative methods in social history. He admittedly has an enjoyable time, both for himself and his readers, in an appendix maliciously entitled 'A Note on Statistics and Conservative Historiography,' and it is true that much of the quantification of the past two decades has been used by right-wing revisionists to take the ideological steam out of historical debate and to prove that things were not so bad after all *before the revolution*. But a good deal of this revisionism, such as that about English enclosures, can stand up to any criticism, and it would be mere obscurantism to deny the role that statistics can, if used with proper scholarly caution and controlled by common sense (which is far from always the case), increasingly play in social history. Though Moore specifically condemns 'the machine-breaking mentality that rejects figures out of hand' his arguments are in fact grist to the mill of the neo-Luddites of our time, who still dominate the historical profession in all countries, and whose prejudices are confirmed by the arrogance and folly of some of the leading cliometricians. Bad statistical history is no better, but also no worse, than bad impressionistic history, although it is certainly duller. Third, he seems old-fashioned in his neglect of demographic change as a critical factor in affecting all social relationships, not least those of lord and peasant. It is demographic growth which leads to land hunger, the flight to the city and agriculture for the market, and a shift of agricultural profit from peasant or tenant to landlord. It is demographic stagnation or decline which reverses the pattern. This fact looms so large in our current interpretation both of the twentieth century and of the past, that writings which ignore it seem as out of date as textbooks in physics which make no reference to the atom. Different societies will react differently to similar demographic circumstances, as did Prussia, France and England in the sixteenth century, but all were carried along on a tidal wave of demographic growth of tremendous force. Moore's interpretation of English enclosures is seriously weakened by his failure to deal with the demographic factor, and other examples from the chapters on China and Japan could also be quoted.

Fourthly, since Moore has willynilly involved himself in a vast panoramic survey of the causes and consequences of revolution and the processes of modernization, his frame of reference, which consists almost entirely of conflicting social forces, seems unduly narrow. A reading of C. E. Black's recent *The Dynamics of Modernization* shows what a wide range of human activity is involved in the modernizing process, and in particular, the important part played by both ideas and institutions. Moore seriously neglects the ideological factor in history, whether it is Puritanism as a cause of the English Revolution, or the importance of deference as a system of patterned behavior in traditional societies, or the role of nationalism as a prime factor behind the Chinese revolutions of the twentieth century.

To end on a note of criticism would be unjust to a book of outstanding qualities. No one has ever before tried to use the comparative method on such a scale, and with so careful a study of the professional literature. Few have ever before defined so clearly the importance of the peasantry in a revolution, or the political significance of whether the alliance of landlords and industrialists is formed under the patronage of or in opposition to the state. Few historians treat those with whom they disagree with the generosity and honesty displayed by Moore. Few historians show such a passionate respect and admiration for humane and liberal values. Most historians, particularly administrative and political historians, tend to be cynical pragmatists with the Hobbesian view of human nature, the function of the state, and the purposes and methods of international relations.

The book must in the last analysis be judged to be a flawed masterpiece. The question it sets out to answer is not the right one, and the answer given misses the significance of the *timing* of the alliance of aristocratic and industrial elites. The geographical range is enormous, but it omits the two key areas, Prussia and Russia; the analysis of the causes of revolution ignores almost entirely the role of ideology; the discussion of modernization can hardly be conducted within the narrow limits of the inter-relationship of social groups, neither of landlord and peasant, nor of three, landlord, peasant and bourgeois, not even of four, landlord, peasant, bourgeois and bureaucrat. The determining force of population growth is hardly allowed for at all. Moreover, the book points to some of the grave difficulties, both methodological and conceptual, of comparative history. Much of it is taken up with straightforward analyses of individual societies, with only a long conclusion to synthesize the whole. And when it comes to the synthesis, the paucity of the examples, the complexity of the variables, and the differences in the patterns adopted by different societies, all make convincing conclusions extremely difficult to draw. But this is largely because comparative history is still in a very primitive and unscientific stage of its development, and no one knows how to do it properly. Perhaps one is tempted to suspect it cannot be done well, although this does not mean that it is not worth trying.

CHAPTER 7 · The crisis of the seventeenth century

Not so very long ago it was possible to believe in a fairly steady linear progression of European history from the eighth to the twentieth century in terms both of economic output and of bureaucratic organization. Today we are uneasily aware that for long periods of time, as long as a century or more, Europe has in fact stagnated or regressed. The first, longest, and most tragic of such intermissions lasted from about 1320 to 1480, and covered the whole of Europe with the exception of Italy. During this dismal period, governmental authority crumbled as local warlordism grew, tax yields declined, and the state became a prey of aristocratic factions. Worse still, a Malthusian crisis, followed by recurrent attacks of devastating bubonic plague, prolonged Anglo-French war, and erratic monetary manipulation combined drastically to reduce both the population and the production and trade of Europe. Population shrank even faster than production so that real income *per capita* rose and the poor were probably economically better off than ever before, or than they were to be again until the mid-nineteenth century. But the psychological price of living in a contracting world, with a horribly low expectation of life, was very high indeed. As Huizinga showed many years ago, the fifteenth century was an age of melancholy and morbid introspection.

All this has been familiar for some time. But surely the arrival of Renaissance, Reformation and nascent capitalism in the sixteenth century ensured a steady progression henceforward? So one would like to believe, but despite the attraction of such a concept, it has recently become clear that the years 1620–1740 witnessed yet another economic and political crisis.[1] Some of the familiar fifteenth-century features recur. Devastating plague and famines cut back the population, particularly in Italy and Spain.

In one country, England, preventative demographic checks (late marriage, no marriage, *coitus interruptus*) seem to have been in operation, for reasons which are at present wholly obscure. In another, Germany, there raged for thirty years a war as destructive of civilian lives and property as any of this century, and much of the area was left in ruins. Brecht was right to choose seventeenth-century Germany as the background for his moral tale about the horrors of war. Even England, which, thanks to the improvement in agricultural productivity and the extraordinary prosperity of its colonial trade after 1660, was only mildly affected by the Great Depression, saw its population stagnate, its trade endure a prolonged crisis of readjustment from 1620 to 1660, and its output of iron, lead and tin level off.

Secondly the mid-seventeenth century saw a crisis in the growth of the nation state. If 1848 was to be the year of revolution, the 1640s were the decade during which major upheavals occurred in England, Ireland, Scotland, France, Sweden, Catalonia, Portugal and Naples, there was a coup in Holland, and Germany endured the final, desperate, convulsions of the Thirty Years War.

This problem of the double crisis of the seventeenth century is of critical importance in understanding the modern world, since out of it emerged both capitalist society and the bureaucratic state. It provides the ideal testing ground for the various models of historical change advanced by Marx, Weber, and others.

There are, basically, three general hypotheses about the causes of this seventeenth-century crisis. The first, the Marxist hypothesis, as propounded by Professor Eric Hobsbawm, with massive documentary support from the Braudel school in Paris, sees the problem in primarily economic terms. The political events are regarded as largely epiphenomena, and Hobsbawn only incidentally concerns himself with the great revolutionary outbreaks of the mid-seventeenth century. According to this view the crisis is one of overproduction in the face of the limited elite markets offered by the so-called 'feudal' society in which wealth was concentrated in the hands of a tiny handful of aristocrats who used their accumulated capital for conspicuous consumption rather than for productive investment. The decline of the independent towns and the reimposition of serfdom in Eastern Europe were two consequences of the built-in limitation on growth of this type of society.

Suggestive though it is, this interpretation of early modern Europe contains too many ambiguities and difficulties to be fully satisfying. No one now doubts the facts of a century or so of economic stagnation in many, but by no means all, regions of

Europe, interspaced between the forward thrust of the sixteenth century and the renewed acceleration of the middle and late eighteenth century. But in the first place, the chronological picture is very vague. The crisis is generally agreed to have begun in 1620, but it is sometimes regarded as being over by 1670, and at other times as trailing on until around 1740. Different parts of Europe and different sectors of economic and intellectual life clearly reacted in different ways and at different times over a very long period. English industrial production may have faltered, but her agricultural output increased rapidly throughout the century. Her commercial boom of the late seventeenth century failed to stimulate any very striking industrial activity, while the Newtonian scientific revolution and planned encouragement of technological innovation petered out by 1720. In the United Provinces the depression hardly touched the soaring fortunes of Amsterdam. In France the crisis of the early seventeenth century hit the south far worse than the north, and it was not until the 1680s that general economic and demographic decline set in. In Eastern Europe the rise of the great latifundia operated by serf-labor proceeded not uniformly, but from area to area over 150 years, ranging from East Prussia in the sixteenth century via Sweden in the seventeenth to Russia in the early eighteenth. Thus one may readily agree that a generally downward turn began about 1620, without admitting that there was any clear or uniform reaction to it.

Nor is the Marxist explanation of this downward turn altogether satisfactory. An alternative explanation in terms of an unfortunate conjuncture of events pressing hard upon a demographically dropsical society seems equally valid. Plague returned to strike hard at the labor force; consumer markets contracted as war devastated ever greater areas of Germany; a shortage of circulating media developed as the silver imports from Peru declined. Irresponsible monetary juggling by Sweden, Spain and the German princes shattered the confidence of the international trading community, and made rational calculation of profit impossible. Everything conspired to turn the years 1619–22 into a major crisis more profound and lasting in its effects than that of 1929. It may be that this prolonged seventeenth-century crisis was more important negatively in pushing Eastern and Southern Europe way behind in the advance towards modernity, than in acting as a positive stimulus to subsequent growth in the key areas of North-West Europe.

It is the second aspect of the crisis, the political, which concerns Professor Trevor-Roper, whose paper in Ashton's collection of essays offers an alternative model to that of Hobsbawm. He sees the political upheavals of the mid-seventeenth century as the watershed between one age and another, the Renaissance and the Enlightenment, a crisis caused by a basic defect in the pre-existing political structure which made it incapable of standing the strains imposed upon it. Both Hobsbawm and Trevor-Roper – the Marxist and the anti-Marxist – are at one, be it noted, in scorning the old Whig notion that constitutional conflicts can be taken at their face value. Both they and the other contributors to the debate are agreed that this is a naive and superficial way of looking at historical change, that behind every constitutional struggle lie interests and passions and prejudices which must be carefully explored and exposed. To Trevor-Roper, the crisis is one between the state and society. By the seventeenth century the centralized state machine – courtiers, officials, bishops and politicians – had become intolerably burdensome and oppressive to the rest of the society. The division between the beneficiaries and the victims of the political system was becoming more and more acute and obvious every day, as the Renaissance court with its ever-increasing train of parasitic bureaucrats laid heavier and heavier burdens on society. When the Hobsbawmian economic recession reduced the size of the cake from which this governmental slice had to be cut, the situation became intolerable and various social groups tried to change the system by revolt and revolution. The cities had been crushed earlier on, in the sixteenth century; now it was the landed classes who fought against the courts. The more successful societies, those of Holland, England and France, adjusted to the situation partly by improving and streamlining the administration and partly by increasing their economic resources by the application of mercantilist ideas. By these means the burden was adjusted to the economic potential of society, and the age of enlightened despotism could begin.

This ingenious and superficially attractive thesis does not stand up to close examination. Like so many generalizations currently made about the evolution of the modern state, the modern constitution and the modern economy, it is the work of an historian taking a model first evolved to fit the unique British experience and then applying it indiscriminately to the very different context of the European continent. First, none of the conflicts under examination, in England, France or Spain, turn out to be simple line-ups of officials versus the rest, as Trevor-Roper lamely admits in a postscript. Second, the picture of an enormously affluent horde of spendthrift courtiers is vastly overdrawn. The spectacular riches of the few have blinded Trevor-Roper to the modest, and often miserable, rewards of the many. And so the burden of the court and bureaucracy, even allowing for the vast submerged iceberg of concealed fees and bribes, was nowhere comparable with the estimated cost of war. Third, it is difficult, if not impossible to view the mid-seventeenth century as a watershed, and as the true revolutionary period as opposed to that of the Reformation, except in the narrow terms of the English experience. Neither France nor Spain were so very different after the upheaval from what they had been before, and the policies remained much the same. Finally, wherever one cares to look, the attempted internal reforms of Strafford, Richelieu and Olivares were triggers for revolt, rather than moves toward the new era, as Trevor-Roper would have them.

If the Trevor-Roper thesis will not do, what is the alternative? The solution tentatively put forward here by John Elliott and others, and supported elsewhere by myself, would lay major stress on the pressures of war. Indeed some scholars, such as Vicens Vives and F.C. Lane, regard the modern state as primarily a war-making machine, created and driven forward by the needs of military preparedness and aggression. It can hardly be doubted that this has been its most successful field of activity over the past four hundred years, and there is nothing in the contemporary world to suggest that any change is in prospect. Vives explains the rise of the Renaissance state in the early sixteenth century as the product of international warfare and internal disorder, and its most striking manifestation as the standing army, often composed of foreign mercenaries. Lane turns the argument into a financial profit-and-loss account. He looks on the modern state as a device for cutting the costs of protection by the acquisition of a monopoly of violence, both internal and external. Once this is achieved, the state can then charge a higher price for protection from enemies designated (and if need be manufactured) by itself, at substantially lower costs. It can thus transfer wealth from the population at large to the officials. This is a model which goes a long way toward explaining the rise of the court system described by Trevor-Roper.

The bureaucratic expansion of the sixteenth and seventeenth

centuries was the product of the needs of all states to recruit, pay, equip, and transport ever-larger numbers of fighting men over ever-larger distances. Since new offices could be sold, the increase of officials over organizational requirements was a product of the needs of war finance. This being so, the conflicts of the seventeenth century were primarily caused by the rising scale and duration of war, which forced all governments to attempt to invade old fiscal and constitutional immunities, in order to appropriate ever-larger proportions of the national resources (which in any case were shrinking because of the general economic recession). In many areas, Scotland, Ireland, Catalonia and Portugal, outlying provinces rebelled against the centralizing process for fear of crushing tax burdens and interference in local liberties. Elsewhere, in England, France and Sweden, competing oligarchies among the elite – nobles, gentry and merchants – fought among themselves for access to or control of the offices, grants and favors at the disposal of the new Leviathan. The final outcome of the conflict varied greatly from state to state, and it is illusory to suppose that the result of such a struggle will necessarily result in the emergence either of a more democratic or a more authoritarian regime.

The appearance of these seminal works by Hobsbawm, Trevor-Roper and others points to a very clear moral. As we move away from the more securely based, but dismally narrow-gauged and unanalytical, biographies and narrative institutional and political histories, as we probe behind what men said to what we think they really meant, as we seek to discover broader and deeper social, economic and ideological forces behind the tide of history, so we run the risk of outpacing our evidence. If we go down this road too far too fast, we fall into the Toynbeean bog of vast, vague, soggy generalizations, whose murky depths cannot be tested, probed and measured by any assemblage of empirical data. A few years ago, it seemed that history was becoming an atomized pile of trivia of no interest to anyone but the narrowest of specialists (and the great bulk of PhD dissertations is still of this order today). But we are now at the stage of being stunned by a barrage of organizing hypotheses of middle-range magnitude, which are supported by a good deal of plausible-seeming data, but which cannot yet be firmly embedded in the historial evidence. To document, to quantify, and to qualify these generalizations is the primary task of the current generation. We need to combine this welcome breadth of ideas with the meticulous scholarship and high standards of evidence that were the glory of the old school of historians.

An excellent case study which may support the military interpretation of the crisis is that of Spain, where the relationship between Castile and Catalonia, the capital and the provinces, has been examined by Professor Elliot in an outstanding work of post-war historical scholarship.[2]

In the 1590s the Spanish empire seemed to be poised on the brink of world conquest. In a hundred years, the arid upland kingdom of Castile had gobbled up the rest of the Spanish peninsula, huge parts of Italy including Sicily, Milan and Genoa, the Netherlands, central and southern America and the Portuguese East Indies. Silver poured in an ever-increasing torrent from the mines in the Andes to feed the greatest bureaucracy and army in Europe. Spain seemed to have a good grip on France, she had stirred up rebellion in Ireland and was seriously threatening England. Fifty years later Bourbon France was a serious rival, England and the United Provinces were prosperous and aggressive, Portugal and the East Indies had broken free and the Catalans were in full revolt. Spain's armies were no longer invincible, her administration was a byword for sluggish incompetence, her finances chaotic, her transatlantic trade in full decline; it looked as if the empire was on the verge of dissolution.

What had gone wrong? So far from being a unified state, Habsburg Spain was a loose confederation, divided by customs barriers and widely differing constitutions. The burden, the glory and the profits of empire were left to the nobles of Castile, while those of Catalonia skulked at home. Protected by their privileges against royal demands for money or men, the Catalans were also excluded from employment and rewards. The rural nobility lost all sense of purpose, and became absorbed in faction-fighting, blood-feuds and banditry.

In 1621 there rose to power in Spain the Conde Duque de Olivares who, with Richelieu and Strafford, was one of the three great architects of absolutism of the age. This tireless but neurotic statesman realized that Castile now lacked the economic strength and the resources in manpower to support alone the vast edifice of a world-wide empire. He conceived the not ignoble ideal of welding the provinces into a unified whole, sharing equally in the profits and burdens of greatness. He saw provincial privileges as instruments for the protection of contemptible private interests and was determined that they should be subordinated to the well-being of the empire as a whole. What he failed to appreciate was the inherent paradox of his program. The only hope of winning the co-operation of the provinces was by giving central offices to the nobility and commercial privileges to the urban oligarchy. But any such move would at once alienate the Castilian aristocracy and the merchants of Seville upon whose co-operation the whole edifice of empire depended. The program was all the more impracticable since it had to be carried out at a time of mounting external pressure culminating in open war with France.

The signal for the collapse of Olivares's grandiose plans was the Catalan revolt of 1640. Maddened by the depredations of unpaid soldiery forcibly billeted on them for the winter to await the next year's campaign against France, the peasantry and the urban mobs turned to violence. They attacked first the troops, then the agents of royal authority, then their own propertied classes. A minority of the latter seized the opportunity to demand confirmation of Catalan privileges and were then driven by fear of reprisals into the arms of France. Inspired by this rising, Portugal broke free and Andalusia threatened to do the same. In the end the Catalan revolt collapsed. The society was too fragmented to cohere in a national uprising, the French ratted, and famine and disease took a terrible toll. But although Spain was thus partially restored and enabled to stagger on into the eighteenth century, the damage had been done. Catalonia was to the government of Philip IV what Scotland was to that of Charles I. Barcelona could not break away from Madrid, but would not unite with her. 'The revolt of the Catalans at once epitomised and foreshadowed the tragedy of Spain.'

A very different case study which provides an exception to all generalizations about a century of crisis, is that of Spain's great enemy, the Dutch.[3] The problem here is how it was that this small province could successfully challenge the greatest power in Europe, could achieve this independence, and could grab the lion's share of world trade, and become the greatest naval power in Europe during the seventeenth century.

Some years ago Pieter Geyl wrote:

History cannot be conceived, and it cannot be written or communicated, except from a point of view conditioned by the circumstances of the historian. One can even argue that, humans being what they are, history can benefit by a close contact of the historian's imagination, or awareness, with contemporary life. The thirteen months Mr Geyl spent in the Buchenwald concentration camp are ample testimony to his involvement in current affairs, and it was a passionately held belief which inspired his major reassessment of the history of the Netherlands over the last four hundred years.

The key to Geyl's achievement lies in the fact that he is a Flemish nationalist, who finds it impossible to accept as natural or inevitable the political division of the Dutch-speaking people. This basic premise led him to look at the sixteenth-century evolution of the Netherlands in quite a new light. In the middle of the sixteenth century the accident of dynastic marriage and inheritance had placed under the Spanish crown a loose agglomeration of provinces and cities, some French-speaking and some Dutch, collectively known as the Netherlands. A few years later an armed revolt began which eventually resulted in the division of the area into Belgium and Holland as we know them today. As interpreted by Geyl, this revolt of the Northern Provinces against the rule of Spain ceased to be a heroic struggle for political independence and religious freedom by a people in arms, as it had been to historians like Motley and Fruin. It became the work of a tiny but resolute minority, imposing its views upon an inert or hostile majority.

For reasons of geographical convenience, a band of Calvinist desperadoes – mostly exiles from the south – chose to set up their headquarters in the north behind the river barriers. There they dug in, held down the Catholic majority by force of arms, found themselves a wily politique of a leader in William the Silent, the head of the noble house of Orange, and grew rich. As late as 1624 a quarter of the population was still reckoned to be Catholic. The political division between north and south did not represent a linguistic or cultural or religious division, for Flanders and Brabant, which were Dutch-speaking and had been the main centers of Protestantism, were left behind the Spanish lines. The division was thus merely one of strategic convenience, the line of military stalemate along the waterways. Mr Geyl concludes that

> it is because the rivers enabled the rebellion to entrench itself in the North, while Spain recovered the provinces situated on the wrong side of the strategic barrier, that in course of time there

sprang into existence the dual system of the Protestant Northern Republic and the Catholic Southern Netherlands, of Protestant Holland and Catholic Belgium.

This interpretation may seem reasonable to us today, when military lines divide Germany and Korea and two different cultures and ideologies consolidate themselves behind them. But it was advanced over thirty years ago, in the heyday of concepts of natural frontiers and national self-determination, when the idea that a nation might be an artificial construct was not merely immoral, but unthinkable. The thesis was consequently inspired not by grim acceptance of the power of the sword, but by a denial of its efficacy to obliterate the cultural identity of the Dutch-speaking peoples. It recognized, however, that history can be thrown off what might be regarded as its normal course by unforeseen catastrophe. This leads Geyl into sharp conflict with the philosophical position adopted by E. H. Carr. Because of his loyalty to frustrated Flemish national-ism, he finds it impossible to accept Carr's teleological dictum: 'It is the sense of direction in history which alone enables us to order and interpret the events of the past.' He rejects the notion that the historian should write 'as if what happened was in fact bound to happen, and as if it was his business simply to explain what happened and why.' This brutal pragmatism is rejected by Geyl, rightly in my opinion. He agrees that history is an unending struggle of opposing forces, but believes that the losers always contribute something to the culture of the winners, and that a denial of the possibility of choice in history not only robs it of much of its instructiveness for the present, but also deprives the historian of an understanding of its true complexity.

Given the premise of an artificial division of the Dutch-speaking peoples, the next question which had to be answered is why the line of division remained virtually unchanged for such a very long time. It did not move north because first Spain and then France lacked the military resources and skill to break through the heavily defended water-barriers against a United Provinces whose wealth could in a crisis be mobilized to pay for a large army of mercenaries. The stability of the line was decisively influenced by the fact that the seventeenth century was a time when the art of war was in one of its static phases, when defensive techniques far outstripped offensive capabilities. When the line was most seriously threatened, by Louis XIV in the early eighteenth century, the English under Marlborough moved in, for their own reasons, to protect the Barrier Fortresses. The line did not move south partly because so many of the Dutch generals were overcautious, but also because the urban oligarchs (the regents) of Holland and Zeeland, particularly of Amsterdam, did not greatly want it to. So long as it remained where it was, the great port of Antwerp was strangled by Dutch control of the mouth of the river Scheldt. A reunited Antwerp would be free to trade again and so would gravely threaten the prosperity of the more northerly ports.

The United Provinces were floated and maintained by the unparalleled economic prosperity of the area, and particularly of Amsterdam. Their ships carried two-thirds of the freight of the Baltic and much of the French and English export trade in Europe, and the city became the center of world trade and world banking. But, as Geyl is careful, and in some ways proud, to point out, Holland lacked a solid industrial base. The prosperity, therefore, depended on the maintenance of the freedom of the seas – except the Scheldt – and the freedom to trade – except for others in the Dutch East Indies; these were principles which would have to be fought for in an increasingly mercantilist Europe.

The Dutch in the seventeenth century were the richest nation in the world. As such they were naturally not loved, even by such co-religionaries as the English, and they were therefore forced into a series of prolonged wars against jealous rivals, first Spain, then England, and lastly France. An important feature of Geyl's re-visionism is a shift in the balance of historical sympathy away from the House of Orange, which provided the hereditary, military and political leadership, and back to the burgher oligarchs. He sees a prosperous, cultivated, civilian bourgeoisie forced to fight war after war to defend its economic interests. To win, it was forced to give power to a military-political complex with a vested interest in aggressive war. To Geyl, the true interest of the United Provinces was commercial expansion, provincial particularism, religious toler-ation, and political control by the regents, not the military adven-turism, centralization, and dogmatic Calvinism promoted by the House of Orange.

In the end the war effort was more than the United Provinces could bear. England found that she could not defeat Holland commercially by fighting her; but she succeeded, perhaps acciden-tally, in doing so by allying with her in the endless wars against

Louis XIV. Not for the last time in history, the alliance of a small and a large country to fight a powerful enemy had the principal result of transferring economic leadership from the small ally to the large, while leaving the enemy largely unaffected in the long run.

Apart from the strain of war with France and the growing competition of England, Dutch economic leadership was also weakened by a shift of psychological attitudes, a withdrawal from the aggressive risk-taking, characteristic of the Dutch East India Company in its early days, and a transfer of capital to less spectacular, more prudent, investments in finance and banking. It was a shift, perhaps an inevitable shift, not so much from the robber baron to the organization man, as from the entrepreneur to the accountant. It was accompanied by a closing of the avenues of social mobility by new regulations and new practices which turned the existing oligarchs into a hereditary clique sharing out between them the offices and resources of town and province. This shutting off of the openings for new talent accelerated the decline in both culture and economic pre-eminence of eighteenth-century Holland.

CHAPTER 8 · Magic, religion and reason

I

In 1938, the great French historian Lucien Febvre issued a call for a reorientation of historical studies, with much greater attention paid to what he called '*L'histoire des mentalités collectives*,' defined as an inventory of the mental baggage of past generations and a sympathetic effort to understand their beliefs and modes of reasoning. Over thirty years have now gone by, but it is only during the last decade that there have been signs that Febvre's advice is beginning to produce results. In 1961, Robert Mandrou published *Introduction à la France Moderne: Essai de psychologie historique 1500 – 1640*, in which he discussed not only the physical and social environment of the average man, but also his psychic attitudes, his '*outillage mental*,' his fundamental beliefs, his ideas about morality and capitalism, his sports and pastimes.[1] At the end Mandrou inserted a long section on 'Evasions,' classified as nomadism, imaginary worlds, satanism, and suicide. Nothing could be further from the traditional emphasis in historical writing on the deeds of the elite as statesmen, bureaucrats, diplomats, soldiers, priests, and thinkers. Meanwhile, Edward Thompson and others were subjecting popular culture to sensitive and sympathetic analysis in an endeavor to reveal what the laboring classes were really like and what they believed,[2] as opposed to what their betters thought they were like and assumed they believed. The Enlightenment is now being turned on its head, and the squalid lives and half-baked ideas of Grub Street scribblers are being given as much attention as the grandiose intellectual constructs and the rich and elegant careers of the great philosophers.

In England, America and France, the three countries where most serious history is conducted, much rethinking is taking place about the history of science and its relationship to rational thought. Most of the basic assumptions of the science of earlier ages have turned out to be wrong, and many of the more distinguished scientists have been found to be full of absurd or irrational notions. Boyle was a great believer in the medicinal properties of stewed earthworms and human urine (the latter taken both internally and externally), and was anxious to interview miners to obtain details of the 'sub-terraneous demons' they had met with. Even Newton spent a vast amount of time on the elucidation of the Book of Revelation and on complex calculations of the measurements of the Temple of Solomon.

The last important development that is relevant here is the attempt to bring history into closer contact with the social sciences. For some years now historians have been conducting successful raiding parties into sociology, and have brought back valuable loot from Weber and Durkheim, and have even found a few nuggets among the dross piled up by more recent sociological schools. It was only a matter of time before some enterprising young historians would lead a search party into anthropological territory to see what men like Malinowski and Evans-Pritchard might be made to contribute.

These three trends – an awakening interest in '*mentalités collec-tives*,' popular literature, and working-class culture; the growing realization that rationality and irrationality, science and nonsense, are not opposite poles, but rather points on a spectrum, or even interacting and interconnecting systems of thought; and a feeling that a revitalization of history may have to come from greater awareness of the theoretical models, the research designs, and the empirical findings of the social sciences – have all now come together in a big book about magic in England by Keith Thomas.[3] Because it represents so many different tendencies in recent his-toriography, because the subject of the decline of the belief in magic is so central to the development of modern technocratic society, because its conclusions are so original and so interesting, because it is built on the solid foundations of vast erudition and primary research and is illuminated by the attitudes and discoveries of anthropology, this book is clearly a major work of modern historical scholarship.

It is now generally admitted that the life of premodern man was the very opposite of the life of security and stability depicted by nostalgic romantics. Both groups and individuals were under constant threat, at the mercy of the hazards of weather, fire, and disease, a prey to famines, pandemics, wars, and other wholly unpredictable calamities. This insecurity produced a condition of acute anxiety, bordering at times on hysteria, and a desperate yearning for relief and reassurance. There are three basic ways by which man has tried to remedy his condition. He has tried to relieve the symptoms of his anxiety by recourse to magic, or by placing his confidence in the providence of God as revealed by religion; and he has tried to remove the causes of his anxiety by expanding his control over his environment through scientific and technological invention. These three remedies are not mutually exclusive; all act and react one upon the other. If struck down by disease, a man may resort to magic ritual, the identification and persecution of a witch, prayers to God, blood letting, acupuncture, or the consumption of pills (most of which are freely admitted by the more honest among the medical profession to have little or no prophylactic value). Which of these remedies a man happens to believe in depends more on the nature of his culture than on the clarity of his logic or the degree to which his behavior is rationally determined.

In the Middle Ages magic and religion were inextricably confused. The late medieval church boasted of a panoply of magical powers and divinities, miracle-working rituals like exorcism or the application of holy water or the sacraments to ward off evil. Whatever the theologians may have thought and taught, in the minds of the people late medieval Christianity was to a very large extent a polytheistic religion in which the omnipotence of the High God was obscured by miracle-working saints, each specializing in the protection of some geographical or occupational group, or in the care of some specific disorder. The local priest often strongly encouraged this development, so that the main difference between him and the sorcerer or wizard was that the former held an official position and the latter did not.

This magical baggage came under violent attack from the early Protestant reformers in England. They denounced the Mass as 'nothing better to be esteemed than the verses of the sorcerer or enchanter,' and their ferocious iconoclasm toward images of the saints and the Virgin Mary was inspired by a passionate desire to purge the church of all hints of magical powers. When William Lambarde identified the Pope as 'the witch of the world,' he was saying something which means nothing to us, but which was of profound significance to his contemporaries. But the extreme austerity of faith, the disclaimer by the established church of all miracle-working powers, was more than suffering humanity could bear. To the extent that the Reformation was a drive toward a more rational view of the world, it was partly abortive. Psychological tensions were probably on the increase owing to deteriorating physical conditions, such as rapid demographic growth, severe Malthusian famines, devastating wars, high social mobility, structural unemployment, and galloping inflation. Moreover, the new doctrine of God's omnipotence, and therefore the elimination of chance in the world, merely made things worse, since misfortune was now officially regarded as God's punishment for guilt – a doctrine more likely to appeal to the successful than to the failures of this world. 'A poor man lies under a great temptation to doubt God's providence and care,' lamented a contemporary. He certainly did, and still does.

A sixteenth-century Englishman was thus faced with greater insecurity – and therefore greater anxiety – than before, but was now deprived of the many-sided consolations of the medieval church – the confession box and absolution, the miracle-working saints, relics and sacraments, the ritual of exorcism. A logical conclusion from such a situation is that the role of unofficial magic in English society must have increased significantly in order to fill the vacuum. This cannot be proved, but at least it has now been shown beyond doubt that an Elizabethan Englishman lived in a world in which every chance event was thought to be caused by magic, which could be manipulated by wizards, 'wise men,' 'cunning men,' white witches – and occasionally black witches. 'If men have lost anything, if they be in pain or disease, then they presently run to such as they call wise men.' These 'wise men,' or witch doctors as they are called today, seem to have been at least as numerous and as influential as the regular clergy, and indeed some of them served in both capacities. The average Elizabethan was probably less worried about the prospects of torment in Hell in the next world than he was about his current sufferings in this world – sickness, poverty, robbery, or cuckoldry. These were matters about which the parson could do little, except to ascribe them to the sinfulness of the victim or the inscrutable providence of God. They were, on the other hand, precisely the things that the black witch was thought to be able to cause, and the white witch to be able to cure.

The Elizabethan world picture was thus one in which misfortune was the work of spirits, demons, and fairies, who had to be entreated, threatened, or conjured by spells, rituals, and charms. To a Shakespearean audience there was nothing the least bit surprising about Caliban or Macbeth's three witches or the ghost of Hamlet's father. Kings and queens of England regularly touched thousands of men and women as a cure for a variety of skin diseases, and cramp rings hallowed by them were thought to be a sovereign cure for epilepsy. Many intellectuals believed in lucky charms, and almost all believed in witches. Elias Ashmole, the founder of the Ashmolean Museum at Oxford, carried around three spiders as a prophylactic against the plague, while a Nonconformist parson put his faith in moss from a dead man's skull. In the late seventeenth century a lord of the Admiralty spent long years searching for buried treasure with equipment invented for him by the fairies, with whom he kept in contact through his mistress. The conjurations of spirits, the casting of astrological horoscopes, the search for the Philosopher's Stone, the production of love potions, the development of rituals for finding buried treasure were all not uncommon pastimes for enterprising dons and undergraduates. An Elizabethan Master of Balliol got into trouble for making money on the side by selling a spirit guaranteed to ensure success in gambling with dice (it is a measure of the gulf which separates that age from our own that even his severest critics would not suspect the recent Master of any such proclivities). The intermediary who controlled the actions of these magical forces was the wise man, the cunning man, the white witch. 'The most horrid and detestable monster is the *good* witch,' wrote the well-known Puritan preacher William Perkins, a view he adopted partly because the former ascribed to his own invention what should be attributed to God alone, and partly because of the threat he posed to the clergy as a professional rival. In spite of this widespread clerical hostility, there was little enough that the church could do about the white witch because of favorable public opinion. It is now clear that the persecutions of white witches in the church courts were almost entirely ineffective.

There is good reason to believe that the counterculture of magic was stronger and more widely diffused than the official culture of Protestant Christianity. The official explanation of the nature of the universe was that it was under the sovereignty of a capricious deity, who for some reason or other allowed a good deal of latitude to an equally capricious devil. The unofficial one was that all inexplicable events were caused by impersonal supernatural forces of unspecified origin or nature, which could be appeased, encouraged, or thwarted by ritual actions of certain human beings endowed with special powers. A third system of belief held that the experience of the individual in the world was predetermined by the movement of the stars. The precise timing both of birth and of subsequent important actions was crucially important. Astrology promised to foretell the future and to reveal the unknown by a judicious combination of scientific astronomical observations and a complex structure of magical assumptions about causation. Like the 'wise men,' the astrologers also came into sharp conflict with the clergy, partly because they offered a rival form of predestination to that of God's grace, and partly because they conducted a large and lucrative consulting practice which threatened the hold of the clergy over their flocks. Here again clerical hostility had little or no effect, for astrologers were patronized by the highest in the land, as well as by such credulous creatures as servant girls and sailors. The Leveller William Overton consulted an astrologer whether or not to launch a popular revolution in April 1648; King Charles II consulted another about precisely when to address parliament in 1673. Even John Locke believed that medicinal herbs were best picked at astrologic-ally determined times.

In spite of the efforts of the early Reformers, magic ritual slowly contrived to seep back into the Protestant churches. The Anglican settlement of 1558 had preserved much of the visual apparatus of the medieval church, including vestments, the use of the cross in baptism, and other practices which the Puritan preachers denounced as popish and superstitious. By the 1630s Archbishop Laud's drive for the 'beauty of holiness' had put the communion table back at the east end of the church and had railed it off from the public, while increasing emphasis was laid on such things as organ music and stained glass windows. On the other flank of the church, the Puritans popularized the public fast in which the population temporarily gave up food, work, sex, and sleep. They also became fanatical in their enforcement of the rigid taboo of the Sabbath, a movement which was undoubtedly encouraged by the widespread belief in the magical properties of time, to which astrology also was addicted. Thus by 1640 magic ritual had re-entered the services of all the contending factions in the church, while some of the more radical Puritan sects were once more laying claim to miracle-working powers.

II

Until the last few years the study of witchcraft has been almost entirely left either to unscholarly cranks or to indignant rationalists, the latter more concerned to castigate the witch-baiters for their credulity and cruelty than to understand what the phenomenon was all about. Mr MacFarlane's study of witchcraft in Essex, illuminated by detailed knowledge of the findings of modern anthropology, the reassessment of the witchcraft outbreak of 1692 in Salem by Professor Hansen, drawing on the findings of abnormal psychology, the examination of the change in attitude of the French magistrates by Professor Mandrou, and Mr Thomas's major survey of the climate of opinion in England on all kinds of magical beliefs – these books at last make it possible to answer some of the basic questions. Moreover by a happy chance they complement one another, since each approaches the problem from a different angle. From the findings of all four, a composite picture can be drawn which has the appearance of plausibility.

Belief in witchcraft reached a higher level of consciousness in the sixteenth century than it had in the Middle Ages. The first reason for this was the enormous increase in belief in the powers of the Devil brought about by the Reformation. The early Protestants indignantly rejected all claims that God could be persuaded or cajoled into interfering for the good in the workings of nature, but at the same time they strengthened claims that the Devil was responsible for all the forces of evil in the world. Thus they rejected white magic for the church, while offering an official explanation for black magic. This paradoxical development arose since an immanent Devil was the necessary and logical complement to an immanent God. While the latter ruled in heaven, the former became, in John Knox's words, 'the Prince and God of the World.' Belief in the supernatural forces of evil abroad in the world were thus reinforced by Protestant doctrine, which soon also spilled over into Counter-Reformation beliefs. Second, the Reformation theologians abandoned the only approved remedies against the machinations of the Devil, namely exorcism, holy relics, and the sprinkling of holy water, thus removing the official means of cure at a time when the disease was officially said to be spreading. Third, the pressure of social and economic change was breaking down the old values of the intimate, 'face-to-face' peasant communities and creating great tension in the villages. In particular, poverty was becoming too widespread to be handled on a voluntary basis, and the moral duty of the rich to give alms to the poor and the moral right of the poor to demand them were both being called into question. As a result of this breakdown there was constant friction between increasingly reluctant alms-givers and increasingly exigent poor old women. The former had residual feelings of guilt at the decline of their charitable impulses and felt resentful toward those who badgered them. If the guilty refuser of charity then suffered a misfortune, he immediately suspected that the rejected alms-seeker had bewitched him. This transferred his guilt back to the alms-seeker and diverted the frustrations felt against the whole system of poor relief on to the persecution of an individual. The psychological mechanism of witch persecution is now clear enough.

Fourth, continental Europe, although to a much lesser extent than England or New England, saw the acceptance among the educated of a comprehensive conspiracy theory, an invention of obsessed priests and intellectuals. This was the notion of a widespread secret society of witches, assembling in covens, making pacts with the Devil, and copulating with him at Sabbaths, to which they traveled on broomsticks. Evidence for this extraordinary farrago of nonsense was soon provided by a flood of confessions, either the product of autosuggestion in hysterics or extracted by the use of the most terrible torture, the increased use of which was the last contributory cause. As we have found out again in the twentieth century, the torturer can obtain detailed evidence of the most absurd conspiracies and the most unlikely conspirators, provided he is told what and whom to find, for in their torment the subjects will freely confess to anything and will accuse any or everyone they know. It is to the credit of the English that the common law legal system greatly inhibited, if it did not altogether prevent, the use of 'the unEnglish method of torture.' As a result, the destructive potentialities of the witch-hunting craze were never allowed to develop to the degree that they did on the continent and in Scotland. Although prosecution was extremely common in England, the death penalty was relatively rare, owing to the care with which the magistrates and clergy normally approached the problem of obtaining satisfactory evidence.

Fear of evil spirits manipulated by witchcraft thus spread in the sixteenth century in a society which believed implicitly that any inexplicable event was caused by magic, in which the church had abandoned its old miracle-working weapons, and in which the powers of the Devil were thought to have greatly increased. It was also a society undergoing great social stress, in which the moral duty of the rich toward the poor was no longer clear, and in which the only resort of the poor against injustice was the invocation of black magic. It is clear that village communities must have spent an enormous amount of time discussing suspicions of witchcraft and ways of dealing with it. The prosecutions were only the top of the iceberg, and below the surface there was a constant warfare in progress between white and black magic. Only if black magic seemed to be unstoppable by other means was there recourse to the courts.

So far, we have treated witchcraft exclusively as part of a system of beliefs whose function was to alleviate anxiety caused by ignorance of causation and incapacity to control the environment. It may also have served a latent function as well, as a restraint upon social conflict. Everything we know about village life, especially in the sixteenth and seventeenth centuries, suggests that it was bad-tempered, quarrelsome, and riddled with hatreds, jealousies, and feelings of guilt. Fear of being bewitched must have acted as a powerful incentive to the financially secure in the prime of life to be kind and generous to the old, the sick, and the poor. Conversely, fear of being accused of witchcraft must have been a powerful incentive to the latter to be amiable and courteous to the former. On the other hand witchcraft allegations deflected aggressive impulses and social tensions away from the maladjusted institutions and conventions that lay at the root of the trouble. In this particular case the root was the economic system which made the poor so demanding and burdensome and the rich so guilty and resentful, and the status system which left women without a meaningful social position. Witchcraft beliefs therefore postponed the necessary institutional and intellectual changes by allowing society to deflect its rage on to the persecution of a scapegoat. As a result these dysfunctional institutions were allowed to struggle on instead of being rapidly transformed.

Those who launched accusations of witchcraft can be seen to fall into three categories. The first, and by far the most common, were simple village peasants who had committed some breach of the social conventions in their behavior toward the accused – usually it was the refusal to give alms or lend money. The accused had consequently let fall some expression of malice – usually a curse – and the accuser had subsequently been struck by misfortune. The sufferer first made application to a 'cunning man,' who helped him to confirm his suspicions of the identity of the witch who was the cause of his troubles. Because of this relationship between the accuser and the accused, the former almost always enjoyed a higher social and economic status than the latter. The second class of accuser was the hysteric, usually a woman, who went into severe fits and spoke with voices, accusing all and sundry of bewitching her. In some of the most sensational cases, it is clear that the predominant role was played by a local epidemic of hysteria, superimposed on a general belief in magic. Hysteria is extremely catching, and as a result from time to time, as in Salem in 1692, or in some French nunneries, whole communities would be shattered by an epidemic of witchcraft hysteria which could well engulf the accused as well as the accusers, and could temporarily blind the authorities to the flimsy nature of the evidence. The literature of abnormal psychology, notably the writings of Charcot and Janet, Breuer and Freud, provide examples of behavior, speech, and physical contortions which exactly parallel those of the afflicted girls at Salem. Totally different experiences can produce similar frustrations with similar visible symptoms. At Salem all the accusers and some of the accused were clearly victims of such an epidemic. In these cases, none of the normal rules applied. Children accused parents and parents children, and some of the accused were citizens of high social and economic standing.

The third and rarest class of accuser was the dedicated ideological witch-finder, armed with the *Malleus Maleficarum* or some similar inquisitorial handbook, who roamed about the countryside terrorizing whole neighborhoods. A fearful example of the havoc wrought in a suggestible population by these men was the mass prosecution of fifty witches in the Manningtree area of Essex in

1645, which was launched by two witch-finders. Because of the presence on the scene of these professionals, this is one of the rare cases in England in which the confessions made mention of those stock European practices of assembling in covens, copulating with the Devil, kissing his arse, etc. On the other hand it is clear that these professional witch-finders with their obvious anal-erotic obsessions were only exploiting and encouraging pre-existing fears and hatreds and delusions within the village community. Indeed, the whole history of witchcraft has been distorted by concentration upon these rare but highly sensational cases, heavily spiced with sex and sadism, which were launched by hysterical women or by professional witch-finders. What has been ignored is the regular flow of complaints and prosecutions from ordinary persons who had suffered inexplicable misfortune.

Those accused of witchcraft can also be fitted into three categories, although the distinctions are by no means as sharp as they are between the types of accuser, and the risk of over-schematization is greater. The first group are the genuine witches, resentful persons of low social status and economic level, who tried to take revenge upon their neighbors, usually for some real injury. By the use of spells, ritual, potions, the sticking of pins into waxen dolls, etc., they seriously tried to induce sickness or death in human beings or cattle. Witchcraft was the weapon of the weak against the strong for, apart from scolding and arson, it was the only weapon they had. Magic, of which witchcraft is a part, only works to the extent that people think it works, for its effects are dependent on the psychosomatic power of belief and not on physical properties. Since society believed in witchcraft, the victims were often suggestible enough to be severely affected by it. There is, therefore, a good deal to be said for the view of skeptics like Hobbes, who denied the capacity of witchcraft to do any concrete harm, but thought that witches should be punished for the malice of their intentions. The second category of the accused was the innocent, who undoubtedly formed the great majority. Some of them denied their guilt to the end, but very many were browbeaten, tortured, or confused by the strength of popular opinion among their neighbors and by the pressure of prolonged interrogation into confessing crimes of which they were not guilty. The third category were the hysterics, often women or pubescent children, who gave free rein in their voluntary confessions to autosuggestive fantasies about affectionate dealings with animal familiars or loveless copulations with the Devil.

It is very noticeable that during the peak period of witchcraft activity and persecution in the West, most of the black witches were women, and most of the white witches and the accusers were men. Unfortunately, anthropologists have so far been unable satisfactorily to identify and isolate the causes why in some African societies today the black witches are nearly all women, in others they are nearly all men, and in others again they are mixed. Theories about the economic predominance of women in Ghana or about generational conflict in Massachusetts simply do not apply to other societies. In this vacuum of scientific theory, the historian can only speculate in the void. Is it possible that the practice of witchcraft was one of the very few ways in which a woman could impress herself on a male chauvinist world, at a time when economic opportunities were limited, the structure of the family was changing only very slowly, and when feminine eroticism was strongly condemned? Is it possible that the decline of witchcraft was brought about to some extent by a partial adaptation of the family in order to give women a greater share of respect, authority, and sexual satisfaction? Is it more than coincidence that witches vanish just at the time when Fanny Hill appears? If so, then the rise and fall of witchcraft in the West has to be associated with different stages of a revolution of rising female expectations, generated in turn by the growth of literacy and the rise of individualism that were accidental by-products of the Reformation. All this is very fanciful, but the sexual element in witchcraft in the West is too obvious to be ignored.

A measure of how far our understanding of the true dimensions of witchcraft has been enlarged by recent work is afforded by comparing the current picture with that offered by Professor Trevor-Roper in 1967. The latter work is written with the author's usual brilliant style and panache, and displays to the full his capacity for bold intellectual synthesis. He is learned, witty, and wide-ranging. He presents a vivid picture of the weirder manifestations of intellectual demonology on the continent, and describes in gruesome detail the horrifying consequences. He is inspired by a *saeva indignatio* at the cruelty and folly of mankind, which is worthy of his models, Gibbon and Voltaire. He offers a seemingly plausible explanation of the rise and fall of the witch craze in Europe. He is 'relevant' in that he specifically draws an analogy with McCarthy-ism and other modern movements of persecution inspired by fear and directed toward scapegoats and dissidents. His essay has all the virtues, and it has rightly been widely praised as a model of historical essay writing. But today it looks both old-fashioned in its approach and wrong or at best overassertive in all of its main conclusions. Trevor-Roper's study is based on no new source materials or primary research, and it concentrates on the old question of who was to blame for the persecutions, instead of trying to see how witchcraft operated in the concrete social setting and what functions it served. It substitutes fine writing and fine sentiments for a patient investigation of the mental climate, the social relationships and the physical conditions in which these strange beliefs flourished. It proposes grand general theories about the relation of persecution to geography or religion which can either be shown to be untrue by the most superficial digging into the anthropological literature, or else are wholly incapable of verifica-tion. And finally it shows a tendency to stretch the evidence as ammunition to support the author's well-known anticlerical and antireligious opinions.

The new work which has just been published suggests that almost all of Professor Trevor-Roper's overconfident assertions are either false or unproven. There is little sign, at any rate in England and America, that the clergy were the prime instigators of the persecu-tion. Professor Hansen successfully vindicates the reputation of the much maligned Cotton Mather, and shows that in Salem the clergy were on the side of caution and restraint, and were overruled by public opinion. Indeed in England and France it was the educated classes, the clergy and the gentry, who first became skeptical and eventually set up strict legal rules of evidence which prevented further convictions. Second, although far-fetched continental intel-lectual theories about pacts with the Devil may have been influential in governing the details of the confessions, they were not of prime importance in explaining the rise of witch persecutions, since most prosecutions were launched not by learned professional witch-finders but by ignorant neighbors in the village. No evidence can be found for a connection between a local conflict of religious beliefs on the one hand, and the persecution of witches on the other. As for the alleged association of mountainous country with witch persecu-tion, the less said about it the better.

It is of some general interest to ask why such a dazzling display of talent should have resulted in such egregious error. All historians possessed of true intellectual distinction – of whom there are not many – from time to time indulge in bold synthetic re-interpretations of problems with which they are only acquainted at second hand, through reading the secondary literature and through perusing some of the primary sources easily available in print. Because they are so intelligent, they sometimes come up with ideas which set the experts and the graduate students off on a wholly new tack. Often their ideas are sooner or later proved to be wrong, but the very effort to prove them wrong enormously enriches the field and leads to the development of a new and better synthesis through the workings of the Hegelian dialectic. But they sometimes fall flat on their faces, their work appearing merely out-of-date and ill-informed. Trevor-Roper's most valuable writings have hitherto consisted of brilliant interpretative essays, most of which have been so suggestive that they have fully justified themselves. The essay on witchcraft, however, is less helpful. It is not merely often wrong, it is very limited in its approach, and as a result is either tacitly ignored or curtly dismissed by the current generation of witchcraft scholars working from new anthropological and psychological perspectives.

III

Why did the persecution of witches decline in the seventeenth century? What is absolutely certain is that the lead was taken by the lay and clerical elite, who were the first to lose faith in the system of beliefs upon which the persecutions were founded. Belief in the efficacy of magic, and therefore of the reality of black witchcraft, survived in the general population until recent times. Indeed there are sound reasons for doubting whether belief in magic has ever died out in the West. The problem, therefore, is how to explain a change in attitude in the seventeenth century not so much among the peasantry who launched the prosecutions as among the elite who controlled the legal process, the clergy and the magistrates. The great strength of Mr Thomas's book is his insistence that the change cannot be considered in isolation, as hitherto it has been, but must be looked at in the light of magical beliefs of all kinds. There is a basic intellectual and practical unity between magic, astrology, and witchcraft. William Lilly, for example, practiced astrology, medicine, spirit-raising, treasure hunting, and the conjuration of fairies. Astrologers, and their rivals, the cunning men, were often called in to diagnose cases of witchcraft.

The question must therefore be broadened, and we must ask not what was the cause of the decline in the belief in witchcraft in the seventeenth century, but what was the cause of the decline in the belief in magic. One possibility is the growth of mechanical philosophy. The trouble with this explanation is that skepticism about magic and witchcraft was growing among clergy, lawyers, doctors, and lay magistrates in the early seventeenth century, before the new natural science had made any real impact. In any case, magical overtones pervaded early seventeenth-century science. Hermetic thought was a stimulus to heliocentric theories, belief in the magical properties of numbers to mathematics, astrology to astronomy. The discovery of magnetism actually increased belief in spirits, since it seemed to prove that physical objects could influence one another from a distance. More important than any scientific discoveries was the change in scientific attitudes, namely the new Baconian demand for experimental proof. The idea that 'there is no certain knowledge without demonstration' slowly eroded belief in all kinds of magical explanations for events, just at the time when the lawyers were tightening up their rules of evidence in a parallel demand for more rigorous proof. But this rational approach to evidence could not develop in a world of arbitrary magic. A prior condition for the emergence of the spirit of scientific inquiry was therefore the development of religious belief in an orderly universe in which God's providence operates according to natural laws.

Organized and established religion must be seen as a system of explanation and recourse parallel to and rivaling those of magic and astrology. Hobbes rightly pointed out that the distinction between superstition and religion is in the eye of the beholder. 'This fear of things invisible is the natural seed of that which everyone in himself calleth Religion; and in them that worship or fear that power otherwise than they do, superstition.' Although religion deals with fundamentals, and magic with particulars, ministers and witchdoctors were clearly rival practitioners in the application of supernatural powers to the problems and miseries of this world. Both tended to blame individuals – the former the sufferer for his sin, the latter the malicious manipulator of spirits. Presbyterians and astrologers offered alternative systems of predestination. Professor Evans-Pritchard has recently suggested that 'when religious beliefs, whether those of spiritual cults or ancestor cults, are strong, witchcraft beliefs are relatively weak.' As we have seen, the distinction between religion and magic was hopelessly blurred in the Middle Ages, and the first stage in making a separation occurred when the Protestant reformers rejected all claims to miracle-working powers for their churches. The second important step, however, was taken at the end of the seventeenth century, when religion became more rational and God's providence was at last regarded as working in strict conformity to natural laws. It was the natural theology of the eighteenth century which finally broke the habit of ascribing misfortune to moral delinquency or malevolent agency.

Another of Hobbes's theories was that
in these four things, opinion of ghosts, ignorance of second
causes, devotion to what men fear, and taking of things casual for
prognostics, consisteth the natural seed of religion, which by
reason of the different fancies, judgements, and passions of
several men, hath grown up into ceremonies so different, that
those which are used by one man are for the most part ridiculous
to another.
It is undoubtedly true that both magic and the various Christian churches and sects all offer explanations to fill the gaps caused by human ignorance of causation, but their scope is not purely determined by that ignorance. If this were so, neither would have shrunk until technological control of nature had increased, but the chronology, as we have seen, is wrong. At the beginning of the seventeenth century Bacon had defined the aims of the new science:
The end of our foundation is the knowledge of causes and the
secret motion of things, and the enlarging of the bounds of
human empire, to the effecting of all things possible.
This was indeed the goal, but during the critical period when magic was in decline and the magical properties of religion also in retreat in the face of natural theology, there was really no great technological breakthrough. Doctors were just about as powerless to cure disease or to prolong life in 1700 as they were in 1500, the means of recovery of stolen property were as inadequate as ever, forecasting the future was as unreliable as ever. What had changed, however,

was man's aspirations and expectations. There was now a belief abroad that the human condition could be improved, partly by social action such as founding hospitals or legislating poor relief, and partly by making technological discoveries. There was also a new willingness to tolerate ignorance, instead of filling the hitherto intolerable void with assumptions about the intervention of demons or angels, or the direct providence of God.

What undermined educated belief in magic, and with it educated belief in witchcraft, was thus not the success of technology in reducing the area of ignorance. It was rather a new religious attitude of self-help, an acceptance of the doctrine that God helps those who help themselves, and that supernatural intervention in the workings of nature was now so rare as to be negligible for all practical purposes. Such are the broad conclusions of Mr Thomas's important book, parts of which are supported by the works of Professors MacFarlane, Mandrou, and Hansen.

There are three important points in which Mr Thomas's model is itself open to question. In the first place it is not altogether certain how far the Reformation in fact reduced the magical content of religion, and thus left the way open for the rise of the cunning man, the wise woman, and the witch. The change may have been a real one, but until we have a comparable study of belief in magic over two centuries in a predominantly Catholic country at roughly the same level of economic and social development, say in France, we cannot be sure that the theory holds good. This is a case in which the only research strategy is a comparative one which examines two cultures, while holding all factors steady except that one was Catholic and the other Protestant. We are at present wholly ignorant about the effect of the Counter-Reformation on belief in magic. Second, the stress laid by Mr Thomas on rising tensions in the alms-giver/alms-seeker relationship as the factor in stimulating recourse to witchcraft in the village community seems doubtful. Although this certainly appears to be true for England, it does not apply in cases such as that at Salem in Massachusetts or at Loudun in France, where the key ingredient was clearly an epidemic of hysteria generated by other causes. Institutionalized poor relief never spread to the countryside in France as it did in England, so that in the former case the decline of witchcraft cannot be ascribed to a rise of more impersonal relationships between the rich and the poor in the village. Moreover, it is clear that intellectual demonology based on the writings of paranoid inquisitors with a conspiracy complex and sado-masochistic sexual hang-ups, and supported by confessions extracted by torture or autosuggestion, played a far larger part in the continental witch craze than it did in England. In this sense, the examples of England and New England are not typical of the West as a whole. In all areas, on the other hand, most cases of witchcraft were brought to the attention of the magistrates by popular protest from the villagers, rather than as a result of investigations by a professional witch-hunter or inquisitor. Mr Thomas's main finding is therefore unaffected, that witchcraft is merely one aspect of a diffused belief in the constant, daily operation of magic in individual human affairs. This is how witchcraft appears to every anthropologist who has investigated it in a modern tribal setting, and this is how historians must certainly treat it in the future.

Third, there is the intractable problem of how to quantify belief. Mr Thomas has shown conclusively that in Elizabethan England there was a magical counter-culture more widely diffused and more deeply believed in than the theories advanced by the official religion. What he cannot prove is whether this counter-culture had increased or diminished by comparison with the Middle Ages. Even his evidence for the decline in the late seventeenth and eighteenth centuries is none too secure, being based largely on the change of attitude of the elite toward witchcraft and on the decline of complaints by the clergy about competition from their ancient rivals, the wise men and the astrologers. This is not ideal evidence, but it is probably as good as we are likely to get. There can be no doubt that in the course of the seventeenth century, the English propertied classes became less fearful and insecure, and less willing to go to extreme lengths to maintain orthodoxy and order. The last heretic was burned in England in 1612, the last political subject was tortured in 1639, the last witch was hanged in 1685, in each case a century or so ahead of similar changes on the continent. It is less certain how long it took for this skeptical attitude to seep down to the public at large, but in the late seventeenth century we certainly hear less than we do in the late sixteenth about witches, cunning men, and astrologers, about familiars, fairies, and horoscopes.

IV

An interesting parallel to the rise and fall of belief in a world torn
between God and the angels on the one hand and the Devil and the
witches on the other was the rise and fall in the belief in Antichrist.
'Next to our Lord and Savior Jesus Christ, there is nothing so
necessary as the true and solid knowledge of Antichrist,' wrote
Oliver Cromwell's best selling schoolmaster. Everyone from John
Pym to Isaac Newton speculated about the identity of Antichrist as
recorded in the Scriptures, and the timing of his overthrow. Luther
and Calvin were positive who he was: he was the Pope, the Great
Whore of Babylon. The most advanced mathematical skills of the
day were harnessed in the search, for the Number of the Beast was
known to be 666 and his overthrow in 'a time, times, and half a
time.' John Napier particularly valued his invention of logarithms,
since it enabled him to speed up his calculations on this subject,
while Newton devoted much of his stupendous talents to the same
futile problem.

In this latter half of the twentieth century, we know all too well
what happens when otherwise sober and prudent statesmen and
rational and clear-headed intellectuals become obsessed with a
Devil-theory: it blows their minds, and the result is bloodshed,
torture, and repression on a scale which seems hardly credible to a
posterity which has freed itself from the particular mythology. The
reason why Devil-theories are so destructive of human happiness is
that two or more can, and usually do, play at the identification
game, label one another as Antichrist, and embark on a holy war of
mutual extermination. Thus it was not long before some English
Protestants were identifying all bishops – even Anglican bishops –
as Antichrist. To escape from them many fled 3,000 miles to the
wilderness of Massachusetts. The next mutation came during the
intellectual and political disintegration of Civil War and Interregnum, when the Parliamentarian leaders and preachers whipped up
enthusiasm by identifying first Archbishop Laud and King Charles,
and then all royalists as agents of Antichrist. Finally the radical sects
in their turn identified all holders of religious or secular authority,
including the Parliamentary leadership, as Antichrist, thus bringing
down on themselves a persecution as ferocious as that of the witches
themselves. This was the end of the road. The great search for

Antichrist, whose elimination would purify the world and open the way for the reign of Jesus Christ, had finally turned out to be a blind alley leading nowhere. Out of the disillusionment emerged a more rational view of the world, and a greater tolerance of men with differing opinions. It is not a mere coincidence that concern with both Antichrist and those agents of the Devil, the witches, decline sharply after 1660. The English were intellectually and emotionally drained by the experience of a century of feverish activity to seek out and destroy Antichrist the Beast and the Devil and his disciples.

We can now see, perhaps for the first time, the complex chronological interaction of magic, religion, and science as rival explanatory systems. The early Reformation renounced the magical powers of religion, and unofficial magic presumably poured in to fill the void. In its official doctrine, however, the reformers greatly stimulated belief in the Devil as the instigator of all misfortune and evil, and of Antichrist as the embodiment of evil on earth, who had to be destroyed before the reign of Jesus could begin. It was only much later on, after a century of turmoil and bloody persecution, that the profounder aspects of the new religion came to the fore. By the late seventeenth century Protestantism's more rational and coherent view of nature and its relationship to God's providence had at last produced a state of mind to which magical or miraculous explanations of events were unacceptable. Later still, this religious-inspired rationalism began to undermine religion itself. The relation of magic and science went through the same two stages of symbiosis and antagonism. For a century, magic went hand in hand with science, but eventually science broke away and destroyed its partner's credibility, at any rate among the educated classes. Much later still, in the nineteenth century, it also broke with religion, which it began to destroy too.

This is not a simple story of heroes and devils, of reason battling unreason, nor is it enough to treat it as one of the more bizarre aspects of human folly. The most deeply held beliefs of the past seem wholly irrational to us, as no doubt many of our own will seem to posterity. When all is said, however, the abiding distinction of the West has been that in the last three hundred years it has gone further than any other society the world has ever known to rid itself of these ancient fears and superstitions. The process is perhaps the most important intellectual change since man emerged from caves. But today, at the apogee of our scientific, rationalist, technological civilization, magical beliefs are spreading once more. Millions of lucky charms hang in cars to ward off traffic accidents; astrological advice is regularly published in the popular newspapers, and courses on the subject are just beginning to appear at the universities in response to student demand; the casting of horoscopes, often assisted by computers, is a booming growth industry; every year huge crowds of the sick pour into Lourdes in the hope of a miraculous cure. Perhaps most disturbing of all is the current faddish revival of interest in witchcraft, evidence for which is provided by the spate of new historical works, reprints of inquisitorial handbooks and of reports of notorious witch trials, imaginative re-creations of historical events by talented novelists like Françoise Mallet-Joris and fashionable film directors like Ken Russell, and the beginning of semi-serious organized witch cults in California. In the light of this current revival of belief in magic and the irrational, neither arrogance nor complacency is in order when one views the long, messy, continuing struggle which has slowly led to what Max Weber described as 'the disenchantment of the world.'

As a result of this struggle modern man now walks upon a knife edge. On the one side is a 'technetronic' society, smooth, impersonal, rational, and scientific, a kind of universal IBM company ruled over by the computer. While it can be supremely efficient, it is also drab and sterile, leaving no place either for the emotions, including the finer ones of love and compassion, or for the sense of aesthetic mystery and wonder which is at the root of all great literature, art, and music. On the other side is a society at the mercy of prejudice and passion, driven forward by wholly irrational beliefs which stunt the mind and prevent effective action for human betterment. While it may be warm and vibrant, it is also full of cruelty, hate, and fear. The naked ape had better watch his step.

CHAPTER 9 · Catholicism

The English Catholic community has not hitherto been well served by its historians or publicists. In this century, the reality of a fascinating story has been hopelessly blurred by the romantic pseudo-medievalism of Belloc and Chesterton and, more recently, by the equally misleading nostalgic snobbery of Waugh in *Brideshead Revisited*.[1] As a result, the history of the community that is current today is roughly as follows. In pre-Reformation England, Catholicism was embraced by the bulk of the population. Over the next two centuries it slowly shrank, thanks to vigorous proselytization by Protestant preachers, reinforced by savage political persecution. Remnants of the medieval faith were preserved among a minority of wealthy landowners, thanks to the heroic efforts of dedicated missionary priests, many of whom suffered martyrdom for their pains. In the nineteenth century the community was transformed and revived by the removal of religious and civil disabilities, the influx of large numbers of Irish urban workers, and the establishment by Rome of a formal episcopal organization. The image is one of a perpetually backward-looking group who dreamed and plotted for a century and a half to restore the pre-Reformation church with the aid of Catholic kings, assassination schemes, and one serious attempt to wipe out, at one blow, the total ruling elite of the nation – the Gunpowder Plot of 1605. It was a dream that failed, leaving behind it little but a record of martyrdom, disappointment and betrayal.

Meanwhile the raw materials for a new and more sophisticated interpretation of the problem were being assembled in the sixty-odd volumes of documents published by the Catholic Record Society, a few notable local studies were being written, especially of Yorkshire by a Benedictine, Hugh Aveling,[2] and anthropologists and sociologists were providing novel theoretical models for the analysis and classification of religious institutions, communities, rituals and behavior. By the 1970s the stage was set – and now Dr Bossy has arrived to fit it all together.[3]

His story bears only the most tenuous relation to the traditional one. According to him, the first 200 years after the Reformation saw the creation of a viable, healthy, and growing sect, arising out of the ashes of the dead pre-Reformation church. This community was a genuinely new one, a sect which owed little or nothing to the church of Cardinals Wolsey and Pole. By 1620 it was led by a close-knit intermarrying group of aristocratic and gentry families, inspired by, but the patrons and masters of, some 700 regular and secular priests. It was an upper-class, lay-dominated, rural, domesticated, non-proselytizing sect – one of several which could not stomach the flabby inertia and lack of spiritual zeal of the Anglican clergy.

It is not at all clear at present just why some landed families took to Catholicism between 1570 and 1620 while others remained carelessly Anglican and others became zealous Puritans. Dr Bossy points out that on the eastern slopes of the Pennine chain of hills, the vales were alternately Protestant and Catholic, which suggests the perpetuation of old local feuds in a new religious form. What is certain is the enormous importance of the role of women in the conversion process, whether to Catholicism or to Puritanism. Both were religions of the spirit, reinforced by rituals of fasting and daily prayer. Both demanded zealous, learned, independent clergy who would speak directly to the soul. Both appealed to women under emotional stress.

In one of his most brilliant chapters, Dr Bossy shows how this lay Catholic community slowly detached itself from the Anglican conformists around it by the observance of a series of separation rituals: a quite different calendar of fasts and feasts; attendance at the Mass; and separate *rites de passage* of baptism, marriage and burial. As he points out, the 'Church Papists' of the Elizabethan period were a breed who could not reproduce themselves. In the face of strong priestly disapproval, they could hardly teach their children to live a life of deliberate duplicity by attending both public Anglican communion and private Catholic Mass, although in the early days it was easy enough for they themselves to do so without moral discomfort.

By the time the separation process was complete, in about 1620, the characteristics of the Catholic community were set for the next

150 years, 'the Age of the Gentry': predominantly controlled by aristocrats and rich squires, but inspired by resident Jesuit chaplains, and supported by itinerant secular missionaries; bunched together in clusters of servants and tenants around great homes with their resident priests; mainly congregated in the upland north, away from areas of new economic activity; largely non-proselytizing and loyal to the English Protestant state. They were, and accepted that they were, a minority group embracing maybe a fifth of the titular nobility and a twelfth of the upper gentry, but only about 1 per cent or less of the total population. Numbers remained static or even declined in the late seventeenth century under the hammer blows of vicious persecution. The priesthood became increasingly a profession drawn largely from the sons of the gentry. Its numbers fell, but this was no great loss since, just as in the Anglican church, there had been a serious surplus of priests to serve the community in the second quarter of the century.

The late seventeenth century was the age of the resident chaplain in the great house, who serviced the community controlled by the lord. There was sometimes friction between the two, if the former was treated like a servant. But things usually ran fairly smoothly so long as the priest did not display a foolish excess of zeal, like the one who tried to persuade the married couples in his congregation to take a vow of chastity. Priests wore secular clothes, and many served useful double lives as family lawyers, stewards, land-agents or tutors, just as chaplains did in Protestant noble households (and as the philosopher Thomas Hobbes did at Chatsworth). Because of the peculiar nature of the social composition and organization of the Catholic community, catering to an educated and leisured class in a household setting, the forms of devotion were more spiritual than magical, and more domestic and private than collective.

This structure survived the public paranoia and official persecutions of the late seventeenth century remarkably well, but it underwent profound transformations in the eighteenth century in response to the economic and intellectual changes of the age. The old rituals of fasting, feasting, and day-long church attendance on saints days could not survive the challenge from the pragmatic work ethic of the age of Adam Smith. As early as 1683, William Blundell, a pious Catholic gentleman, was calculating the cost of such behavior in terms that were as materialistic as those of any hard-boiled, contemporary political economist. He estimated that in

England and Wales the work of the whole population for one day
'will amount to £100,000, so that the difference of working and not
working ... is no small matter as to civil and political respects.' In
the face of this sort of calculation, the more time-consuming
separation rituals were drastically reduced. Second, the priests were
increasingly drawn from classes below the gentry, increasingly
turned their attention from the gentry to farmers and laborers, and
increasingly shifted the center of their activity from dispensing the
sacraments to moral catechizing, in conformity with the more
rationalist currents of the age. Third, numbers increased.

After 1770 the pace of change picked up. Penal restraints on
Catholic worship were removed, missionary activity increased, and
the Catholic population shifted from the countryside to the new
industrial areas in the cities, especially in Lancashire. One reason
for this shift was the enormous influx of Irish immigrants after
1790, but Dr Bossy provides plausible reasons for thinking that the
change would have taken place anyway, as surplus English Catholic
laborers were forced to leave their villages and emigrate to the cities
to take up industrial occupations. The result was that the Catholic
community grew from about 80,000 in 1770 to 750,000 in 1850, a
tenfold increase in 80 years. The size, the social composition, and
the geographical distribution of both the lay community and the
priesthood had been radically altered.

With the lifting of all civil disabilities in 1829, the sect became a
denomination, just one among the many that made up England's
extraordinarily pluralistic religious configuration. Clerical influence
increased and lay control declined, just as it did among the
Protestant churches in the early nineteenth century, culminating in
the imposition of episcopal organization by Rome in 1851. This was
not due to any economic decline among the Catholic aristocracy
and squirearchy, who if anything were getting richer as the
survivors in the male line gobbled up the estates of more and more
Catholic heiresses. It was part of a broader movement to clerical
power in early Victorian England, reinforced by the Gothic revival,
the shift of the center of gravity from the countryside to the towns,
and the increase of numbers outside the orbit of the household and
tenantry of Catholic landlords. A third possible organizational
structure was Congregationalism, controlled by middle-class farmers and businessmen who built the chapels and organized the
necessary fund-raising. This was a real possibility for a while, but it

was defeated partly by energetic counter-attack by the priestly hierarchy, and partly by the prevailing sentiment of the times which favored clerical claims.

In his conclusion, Dr Bossy sketches a broad schema into which to fit his picture of the Catholic community. He points to the persistent pluralism of English religious history, the fact that ever since its establishment, the Anglican state church has failed to satisfy the spiritual aspirations of the whole of the population. This was one Renaissance state in which the doctrine of *cuius regio, eius religio* did not apply. Dr Bossy would like to abandon the traditional division of dissenters into the Catholics on the right and all the others on the left. He would regroup them into two divisions, one of which was composed of those who accepted at least two of the three major tenets of Protestantism, the prime authority of the bible, justification by faith, and the priesthood of all believers. This leaves out the Catholics, Quakers, and Unitarians, but includes Presbyterians, Congregationalists, Baptists and Methodists. He argues that it was the rigidity and unwillingness to compromise of the Anglican church that spun off this diversity of dissenters century after century. Finally he suggests, almost as a postscript on the last page, yet another way of grouping dissenters, this time according to the principles of structural anthropology. There were those whose relation to a Divinity, in some way continuous with humanity, were mediated through nature; and those whose relation to a Divinity, fundamentally transcendent and different from humanity, were mediated through culture, namely the text of the bible. The practical result of this division is the same as before, with the same two spectra running from Unitarians through Catholics to Quakers on the one side and Presbyterians through Congregationalists to Particular Baptists on the other.

What are we to make of this remarkable book? The first thing which strikes the reader is how very different a picture it presents from the traditional story, in the sense that persecution, and the slow relaxation of persecution, culminating in full toleration in the nineteenth century, plays almost no part, while social factors and internal lay/clerical tensions bulk large. The Tower, the rack, Tyburn, the Gunpowder Plot, the Popish Plot, the rebellions of 1715 and 1745 are scarcely mentioned and then only in passing. This involves a drastic and deliberate rejection of *histoire historisante*, the narrative of external events. Here I think Dr Bossy has thrown the baby out with the bathwater. The evolution of the Catholic community is just not fully intelligible except in the context of a century and a half of official persecution and popular hatred. After the Gunpowder Plot, Catholics were generally regarded as traitors to their country, and vicious conspirators capable of almost any criminal act. For example, the fiction of their responsibility for the Great Fire of London of 1666 is officially cut in stone on the base of the Monument, for posterity to read to this day. Any breakdown of law and order, in 1640–1, and 1688, immediately led to the looting of Catholic country houses by infuriated mobs. In 1639 a suspected Catholic officer was flayed alive by his troops before an approving crowd in the public square of Wellington in Somerset. The mass hysteria generated by the Popish Plot has few historical parallels, apart from the storm whipped up by Senator Joseph McCarthy and so skillfully exploited by the future President Nixon.

Only this background of persecution, and the psychological characteristics of a persecuted minority sect, can explain the concentration of the missionary priests upon the aristocracy and greater gentry, who alone could provide the necessary local protection; and the insistence by these patrons that active proselytization of the population at large should cease, for fear of bringing further troubles upon their heads. It was persecution which decimated the Jesuits and led to a probable decline in total numbers of the community in the late seventeenth century. It was the easing of persecution which permitted the restarting of missionary work in the early eighteenth century, and it was the abolition of the penal laws against Catholic worship which allowed the priests to exploit the opportunity offered by the Irish immigration after 1790. It was the idleness and powerlessness of the Catholic nobility and gentry because of their exclusion from public office, and their desire to play their natural role as leaders of the society and supporters of law and order which tempted a steady trickle of them to abandon their faith and conform to the Anglican church in the eighteenth century. Some families were endlessly torn by this dilemma, the most striking example being the Howards, Dukes of Norfolk. Between 1570 and 1850 there were thirteen heads of the family, all but one of whom adopted a different religious faith from that of his predecessor, who was usually his father. This can hardly be interpreted as an extreme case of hereditary oedipal rebellion. Rather it shows the tension between loyalty to their religion and loyalty to the natural responsibilities of their class which tormented these families from generation to generation, a tension which was only relaxed in 1829, when it was already too late to be of use.

At every point, therefore, from 1570 to 1850 the burden of persecution and exclusion influenced the evolution of the Catholic community in England. Virtually to ignore this fact is rather like writing the history of the Jews of the Pale, ignoring the existence of anti-Semitic laws and intermittent pogroms.

Despite this one obvious flaw, Dr Bossy's book in one giant stride drags the history of the Catholic community in England into the forefront of modern historiography. It is a formidably intelligent work in which the author argues with his reader on the printed page and calmly persuades him by logic and example. It is revolutionary in its interpretation, subtle in its conclusions, learned in its scholarship, and wide-ranging in its discriminating borrowing from anthropology and sociology. It is a very fine book indeed, and I believe that in almost all important respects it is right.

CHAPTER 10 · Puritanism

One aspect of the massive historical assault on the problem of Puritanism over the last thirty years has been the endeavor to explain its causes, not so much in ideological as in political, institutional and economic terms.

Despite some excellent studies of the ideology of Elizabethan Puritanism, no detailed examination of the movement as a political force existed until the publication of Dr Collinson's masterly study.[1] What he does is to confirm the growing impression that the older interpretation of the English Reformation as an act of state is largely misguided, a product of the congenital myopia of administrative historians. Professor Dickens has demonstrated the groundswell of popular religious feeling upon which the Reformation was carried, Professor Hexter has postulated a general intensification of religious emotion that lay behind both Reformation and Counter-Reformation, and Dr Collinson's book on the Puritans in the late sixteenth century provides further proof of the importance of religion acting on society, irrespective of the will of princes and potentates. Few devout Englishmen could accept the Anglican settlement, with its botched-up doctrinal compromises and its confirmation of all the abuses in organization and administration of the late medieval church. They demanded a further reformation to create a truly purified church, and since they had support in high places, reaching up into the bench of bishops, the Privy Council, and both Houses of Parliament, they could with impunity set out first to persuade the queen to change her policy, and then, when that failed, deliberately to create a church within a church. Dr Collinson perhaps exaggerates the conspiratorial nature of the Presbyterian underground organized by John Field, and is perhaps too intrigued by parallels with twentieth-century communist cells, but he tells a fascinating, and plausible, story of the rise of a revolutionary movement and its ultimate destruction by forceful police action by Elizabeth and Archbishop Whitgift. He also shows how illusory was this facile victory, so that the crushing of the organization merely drove the movement deeper into the heart of English society, which continued to grow and spread its roots. Forty years after the Queen's death, it contributed to the overthrow of the Anglican church and the making of a Civil War, and after the Restoration it created a permanent split in English religious life that has affected our history from that day to this. Responsibility for this development lies largely with the obstinacy of Elizabeth and James, and the bench of bishops. It is the story of what momentous consequences may follow from a simple refusal to negotiate at the appropriate time.

If Puritanism is to be put in its proper perspective, and if its astonishing popularity in the early seventeenth century is to be explained, it is clearly as important to investigate the shortcomings of the established church as it is to demonstrate the attractiveness of Puritanism. This is particularly so since the only thing that held the different bands of Puritans together in the early 1640s was a strong antipathy to the Laudian church.

An extremely important aspect of the shortcomings of the Anglican church was its economic difficulties, whose roots lay far back in the time of the Reformation.[2] In England, as elsewhere in Europe, the sixteenth century witnessed a massive secularization of ecclesiastical property. Monasteries and chantries were swallowed by the crown. Bishop and dean and chapter, having narrowly weathered the reign of Edward VI, found themselves, under Elizabeth, subjected to less open but almost equally effective attrition at the hands of the courtiers and nobility. Meanwhile, the parish clergy were also hard-pressed by the price revolution and by impropriations which transferred much of their income to the pockets of the gentry, nobility, and colleges. As a result the social status and the educational and moral qualifications of both clergy and episcopacy failed to satisfy the new generation, and the cry arose to abolish the latter in order to subsidize the former. In this crisis in its history, in the latter years of Elizabeth, the Church suddenly found itself some powerful allies. First the crown, and then a section of the wealthy laity, realized that the Church, and particularly the episcopacy, was an integral part of the Establishment whose fall might well endanger the position of both peerage and monarchy. The landed classes were at last brought face to face with the ambiguity of their position. As devout Christians they deplored the ignorant condition of the clergy and were opposed to simony, pluralism, and non-residence; but as lay impropriators, patrons of advowsons, and potential courtiers their own economic interests were bound up with these very abuses. As Calvinist reformers they were highly suspicious of the powers and wealth of the bishops; but as members of the propertied classes they feared that the abolition of episcopacy would unleash similar attacks on their own authority and vested interests.

This stalemate continued until the end of the 1620s, only to be broken by serious attempts on both sides to attack the problem at its roots. The Puritans began to put their consciences before their purses. They set up a company financed by public subscription, which began buying up lay impropriations and restoring the money – but not the authority – to the church; and as individual patrons or as congregations they began to increase the salaries of the clergy – of their own choosing – by voluntary augmentations. Against these developments Laud set in motion the full powers of the state. He crushed the scheme for buying impropriations, attacked augmentations as the thin edge of the wedge of independency, and attempted to restore the financial health of the church by force. He tried to squeeze increased tithes out of the towns, especially London, and increased salaries out of impropriators. The result was, as Dr Hill puts it, that 'Protestantism, patriotism, parliamentarianism and property all worked together against Laud's attempt to reverse history.' And so in the 1640s bishops and deans and chapters went down, but, significantly enough, tithes survived.

The most serious objection to this powerful and heavily documented analysis is whether this concentration on the economic problems of the church, necessary as it was for the task in hand, really succeeded in achieving a judicious symbiosis of economic and religious factors. Thus there is overwhelming evidence of the poverty of the Elizabethan parish clergy, resulting in their lamentable ignorance and their low personal quality. But the parish clergy had been in this brutish condition throughout the Middle Ages. Was it not the rise of the Calvinist conscience with its emphasis on the importance of the moral qualities of the priesthood that at last made the issue one of burning importance? Again, before the civil war lay patrons were filling livings with men of their own religious persuasions, and as a result 'lay patronage made Puritanism an issue

within the church.' But could it not equally well be urged that
'Puritanism made lay patronage an issue within the church' by
alarming conservatives like Laud? Lastly it is not enough to describe
in detail the economic pressures exerted by Laud, without also
examining the parallel drive for the 'beauty of holiness,' the
encouragement of organs and altar-rails. Who is to say which did
more to alienate men's minds?

Be that as it may, one of the results of the organizational,
educational and religious weaknesses of the Anglican clergy was
that the spiritual vacuum they left was filled by a growing army of
zealous young Puritan lecturers.[3] One of the keys to Puritanism
was belief in the value of preaching the word, as the sole efficacious
method of winning souls and preventing their subsequent backsliding. The Sunday pulpit was the principal instrument of religious and
political propaganda, and control over it therefore became the
subject of bitter conflict between the crown and the bishops on the
one hand, and the Puritan laity and ministers on the other. Queen
Elizabeth, it was said, 'used to tune the pulpits,' and James I,
Charles I, and Charles II were all too well aware of the importance
of this vital instrument for the molding of public opinion. The
trouble was that the laity controlled the patronage of about four-
fifths of all the livings in the country, and if they chose to use this
power to protect subversive clergy, there was not a great deal the
authorities could do about it. Worse still, from the official point of
view, was the practice, which developed rapidly after 1575, for a
parish or town corporation to agree to provide funds from local
taxation, independent of the incumbent clergymen and the official
establishment of the church, in order to hire a lecturer to preach on
Sundays or weekdays. This was particularly important in London,
where the vast majority of the livings were in royal or episcopal
patronage. The only way the London laity could get the preachers
they wanted was to set up a parallel church organization, hiring
their own men for their own purposes.

Two things stand out in the story, of which the first is the
extraordinary degree to which the new institution took root, at any
rate in the towns. At one time or another most provincial corporations and nearly all the London vestries hired a lecturer to preach to
them outside the regular services of the official church establishment. Mr Seaver has evidence that at least seven hundred men
lectured in London alone in the century 1560–1662, nearly two-

thirds of whom are definitely known to have been Puritans. They include the great majority of the better-known Puritan preachers who often later moved into church livings in town or country. The measure of the change that this makes to our thinking can be illustrated very easily. In 1961 Mrs Pearl, in her definitive book on *London and the Outbreak of the Puritan Revolution* had this to say about the lecturers in London in 1640–2: 'no other London parish besides St. Antholin's supported a lecture every week day. A few, however, supported one or at most two Puritan lecturers.' Mr Seaver shows that in fact there were over seventy of them in 1640 rising to over ninety in 1642, at least seventy of whom were definitely Puritan. A whole new world has been opened up before us.

The second conclusion is the relative impotence of even the most vigorous episcopal persecution to do more than temporarily stabilize a deteriorating situation. The power of the lay patrons was so enormous that nothing short of a major social transformation would have brought victory. In retrospect, Laud's policy was an abject failure, the only result of which was to stimulate the religious and political radicalism of the lecturers. In the 1630s, at the height of the Laudian persecution, some forty-six were still delivering sixty sermons a week in the dense urban area of one square mile. An enthusiastic Anglican official wrote in 1636: 'If his majesty shall in his princely care abolish that ratsbane of lecturing out of his church . . . we shall have such a uniform and orthodox church as the Christian world cannot show the like.' The idea was sound but the hope was vain, for it flew in the face of social realities.

It is difficult to exaggerate the importance of these findings in explaining the religious configuration of seventeenth-century England. We now see more clearly than ever before the enormous obstructive power of lay patronage, the impotence of even the most vigorous of Anglican bishops to gain control of the church, and the efficacy of this battery of words pouring out on holy days and weekdays, in encouraging an already receptive urban middle class to Puritan piety, and eventually to radical political action. In the middle of the seventeenth century, some Royalists claimed that it was these Puritan lecturers who had preached King Charles out of his kingdom.

These efforts to understand the causes of the rise of Puritanism, emerging out of the weaknesses of the Anglican church, the organizational skills of the Puritan leaders, and their unremitting proselytizing zeal, have been overshadowed by the even greater efforts to understand the consequences of the rise.

Over the last half-century, some of the best minds in both history and the social sciences have applied themselves to the problem of Puritanism in seventeenth-century England. Regarded as an ideology, a way of life, or a psychological condition, it has been associated with the rising bourgeoisie, the spirit of capitalism, the scientific revolution and applied technology, political democracy, social egalitarianism, religious toleration, mass literacy and extensive higher education, the conjugal child-centered family, and institutionalized philanthropy for social betterment: in other words, with all the elements which together have been transforming human society over the last two hundred years.

According to Dr Hill the core of the Puritan movement was 'the industrious sort of people,' namely the small merchants, the self-employed shopkeepers and manufacturers, and the artisans.[4] Inspired by a hatred of clerical pretensions, the Puritans placed supreme emphasis on preaching as 'the only means and instrument for the salvation of mankind'; and thanks to their control of a good deal of church patronage, much of the educational system, and ample financial resources, they managed to hold the pulpits in the face of mounting episcopal and royal persecution. The doctrines preached by the Puritan clergy were those which suited the economic interests of the class: the reduction of feast days and the concentration of leisure upon the Sabbath helped to step up and regularize production for a modern economy, but protected the small man from unfair competition; traditional sports and games were frowned on as leading to economically harmful indulgence. That England should have been outstanding in its Sabbatarian zeal, far outstripping Holland in this respect, is ascribed to the greater industrialization of the former. Idleness was a crime in the new capitalist world, hence the punishment of beggars and condemnation of the poor as morally degenerate. The replacement of formal oaths by contractual obligations and the recognition that honesty is the best policy also matched the business needs of a possessive market society. The assumption by the head of the household of direct spiritual and economic control over its members was a by-product of the overthrow of the priesthood which fitted in neatly with the demands of the small man to accumulate capital and keep a close eye on his family business. The political theories of the Puritans demanded the transfer of power from nobles and priests to a wider oligarchy of propertied householders, though certainly not to women, children, servants or the poor. Religious toleration was 'the natural concomitant of the emerging economic order of free industrial production and internal free trade.'

It is impossible to deny the force of this massively documented and powerfully argued thesis. One may seriously question, however, whether the picture it presents both of Puritanism and of the seventeenth century scene is more than one aspect of a more complex and ambiguous reality. In the first place, the Puritans are throughout assumed to consist of small merchants, manufacturers and artisans. But a crucial element in the Puritan movement was the landed nobility and gentry who provided the patronage, the protection, and the political weight. Second, it is assumed that in the seventeenth century English society ceased to be rural, agricultural, and feudal, and became urban, industrial, and capitalist. Now a good test of modernization is the degree of urbanization. But, even allowing for the explosion of London, the proportion of the population living in towns in 1650 was probably not so very much greater than in 1550; the major shift had to wait till the late eighteenth century. The economic and psychological problems of seventeenth-century England were not yet similar to those of nineteenth-century England or of twentieth-century Russia, Ghana, Cuba and India. Third, even if we admit, as we have to, that a middle-class culture and a middle-class ethic developed in the course of the seventeenth century, there is a lot of evidence to suggest that the dominant political and social interest and the dominant value-system remained that of the landed classes well into the nineteenth century. And fourth, this cool, rational analysis of Puritanism as a sensible preparation for the new capitalist environment fails to go to the heart of the matter. Where is the blind fanaticism that tormented witches and tore down maypoles, where the stunning pedantry of Bibliolatry, where the searing introspection? Where can one fit the striking correlation between the outward signs of Freudian anality and the principal characteristics of the Puritan? Was Sabbatarianism really so *very* useful to small industrialist capitalism? Is the Saturday-night blind, so much abhorred by the Puritans, any less characteristic of modern urbanized proletariat than of traditional rural peasantry? Were the ruthless attempts to suppress fornication related to any supposedly harmful effects on productivity?

Another suggested linkage of Puritanism to secular affairs is that it acted as a powerful stimulus to radical political thought. According to Professor Walzer the connection can be made with the aid of social psychology.[5] According to him the essential innovation of the Puritans was the ideological party, combining fanaticism in belief with discipline in organization, and consciously directed toward political action. This novel instrument of power, which is still very much with us today, has been the most successful agent of revolution the world has ever seen, and the similarities between Puritans, Jacobins and Bolsheviks has been obvious ever since Crane Brinton pointed them out over a generation ago. All sought totally to destroy the old order and to set up a new, more moral, world; all were intelligent, virtuous, self-disciplined, hard-working, dedicated, and in many ways wholly admirable men; all resorted to tyranny and oppression, and may well have increased rather than diminished the toll of human suffering and injustice. But what made them tick? Walzer argues that these seventeenth-century radicals were a by-product of the social and religious dislocation of the era of the Reformation, as values and institutions crumbled. The church, the sacraments, the priesthood, the father, the village community, the guild, were all suddenly called into question or undermined. The result among anxiety-prone, literate, thinking men, was anomie, rootlessness, alienation, call it what you will. Out of this crisis of modernization emerged two new social groups, whose psychological and ideological characteristics were formed and fired in the crucible of exile on the continent during the reign of Mary. These two were the professional intellectuals, and the educated laity, from whom the dedicated Puritans – the Saints – were drawn. Calvinism provided the ideal support for these new groups, since it internalized controls and restored confidence in a morally secure and orderly world. If only the Saints could convert society as a whole to their own pattern of behavior, then the Hobbesian state would become superflous. 'Would that all the Lord's people [meaning the English!] were Saints,' groaned Cromwell once, as he surveyed his troubled and sinful realm. These were the groups and forces which turned away from the corrupt Caroline court and the popish Laudian church in the early seventeenth century; who set out first to create a new and godly society in Massachusetts, and then to make over the evil old world itself.

Calvinism, then, was not modernizing in itself, as Weber and Tawney saw it, not a cause of the rise of liberalism or bureaucracy or capitalism, but rather a psychological reaction to the stresses of social and religious change, which accidentally prepared the way for these developments. Puritanism was not part of the new order, but a product of disorder which in turn made the new order possible. Puritanism did not mold the thought of Benjamin Franklin, but it made that type of thinking possible.

The full complexity of this brilliant and original work has been partly lost in summary, but enough has been said to show its importance and its novelty. Is it true? The only answer one can make at this stage is: Perhaps, even probably, but it has not yet been conclusively proved. What needs to be done now is to demonstrate in concrete historical instances the linkage between social disturbance, personal anxiety, and the sudden blinding conversion which for many marked their acceptance of Puritan ideology. In particular, why did apparently rich, assured, well-established gentry and aristocracy embrace this deeply anti-aristocratic creed in such large numbers? Second, is it correct that the Presbyterian Calvinists were truly radical and revolutionary until just before the end, before the 1630s, or even 1640s? There is reason to doubt it. Three whole generations lived and died in uneasy conformity to the established church and the sovereign state, before passing over into revolutionary activity. Third, where do the Independent sectaries fit in? It was they who were the true sixteenth-century radicals, and they who captured first the army and then political power with Oliver Cromwell, but Walzer dismissed them as irrelevant cranks. All this does not mean that the Walzer thesis is unacceptable, but rather that there are important loose ends which have still to be tied up.

CHAPTER 11 · Court and Country

What happened in England in the middle of the seventeenth century? Was it a 'great rebellion' as Clarendon believed, the last and most violent of the many rebellions against particularly unprepossessing or unpopular kings, that had been staged by dissident members of the landed classes century after century throughout the Middle Ages? Was it merely an internal war caused by a temporary political breakdown due to particular political circumstances? Was it the Puritan revolution of S. R. Gardiner, to whom the driving force behind the whole episode was a conflict of religious institutions and ideologies? Was it the first great clash of liberty against royal tyranny, as seen by Macaulay, the first blow for the Enlightenment and Whiggery, a blow which put England on the slow road to parliamentary monarchy and civil liberties? Was it the first bourgeois revolution, in which the economically progressive and dynamic elements in society struggled to emerge from their feudal swaddling clothes? This is how Engels saw it, and how many historians of the 1930s, including R. H. Tawney and C. Hill, tended to regard it. Was it the first revolution of modernization, which is the Marxist interpretation in a new guise, now perceived as a struggle of entrepreneurial forces to remould the institutions of government to meet the needs of a more efficient, more rationalistic, and more economically advanced society? Or was it a revolution of despair, engineered by the decaying and backward-looking elements in rural society, the mere gentry of H. R. Trevor-Roper, men who hoped to recreate the decentralized, inward-looking, socially stable and economically stagnant society of their hopeless, anachronistic dreams.

In the last half-century the historiography of the English Revolution has gone through three fairly well-defined stages. First, we had the political narrative, worked out with meticulous care and scholarship by a great Victorian historian, S. R. Gardiner. This religio-constitutional interpretation came under massive attack from the Marxists just before the Second World War, and the comfortable old Whiggish paradigm collapsed, to be replaced by a clear-cut conflict between rising bourgeoisie and decaying feudal classes. Next came a short post-war period of dazzling and wildly contradictory theorizing on the basis of the most slender of documentary evidence, until the areas of agreement on every aspect of the problem were reduced almost to zero, and the English Revolution lapsed into the sort of fragmented chaos in which the historiography of the French Revolution wallows today. With both revolutions, once historians have realized that the Marxist interpretation does not work very much better than the Whig, there has followed a period when there is nothing very secure to put in its place. The last twenty years, however, have seen the most remarkable efflorescence of specialized historical monographs, the work of scholars on both sides of the Atlantic who have been prepared to take the infinite pains required for any historical research of enduring value, and who have also had the insight, imagination and intellectual capacity to marshall their findings and to generalize from them. As a result a good deal of light is at last beginning to penetrate the fog: truth – partial, imperfect, provisional truth – is starting to emerge.

One interpretation of the events leading up to the political breakdown of the mid-seventeenth century, was first put forward by Professor Trevor-Roper and later developed at book-length by Professor Zagorin.[1] This regards the rise of the opposition in terms of the polarity between 'Court' and 'Country.' But these are bland and vague concepts which have all kinds of ideological, religious, moral, and even aesthetic overtones, over and above the conflict of interest and power. So malleable and accommodating a polarity needs the most careful analysis and definition if it is to illuminate historical understanding.

The Court is easy enough to define: all those ministers, courtiers, officials, servants and financiers of the crown. However, it also presumably includes the titular aristocracy, the bishops, and those merchants who benefited from royal monopolies and who controlled local corporations by virtue of restrictive royal charters. In short it is what today we would vaguely call 'the Establishment.' The main objection to using the word 'Court' is that, although it can be made to embrace a series of elites, they were far from unified in background or thought or political behavior. Great hereditary landed aristocrats, low-born archbishops who had fought their way to the top by the patronage of a favorite, busy bureaucratic officials from the middling ranks, common law judges and the mayors and aldermen of the big cities did not form a solid phalanx of vested interest, ready to line up shoulder to shoulder to oppose demands for political change. When the crisis came in 1640–2, we now know for certain that these groups split apart, the judges taking up different attitudes, most of the city corporations trying above all to cling to office, many bureaucrats siding with parliament or staying on the side-lines. Even the House of Lords did not form a united body; for Laudian bishops and anti-Laudians like Bishop Williams took very different positions; the lay peers deserted the bishops in the crisis; very many aristocrats stayed neutral, and an influential minority sided with parliament. Common membership of a putative establishment called the Court is only one indicator among many of which way a man was likely to jump in 1640–2. Individual or family friendships or hatreds, religious convictions, local influences, constitutional beliefs, trust in or distrust of Charles I as a person, desire to protect one's property and position at whatever the sacrifice of political consistency – all these make it impossible to speak of the Court except in the same general and vague way we use the word 'establishment' today.

It is even more difficult to define 'the Country.' To do so, we have to go away from Westminster, back into the shires, which is an area into which Mr Zagorin did not venture. We will not find out by looking at the 'citizen element,' to which Mr Zagorin devotes a chapter, since, as he is careful to point out, they merely composed one element of both the supporters and the opponents of the crown in 1640. We will not even find out by looking at the Puritans, to whom he devotes another chapter, since they were a lot of clergymen and a divisive minority of the Country, who supplied it with its radical passion for change. And we will not find out merely by looking at the people who turn up in parliament calling themselves 'the Patriots' or 'the Country.' We will have to dig a good deal deeper.

The Country is first an ideal. It is that vision of rustic peace, simplicity and virtue, that goes back to the Roman classics and which fell on the highly receptive ears of the newly educated gentlemen of England. To it was opposed the bustle and activity and smog and filth of the City. It is also a vision of moral superiority, of honesty, frugality, probity, sobriety, and chastity, all allegedly country virtues which stand in contrast to the many vices of the degenerate sycophants who haunt the purlieus of the court. Second, and this is important, it began to become an institution. Almost without exception, whenever an Englishman in the early seventeenth century said, 'my country,' he meant 'my county.' And what we see in the half-century before the civil war is the growth not only of an emotional sense of loyalty to the local community, but also institutional arrangements to give that sentiment political force. The causes of this growth of the county community are twofold. The first was the decline of the family or household community of 'good lordship,' by which the late medieval gentry had been attached to the families of great magnates, crossing county boundaries, splitting counties, and creating personal rather than geographical loyalties. The decline of the aristocratic magnate household freed the gentry for new psychological and political orientations, and made way for new patterns of education at school and university. The second was the growing burden placed on the local gentry by the state, as it expanded its statutory, social and economic controls without setting up a paid local bureaucracy of its own to handle them. The result was the development of the county bench of justices as administrators and judicial authorities, who slowly began to attach a political identity to their membership. This development was greatly fostered by the growth in the numbers of resident gentry in the countryside and by marriage patterns showing very high endogamy within the local county gentry group. The paradox of English history – and by osmosis of American history – is that the growth of power in and loyalty to the center has been exactly commensurate with that of power in and loyalty to the local communities.

But the Country did not only mean sentiment for an institutional arrangement to express particularist local feelings. It also meant a growing feeling for the national community expressed in a heightened interest in the national political institution of parliament. Consequently the third element in the phrase 'the Country' is a political program. Because of the growing financial, political and religious interference of the central government, the gentry developed a program of their own, which they brought with them to Westminster. When these wealthy and influential local squires met in their alternative capacity as members of parliament, they

increasingly came to look upon themselves as representatives of the
gentry constituents they left behind them. Their program was one
of political and institutional decentralization. To be more specific,
the Country wanted local office left in local hands, the removal of
economic controls exercised by the central government, the end of
interference in local lay patronage in the church, some restriction on
the taxing powers of the central government and also a thoroughly
Protestant – but inexpensive – foreign policy.

The Court/Country polarity in politics is, therefore, little more
than a version of the normal state of tension that exists in all
organized societies between the centralizing and the decentralizing
forces: between Hamilton and Jefferson, for example. Since the
polarity continued to play an important political role in England at
least for another 75 years after 1640, it cannot be regarded as the
exclusive cause for a breakdown of government. This is especially
so, since when the crisis came, the lines of division did not run with
mathematical precision between the country gentry and the courtiers. Many gentry saw the virtues of strong monarchical rule, and
not a few courtiers fell off the bandwagon when it began to totter.

In order to provide a convincing interpretation of the collapse of
the central government in 1640, the other forces have therefore to
be brought into play. The collapse was caused not only by the
undeniable ineptitude of Charles and his advisors, but also by
certain specific historical trends. Unfortunately for the crown, the
ideals, interests and programs of the Country found powerful allies
in two other ideologies and three other interest groups: Puritanism
and the Puritans, the Common Law and the common lawyers, and
the new West Indies and American trade and the merchants engaged
in it. The objectives of none of these groups were the same as those
of the Country, but they became linked to them by a process of
convergence which owes more to historical accident than inexorable
necessity.

As for the Puritans, had Elizabeth, and later the Stuarts, continued to keep their options open, to admit aristocratic and
bureaucratic Puritan sympathizers to the privy council and the
court, to go easy on the persecution of Puritan dissidents, and to
keep the official doctrinal policies and religious ceremonies on the
fairly Low Church lines of early Elizabethan Anglicanism, the
intimate association of Puritanism with the Country might not have
taken place. There was a long prehistory of elective affinity between

the two, but there is now little doubt that it was the policy of Archbishop Laud and his associates which finally drove them together in the 1630s. And even so, the gentry still remained solidly Erasmian and had no sympathy for the theocratic pretensions of the Puritan clergy.

As for the lawyers, they had their own grievances against the crown and the prerogative courts, notably their hostility to the interference of the church courts in common law business. They also strongly resented the competition to the common law courts by the overlapping jurisdictions of the two regional prerogative courts and the several courts at Westminster dealing with particular types of clients, like Admiralty or Exchequer or Wards, or certain types of offenses, like the Star Chamber. This intra-mural dispute between lawyers would not have taken on political overtones had the crown not come too readily to the help of the embattled prerogative courts and of Chancery, and if its search for extra revenue had not led it to stretch its own prerogative powers too far. The result was the growth of a 'Magna Carta' ideology among some lawyers about the nature of the constitutional balance, and an alliance of these common lawyers with the gentry and the Puritans. But once again the basic objectives of the lawyers were not those of the Country; the two were merely tactical allies in a joint battle for control over the central direction of the state.

The third group of allies of the country gentry in their political battle were drawn from the merchant community. They were men who lacked an ideology, but possessed a program. Most merchants stayed on the sidelines, part of the vast silent majority which stood idly by as the tides of war and revolution lapped ever closer around their feet. Others were tied to the royal side by dependence on trade monopoly favors, or on support for the oligarchic control of their own communities in the face of rising pressure from below. But other important merchant elements can now be identified, men interested especially in the American trades, in New England colonization, and in breaking the monopoly of the East India and Levant Companies. They were new men in new fields of entrepreneurial endeavor who chafed at the political and economic stranglehold of the older established monopolistic oligarchies. They were usually Puritan in their religious opinions, they wanted to reorient English foreign policy and commercial policy to a more aggressive and dynamic thrust toward the Americas, and they wanted to open up the Mediterranean and Indian trade to new-comers. These men were important members of the group of radicals who seized control of London at a critical moment in 1641, and so swung the power and influence of the City decisively on the side of parliament. The City was an ally without whom the Country would not have dared to launch a war on its own; indeed parliament would have been defeated in a matter of weeks without the support of London. On the other hand, these merchants had little except a leavening of Puritanism, an interest in North American colonization, and a common enemy to bind them to the grandees of the Country.

Although used by contemporaries to describe the political opposition to the Early Stuarts, the term 'Country' is, therefore, little more than a convenient portmanteau expression which conceals a wide variety of interests and ideas, to only one of which it properly belongs. By adopting it, it is possible powerfully to illuminate many things which were hitherto obscure, but only at the expense of obscuring many others.

CHAPTER 12 · The new eighteenth century

I

The 'long eighteenth century' from 1660 to 1800 has always been something of an enigma in English history. Before it, there came world exploration, the first settlements in North America, agricultural, commercial, industrial, and demographic growth, the Reformation, the rise of Puritanism, the formation of the Tudor state, and its temporary collapse in the violent upheavals and astonishing intellectual foment of Europe's first Great Revolution. But what happened next? What filled the mysterious century between the end of feudalism and the establishment of capitalism, to use Marxist terminology; between the century of revolution and the Victorian age of radical improvement and reform?

In some ways it could be argued that England blew it. It first conquered an empire, then lost it; it fought the first half of a new hundred years' war with France for world hegemony, but failed to achieve clear victory; it was the first great power to consolidate political liberties with the Glorious Revolution of 1688, but then declared the constitution, laws, and institutions to be perfect – a doctrine sanctified by 'everything-as-it-should-be Blackstone,' as Bentham later described this great mid-eighteenth-century legal pundit. As a result, for a century the elite resisted all suggestions of a need for any further change. During the middle and late seventeenth century, England had adumbrated or developed the basic ideals of the Enlightenment: rationalism and religious toleration; a rejection of superstition and a horror of enthusiasm; a disclaimer to any God-given mastery over nature and a recognition of man as a part of the natural world; economic and affective individualism and even hints of sexual libertinism; contractual sovereignty and propertied democracy; empirical scientific investigation and Newtonian cosmology. Having accomplished all this, England left it to the French and Scottish intellectuals of the eighteenth century to adopt and develop the ideas, invent the name Enlightenment, and take the credit.

On the other hand, England was the country most admired throughout Europe in the eighteenth century for its political freedom, its respect for the law, its widely diffused opulence and ostentatious luxury, its talented novelists, the cultivated *douceur de vivre* of its elite, and its huge naval power. It was also the country where from 1770 onward the Industrial Revolution first began in cotton mills, ironworks, and coal mines, and where, at about the same time, there can first be detected the beginnings of the great tidal wave of the Victorian moral and religious backlash. The era was, and in part still remains, a puzzle, but much has been clarified by an astonishing surge of historical research over the past two decades.

Thirty years ago, the historiography of eighteenth-century England was a desert dominated by a monopolistic corporation, Namier, Inc., named after its founder and director, the historian Sir Lewis Namier. The corporation based its program on a series of hypothetical propositions: first, the only history worth studying is political history; second, political history is the exclusive concern of an elite of male power-brokers, a subject in which popular opinion counts for nothing; third, politicians have no ideals or general principles, and are motivated exclusively by self-interest, personal advantage, and family connections; fourth, political conflicts are not between parties of principle, but between rival factions of ins and outs jockeying for possession of the power and money and privilege that go with access to the authority and resources of the state.

This historical model was first put forward by Namier in 1929 to explain politics at a particular time, namely the 1760s, for which it had, and still has, considerable plausibility.[1] As the Namier corporation expanded its hold in the postwar years, however, students working for the firm and within its guidelines extended the model backward to the reign of Queen Anne and forward into the 1780s. Thus a model that discounts both popular feelings and political and religious ideology was imposed on the period of intense and public political conflicts of the years between 1679 and 1721 and the period of the American Revolution as well, when the first British empire went down to humiliating defeat at the hands of a band of ill-armed and ill-disciplined rebels, in a war that many Englishmen thought should not have been fought in the first place.

More recently, a powerful assault has been launched on the ideological props of the Whig interpretation of English history, in order to show that the 1688–89 constitutional upheaval was a very conservative affair, rather than one that established a monarchy whose legitimacy depended in theory on a contract with the people, and in practice on the will of Parliament. This assault has resulted in downgrading John Locke and his popularizers to the position of little-read and little-respected radicals, and elevating the long-discredited Tory party and ideology into the mainstream of English politics and political thought, at any rate up to 1714.[2]

The first major attack on the neo-conservative historiography of the eighteenth century came from the far left, and from the new social history. Using an idiosyncratic neo-Marxism of his own devising, E. P. Thompson took the Namierite paradigm and, in a brilliant series of essays, stood it neatly on its head.[3] To Namier, eighteenth-century England was the England of superbly self-confident Whig aristocrats in their country houses. Hardly anyone else counted, and if they did, they could be seduced by cash or favor. To Thompson, the poor filled the center stage, and the Whig oligarchs – now labeled 'patricians' – were ruthless capitalist oppressors and exploiters of the 'plebeians,' using their political power and their control of the machinery of the law to evade taxation, to accumulate wealth through force and fraud, and to acquire and enclose the land. But the poor fought back with a strongly resistant culture of their own, using mob violence as the weapon of last resort. Thus the cynical, conservative, elitist model of Namier now acquired its mirror image in the morally driven, neo-Marxist, populist model of Thompson. The great accomplishment of Mr Thompson was to free eighteenth-century historiography from the stranglehold of the Namierites, and open it up for exploration by the best writers of the new social history. He made the eighteenth century interesting again.

But Thompson was not the only one. Since 1967, the politics of the period have become a major historical battleground. First it has been established that the Glorious Revolution of 1688 was indeed the decisive event in establishing parliamentary checks on royal absolutism. It paved the way for a financial settlement that effectively tied the crown to annual parliaments in order to keep going, and for a financial and banking revolution that allowed England to fight and win its great wars with France largely on credit. The revisionist denigration of the long-term significance of the Glorious Revolution has been effectively routed.[4]

Next, Professors Geoffrey Holmes and W. A. Speck demolished entirely the efforts to apply the Namierite model of politics to the period between 1679 and 1721. They demonstrated the intensity and violence of party conflict over numerous issues of deep principle: Church vs Dissent; Crown vs Parliament; the army vs civilians; the court vs the country; war vs peace; the moneyed interest vs the landed interest, and so on.[5] In a brilliant little book, J. H. Plumb explained how and why this ferocious infighting died away around 1720, to be followed by an era of almost unprecedented political calm. He also explained how the electorate during the reign of Anne became not only the largest and the most frequently consulted of any in Europe, but proportionately larger than any to be seen again in England before the late nineteenth century.[6] By the 1970s, the Namierite interpretation of the reign of Queen Anne was dead.

Just recently, the mid-eighteenth-century Namierite stronghold has come under attack from three directions. First, Professor Linda Colley has pointed out that the political tranquility that existed under the rule of the Whig oligarchy was not quite as tranquil as all that.[7] The landed elite remained divided, with a small but fairly cohesive Tory party still present, still defending the Anglican church, still collecting votes, and capable on occasions, although only with the aid of a group of renegade country Whigs, of defeating the main-line Whig administration. We are now forced to recognize that not all eighteenth-century squires joined the Whig cause: there remained a permanent split in the elite, with a significant minority loyal to the Church, opposed to major wars for empire financed on credit, and hostile to Whig government in general.[8]

The second line of attack came from Professor John Brewer, who demonstrated first that ideology mattered in the mid-eighteenth century, and second that the aristocratic client system could on occasion be successfully challenged by an extraparliamentary popular protest, namely the Wilkite movement.[9] This proved that both the electorate and the disfranchised could make their voices heard, and that there was more to English politics than infighting among factions of Whig aristocrats. Public opinion existed out there, now well informed, thanks to growing literacy (up to 1760) and the rapid spread of coffee houses and provincial newspapers. It was a public with ideas of its own about taxation, war, and the proper distribution of both political authority and the spoils of office.

The argument has been pushed too far, for the Wilkite movement, despite its phenomenal success, was an ephemeral affair whose connection with the radical agitation during the French Revolution in the 1790s, the parliamentary reform movement of the 1820s, and the Chartists of the 1840s is almost impossible to trace. Although the Wilkite agitation shook the Government, it was in large part, as Professor Brewer admits, 'a brilliantly orchestrated and skillfully advertised soap-opera.' It relied heavily for its success on the exploitation of new marketing techniques to whip up popular support, and on the reluctant support of the judiciary in enforcing the law without fear or favor. Judicial impartiality is a peculiar feature of eighteenth-century English life, and it is currently the subject of sharp controversy between Marxist and non-Marxist legal historians, the former explaining it away as astute tokenism on the part of the judiciary to retain elite hegemony, the latter insisting that the records tell a different and morally more attractive story.[10]

The third attack on the Namierite position arose from a close study of the urban electorate in the 1780s, *Electoral Behavior in Unreformed England*, which showed that in some of the boroughs that returned the majority of the MPs the electorate was sharply polarized. According to a less-than-adequate sample of four, what divided them was not class or interest or clientage loyalty, but that hoary issue, religion – that is to say, the conflict of Church vs Dissent.[11] Whether this was a nationwide phenomenon, however, remains to be seen, and is perhaps unlikely.

As a result of this three-pronged attack, Namierism as a political model now preserves its full credibility only for the mid-century point. But even here it looks very different in the light of new understanding of the true complexity of eighteenth-century English society and a better appreciation of the richness of political ideology in that period, a subject to which enormous attention has recently been paid by a number of brilliant scholars on both sides of the Atlantic, led by John Pocock and Bernard Bailyn. What has chiefly

interested American historians is the way the 'country' ideology
of the dissident Whigs provided, with suitable modifications, a
justification for the American Revolution.[12]

Even more striking has been the new emphasis on social problems
that has changed our views of so many aspects of eighteenth-
century English history in recent years. For beneath the revisionism
in politics and political theory lies a major revaluation of the nature
of English society in the eighteenth century. The first important
discovery was the astonishing revival of the aristocracy. In 1649,
they seemed finished – their country houses mostly looted, their
deer parks emptied, their estates confiscated or subject to heavy
fines, their House of Lords and the privileges and titles that went
with it abolished. Great nobles of ancient title went skulking into
corners, trying to avoid arrest for debt. A century later they were
perhaps at the height of their power, prestige, wealth, and control
over the political and financial patronage structure, a position to
which they clung, more or less successfully, until 1880. It is one
of the most important and most extraordinary stories of the history
of England, and one central to the very peculiar social, political,
and cultural development of that strange island.[13]

The English country houses of the eighteenth century remain
as an astonishing visual witness to the self-confidence, arrogance,
opulence, elegance, and taste of the English grandees of that epoch.
These great mansions, their grounds and deer parks, and their
furnishings, pictures and statuary, are an enduring memorial to the
more admirable qualities of that now vanished civilization.[14] It has
only recently been recognized that under the leadership of this
enlightened Whig elite, England forged rapidly ahead to create the
most powerful state in the world. Its finances rested on heavy
but relatively equitable taxation affecting both the landowners and
consumers, and a flexible credit mechanism through the Bank of
England. The money was spent in creating the greatest navy in the
world, built and repaired in the royal dockyards which became the
largest and most efficient industrial plants in the country. England
developed one empire in America, lost it, and then almost immediately conquered another, even richer one in India, while at the
same time spreading its merchant fleet around the globe. All this
was achieved while maintaining the rule of law, and protections for
internal liberty so extensive as almost to teeter on anarchy, as

was shown in the Gordon Riots in 1780. It was an astonishing achievement, and the envy of Europe.

A second key to an understanding of eighteenth-century England is recognition of the unique importance of the growing numbers, influence, wealth, and cultural attainments of the so-called 'middling sort.' These people were not the mythical 'ever-rising bourgeoisie' of the older textbooks: they were the professionals, merchants, tradesmen, small manufacturers, clerks, surveyors, attorneys, journalists, skilled artisans, yeomen farmers, and the like whose existence was a never-ending source of astonishment and admiration to foreign visitors to England. In 1741, Horace Walpole remarked that 'there was nowhere but in England the distinctions of the middling people.' John Bull was one of them. Below them there may still have been a third of the population on the edge of destitution – the plebeian mob – but they were taken care of by the most elaborate and expensive poor-relief system in Europe. No one starved to death in eighteenth-century England.

The critical novelty was that by 1800 there were at least half a million 'middling' families, well educated, fashion conscious, and with money to burn on luxuries. English political stability depended on the fact that they were not 'rising.' They were not seeking to overthrow their betters, the landed elite, but rather to absorb the culture and the values of their social superiors. All they wanted was to gain respect as worthy of admission to the vote, and to place limits on the corrupt exploitation by the landed elite and politicians of the spoils system of pensions and sinecure offices. They were denied the first until 1832, but obtained a little satisfaction about the latter, thanks to the 'economical reform' movement and the efforts of the younger Pitt.

II

One component element of this 'middling sort' was the professions.[15] Unfortunately, however, so opaque are the statistics that it is not entirely clear whether there was an increase at all in some of the older professions. Thus the number of Oxbridge Fellows and Professors grew only minimally as student enrolments shrank. The number of barristers – whose work was limited to pleading in court – fell by more than a half between 1660 and 1760 as private litigation declined and as attorneys – who dealt directly with their clients – took over many of their functions (a decline that also affected the Society of Advocates in Scotland).[16] The number of beneficed clergy also shrank as the practice of pluralism, of holding two livings at the same time, grew rapidly to satisfy the greed of the influential few.[17] What seems to have been happening is that this shrinkage at the top of the older professions was more than compensated for by expansion in the lower levels; attorneys and solicitors and their clerks in the law, apothecaries, barber-surgeons, and quacks in medicine, schoolmasters in education, curates in the church.

The officer corps in the military certainly grew, as the standing army became an entrenched feature of the English state, but it expanded and contracted like a concertina with the ebb and flow of war and peace, with thousands of officers eking out a living on the edge of gentility on half-pay during the long lulls in the endless war with France. There was also some expansion in the civil service, especially in the Excise Office to collect taxes, and in the Admiralty to mobilize resources for war. But the totals by 1730 are not all that impressive when compared with those in 1688, and the income of the majority was barely enough to keep them in the ranks of the respectable 'middling sort.'

In 1730, there were about 60,000 adult men (out of about 1.4 million) employed in what we would today recognize as a profession. At their lower levels, professions were important avenues of social mobility, but they are mainly of historical import-ance because their members constituted an educated, literate body of townspeople who provided part of the market for English cultural products, from novels to newspapers. This one section of the 'middling sort' can be seen as it organized itself, obtained social status, and developed formal hierarchies of recruitment, salary, and promotion, a process that was to continue throughout the eight-eenth century.

Another piece of evidence of the rise of the 'middling sort' was the growing urbanization of England in the eighteenth century, a neglected feature of the age, which has only recently been brought into focus.[18] Apart from the altogether unique city of London, towns seem not to have prospered in the sixteenth and seventeenth centuries. But in the eighteenth century, the proportion of the English population that became urbanized rose from about 20 percent to 30 percent, the increase being distributed among the provincial cities, while London maintained its position as the residence of about 11 percent of all Englishmen.[19] The increase came from immigrants, since high urban mortality prevented towns even from reproducing themselves. Most of the immigrants from the countryside were not, however, cottagers ejected from their holdings by enclosure of the village by a ruthless landlord, as we used to believe. It is now clear that about 70 percent of England was already enclosed by 1700, and only another 13 percent or so went the same way in the eighteenth century.[20]

The economic base of these towns was mostly diversified, depending on marketing, small manufacturing, or overseas trade, but some of it was more specialized, as in dockyard towns, spas, or seaside resorts. Indeed, the royal dockyards were the largest economic organizations of the age, larger than anything seen in Europe since the Fall of Rome. But whatever their economic functions, most of these towns acquired a generous cultural infrastructure: physical plants like coffee houses with the London newspapers, bookshops, theaters, assembly rooms, lending libraries, churches, and meeting houses; and community associations like philosophical societies and reading clubs. This active cultural life, this urban renaissance, is the most striking feature of the provincial English town in the eighteenth century. It is no accident that this is the period when the words 'civility' and 'urbanity' changed from meaning mere residence in a town to take on the moral and aesthetic connotations of culture, politeness, and social polish which they still retain today. Ambitious urban planning became a reality, best seen today at its grandest in Bath, the West End of London, and Edinburgh, and on a more modest scale in Blandford Forum, Dorset.[21]

Apart from the cultural efflorescence of the towns, the most striking evidence of the rise of the 'middling sort' is provided by the growing demand for luxury goods and services. This can be seen in the spectacular growth of the spa town of Bath, a product of the leisured pleasure-seeking clientele who flocked to the city, the entrepreneurs who built it, and the building craftsmen, artisans, tradesmen, porters, and domestic servants upon whose labors the whole enterprise depended.[22] But Bath is only one by-product of the commercialization of leisure and the growth of a consumer society which are such central features of eighteenth-century England.

The facts of this consumer revolution are hardly in doubt. There occurred a remarkable growth of sophisticated advertising and marketing techniques. Fashion drove the market. It altered from year to year, almost from month to month, so that suppliers, Josiah Wedgwood for example, were obsessed with the need to keep up with the fickle winds of change in taste, dictated to the provinces by the great capital city of London. By 1786, a female foreign visitor could rhapsodize upon 'lovely Oxford Street' where 'behind the great glass windows absolutely everything one can think of is neatly, attractively displayed.' So sophisticated had the artifices of fashion become that, by the late eighteenth century, women seeking to add to their sexual attractions could purchase not only spring-loaded false bosoms but spring-loaded false buttocks as well. Other examples are Wedgwood and Boulton's phenomenonal success in marketing luxury pottery and fashion goods, and the growth of provincial theaters, music festivals, horse racing, tourism, and the production of children's toys and books.[23] It can plausibly be argued that all this was man's first big step to modern consumerism: the insatiable eighteenth-century English demand for frivolous as well as useful goods and services created a world that is recognizably our own.

If this is so, then the three key questions are who were the consumers, what were their motives, and what were the effects of the new demand for luxuries? The first two, unfortunately, remain wrapped in obscurity. We do not know exactly who bought or what really impelled them to do so. A description of demand-side economics, demonstrated from evidence of what supply-side manufacturers and servicing trades thought their customers wanted, is hardly sufficient to identify who the latter were. Only a study of household inventories and personal diaries will provide a more precise picture of who wanted what, and why. We need to know how large was this market, and how far down the social scale the consumer revolution penetrated. Thus Thompson's work has fundamentally altered our vision of the cultural baggage of the eighteenth-century poor, but a case can be made that he has exaggerated its nostalgic defensive quality, its opposition to the inroads of capitalist consumerism. The laboring people adapted readily to new market values and mass-produced goods, for example in the

way they shifted their drinking habits from home-brewed products
of varying quality to standardized beer produced by huge, heavily
capitalized urban breweries.

We also need to know why the customers were so eager to buy.
Is the pull of London, the alleged high rate of social mobility, and
advertising in a free press, sufficient to explain so remarkable a
phenomenon? McKendrick seems to favor a Veblen model of
conspicuous consumption stimulated by status competition. But he
admits that the suppliers were not only satisfying a pent-up demand
with their skillful campaigns and marketing tactics, but were actually stimulating a demand for goods that had never existed before.
The mechanism, according to McKendrick, was an internal
'demonstration effect,' namely the desire of the 'middling sort' to
follow the fashions set by the rich, just as we do today. As Mandeville put it in 1714, when the process was just beginning: 'Luxury
employed a million of the poor, and odious pride a million more.
Envy itself and vanity were ministers of industry.'

But is Veblen's theory of competitive conspicuous consumption
enough? Do not people spontaneously enjoy buying things as a
form of self-gratification? If so, consumerism may be seen as a
product of the rise of new concepts of individualism and materi-
alism, or of the herd instinct to imitate, but not necessarily of the
frenzy for conspicuous competition. Thus both the market and the
motives at present remain rather obscure. Only the economic fact
of an unprecedented consumer demand is clear.

Finally, what were the consequences of this consumer demand?
McKendrick claims that it 'goes a long way toward explaining the
coming of the Industrial Revolution.' But does it? What, for
example, has the production of high-quality pottery by Wedgwood
and toys by Matthew Boulton to do with the development of iron-
manufacture or textile mills? It is perfectly possible to have the
psychology and reality of a consumer society without a heavy
industrial sector.

The problem of the antecedent causes of the Industrial Revolution has much bothered historians lately. Once they got away from
W. W. Rostow's deceptively simple model of an economic process
of 'take-off' led by the textile mills, they were still at a loss for an
explanation. At this point, they were rescued by a new hypothesis
and a new word: proto-industrialization.[24] For over a decade, this
has seemed the solution. By proto-industrialization is meant a

regional setting for rural industry – usually textiles – worked by peasants in their homes. Other peasants were drawn into commercial agriculture to feed the industrial workers, the regional towns supplied both the market and the capitalist entrepreneurs who financed the whole enterprise, and the products were exported, not sold locally. The result, so it is argued, was increased population growth through the stimulus to earlier marriage, an eventual shift to workshops organized for greater efficiency and reduction in costs, the development of a cadre of export-oriented merchants, and a commercialized agricultural sector. Result: all the groundwork for an industrial revolution.

Unfortunately, empirical testing in England leads to the conclusion that proto-industralization flourished here and there at various times from the thirteenth to the eighteenth century, but in most cases it eventually just petered out.[25] Proto-industrialization, in short, seems to have been neither a sufficient, nor even a necessary, cause of industrial revolution. The heretical suggestion has even been made that the Industrial Revolution in England was an accident, not very closely related to the general economic, psychological, and social modernizing processes that were admittedly going on in eighteenth-century England. For example, there appears to have been an inverse correlation between literacy, the key indicator of modernization, and industrialization, the former actually at its maximum in remote and barren Westmorland and declining in the areas of high industrial growth from 1760 to 1840. After all, who needs to read in order to work as a laborer in a textile mill or coal mine or ironworks? On the other hand, the geographical accidents of a plentiful water supply to power mills, or the close proximity in the ground of iron and coal, do seem to be necessary causes, although certainly not sufficient ones.[26]

III

What of the poor, that bottom third of the population, the casual laborers, domestic servants, abandoned or widowed wives and mothers, the sick, the destitute? Before industrialization most of them drifted aimlessly from job to job, the women from domestic service to needlework to taking in laundry to prostitution and back again, the men from casual labor in the fields or workshops or the building industry or porterage, to spells of unemployment, vagabondage, and petty pilfering. That the deserving poor were taken care of by a national system of poor-relief is now beyond dispute, although the degree and quality of that care varied from parish to parish.

The study of the poor, history from the bottom up, has been the hallmark of the new social history of the past thirty years. It is therefore astonishing to find that the best book on the subject was first published in 1925, a brilliant picture of low life and high death in London.[27] Mrs George fastened on such 'modern' topics as fertility and mortality, crime and punishment, disorder and mob violence, alcoholism and popular amusements, hospitals and prisons. It is a truly extraordinary achievement. Recent work, inspired primarily by E. P. Thompson, has also focused on crime and the law, and the values, beliefs, customs, and habits of the poor. Thomspon has coined phrases that are now a standard part of every historian's vocabulary: for example, 'the moral economy of the crowd,' by which is meant a concept of natural justice and a just price, which was accepted by both poor and rich alike, and served as the motivating and justifying ideology behind grain riots and anti-enclosure riots. He and others have demonstrated a commonly shared sense of a moral economy of the proletariat, with recognized rights and freedoms, provided clear proof of the early origins of trade unionism deep in the heart of the eighteenth century, and unearthed a thin but perceptible stream of radical opposition to the social injustices of emergent capitalism.[28] But whether there was a growing split between the mental and cultural worlds of the elite and the poor, as suggested by Mr Thompson and his followers, is still very uncertain. An argument has been made that folk customs like the charivari, a popular demonstration against persons who had violated communal norms of behavior, bear witness 'not to cultural conflict but to areas of shared culture.'[29]

This is one reason for disputing Mr Thompson's definition of the eighteenth century as 'patrician society, plebeian culture.'[30] Another is that in this bipolar model of English society, he totally ignored the emergence of a recognizable middle-class culture of respectability, which allied itself with the elite, the patricians, to help stamp out working-class cultural habits and customs and pastimes, ranging from the abolition of contractual and clandestine marriages to the suppression of 'cruel' sports like bear-baiting (but not, of course, fox-hunting or boxing).[31] Thus the faint outlines of Victorian bourgeois culture and morality were already visible in the middle of Georgian England. It was as early as 1770, for example, that Wedgwood decided that the middle-class consumers of his pottery would in future prefer that Greek gods and goddesses be modestly covered with fig-leaves and draperies instead of being displayed nude, as before.[32]

As a result, by the end of the century the 'middling sort' were beginning to define themselves and their values as 'middle class,' and the 'lower orders' to be seen and to see themselves as 'lower class.' What confuses the situation, however, and casts doubt on Thompson's idea of *The Making of the English Working Class*, is that that class was itself being split between the 'respectable' and the 'rough,' with different patterns of behaviour, concepts of honor, and aspirations in life. Whereas the former tried to follow the code of the middle class, the latter preserved its own working-class cultural values regarding work habits, drink, kinship, domestic violence, and sexual behavior. There was certainly a hardening of social frontiers as moral paternalism gave way to legal compulsion in the late eighteenth and early nineteenth centuries, but that frontier ran right through the middle of the working class, while at the top another frontier divided the landed classes, the professions, and the old mercantile and banking bourgeoisie from the new industrialists and entrepreneurs from the North. Thus the cultural frontiers split both the upper class and the working class, to the infinite confusion of all historians, but especially Marxists. A good case can be made for arguing that a society based on class consciousness did not – and could not – have emerged before the general spread of the factory system in the late nineteenth century, which at last sharply divided the wage-earning proletariat from the owners of these large-scale means of production.

IV

A major contribution to our understanding of the eighteenth century has come from another discipline altogether, that of demography. In their monumental study of England's population, Professor Wrigley and Dr Schofield have assembled a vast mass of

information, not raw but carefully adjusted and modified, and have
set out the broad facts of demographic change over a period of 330
years.[33] It is not too much to say that English history will never
look quite the same again, and that the book will set the agenda
for debate for the foreseeable future.

Lack of expertise in these arcane matters makes it impossible to
do more than express uneasiness about the heroic manipulation of
admittedly inaccurate data from parish registers by the use of a
mysterious procedure called 'back projection.' One can only note
that an earlier claim of statistical proof from parish registers that
between 1650 and 1740 the population of one English village practiced contraception, has, after nearly twenty years of confident
acceptance and dissemination in standard textbooks, been proved
to be without foundation.[34]

Assuming that their adjusted data are approximately correct,
what changes have Wrigley and Schofield discovered during the
long eighteenth century, and what are their explanations for them?
They see a period of demographic stagnation or decline running
from 1650 to 1740, followed by a huge surge of population growth
that ran on through the Industrial Revolution well into the late
nineteenth century.

Their central claim is that changes in mortality played only a
minor role in this story, and that the key factor was changes in
fertility, which in turn depended on what proportion of young
people married and how early in life they, and especially females,
did it. They explain changes in age of marriage and nuptiality
purely in economic terms: in good times more people married, and
they married at a younger age. In bad times, fewer married, and
those who did so postponed their marriage to a later age. Wrigley
and Schofield therefore tie the fall and the rise of fertility in England
in the late seventeenth and eighteenth centuries to changes in real
wages rates – with a thirty-to fifty-year time-lag for perceptions to
catch up with reality. Thus, they argue that the fall in English real
wage rates, which reached their nadir in the early seventeenth
century, caused the postponement of marriage late in the century.

There are two reasons why this economic explanation does not
carry conviction. The first is that the application of the lag theory
means that people were delaying marriage for economic reasons at
a period when the bad times were already over, for example after
1660, when real wages were rising, food was plentiful, land was

cheap, and the economy was buoyant. Conversely, the argument has to posit an increase in nuptiality and a decline in the age of marriage between 1750 and 1815, at a time of rapidly rising food prices, heavy taxation for war, population pressure on available housing, and stable or declining real incomes.[35] The second reason why the lagged real wages theory does not work is that the same marital behavior can be seen among the landed elite, who were certainly entirely unaffected by changing real wages among the laboring classes.[36]

Others, particularly the French, have produced evidence that casts doubt upon the emphasis placed by Wrigley and Schofield upon changes in fertility rather than in mortality as the principal control mechanism in governing the rise, fall, or stability of populations. Perrenoud has established that in other European countries where good data are available, that is, France, Sweden, and Norway, a change for the better in the mortality rate of children under the age of ten seems to have been 'at the origins of population growth' in the last half of the eighteenth century.[37] He points out that Wrigley and Schofield themselves demonstrate that there was a massive rise in mortality in England in the seventeenth and eighteenth centuries, and that in consequence the expectation of life enjoyed in England in the late sixteenth century was not achieved again until the late nineteenth.[38]

The causes of the rise and the fall of mortality in the seventeenth and eighteenth centuries remain obscure. In explaining the latter stage, the fall, which occurred all over Europe, but especially rapidly in France, medical advances can be ruled out except for the possible effect of mass inoculation in stemming the scourge of smallpox.[39] Nor can cultural, social, or economic factors be held responsible, since countries as different in their levels of development as France and Sweden experienced the same decline. Modernization theory, based essentially upon a concept of stages of economic growth, consequently does not seem to be the answer. Some scholars like Perrenoud therefore fall back on exogenous biological variables, that is, bacterial and virus mutations and changes in the levels of immunity and resistance to disease among human populations. Over twenty years ago, Le Roy Ladurie suggested that the rise in European mortality in the seventeenth century might be the result of 'the microbian unification of the world' caused by the expansion of overseas trade.[40]

No one can question the magnitude of the achievement of
Wrigley and Schofield in tracing the long and complex history of
English demography in the maddeningly inaccurate records of
parish registers. But even if one accepts their 'back projection'
technique for cleaning up the data, legitimate doubts persist
whether they are right to put such stress on fertility changes as the
prime causal factor rather than on mortality; and their economic
explanation of those changes in fertility seems demonstrably
inadequate.

                                    v

Only one attempt has so far been made to pull this disparate welter
of the new social history together into a single volume, to tie
together into a coherent whole demography, family, sex, poverty,
death, leisure, culture, printing, literacy, the arts, consumerism,
mentalité, and class. Dr Porter even, rightly, tries to weave politics
into the picture.[41] That he has not altogether succeeded is due
largely to the chaotic and centrifugal state of social history today,
which is flying off in all directions with no larger structure to hold
it together – not the nation-state or Marxist class conflict. Nothing
is left but a ragbag of miscellaneous topics, all fascinating in themselves, but without anything to bind them together.

But Dr Porter has done well, producing a vivid, witty, and
entertaining volume that combines great erudition with intellectual
brilliance. He has read and absorbed virtually everything; there is
not a book or an article that is not somewhere incorporated in his
text. There is also a wisecrack or joke on almost every page. For
example: bluestockings – 'the air of their levées was as blue as their
stockings later became'; death – 'the grim reaper was no snob';
traveling – 'the unfortunate traveller shared his bed with strangers
and fleas, and his road with gibbeted corpses and highwaymen';
behavior – 'as a national institution the stiff upper lip came later';
and so on. The conclusion, however, is fairly clear. 'It was a
society which was capitalist, materialist, market-oriented, worldly,
pragmatic, responsive to economic pressures. Yet its political institutions and its distribution of social power, unlike those of more
modern times, were unashamedly hierarchical, hereditary and privileged.' English social life was stretched by social and intellectual

conflict, the rise of individualism and the decline of deference, the demands for political participation by the 'middling sort,' and the runaway economic growth. And there was a persistent undercurrent of riot, robbery, and general disorder inevitable in a society almost entirely lacking a police force, or any instruments of law and order other than the constable and the JP, a small standing army, and a nominally ferocious penal code.

But there was also a darker side to the eighteenth century: the physical squalor, the disease, the alcoholism, and the bestial cruelty depicted in Hogarth's savage engravings of John Gay's *The Beggar's Opera*. Even the growth of reason had its drawbacks. For example, in an age of religious indifference, religious enthusiasm became equated with madness, and the victims of both were incarcerated and subjected to the standard, wholly ineffectual but theoretically 'rational' therapies of bleeding, purging, and vomiting.

Nor is sufficient stress laid on the pervasive stink of corruption at all levels of elite society and government. In 1751, Henry Fielding made a character in *Amelia* remark, 'Do you not know that this is as corrupt a nation as ever existed under the sun? And would you think of governing such a people by the strict principles of honesty and morality?'[42] This was one aspect of the Namierite view of the English polity, and its truth is undeniable. The important role of 'virtue' in the ideology of the American revolutionaries was in part based on a horrified reaction to this luxury and corruption.

Concurrent with this corruption was the rise of oligarchy in politics. The decline of the parliamentary electorate is demonstrated by the fact that in 1761 the seats in only 18 out of 201 small boroughs were contested, and that in 1780 there were contested elections in only two counties. Unlike the situation in the reign of Queen Anne, a sophisticated political machine run by the social elite now held the reins of power, and had squeezed out the electorate. It was the rule of a small landed elite of some 1,500 families. The central government left the countryside to be run by the amateur JPs, but it siphoned off more and more of the GNP to pay for war: 7 percent in 1715, but up to 27 percent by 1811. Per capita taxation doubled during the century. Meanwhile, the poor were kept quiet by welfare payments, the cost of which multiplied sixfold in a hundred years.

It was a society run in the interests of property owners, who passed more and more ferocious legislation to punish thieves and robbers. But their bark was far worse than their bite, and the number of hangings dropped dramatically once the alternative punishment of transportation, first to America and then to Australia, came to seem an equally efficacious and more humane way of ridding England of these undesirables. It cannot be emphasized too often that Britain was a society that was under the law, and whose freedom and wealth were the admiration of Europe. The Whig landed elite were extraordinarily adaptable in riding the whirlwind of economic growth, naval expansion, and individualism in personal relations; at the end, they managed somehow to remain still firmly in the saddle.

'The Thing,' as the radical William Cobbett disgustedly called them, survived, thanks to the dexterous use of political power to satisfy both the landed and moneyed interests, and the equally dexterous use of patronage, clientage, and corruption to manage the electorate and the elected. They also demonstrated respect for the law as applicable to all classes, including themselves, as well as restraint in the economic exploitation of their inferiors; a willingness, that is to say, to provide not only a plausible appearance but a reality of the most just and free society in Europe. But above all, the nation got rich, and those riches, along with personal freedom, were spread widely throughout the top two-thirds of the nation. It was trickle-down economics and ideology, and it worked.

In 1777, an anonymous Englishman complacently described his country as 'a nation whose constitution is founded on the principles of liberty, whose commerce is extended over the whole circumference of the globe, whose internal wealth, as consisting in landed property and moneyed interests, is great almost beyond example.'[43] It is indeed upon this unique combination of respect for liberty and law, a rich and powerful state, a great navy, and an aggressive imperial foreign policy, booming overseas commerce, unprecedented domestic affluence for the majority, and rocketing expenditures on war and poor relief – as well as rising corruption, declining cruelty, persistent poverty, and fluctuating alcoholism – that historians are still commenting today. Eighteenth-century England provided the first fumbling prototype of the warfare-welfare state which has become the standard model for the late twentieth century.

CHAPTER 13 · The Law

About a quarter of a century ago many historians decided that it was high time to study rather more of the population than the top 2 per cent or 3 per cent from whom were drawn the political and social elite: the kings, generals, nobles, judges, bishops, politicians and local magnates whose (mostly bloody) deeds had hitherto filled the history books. The trouble was, however, that very few of the bottom 97 per cent have left any trace of themselves in the records, except the bare facts of their birth, marriage and death. As a result, much of the early work on the poor was aridly statistical in nature. But it fairly soon became apparent that reducing the vast majority of the population to a set of numbers in a table was hardly more enlightening than ignoring them altogether. We still did not know anything about what they thought or felt.

One way out of this dilemma was to turn to the records of the law, for here alone can the authentic voices of the poor be heard, if only as voluble witnesses, angry plaintiffs, and fearful defendants. Treated with care, these documents can act as 'a point of entry into the mental world of the poor.' The results have begun to emerge in the form of case histories, of which the most famous is Emmanuel Le Roy Ladurie's *Montaillou*.[1] Historians strike the richest lode in societies which practiced Roman law, with its written interrogations and depositions, had a well-developed police system, and used torture to extract information. The records of the Inquisition are ideal, since this institution possessed all these characteristics and was also obsessively interested in what people – even humble people – thought. In Anglo-Saxon countries hardly any of these benefits (for historians) apply, but it is still possible to glean a rich harvest from a patient study of legal documents.

Apart from illuminating the *mentalité* and behavior of the poor, legal records can also throw light on the relationship of authority and society. In particular they can show how the law was perceived by different social layers and how, and in whose interest, it was applied in practice. This opens up new vistas on the nature and function of the law, and on the perceptions of different groups as to what constitutes natural justice.

There are two possible ways to go about tackling legal records. One is to break crime down into a series of categories and to quantify indictments over time, in order to produce the sort of statistics in which the late J. Edgar Hoover used to delight.[2] Even today, however, this is a very dubious excuse. We know that the number of indictments bears little relation to the number of real acts, and we strongly suspect that the relationship has varied widely over time. Second, the numbers used are usually quite small, since they are so tedious to extract, which leads to false deductions being made from insignificant and perhaps random fluctuations. Third, our aggregate population estimates are very shaky, which makes it very hard to compare rates of crime per 1000 from decade to decade or century to century, although we can be certain that the murder rate in medieval Oxford was very much greater than in the most dangerous areas of the most dangerous cities in America today. A far more rewarding way to use this material is to extract from it a series of case histories, which illuminate the way the authorities administered justice and the attitudes of the public toward crime and the law. This approach forms an essential bridge between social history and political history, which for a long while now have been proceeding on more or less separate tracks, to the serious detriment of both.

The conceptual framework in which these problems are currently seen during the early modern period in general, and in eighteenth-century England in particular, has been laid down in some brilliant pioneer work by Mr Edward Thompson. To him, eighteenth-century English society was divided between 'Patricians' (the top 5 per cent of landowners and wielders of power) and 'Plebeians' (the rest), who were locked both in an unending conflict – 'class war without class,' and in a culture of paternalist reciprocity.[3] According to this paradigm the law was an instrument created and used to keep the plebeians in their place and to advance their own interests by persons described as 'Patrician-banditti' and 'Courtier-brigands.' The law was 'a selective instrument of class justice.' This is the theme of both Mr Thompson's book on *Whigs and Hunters* and the companion volume of essays by himself and a group of his students. It has to be admitted that in the last twelve pages of his book Mr Thompson suddenly reverses himself, and concedes that 'there is a very large difference ... between arbitrary extra-legal power and the rule of law.' On the one hand, the law is unquestionably an instrument and a legitimation of class power. On the other hand, 'the rhetoric and rules of a society are something a great deal more than a sham ... The law mediates these class relations through legal forms which imposed, again and again, inhibitions upon the actions of the rulers.' Mr Thompson finally concludes that it was this ingrained respect for the law which obliged the English ruling class to make the necessary concessions rather than to persist in reactionary policies enforced by the arbitrary exercise of naked force, when social conflict came to a head in the early nineteenth century.

But this astonishing *volte-face* bears little or no relation to the previous tone and content of his book, nor to the premises underlying the essays of his students, nor to his own subsequent writings, all of which stress the polar class conflict of predatory patricians and oppressed plebeians. Apart from this brief Whiggish recantation therefore, Mr Thompson's position seems to be a consistently neo-Marxist one. The second part of the Thompson paradigm states that crime can be divided into two types, nefarious crime for personal gain, and 'social crime' which conformed to community standards, received widespread protection and support in the locality, and was often used to pressure the authorities to adopt popular concepts of natural justice. According to Thompson and his followers, a whole range of violent popular activities, from grain riots to poaching to smuggling, were expressions of 'the moral economy of the crowd' or of 'social banditry' of the Robin Hood type.[4]

What was the social role of the criminal law in the eighteenth century? The solution lies in the study of two paradoxes. Why was it that although the legislature kept adding – from about 50 to 200 – to the number of offenses against property which carried the death penalty, yet the number of hangings was only about a quarter of what it had been in the seventeenth century, and if anything was tending to fall? Second, why did the propertied classes so obstinately refuse, until the 1830s, to alter this archaic system, in which practice was so wildly at variance with the statute law, despite overwhelming evidence that a milder but more regularly enforced system of punishments would protect their property more effectively and would be more in accord with natural justice and Enlightenment thought?

The answer to both questions lies in the true functions of law in that society. In 1688 the ruling elite had finally rejected, as an unacceptable threat to its own power, the imposition of a Continental legal apparatus, including the abolition of the jury system and the establishment of a ubiquitous police force. This being the case, social control over the remaining 97 per cent of the population had to be maintained by a mixture of terror tempered by mercy, consensus in the rough justice of the system, and an awesome display of the majesty of the law. The passage of more and more penal legislation was not intended to increase the number of hangings, but merely to expand the area of the arbitrary exercise of mercy. Only about half of those condemned to death were actually hanged, the remainder being either pardoned or transported to the colonies on the petition of the local elite and the judges.

This placed enormous powers of patronage in the hands of the elite to prosecute or not to prosecute and to withhold or to grant support for a plea of mercy, as personal feelings and local conditions might suggest. This flexible power reinforced the whole social system of deference and dependence, and also made it possible to adjust the law to the winds of public opinion. Another factor was the behavior of the judges themselves, who leant over backward in favor of the accused if the slightest technical fault in the wording of the indictment could be discovered. In doing so they were protecting the arcana of their profession. In view of these enormous benefits to influential groups, it is not surprising that the rationalist reformers made no headway.

The third factor was the habit of juries to refuse to convict, in plain defiance of the facts, especially by setting the value of stolen property below the minimum that carried the death penalty. The fourth was the accidental by-product of empire – the opening up of a conveniently remote dumping ground, Georgia, to which felons could be transported, never to be seen or heard of again, which alone made such flexibility in the exercise of mercy possible.

The book of essays and Mr Thompson's own book are illustrations of this central theme of the relationship of the social hierarchy to the law and to crime. They examine the nature of crime and the criminals, and the way the law was framed and used to suit the needs of the ruling class without alienating the sense of natural justice of the population at large. This last result was achieved by shrewd tokenism, namely the occasional enforcement of the full rigor of the law against a member of the ruling class, the classic and much quoted example being the hanging – and subsequent dissec- tion of the body – of Lord Ferrers for murder in 1760. Both the use of juries and these occasional sacrifices of a member of the elite made it credible to believe that the law was an impartial instrument of natural justice. It was also, of course, a powerful defense against any despotic tendencies on the part of the king and his ministers in London.

Another study concerns the grisly details of the struggle at Tyburn between the surgeons, anxious to obtain the bodies for anatomical dissection before their students, and the mob, which resented such activities. The other essays all deal with various types of crime: smuggling, which became an activity almost on the scale of the bootleg liquor industry during Prohibition; the wrecking and looting of ships; game poaching; and the writing of anonymous threatening or blackmail letters. Here are some of the darker realities of low life in the Augustan Age.

Several of these essays are examples of that most dismal kind of historical writing, the emptying out on the page of the contents of boxes of note cards. But the overall impression from both books is stunning – and yet is somehow missed by all the contributors, since they insist on looking at the situation exclusively from below. Mr Thompson, for example, takes pains to make clear that external deference to superiors was often a veneer covering deep-seated resentments and hatreds. But even he fails to draw the obvious conclusion about the extreme precariousness of the balance between the forces of law and order and those of crime and anarchy in eighteenth-century England. In the coastal areas of Sussex, the smuggling gangs terrorized the countryside, and outnumbered and outgunned the troops sent to crush them. In Hampshire, gangs of deer stealers rode about at will, and generally meted out their own rough justice. In Cornwall, ship-wreckers were uncontrollable and were left free to plunder as they pleased. In London, mobs of seamen roamed the streets, destroying bawdy houses they thought had cheated them. Large-scale pitched battles took place at Tyburn for possession of the bodies of the hanged. In years of bad harvests, food rioters took over the markets and ransacked private granaries.

Besides these group activities, regarded by Thompson and his

followers as 'social crimes,' there were the more personal crimes of
the underworld, the work of the swarms of pickpockets and petty
thieves; the muggers who prowled the streets of London with even
greater impunity than those in New York today; the footpads and
highwaymen who regularly waylaid and robbed travelers on the
highroads. These working men were not of a kindly disposition.
Sussex smugglers caught and tortured slowly to death an exciseman
and an informer; a mob of London weavers stoned to death an
informer; Cornish wreckers stripped and murdered a helpless
woman cast away on a beach; anonymous blackmailers were
constantly using the threat and reality of arson to extort money or
concessions; muggers maimed and murdered; highwaymen and
footpads shot to kill if resistance was offered to their demands. Nor
was the society within which these criminals moved, like Mao's fish
in the water, particularly gentle. On several occasions, for example,
crowds stoned and beat to death persons put in the pillory for
particularly unpopular offenses like sodomy or the keeping of
brothels. As for the crowds at a hanging, they were merry and
drunken, and enjoyed the spectacle.

Some geographical areas remained wholly outside the law in the
early eighteenth century, for example Kingswood forest, just
outside Bristol. The coal-miners there lived a savage, untamed life,
untouched by gentry or the church, brawling, fornicating, drinking, and occasionally marching into Bristol, to the terror of the
citizens. It took the heady brew of Methodism finally to tame them
and to allow the penetration of law and order. In the eighteenth
century riot was as much a part of the tactics of the plebeians in the
negotiating process as the taking of hostages has become today.
Both are used to equalize power in a conflict, and in doing so to
publicize a perceived injustice.

This was a society forever teetering on the edge of anarchy; and in
view of this, it is not surprising that the legislature resorted
increasingly to the threat of 'Albion's Fatal Tree' – the gallows. The
real surprise is that they did not in practice use it more often. As it
was, they most skillfully managed to keep this unending conflict
between the haves and the have-nots from developing into an open
and bloody class war. The English propertied classes of the
eighteenth century were prepared to put up with a level of casual
violence from their inferiors which would lead to martial law and
the suspension of civil rights were it to occur today. The idea that

there is something historically unusual about the level of late twentieth-century violence in America is sheer nonsense, as these books amply prove.

In *Whigs and Hunters*, Mr Thompson circles around and slowly narrows in on a single Act of Parliament, the Black Act of 1723, which at one blow created fifty new capital offenses, all concerned with threats to property. To explain the Act he found himself obliged to study deer-hunters, forest government, courtiers and their parks, and finally the Whig government in London. In the process, he throws the gauntlet down to generations of Whig historians and particularly to Professor J. H. Plumb's two-volume work on Robert Walpole's establishment of Whig power under George I and George II. He flatly declares, 'I am at a loss to know who ... benefited from Walpole's administration ... beyond the circle of Walpole's own creatures.' Here is historical revisionism with a vengeance, challenging one of the most established dogmas of the past decades, that Walpole was the architect of English political stability, prosperity, the rule of law, and political liberty for the men of property, which was the envy of the civilized world at the time. It was a state and a society that was particularly admired by French philosophers and reformers, although some of them also noted that an extraordinarily large number of Englishmen seemed to end up on the gallows or transported to America for life.

The ultimate moral issue raised by these books is whether such practices were a price worth paying for the benefits received. In a key passage, Mr Thompson identifies his subject as a conflict between on the one hand 'the petty predators' – deer-poachers, turf-cutters, wood-stealers, horse-thieves, venison-traders, armed petty blackmailers – and, on the other, 'the great predators.' These he defines as the great Whig oligarchs, such as the Duke of Newcastle and Sir Robert Walpole, men scrambling for office, money, perquisites, and patronage, and enclosing Crown and public lands in the process. 'Their depredations were immeasurably larger and more injurious ... than the depredations of the deer-stealers.' Mr Thompson goes even further to argue that

political life in England in the 1720s had something of the sick quality of a 'banana republic.' This is a recognized phase of commercial capitalism when predators fight for the spoils of power, and have not yet agreed to submit to rational or bureaucratic rules and forms.

There are many things wrong with this neo-Marxist conception of eighteenth-century law and society offered by Mr E. P. Thompson. Perhaps his view of the sinister Patrician class should be cleared out of the way first, so that the more serious historical issues can be put in the right perspective. Twenty years of intensive investigation of English social history of the early modern period suggest that England in the 1720s was no more corrupt, no more swarming with 'great predators' than it had been at any time in the previous 180 years or was to be for the next fifty. Walpole was, in fact, the last English chief minister to make a great fortune out of his office – and we now know that the Duke of Newcastle made nothing.

Only a historian looking back from the more respectable and bureaucratized period of the Napoleonic wars would see anything especially corrupt about the England of the 1720s; one looking forward from the 1540s or the 1620s would see a positive improvement. Nor is it fair to describe the Whigs in the 1720s as 'a curious junta of political speculators and speculative politicians, stock-jobbers officers grown fat on Marlborough's wars, time-serving dependents in the law and the church, and great landed magnates.' No political party leadership is a very pretty sight when examined at close quarters, but the Whigs had the support of the political nation – and rightly so – as the barrier against religious persecution, arbitrary monarchical government, police repression, dependence on France, and military adventures leading to high taxation and reduced trade.

Although they hardly ever come right out and say so, the six authors of a new collection of essays provide the material for a major critique of other aspects of the Thompson paradigm.[5] In the first place the patrician–plebeian dichotomy is shown to involve a serious distortion of the eighteenth-century English social structure. It completely ignores the central change of the period, mainly the remarkable, and probably unique, rise in numbers, wealth, leisure and education of 'the middling sort,' minor gentlemen, large tenant farmers, small professional men, business men, monied men, small merchants, shopkeepers, clerks, apothecaries, scriveners, surveyors, auditors, artists, engravers, and so on. These are the law-abiding people of property whose demands for equal justice for all, due legal process, and participation in the political system led to the enormously popular Wilkite movement in the late eighteenth century, and ultimately to the first Reform Bill of 1832. Second, it is misleading to treat the law in seventeenth and eighteenth-century England merely as an instrument of class oppression, a view which can be made to seem plausible only by narrowing the focus to the criminal law. England was a profoundly legalistic society, and the patricians were as bound by the rules of the common law as were the middling sort or the plebeians. The law was a universally revered ideology which in its civil aspect both legitimated and at the same time limited the authority of the patricians. The common law created a multiple-use right, as easily exploited by the accused as by the accuser. One of the most remarkable demonstrations of this is the way the radical John Wilkes, acting as a strict constructionist, used the letter of the common law to baffle Chief Justice Mansfield, with his equitable view of his function as a judge.

No one can read this essay by Brewer and still believe that the law was merely a tool for social oppression by the patricians. This conclusion is supported by another essay on the Yorkshire coiners, in which it is shown conclusively that the elite was divided in its interests and opinions and that the coiners made skillful use of the niceties of the law. Even when the coiners – respectable tradesmen all – clubbed together to hire some ruffians to murder an over-zealous exciseman, the forces of order were unable to persuade a local jury to convict the murderers, who had to be discharged. The leading coiner, 'King David', was indeed convicted and executed and the murderers finally convicted (five years later) – of robbing their victim's body – but huge crowds collected to prevent the authorities from hanging the corpses of the executed murderers in chains. Clearly, institutions like the jury and the pillory, to say nothing of mob rioting, added an element of popular participation to the whole judicial and penal process.

It is now abundantly clear that both the law itself, and its administrative procedures, severely limited the power of the patricians. Most of them certainly wished to establish a deferentially harmonious society, but they were unwilling to pay the price of an authoritarian state apparatus to obtain one, and unable to get their way through the law. In the locality, the agent of enforcement was the amateur constable, supervised vaguely by the amateur JP. Both tended to concentrate on avoiding conflict and letting sleeping dogs lie. 'Patrician' JPs were passive resistors to unpopular state laws passed by 'Patrician' MPs about such matters as alehouse licensing, gambling, profanity, breaking the sabbath, sexual misdemeanors, and absence from church. Only those outside the 'moral community' of the village tended to get prosecuted.

Finally the distinction between nefarious and 'social' crime turns out on close inspection to be sometimes hard to draw and not very helpful as an analytical tool. Footpads who used their truncheons to break their victims' heads for personal gain clearly fall into the former category, while the often female rioters who seized and sold grain at a 'just price' equally clearly fall into the latter. But what about the highwaymen, who were often popular heroes because of their gentlemanly bravado and their skill in preying upon the rich? Are they Hobsbawm's 'social bandits'? And what about the Cornish wreckers, who also enjoyed wide community support and moral vindication? Are they therefore to be classified as 'social' criminals, although they were men who lured ships in a storm on to the rocks, and stripped naked and/or murdered the survivors as they struggled ashore? The case of the Yorkshire coiners shows how the distinction between normal crime and 'social' crime is hopelessly blurred, since the coiners were making money by forgery and undermining the national economy by doing so. And yet they were providing the local community with a necessary means of exchange which should have been supplied by the government itself, and so received widespread local support.

What remains untouched of the Thompson paradigm is first the not very surprising fact that the criminal law – but not the civil law – was indeed in the last resort an instrument of the elite to protect their own and other people's lives and property by the use of selective terror. What else has the criminal law ever done? Second, there was undoubtedly a 'moral economy of the crowd' which animated grain rioters, prisoners for debt and certain other local groups who felt that the law did not coincide with natural justice. This again is hardly a novelty.

Freed from the constraints of the neo-Marxist paradigm, we are now moving into a new stage in the historiography of the workings of the eighteenth-century legal system. We are now free to study the interaction of an increasingly complex and middle-class eighteenth-century society and its government, and the conflict between ideas about property, authority and deference on the one hand and ideas about equality before the law, freedom and natural justice on the other. England in the eighteenth century emerges as an unruly, disorderly, almost anarchic, society, tenuously held together by profound and shared respect for the common law, by a partly shared consensus about the legitimate but limited rights of paternalism, by shared assumptions about social relations, and by the intermittent use or threat of terror. This new work has shattered first the Namierite and now the neo-Marxist interpretations of eighteenth-century English government and society, and their attitudes towards law, crime and riot. The result is a much more sophisticated and more nuanced understanding of the relationship of law to society.

CHAPTER 14 · The university

What was the purpose of the English university in the sixteenth and seventeenth centuries? Its medieval function had been to serve as a professional training school. Its *alumni* moved on to the civil and common law, and into the higher ranks of the clergy, for a degree in canon law was becoming increasingly desirable for those aspiring for promotion. Of those who left the university without a degree, many became parish priests.

Since the curriculum was exclusively scholastic and legal, the upper-class elite tended to steer clear of the universities, which had little or nothing to offer them unless they were seeking a career in the church. The students, therefore, came from fairly humble homes. Some of them were cooped up in colleges for secular or monastic clergy, but the majority lived free and unregulated lives as members of loose-knit communities known as Halls.

During the Reformation this medieval university disappeared with startling suddenness. The monastic colleges were suppressed when the monasteries were dissolved, and the Halls also mostly disappeared. A considerable number of new colleges were founded, of which the two novel features were that the students now included a large number of gentry pursuing a secular career and that a strict discipline was imposed upon them, enforced by high walls, a hierarchical constitution, and severe penalties for disobedience, even including – *mirabile dictu* – corporal punishment. The old freewheeling life of the medieval student came to an end.

The last stage of this institutional tightening up was to come in the 1570s at Cambridge and the 1630s at Oxford, when new university statutes radically changed the distribution of political power: the final voice in decision-making was removed from the old participatory democracy of the junior faculty and given to a narrow oligarchy of heads of colleges. The growth of order and hierarchy in Tudor society and politics generally was thus closely paralleled by the growth of order and hierarchy in the universities.

As the Reformation crisis deepened, the state decided that what
went on in the universities was too important to be left to the
academics, and it began to interfere directly and vigorously. Since
the stock-in-trade of intellectuals is ideas, they inevitably find
themselves subjected to severe pressure from all sides at times of
political and religious crisis, whereas in quieter times, when
economic interests tend to dominate, they are left more or less in
peace. The faculty of a university is always largely composed of
conservative and unimaginative men, only too anxious to steer their
course according to the established rules, but it usually also contains
a sprinkling of people whose product is intellectual innovation. At
times like the sixteenth and seventeenth centuries, such men are
closely watched to make sure that the ideas they produce are
congenial to the authority of the day.

Furthermore faculty members were important in another way,
since they had charge both of the future opinion-makers and
propagandists – the clergy – and also of the secular power elite in
what is supposed to be their most impressionable years. And so the
dons of the sixteenth century were subjected to considerable
pressure from the state to ensure their religious and political
conformity. Through the powerful influence of the chancellor of
the university, who was always a leading political figure, and
through the expanding patronage system of the court, the English
government increasingly interfered in the election of headships of
houses, fellowships, and scholarships by letters of recommenda-
tion, lobbying, and even threats.

Two huge and wealthy royal establishments, Trinity at Cambridge and Christ Church at Oxford, gave the crown a powerful
patronage lever within the universities, which was further aided by
the creation of Regius Professorships in subjects which the crown
was anxious to foster. This multiple invasion of the university by
the state during the late sixteenth century was even more far-
reaching in its consequences than the second invasion, in order to
promote science and scientists, in the late twentieth century.

Into this new institutional structure there poured a rising flood of
students drawn from two social groups. The first was a lower-
middle-class element, sons of traders, shopkeepers, yeomen, hus-
bandmen, and superior artisans, who were often financed by
scholarships or by menial service around the college. We assume –
though it has yet to be proved – that many, if not most, of these

men were aiming at a degree and a career as a clergyman in the new Anglican church. Now that the laity were making wholly unprecedented demands for an educated and responsible clergy, a university degree was becoming more and more desirable, even for a parish priest. Another occupation open to a low-born graduate was as schoolmaster to teach literacy and Latin grammar to the growing number of children whose parents were willing to pay for such things.

The second major and rapidly increasing element in the student body was the sons of the lay elite from nobles to gentry, who now for the first time in history sent their sons to the university for two or three years, although mostly with no intention of taking a degree. What these men hoped to get out of their stay at the university is not entirely clear, but it certainly included a sound grounding in rhetoric, the Latin classics, and the bible. From the university they would move on to the Inns of Court to pick up some Common Law, and perhaps later still to the Grand Tour in order to acquire social polish, languages, and an experience of the world.

As a result of this huge influx of gentry, the universities found themselves playing a dual role: training about half the student body toward an examination and a degree with a view to a professional career, and giving to the other half what they thought they needed before assuming their hereditary places among the ruling elite. This dual function should be familiar enough to us today since it has been normal for Oxbridge and the Ivy League between the middle of the nineteenth century and the middle of the twentieth.

These organizational and social changes in the university are now fairly well established. It is far less clear, however, just what it was that the students studied. The education of the clergy remained a prime function of the university, but just what they and the newly arrived gentry were to be taught was a matter upon which the dons received a good deal of contradictory advice: from the secular humanists to teach the classics, especially Cicero; from the Christian humanists to combine the classics with biblical studies and ethics; from the Puritans to teach the bible and Calvinist biblical commentaries; from the academic conservatives to stick to scholasticism and Aristotle; from the scientific innovators to teach Baconian pragmatism; and from the social reformers to give the upper classes a 'useful' education in modern European languages, literature, politics, and history.

The most important change that can be clearly documented was that the teaching of canon law was positively forbidden by the state soon after the Reformation, thus abolishing at a stroke one of the main functions of the universities in the Middle Ages, the training of canon lawyers. The accidental result was to give the Inns of Court in London a clear monopoly of all legal education in the country. To find out what actually happened apart from this, we have to seek such enlightenment as we can get from the few surviving guides to students and the many student notebooks.

According to Professor Kearney the mid-sixteenth century sees a clash of two humanisms.[1] The first, which he labels 'Court Humanism,' demanded a close study of the classics in order to strengthen the gentry's loyalty to the state and to the established doctrines. This flourished in the 1530s to the 1550s, to be replaced by 'Country Humanism,' which stressed godliness and virtue over learning and which laid greater stress on biblical studies and history. The Elizabethan period saw the introduction into Cambridge, although hardly at all into Oxford, of Ramism, a sort of plain man's logic with which to assail both the linguistic and grammatical obsessions of the humanists and the slavish pedantry of the Aristotelians.

Ramism stressed content rather than form, but it became associated with religious radicalism – quite how is not clear – and was therefore effectively suppressed, both in England and in Scotland, around the turn of the century. In the 1590s there developed a strong reaction back to medieval scholasticism, which Professor Kearney sees as part of a general conservative trend in the early seventeenth century.

Professor Kearney admits that in the revolutionary decades of the 1640s and 1650s Baconianism had a brief vogue among a minority of dons, but he argues that in educational practice nothing much changed at the universities. Even the scientific leaders themselves believed that science had no place in an undergraduate curriculum. Seth Ward, the future historian of the Royal Society, asked bluntly, 'Which of the Nobility and Gentry desire when they send their sons hither that they should be set to Chymistry or Agriculture or Mechanicks?'

Which indeed! In any case, the ruling class was hastily falling back by then on traditional scholasticism as a bulwark against the socially subversive ideas of the extremist sectaries. On both sides of the Atlantic universities were coming under attack from the sects, which denounced the 'Ninnyversity' as the spawning ground of a tight professional class of ministers, lawyers, and doctors who were incapable of speaking plainly and clearly to the people, and who used their learning to protect and further their own selfish interest. But the dons and the members of the professions fought off this assault with the aid of the lay power – John Winthrop in Massachusetts and Oliver Cromwell in England – and the old curriculum survived virtually intact.

The post-Restoration dons and students, therefore, inherited a curriculum made up of scholasticism and the classics, 'the Ancients,' which they vigorously defended against the assault of the 'Moderns,' such as languages, history, and the classics in translation. In a frenzy of reactionary zeal, Oxford University in 1683 forbade students to read, and ordered to be publicly burned the works of such diverse enemies of safe thinking as the Independent Milton, the Presbyterian Baxter, the Catholic Cardinal Bellarmine, and the skeptic Hobbes. The reason for this all-embracing conservatism in the universities in the late seventeenth century, according to Professor Kearney, is that they were composed of two declining social groups, the gentry and the clergy, who were now being outnumbered and overtaken by the monied and commercial classes and the dissenters.

Under the stress of this social threat, the dons and the students retreated into reactive conservatism, as a last-ditch defense against the wave of the future. By fleeing to scholasticism and the classics, they hoped to preserve the old clerical/gentlemanly values in an alien capitalist world whose intellectual mouthpieces were Descartes and Locke. In the battle of the Ancients and Moderns, the supremacy of the former within the universities and of the latter without is therefore of profound social significance, and should not merely be regarded as an epiphenomenon of the history of ideas.

In Professor Kearney's view, the effect of the universities over this two-hundred-year period was to strengthen the forces of social and intellectual conservatism. They were the principal instrument which polarized society into two distinct status groups and subcultures, the gentlemanly members of 'polite society' and the rest of the population, separated by a gulf defined by a leisured style of life whose most visible characteristic was a running acquaintance with Latin.

Plebeians could acquire gentle status by a university education and a career in the church, an institution now controlled by the lay elite, and in which advancement depended on the favor of gentry patrons. Their stay at the university gave the gentry a common educational experience and served to create a national elite which was both unified in outlook and culture and clearly distinguished from the rest of the nation. Moreover, the curricular trend back to scholasticism which set in at the end of the sixteenth century created the intellectual background for the authoritarian regime of Charles I and Archbishop Laud in the 1630s. This trend also explains why the revolutionary leaders of the 1640s were angry old men, nearly ten years senior to the Royalist supporters. According to Professor Kearney, the former had been bred at the universities on the Elizabethan biblical curriculum, the latter on scholastic theology and the Fathers, the former being interpreted as an incentive to radicalism, the latter to conservatism.

Professor Kearney has propounded a thesis of great boldness and originality, which offers a key to unlock the door to many mysteries about English social and intellectual history over a critical two-hundred-year period. This is in many ways an original and exciting book which will provide themes for discussion and investigation for many years to come. It is enlivened with sudden flashes of insight and provocative assertions. But impressive as is the intellectual tour de force which has produced so attractive a synthesis, there is unfortunately reason to think that the methodology is unsound and that many of the conclusions are unproven or untrue.

There are four methodological flaws in Professor Kearney's book, any one of which would alone be sufficient to detract seriously from its value. First, it is based on a fixed presupposition, namely that the university is an institution which not only was intended to operate, but which in fact did operate, as a social and intellectual control system to strengthen the monopoly of the existing elite over high status positions, to formalize and reinforce class distinctions, and to propagate conservative ideology. The university is assumed to have been, both in intent and in practice, one of the most important elements of the system of repression which maintained the social status quo.

That governments and ruling elites have in the past tried to use the educational system for such purposes is a matter of historical record. It is only in the twentieth century that liberals have tried to use the system to create a society based on equal opportunity and high social mobility. But the extent to which the universities did in fact operate in this way and the degree to which there were internal resistances and slippages are quite other matters.

In practice, universities have nearly always performed two directly contradictory functions. On the one hand, they have served to channel the children of the elite into elite positions, and thus to harden the social structure; and they have also transmitted the inherited traditional culture of the past to each new generation. On the other hand, they have provided avenues, broad or narrow, by which talented children of relatively humble origins (but usually not from the manual laboring class) may enter the ranks of the elite; and they also have provided relatively safe havens of intellectual freedom in a heavily censored universe, from which can emerge new ideas and new facts which challenge both the existing social system and the existing set of values.

Without recognition of the essentially ambivalent role of the universities – socially a block and a sieve, intellectually a buttress and a land-mine – it is impossible to understand the role the universities have played in Western society in the last 300 years. Exclusive stress on the second, innovatory and socially mobile role leads to the exaggerated claims of twentieth-century liberals for the university as a force for social and intellectual change. Exclusive stress on the reactionary and socially stabilizing role confirms the Marxist denigration of the importance of freedom of thought and expression in the university, since it is regarded as no more than an epiphenomenon of bourgeois culture. 'To state that the school is above life, above politics, is a lie and a hypocrisy,' wrote Lenin, who therefore proceeded to crush freedom of thought in Russian universities. This doctrine has now been taken up again by the more radical students of Europe and America, who also regard the university itself, and freedom of opinion within it, as mere façades and supports for the existing military-industrial complex.

Serious historical mistakes follow from the adoption of the assumption that 'universities are the intellectual organs of the ruling elite.' Thus despite the efforts of the government to suppress dissent, the English universities in this period played an absolutely vital role in the dissemination of Puritanism throughout both lay and clerical societies. Puritan intellectuals filled college fellowships, and from there they indoctrinated generation after generation of gentry and parish clergy with their subversive ideas.

Similarly, the attack of the free-will theorists on the accepted Calvinist ideas about predestination was also launched within the universities, despite the fact that Calvinism was part of the official Anglican doctrine. And when Arminianism finally became official in the 1620s, opposition to it continued from inside the universities, even at the height of the Laudian tyranny. The universities only became fully conformist in the late seventeenth century, and then they overdid their enthusiasm for the status quo to such a degree that they had the greatest difficulty adapting to the revolution of 1688, and thereafter tended to lapse into centers of High Tory disaffection.

As for the role of the universities as agents of social mobility, the very large number of men of humble origins whom they enrolled sufficiently speaks for itself. Whatever else they were at this period, the colleges were not exclusive havens for the social elite.

The second flaw in Professor Kearney's book is his organization of intellectual history around a Hegelian dialectic of conservative and radical opposites. In the first place his categories are all wrong. It is false to identify classical studies with conservatism in the seventeenth century, however much this may be true today. Indeed, Hobbes argued the opposite, that the English Revolution was caused in considerable measure by too much reading of such subversive republicans as Cicero, Tacitus, and Seneca.

It is unreasonable to call Eliot a 'Court Humanist' and Lawrence Humphrey a 'Country Humanist,' since they merely represent different stages in the acclimatization of an Italian prototype rather than distinctive intellectual positions. Humphrey was merely adapting a Renaissance model to a Reformation society, and, as the protégé of the Earls of Leicester and Warwick, he cannot be described as any less a 'Court figure' than Eliot. As for scholastic theology, it is true that the Early Fathers are less dangerous literary fare than the New Testament. But slavish reliance on the bible as the source of all authority is hardly more liberating a doctrine than one of slavish reliance on Aristotle. Dr Kearney's opposites are by no means as contrary as he claims, nor are the consequences of adopting them as obvious.

Moreover, he mysteriously ignores theology altogether and consequently fails even to notice the main intellectual quarrel which was tearing Oxford and Cambridge apart between 1590 and 1640, namely the battle between predestinarian Calvinists and free-will Arminians over the Doctrine of Grace. This was one of the most hotly debated issues of the period, and one which was to have the most serious political consequences once Charles I swung the whole weight of Court influence behind the Arminians.

Nor is it good enough to treat Ramism, Baconianism, Cartesianism, and the Moderns as interchangeable parts of an intellectually progressive machine. Ramism cannot easily be fitted into a left-right spectrum, except in so far as at Cambridge it was clearly associated with the Puritanism of Cartwright and his followers. The Baconians and the Cartesians were opposites in their approach to the scientific method, and many Moderns rejected science as unsuitable for the education of a gentleman. In order to make his conservative/progressive dichotomy stick, Professor Kearney is forced in places to indulge in anachronistic thinking. For example, he regards a belief in astrology, in the effect of the heavenly bodies upon the character and fortunes of the individual, as evidence of conservative thinking. But this was a standard assumption of the seventeenth century, common both to many of the new scientists and to the Aristotelians, and nothing whatever can be deduced from it.

In any case, even if Professor Kearney's categories were correct, which they are not, his system of polarities is false, since it is not how ideas work. New ideas permeate old ones, run underground and pop up in unexpected places, mingle surreptitiously, or even coexist side by side without either conflict or conflation. One system of beliefs or values rarely challenges another directly and finally overthrows it in a single cataclysmic struggle. It is more a matter of guerrilla warfare, secret infiltration, and eventual mutual accommodation.

The third error is the crude way in which Professor Kearney relates ideas or sets of ideas directly and functionally to the alleged interests of certain classes. This bull-in-a-china-shop approach to intellectual history is no way to advance our understanding of the sociology of knowledge. Under this reductionist treatment the intellectual disappears as an individual with a personal and unique contribution to make, and becomes merely the symbol of a class or interest.

Thus Professor Kearney not only associates the classics, Aristotelian scholasticism, and the Early Fathers with conservatism; he also associates conservatism with the gentry. Everything else – biblical study, Ramism, Cartesianism, Baconianism, the Moderns – is regarded not only as potentially subversive, but also as associated with the merchants. This attachment of specific curricular programs to specific social groups like gentry and merchants is pure poppy-cock, unsupported by any shred of evidence. For example, how is it possible to argue that the strength of Locke's position 'depended essentially upon the appeal which he made to new social groups ... the monied interest' (p. 159)? In his treatise on education, Locke is specifically and exclusively concerned with the bringing up of a young landed gentleman, and his undoubted links with the Whig Party leaders hardly turn him into an educational reformer in the mercantile interest.

The social bases of the model are not any better founded than the intellectual ones. The shrinking enrolment of the upper-class students after 1670 cannot be explained by any hypothetical decline of the gentry in the face of merchant competition. If the lesser gentry were indeed in financial difficulty at this time, the greater gentry and nobility were in a flourishing condition, and yet the latter were fleeing the universities as fast as the former. What we see in the late seventeenth century is a wholesale rejection of the value of a university education as a preparation for life as a member of the elite. Attendance of gentry at the university declined not because they represented a declining social class, but because they no longer chose to send their sons there.

As for the second allegedly declining class, the clergy, their numbers were stationary, and their status was rising, while their finances were certainly not getting worse and were soon to improve with the aid of Queen Anne's Bounty. They were rapidly becoming the social associates of the gentry, the solid backbone of the Tory Party, and were beginning to infiltrate the Bench of Justices. What sense does it make to describe the post-1689 period as 'The Age of Dissent' (p. 158), when in fact it saw the solidification of squire and parson as the dominant elite of the countryside?

It is false to assume that there is a one-to-one correlation between what goes on in the university and the needs of outside society. This is to take the misguided functionalist notions of modern sociologists far too seriously. As every historian knows, all the institutions of society are partly functional and partly antiquated, vestigial, or even frankly 'dysfunctional.' This is because they all have a history and a life of their own, and their response to outside pressure is consequently imperfect, stumbling, tardy, and even reactive.

The history of higher education in the West over the past four centuries does not support the assumption that the things that are taught in a university are directly and functionally related to the needs of society. The three great and unquestioned contributions of the university to society have been the preservation of the cultural heritage of civilization; the advancement of learning, meaning the increase in factual information, and the formulation of new ideas about both nature and society; and the technical preparation of graduate students for the professions – until quite recently for the church, law, and medicine, and now for a whole range of new occupations from engineering to the professional study of history. These are three services without which no advanced society can function, and which have usually been supplied in the West by the universities.

It must be admitted that the cultural heritage in art and music and creative literature has hitherto always been transmitted outside the university through an informal apprenticeship system. It must also be admitted that some of the most innovative thinkers of modern times – Marx and Darwin and Freud, for example – have lived and worked quite outside the academic profession, and that at one period, the eighteenth century, the advancement of learning took place almost entirely elsewhere. But over the last century, the university has been acquiring a more and more exclusive monopoly over all three functions, evidence of which are the creative arts and creative literature programs, the research-oriented faculties in the major institutions, the rise of professional schools in law and medicine and business, and the growth of the graduate programs, which effectively control admission to the various academic disciplines.

The university also supplies a fourth service to society, the general education, until recently, of a tiny social and intellectual elite, and now of a rapidly increasing proportion of the masses. In this case the specific curricular methods adopted are by no means so obviously related to social purpose as they are in the case of the other three. Indeed it is the lack of 'relevance' of the undergraduate education which is one of the main burdens of student complaints. But this problem of relevance was far more glaring in the past than it is today. To give the most obvious example: what has been the functional purpose, in educational and intellectual terms, of giving the ruling classes of the nation states of northern Europe and America a painfully narrow training in the dead language of a long-extinct Mediterranean empire? The classical authors certainly contained most of human wisdom as it was known in the early modern period, but as the contemporary critics kept pointing out, almost all of them were available in translation and the stress on the linguistic and grammatical forms tended to obscure their factual and philosophical content.

A remarkable volume of fresh educational thought was generated during the Puritan Revolution.[2] Most of the reformers were hostile to the current classical curriculum, some from a utilitarian wish to make education more relevant, others from a desire to break down existing social distinctions. As they pointed out at the time, and as has been pointed out many times since, the value of learning Latin in creating and preserving class distinctions is clear enough, but to label such a grind a 'liberal education' is merely a hilarious early example of double-think. Indeed a cynic might suspect that a good deal of what has been taught to undergraduates at the university throughout most of history – including the present – has been about as useful to the society and as beneficial to the individual as the practice of female circumcision.

In any case, it is an open question to what extent the things students learn in the university classroom influence their subsequent political and religious beliefs. Is it possible to deduce the future political positions of an Elizabethan gentleman from whether he was fed at the university on a diet of Scheibler, Burgersdicius, and Zabarella, or one of Scribonius, Freigius, and Beurhusius? Maybe it is, but the connection has yet to be made.

Changes in the content of the sermons in the college chapels probably had a greater influence on attitude formation than changes in the content of reading lists in the classrooms. Similarly today, the fact that most academics at the better universities are liberals in their political and moral attitudes is more important in shaping the values of undergraduates than the subject matter of the textbooks they prescribe. (Even so, these attitudes have been prevalent for forty years, without doing anything very obvious to alter the Republican and conservative views of the alumni.)

Some academics consequently give up altogether. In the late seventeenth century John Aubrey decided that it was a waste of time to try to teach adolescents anything at all, since at that age their minds are so obsessed with images and fantasies of sex that they are incapable of paying attention to any other subject. There is reason to think that he was exaggerating, but even so, the impact of changes in the curriculum on student values is a subject about which virtually nothing is known. All academics assume that they have profound effects, but none of us can prove it, and Sir Osbert Sitwell's description of his education as taking place 'in the holidays from Eton' is perhaps not all that unusual. What goes on outside the classroom, in private reading, conversations with fellow students, informal discussions with the faculty, and extracurricular activity, may be more important than what goes on inside it.

Serious questions can be asked about the use made of student notebooks. It is by no means certain that the intellectual development of an individual at the university can be reconstructed from the perusal of one or two of many books of notes on lectures attended and books read for class (I am certain mine could not). Even if we assume that it can be, it is essential to distinguish the notebooks of students proceeding to a degree and a donnish or clerical career, from notebooks of young gentlemen in temporary residence to pick up a liberal education.

It is very dangerous to use the argument *ex silentio*, making deductions from what is not in them, when we clearly can never be sure that the same student did not own other notebooks on the same or other subjects which are now lost. This is particularly important since the 'Guides to Students' suggest that the curriculum was very mixed, so that one notebook might easily contain Aristotle and Galen and another Harvey, Galileo, and Gassendi. Where the evidence is reasonably abundant, we find different reading lists being given to different students by different tutors in the same college. This is what we might expect, but it casts doubts upon any stage model.

For example, the late seventeenth-century guides to students at Oxford include, along with the traditional authorities, works on Cartesian logic, neo-Platonist ethics, the Lockean assault on metaphysics, and a large range of modern scientific writers. There is therefore some reason to think that the universities may not have been quite so reactionary after all in the late seventeenth century, except for the bad period of the mid-1680s, which was one of acute political crisis. If this is so, one of the main props of the model falls to the ground.

If parts of Professor Kearney's model are unsound, what is there to put in its place? The answer is, not much, except what remains of his own structure plus some suggestions from elsewhere. We now know that in most parts of Europe between the middle of the sixteenth and the middle of the seventeenth century – the exact dates vary from country to country – men were flooding into the universities in numbers which, taken as a proportion of the male age group, were not matched until the 1930s or afterward. This is certainly true of England, Germany, Spain, and Massachusetts and is probably true of France and Italy. The vast majority of this mob of students became dropouts, either because of poverty or because they were not seeking a degree in any case. Why they came, how they supported themselves, what they did afterward are questions which are still obscure. It is tempting to see in this movement a fashion or a fad, first propagated by the Humanists, and later encouraged for quite different reasons by the Puritans, the Jesuits, and the secular state, but a fad which eventually got out of hand.

The social consequences of the influx were ambiguous. It is true that knowledge of Latin became a passport to gentility, and that classical studies therefore helped to polarize society. But the enormous extension of opportunities for the relatively humble to acquire a classical education at grammar school, private school, and college was a factor making for greater social mobility rather than less. The intellectual significance of curricular changes is even more ambiguous. The Latin classics can and could be regarded as leading to either conservatism or subversion, according to taste; Ramism's association with Puritanism at Cambridge may be fortuitous, and it certainly was not a radical force in, say, eighteenth-century Yale; reliance on the bible is perhaps even less liberating intellectually than reliance on Aristotle; and the relationship of the new science to political and religious opinions is at best unproven and at worst non-existent.

What is beyond dispute is that over the greater part of Europe (except for the Calvinist areas) the higher education bubble burst in the middle years of the seventeenth century. One reason was that far too many men were being educated to far too high a level and in far too nonvocational subjects such as the classics for these under-developed societies to find them satisfactory employment after-ward. The state began to worry about the threat to social stability of a class of alienated intellectuals – curates, lecturers, schoolmasters, drifters – while the Jesuits and the Dissenters set up their own rival establishments to the universities. The poor no longer saw higher education as an open avenue to social advancement, and the number of entrants fell to match the limited openings in the church and the declining opportunities in schoolmastering.

There was a downward spiral of university education and job opportunities for the educated. This is because, like all educational booms, that of the sixteenth century was partly feeding on itself, in the sense that many graduates entered the expanding teaching profession. But disillusionment with higher education also spread to the grammar schools, large numbers of which abandoned the teaching of the classics in the late seventeenth and eighteenth centuries. As a result, the proportion of the male population which was acquainted with Latin in 1750 or 1800 must have been very significantly less than it had been in 1650.

Moreover, the rich, who had never looked to higher education for vocational training, were now cured of that respect for classical learning as such which had been propagated with such zest by the Humanists. They were now demanding no more than an all-round training in the liberal arts, the shallower and broader education of the quintessentially amateur virtuoso, which was something that the universities were ill-equipped to offer. Locke urged parents to keep their children at home with a private tutor, others recommended one of the academies abroad. Furthermore, the second quality that universities could claim to foster, namely piety through biblical and exegetical study, was no longer so highly prized by the secular elite as once it had been. The age of religious indifference had set in by the late seventeenth century.

By the eighteenth century the universities were, therefore, back to where they began in the Middle Ages, as fairly small training schools for the professions, mainly the church. Since the gentry were also deserting the Inns of Court, one of the social conse-quences must have been a growing isolation of the professional classes, clergy, lawyers, and doctors, from the landed elite which they serviced. They may have come from much the same social class, but they no longer went to college together. It may well also be that the higher ranks of the squirearchy and the nobility, who continued to get an education at home with a tutor, at an academy abroad, and on the Grand Tour, became more and more culturally distinct from the lesser parish gentry, who now terminated their education at school level, before settling down in the countryside to the pleasures of the chase and the bottle.

As a result of this flight from the universities of the social elite, less than half of the men who achieved sufficient eminence in the eighteenth century to win an entry in the Dictionary of National Biography had attended Oxford or Cambridge while less than three-quarters had attended any university at all (the additional university men being drawn from the Scottish and Irish universities).

The intellectual consequences were hardly less serious than the social. With the end of ideology, the state again lost interest in the dons, who were no longer useful in its propaganda wars, and the flood of polemical literature produced by the latter subsided. From being the intellectual powerhouses of Europe, universities sank back to obscure backwaters, hardly stirred by the great movement of the Enlightenment, which came out of circles in the capital cities and on the margins of the *haut monde*. It was not until the age of Napoleon that the universities began to revive again, intellectually, socially, and numerically.

CHAPTER 15 · Madness

1

During the last fifteen years, a series of semi-independent intellectual trends have come together to transform the history of what
society has thought about madness and how it has treated those it
considers mad. Once upon a time, the history of medicine was
regarded, like that of pure science, as largely 'internalist,' a story
of how a progressive endeavor by a handful of gifted intellectuals
slowly replaced superstition and error by empirical proven truth.
More recently, however, historians have begun to fit the protagonists in these ancient intellectual battles more deeply into their social
settings. In the process, they have revealed a welter of unproven
pseudo-scientific theories, professional or national rivalries, institutional jealousies, personal and professional ambitions, cultural
conditioning, sexist and racist prejudices, political exigencies, economic incentives to save money, and religious biases, out of which
new and powerful scientific and medical paradigms have emerged.

Some now argue that medical progress has been a power grab
by the medical profession, and institutional treatment for the
purpose of better care has been relabeled the 'great confinement.'
It is now credibly believed that hospitals were lethal death traps
before Pasteur demonstrated the importance of a sterile environment. It is now also generally recognized that doctors may –
presumably unwittingly – have killed more patients than they
cured, certainly before the early nineteenth century, and maybe
before the invention of antibiotics in the mid-twentieth, and that
their most valuable contribution to public welfare was psychological reassurance that help was on its way.

The most ambitious attempt ever made to examine the
demography of early modern England concludes that the prolonged

growth of population which began in the 1740s and only petered
out during the last few years owed little, at any rate in its early
stages, to a decline in the mortality rate. Medicine, therefore, can
have had no part in the beginnings of the great demographic
transition.[1]

The beneficial effects of the medical profession are now thrown
into doubt, and scientists generally are no longer regarded simply
as wise men battling the mysterious forces of nature with supremely
elegant conceptual thinking, and incredibly patient and exacting
testing and retesting of data. Newton is now known to have been
as concerned to establish the measurements of the temple of
Solomon or to unravel the meaning of the Book of Revelation as
he was to elucidate the laws of gravity or optics. James Watson's
frank disclosures in *The Double Helix* of the strength of personal
ambition as a compelling motive behind scientific research has
forever destroyed the image of the detached scholar selflessly dedicated to the pursuit of truth. The self-evident fact that exploitation
by politicians of the recent discoveries of nuclear physicists is quite
likely to result some time in the next few decades in the destruction
of civilization, and possibly of most life on earth, merely reinforces
this atmosphere of cynicism and suspicion.

The second trend has been a turning away from the history of
elites, whether intellectual or political, to the history of the poor
and downtrodden, a trend in which the nature of surviving documentation has inevitably also led to a focusing on social 'deviants,'
such as homosexuals, criminals, and the insane. One effect of this
more catholic approach has been, in the case of the history of
medicine, no longer to limit it to the study of orthodox medicine
(as practiced, in England, by the members of the Society of Apothecaries and the Colleges of Physicians and of Surgeons) but to
include also popular medicine, which antedates Galen and
continues to this day to be far more widely used than orthodoxy
likes to admit. Some of its practitioners were wise women, white
witches, whose full significance has only emerged as a byproduct
of yet another contemporary trend, a sudden revival of interest in
the irrational in general and witchcraft in particular. Today the
distinction between magic and science is no longer as clear-cut as
it used to be, now that seventeenth-century science is seen as

emerging from a strange brew compounded of Hermeticism, alchemy, and astrology.

Finally, interest in problems associated with madness and its treatment have been stimulated by the writings of Michel Foucault.[2] According to him, the whole post-Enlightenment attempt to treat the mad more humanely, and to devise positive ways to cure them, was largely an aspect of a drive to confine and isolate all deviants in society, to lock them up and throw away the key. It was part of what he calls 'the great confinement,' other parts being the extensive growth of workhouses, schools, and prisons. In the eighteenth century, he says, the mad replaced the medieval lepers in isolation hospitals on the outskirts of cities. There is, he claims, an identical attitude of mind behind the treatment of the two, and the places of isolation were the same.

Foucault is certainly correct that Enlightenment hopes of devising ways to reform criminals or cure madmen through incarceration have proved a gigantic failure. Today no one really knows what to do with either, except to lock up the former and drug the latter. Yet the residual belief remains that a test of the moral worth of a society is the way it treats its more impotent members, the indigent, the sick, and the mad. The battle has thus been joined between post-Enlightenment optimism about the power of society to provide remedies for human pain and suffering, and a cynical suspicion that any change is liable to be for the worse. The former effort reached its apogee in the mid-twentieth-century welfare state, and in America with President Johnson's 'Great Society.' Today, in 1982, there has re-emerged the older, more pessimistic view that nothing much can or should be done, and that whatever is done is morally corrupting to the recipients and financially crippling to the donors. So far as the mad are concerned, we are just about where we were five hundred years ago, when, in about 1450, a Lord Mayor of London concluded that 'some be restored unto their wit and health again. And some be abiding therein for ever, for they be fallen so much out of themselves that it is incurable unto men.'[13]

What is not by any means so certain, however, is whether there is any firm basis in reality to Foucault's vision of the 'age of confinement.' Was there a major disjunction in Western treatment of deviants in about 1650, based on a new principle that madness is shameful, and that the best treatment is forcible isolation from society under management by professionally trained doctors? If this is so, was it merely the result of a conspiracy of professionals to seize power for themselves to lock people up and determine their treatment? That there was a trend toward confinement is undeniable, but the motivation is questionable. The mad were put into institutions at least partly in order to save them from exposure to great cruelties at the hands of the public or their families. In any case, the few dangerously mad had been locked up in cages like animals from at least the late Middle Ages. Far from being isolated, the twenty-odd manacled madmen gibbering and rattling their chains in their filthy cages in Bedlam were one of the great tourist attractions of London from the early sixteenth century to the early nineteenth. It was one of the standard sights of the city, on a par with the royal tombs at Westminster Abbey, the lions prowling in the moat in the Tower of London, the flogging of half-naked whores at Bridewell, and the bull- and bear-baiting over the river at Southwark.

It has also been pointed out that there were enormous differences in the degree and organization of incarceration from country to country, England leading the way in private madhouses in the eighteenth century, and France in huge state-supported institutions. Moreover, the chronology is complicated, since the poor were the first to be incarcerated in large numbers in the seventeenth and eighteenth centuries, but the mad only in the nineteenth. In England in 1810, the total number of mad persons in confinement was only 2,500 out of a population of 9 million, or about 30 per 100,000, and the numbers did not begin to rise rapidly until the 1830s.

Foucault's comparison of treatment of the mad during the early modern period and that of lepers during the Middle Ages does not stand up to close examination. Early modern madhouses were not disused leprosaria but evolved out of medieval hospitals, based on Arab models. Bethlem Hospital, or Bedlam, is one example. Lepers were condemned to lifelong isolation from the community, whereas very large numbers of the mad have always quickly come and gone. During the year 1788, for example, Bedlam held 282 different inmates, but it admitted 219 and discharged 205.[4] This transit camp of the mind, with its constant turnover, was entirely unlike the lifelong prison of the medieval leprosarium.

Finally, Foucault's attempt to link the treatment of schoolchildren, the poor, criminals, and the insane under a single conceptual umbrella, since all were subject to confinement, is both unhistorical and misleading. No serious scholar would doubt that the poor, in or out of workhouses, have been substantially relieved of the crushing burden of indigence in the last two hundred years, or that children, at least up to the 1960s, were increasingly better educated, and thus better prepared to take their place in society and better able to improve their chances in life. Moreover, poor parents willingly paid money to send their children to school, since they knew it gave them moral precepts, behavior discipline, and learning skills that would come in very useful in later life. Whether criminals and the insane have either benefited or suffered much from incarceration is an open question.

The central challenge of the Foucault model is to the humanitarian values and achievements of the eighteenth-century Enlightenment. The acute sensitivity to cruelty, and the vaulting ambition to cure social ills by the use of planning and science, were first made possible by the decline of religious faith in the late seventeenth and eighteenth centuries, which opened the way to a more secular view of human ills and their possible amelioration. Sins against the Holy Ghost and violations of God's law such as heresy now took a lower priority than acts that were harmful to sentient creatures. It has to be admitted, however, that this desacralizing of traditional morality also opened the way to the use of cruelty as a value-free means to secular ends – political for Machiavelli, sexual for Sade, racial for Hitler.[5]

Despite these possibilities, the Enlightenment was a force that in Western Europe resulted in the substitution of imprisonment for torture, mutilation, or death as the main punishment of poor criminals; the abolition of the slave trade; the reform of conditions in the prisons, which reduced opportunities for hideous cruelty (as well as those for easy-going tolerance of irregularities); the reduction and final abolition of the appalling floggings (up to 1,000 lashes) which were common in the armed forces; and the introduction of moral therapeutic methods of treatment of the insane.

The hostility to cruelty in the late eighteenth century covered so wide a front, ranging from the treatment of soldiers to that of criminals, chimney-sweep boys, boxers, women mine workers, and baited bears, that denial of its reality flies in the face of the evidence.

It also undercuts the basis of the whole liberal enterprise of the last two hundred years, which has done so much to diminish man's personal and legal inhumanity to man. One has only to read how the medical profession treated King George III when he went mad – encasing his body in machinery, chaining him to a stake, beating him, starving him, threatening him, blistering and bleeding him, giving him digitalis, tartar emetic, and other noxious medicines – to recognize that the shift to 'moral' treatment of the insane was a major amelioration of the human lot, regardless of its practical efficacy in making long-term cures, which admittedly was not great. It is not enough to advance the valid argument that more humane treatment of the insane depended on the revolutionary notion that the loss of reason was neither irreparable nor a cause to treat a human being like an animal, and that the cure depended on treating the mind rather than the body. It is perfectly true that theory determines treatment, but the wide extent of the humanitarian trend is still undeniable.

Foucault and his followers argue that it was the doctors who were behind the great confinement of the insane, whereas in fact a better case can be made that they were merely responding to social demand. Society was willing and anxious to pay for incarceration. The private madhouses that sprung up all over England in the eighteenth century were run by entrepreneurs who supplied an expensive need of society. Large numbers of well-to-do families were now willing to pay to have their mentally defective children, or hysterical or merely redundant wives, or senile parents taken care of by someone else, out of sight and out of mind. There was push more than pull at work in the creation of the English private madhouses of the early eighteenth century, and even more in the building of the huge public asylums of the early nineteenth century. Moreover, all the children in school, as well as the insane in madhouses, were paid for by their relatives or by the parish under the conviction, often fulfilled, that the experience would do them good. As for the helpless poor, some of whom were confined in workhouses, it is hard for anyone who has read about their conditions in eighteenth-century London or in France to believe that their lot has not improved since the age of confinement. This leaves only the poor criminals, and even they, if asked, would probably choose prison rather than the alternative penalities of severe flogging, multilation, or execution.

Foucault thus provides us with a dark vision of modern society which accords with only some of the historical facts.[6] Abstract and metaphoric in expression, unconcerned with historical detail of time and place or with rigorous documentation, Professor Foucault's work has had an enormous and disturbing influence upon traditional views of recent Western history. By challenging the conventional wisdom of the Whig interpretation, he has forced the historians to turn to a careful investigation of the facts. He deserves full credit for drawing attention to the growth of confinement of a variety of deviants over the past two hundred years, for casting doubt on the motives of professionals, and for focusing attention upon the history of the treatment of insanity. It is he who has set the agenda for the last fifteen years of research.

2

There are several possible ways of tackling the history of madness. One is by institutional histories of the places of confinement, the private madhouses and their successors the public asylums. Another is by a study of ideas about madness, particular types of madness, and how to treat them, in order to display changes in the underlying conceptualization of the mind/body problem, and changing roles of revealed religion, magic, and scientific medicine. A third is by seeking out the rare records of the host of unqualified practitioners, to see how they regarded patients, how their patients regarded them, who those patients were, and what treatments they were prescribed.

One type of madness, so-called 'possession' in the sixteenth and early seventeenth centuries, has been made the subject of a brilliant little book by D. P. Walker, the implications of which are very far-reaching.[7] Possession was a species of madness which could *only* be dealt with by magical means, since it was thought to be the involuntary occupation of an individual by a devil. The marks of possession were speech in an unknown language, knowledge of hidden secrets, supernatural strength, and horror at the use of sacred objects or words. Many of the possessed denounced their neighbors as witches, which led to the death of many innocent people. If fraud was not involved, the only possible explanations for such symptoms were possession by the devil, or some physical disease, such as epilepsy or hysteria. The Catholics chose the devil theory, and threw him out by the use of exorcism, a magical process using the Eucharist and other sacred objects and words to put the devil to flight; and the treatment often worked. Protestants, who believed that miracles had ceased with the apostles, had no such remedies to offer to the possessed.

Medical practitioners hastened to fill the void, for example in 1589 when the Throckmorton children were diagnosed by Dr Barrow of Cambridge University as bewitched, on the basis merely of a urine specimen. The children caused the executions of three members of a family as witches, before 'these abominable little girls,' as Dr Walker rightly calls them, decided that the game had gone on long enough. Belief in possession was closely linked to belief in witchcraft. In 1600 a number of English writers were casting serious doubts upon possession as anything more than a mixture of melancholy and ambition for notoriety by young girls, working upon a popular belief in the stereotype of the witch as 'an old weather-beaten crone, having her chin and her knees meeting for age . . . going mumbling about streets, one that hath forgotten her pater noster and hath yet a shrewd tongue in her head.'

But denial of the reality of possession led to denial of the reality of the devil, and denial of the reality of the devil was an encouragement to atheism, for 'if no devils no God.' Dr Walker suggests that women were particularly liable to possession since it was the only way they could draw attention to themselves, and get the chance to preach to a large audience. But in the long run the rejection of miracles by Protestants led to skepticism about possession; skepticism about possession led to skepticism about devils; skepticism about devils led to skepticism about witches; skepticism about witches led to a more rational religion; and a more rational religion opened the way to the development of early modern science. As John Aubrey remarked at the time, 'Printing and gunpowder have frightened away the fairies.'

3

Another way to approach the history of madness is to investigate the vast underworld of unlicensed practitioners – wise men or women, magicians, astrologers, amateur clergy, and downright quacks. Taken all together, it is clear that in the towns the total number of these practitioners per capita was very large indeed, even by modern standards, perhaps as high as one per 250 to 400 inhabitants. The quantity was therefore ample, whatever may be said about the quality of the treatments prescribed. In sixteenth- and seventeenth-century England, even country people had someone to turn to – more often than not an unlicensed prac- titioner – within five miles.[8] The problem for the historian is to find out about these practitioners and their patients, since the former did not normally keep records, and if they did they tended to be destroyed.

Every now and then, however, an inquiring scholar stumbles across some unknown and revealing cache of documents, and if he has the imgination to see the possibilities (and the stamina to carry out the enterprise) he stakes out his claim and starts digging. About ten years ago, Professor Michael MacDonald found one such gold mine – a series of detailed casebooks of 60,000 consultations over a period of thirty-seven years from 1597 to 1634, kept by the most popular practitioner of both physical and psychiatric healing we know of in early seventeenth-century England. What makes this study so important is not only the scale and detail of the document- ation but also the intellectually ambiguous position of the prac- titioner himself, the Reverend Richard Napier.[9]

Napier was teetering unsteadily on the edges between magic, astrology, alchemy, religion, and the contemporary medical phar- macopeia, and was uncertain in his own mind where truth and efficacy lay. He was a learned Anglican theologian – a Master of Arts of the University of Oxford, and the parson of a rural parish in Buckinghamshire. He was an astrologer who told horoscopes. He was an alchemist, a mathematician, and a conjurer of spirits, using an archangel as a medium. He was one of the last Renaissance magi, an expert in a whole series of now wholly discredited but at the time highly sophisticated and respected intellectual systems, Galenic, Rosicrucian, alchemical, Hermetic, cabalistic, Neopla- tonist, and also Christian. To some contemporaries he was suspect as a 'necromancer,' a 'conjurer,' whose activities were challenged by the 'piss-prophets,' the professional doctors with their urine specimens.

His eclectic notion of causation was soon to be dissolved in the light of the new Baconian scientific method, the new Newtonian scientific theory, and the new Latitudinarian and rationalist religious atmosphere of the post-Restoration period. The Reverend Richard Napier would not have fitted easily into the world of Samuel Pepys and King Charles II. He was a product of a specific period of history: one of home care rather than confinement, of amateurs rather than professionals, and of therapeutic eclecticism rather than pseudo-scientific medicine. He is important both as an exemplar of the intellectual climate of the early seventeenth century and also as a careful note-taker who opens a window for us on a hitherto unknown world, that of the humble, or not so humble, patients themselves, of whom this book deals only with those who were psychologically disturbed rather than physically ill. Napier's clients were drawn from those classes able to afford to pay his modest fees of six to eighteen pence per consultation – that is, the top three-quarters of the population, excluding the very poor. Half of them came from within ten miles, and almost all from Buckinghamshire or neighboring counties. They are thus a good sample of a rural population not too far from London.

The first surprise is how relatively few of Napier's patients were psychologically sick. Today it is reckoned that about one-third of all patients who consult some kind of medical practitioner are either overtly psychologically sick or suffer from some mental disorder that finds expression in physical symptoms. Only 5 percent of Napier's patients, however, have been classified by MacDonald as suffering from mental as distinct from bodily illness. This suggests that the frequency of psychological illness in pre-modern societies may have been relatively low compared with those of the contemporary, modernized world. Nearly two-thirds of the psychologically disturbed patients were women. This was explained by medical theory, which recognized that physical disorders connected with the uterus, which they mysteriously called the 'suffocation of the mother,' caused psychological symptoms.

Melancholia was the great affliction of the elite and intellectuals in the early seventeenth century, but Napier's casebooks shows that it was equally common lower down the social scale. Many women were plunged into depression by their oppressed lot as females in a patriarchal society, at the mercy of their parents or husbands. One seventh of both sexes were disturbed by the threat of economic disaster, especially ruin and imprisonment for debt, which was an ever-present menace to the small shopkeeper and trading classes, in an age in which interest rates were high, price fluctuations and environmental hazards great, and insurance nonexistent.

Napier's records shed a fitful light on problems of family history in the early modern period. A number of the mentally disturbed were troubled by the usual misfortunes of mankind, fear and jealousy, marital disputes, disappointment in love or marriage. Bereavement, however, did not loom large as a cause of anguish, presumably because it was so common. It was the cumulation of misfortunes that was too much. Take, for example, William Stoe, about whom Napier's note runs: 'Much grief from time to time. Had a wife long sick who died after much physic. Lost much cattle which died. Had the plague in his house: two children died [and he] himself had it. . . . Never well since.' The death of children disturbed a number of female patients, but it is noticeable that all the recorded cases are of children over the age of four. Infants died so frequently that few parents were seriously disturbed by their loss, but young children at their most bewitching age had a better expectation of life, and developed strong bonds of maternal affection. Napier thought it a sign of mental abnormality if a woman 'careth not for her children. Can take no joy of her children.' But then she was so depressed that she was 'tempted to hang herself.'

Frustrated love was a not uncommon cause of mental strain, even if few rejected lovers went as far as Thomas May: 'Grief taken for a wench he loves. He sayeth if he may not have her, he will hang himself.' A significant number of the lower middle classes certainly fell in love in the early seventeenth century. But the problem left unsolved by these case studies is whether they represent a social norm of courtship and marriage for love, or are merely a small minority of eccentrics who were bucking the system of arranged marriage for money. Did they themselves believe that to be lovesick was a form of madness? It is noticeable that about a sixth of those distressed by courtship or love were frustrated in their wishes by the adults, such as a young man who was prevented by his father from marrying his lover and 'fell distracted.' Did a minority of the young fall in love but the majority obediently follow the advice of their elders? We still do not know. More were disturbed by cruel or drunken or diseased or otherwise unsatisfactory husbands, but this may have had more to do with day-to-day survival than with love itself.

Those who believed themselves bewitched by a neighbor were twice the number of those disturbed by frustrated love or marital mistreatment. Indeed, a third of all Napier's mental patients thought they were bewitched, a statistic which throws a vivid light upon the degree of bitterness and malevolence prevalent in an early modern village. Professor MacDonald is one of those who believe that 'hatred, fear and violence were endemic in rural England before the Industrial Revolution' – a view with which I wholly concur. It was a world of suspicion, intrigue, petty jealousy, sudden brawls, and vindictive revenges for assumed slights or injuries.

When it comes to analyzing the recorded symptoms of mental disease, vast chasms of incomprehension begin to open up between ourselves and the inhabitants of the seventeenth century. Robert Burton, with his scholar's compendium of madness in *The Anatomy of Melancholy*, and Richard Napier with his practitioner's notes of actual cases, are equally difficult to decode. Napier recorded his clients mostly as 'troubled in mind,' 'melancholy,' 'mopish,' 'light-headed,' in that order, running down through 'senseless,' 'grieving,' 'weeping,' 'frantic,' 'distracted,' 'furious,' to 'solitary,' 'suspicious,' or 'wandering.'

It can be seen, however, that Napier's universe of the mad contained two basic types. There were those with uncontrollable violent energy or mental incoherence, who might be a danger to others or be incapable of caring for themselves. And there were those who suffered from physical torpor and emotional delusions and disorder – those he characterized as 'melancholy' or 'mopish.' Only a tiny handful of his patients were defined by him as 'mad' in the sense that they lacked all sense of the links between personal behavior and the norms of society. It was these, and these alone, whom the seventeenth century locked up, chained, and physically punished to try to bring them to their senses. Thus only twenty of the 2,039 mental patients who visited Napier had been either chained or beaten. It was persons like those who composed the twenty or thirty in Bedlam in 1700 – who were visited by some 96,000 tourists a year. To contemporaries, madmen were men reduced to the level of animals, since they had lost the power of reason and thus their soul.

Both the patients and their learned advisers like Napier held one thing in common with modern man. Both believed that there is no rigid distinction between mind and body, and that the two interact upon each other. Thus a near contemporary of Napier, a more colorful and eccentric character called Simon Forman, who also ran a large consulting practice, diagnosed a woman in 1597 in the following terms: 'Much subject to melancholy and full of fancies. . . . She hath not her courses, and the menstrual blood runneth in her head. And she thinks the devil doth tempt her to do evil to herself.'[10] Whether Forman himself believed in the devil is not clear, but the huge number of Napier's patients who thought themselves bewitched is proof of how widespread was a magical view of causation among the population at large. Napier's eclectic treatment, which included magical amulets, Christian prayers, astrological horoscopes, and Galenic medicines, shows his own uncertainty about where the truth lay.

In his concluding chapter, Professor MacDonald peers beyond into the late seventeenth and eighteenth centuries, the age of the monopoly of treatment by the medical profession, and of increasing care in private madhouses. He sees two interlocking trends at work. The first, stimulated by the religious excesses of the English revolution, was a rejection by the elite of religious enthusiasm, and by extension of all religio-magical explanations of how the world worked. The theory that the devil was at work in the possessed or in witches was no longer regarded as credible. After the experience of the Civil War, irrational systems of belief were seen as threats to the established social order, which the ruling classes were determined would never again be subject to such radical challenge. Religious zeal was now equated with 'enthusiasm,' and regarded as a form of madness, while demonic possession was treated as mere delusion or hypocrisy.[11] Suicide ceased to be regarded as a sin against the Holy Ghost, instigated by the Devil, and to be punished by burial in unconsecrated ground and seizure of property. Jurymen now declared that suicides were non compos mentis.[12] 'Reason' was now king, and since medicine was allegedly scientific, it was the medical profession that naturally took charge of the insane, and confined the worst cases, according to the prescribed rules of their profession.

Despite the total lack of any evidence of the practical effectiveness of curing the insane by purges, bleeding, emetics, and chains, professional medical theory fitted neatly into post-Restoration elite culture, compounded as it was of rational religion, neoclassicism, and natural philosophy. By now, Richard Napier and all his works were a hopeless anachronism, bypassed in the rush to supposed modernity.

Dr Walker and Professor MacDonald have rediscovered an important but lost piece of the intellectual and cultural history of the West, one which offers a plausible explanation of the triumph of professionalism in the late seventeenth and eighteenth centuries, and the modest spread of private madhouses. These two studies fit these changes into the changing cultural patterns of an increasingly secular and optimistic age. This makes much more sense than attributing them to an evil conspiracy of the early modern bureaucratic state and professional elites to enslave the multitude.

Among the poor, however, the old system of semimagical beliefs persisted. Bacon himself had expressed skepticism about the efficacy of medicine, 'a science which hath been more professed than laboured, and more laboured than advanced,' a point of view which opened the way to innovations in anatomy and chemistry. The poor, however, remained wholly skeptical, and a popular almanac for the year 1688 predicted that physicians 'would all be busy killing sick people.' As a result of this conservatism, there emerged in the late seventeenth century a major dichotomy between elite and popular culture with respect to the efficacy of doctors and the treatment of the insane.

Nor were the poor altogether wrong in their rejection of the new order of things. Private madhouses were indeed often a public scandal, and it was not until 1774 that Parliament passed the 'Madhouse Act' to set up a system of licensing and inspection. Foucault is almost certainly right to believe that confinement in the eighteenth century was a retrogressive step by which more and more of the mentally ill were subjected to the treatment hitherto restricted to the dangerous lunatics. Moreover it was now easy to abuse the services of private madhouses out of personal spite, and nothing was more common in the eighteenth century in a marital quarrel than for a husband to threaten to lock his wife up in a madhouse.

On the other hand, the great humanitarian movement of the late eighteenth century appeared to change all that; it provided the basis on which the state built larger and more elaborate asylums. The 'moral' methods of leniency and kindly treatment were first introduced by William Tuke at the York Retreat in the late eighteenth century, and as a result the Victorians were convinced that the bad old days of medical mistreatment of the insane in madhouses were over. They reflected complacently on how in the eighteenth century 'coersion for the outward man and rabid physicking the inward man were specifics for lunacy. Chains, straw, filthy solitude, darkness and starvation . . .; nothing was too wildly extravagant, nothing too monstrously cruel, to be prescribed by mad-doctors.' Nonmedical practitioners now tried to work on the mind rather than on the body, and by gentle rather than forceful methods – which was a direct challenge to the monopoly of treatment now claimed by the medical profession. The *locus classicus* of this great reform is the picture of Pinel striking the chains from the lunatics at Bicêtre in the middle of the Terror in Paris. Lunacy was now regarded as a curable disorder, given the right physical conditions and the right psychological treatment. Unfortunately, however, this optimism was unjustified, and the Victorian asylums slid imperceptibly back into holding-pens for persons patently incurable. Attention of the well-meaning was therefore focused on the humane treatment of the inmates, rather than upon their cure.

There followed the rise of psychiatry as a profession to deal with the sick mind, an endeavor that has had only very limited success. Today, we are back to where we were in the seventeenth and eighteenth centuries, restoring the mind by treating the body with chemicals instead of purges and emetics, and electric shocks instead of whips and chains. Thanks to drug therapy we are also emptying the asylums, and releasing their inmates once more into the streets, where they had been up to the eighteenth century, before the great confinement began.

Some aspects of the nineteenth-century phase of these developments in the treatment of madness are illustrated in a useful series of essays about particular institutions and personalities edited by Professor Scull.[13] Over the entire collection, however, looms the brooding figure of Professor Foucault, whose creative, if pessimistic, imagination still dominates the field. One very serious result of the current mood of denigration of doctors and scientists is a downplaying of the crucial distinction between truth and falsehood. Some treatments of the insane used today seem to work; almost all used in the seventeenth and eighteenth centuries did not. It is one thing to overthrow the simplistic Whig interpretation of history, but another to put in its place an equally simplistic pessimism that seems unable to distinguish antibiotics or insulin from charms, prayers, or whips. The strength of the work of Walker and MacDonald is the sophistication of their interpretations and the close attention they pay to the sources. In their hands insanity becomes a window through which to observe fundamental changes in the intellectual and social life of the West, as rationality slowly took the place of faith, magic, and superstition. Whether this was a change for the better or the worse is, unfortunately, still very much a subject of dispute.

PART II

An Exchange with Michel Foucault

1   Letter of Michel Foucault

(1) You ascribe to me the thesis that, as from 1650, a new principle emerged according to which 'madness is shameful' and 'the best treatment is forcible isolation from society under management by professionally trained doctors.' This view is precisely the opposite of that which I have set forth as the main argument of my book and enlarged upon through the full five chapters of the first part. Namely, that the procedures and institutions of confinement evolved throughout the whole of the sixteenth and seventeenth centuries, and did not begin in 1650; that they were essentially extramedical; that the results aimed at were only partially therapeutic. The dates, conditions and regulations of these nonmedical confinements are analyzed on pages 56–123 of my book; the limited space allotted to medical practice is analyzed on pages 124–77. Why do you not take into account these 120 pages which utterly refute the thesis you credit me with? And why do you ascribe to me an untenable thesis, never, to my knowledge, maintained by anyone and certainly not by me?

(2) You credit me with the idea that this was merely the result of 'a conspiracy of professionals to seize power for themselves to lock people up.' This is, once again, the exact opposite of what I have said. To begin with, I never had recourse to the notion of 'conspiracy' to analyze this historical phenomenon, or any other. Moreover – and this forms the subject matter of my book – I have attempted to show the length, the diversity and the complexity of the processes which finally, after a century and a half or more, led to the setting up of a specialized psychiatry and of a body of alienists who were able to claim the exercise of medical authority within the framework of the institutions of confinement. What I wrote is therefore not the description of a conspiracy; I never set down 1650 as the date of a medicalization; and I never considerd doctors to be the sole agents of such a medicalization. You are entirely mistaken on all three points. Why?

(3) You raise the objection that there is evidence of the confinement of madmen during the Middle Ages, as if I did not know or mention such facts. Now, I refer precisely to such accounts of confinement as can be found and I point out that there existed, in this respect, a very old tradition that assumed, in later years, another dimension; I mention a certain number of examples on pages 20–1 and 125–7; I also point out (pp. 161–2) that, throughout the Middle Ages, madmen were sometimes locked up and displayed like animals. Assuming that you have read my book, could you have copied what I said the better to reproach me with not having said it? Or should I believe that you have not read it?

(4) Yet another objection on your part: madmen were not 'isolated' since tourists went to see them where they were kept in chains.

Two comments:

(a) Do you really believe that locking people up and making an exhibition of them proves that they are not submitted to segregation? Just tell me, fettered and howling in a yard or writhing behind bars, subject to the jibes of gawking onlookers, you would not feel slightly isolated?

(b) Now, it so happens that I have mentioned, with appropriate references for both France and England, these visits to madmen made a show of in this way (pp. 161–3). I consider these facts as an aspect of the complex attitude toward madmen: they were hidden away and at the same time exposed; both attitudes are borne out by my references.

A little more attention would have prevented you both from over-hastily leveling at me an ill-founded reproach, and from supporting the said reproach with such a wondrous strange chain of reasoning.

(5) You argue that there are 'enormous differences in the degree and organization of incarceration from country to country,' England specializing in private institutions and France in state-supported ones. Now, on pages 67–74 and 483–96, I insist on the pronounced differences between a country like France and a country like England where religious organization, legislation, institutions and attitudes provide much more scope for private initiative; I point out, in particular, the long tradition with which Tuke is in keeping and which evolved throughout the eighteenth century. Nevertheless, you are wrong in thinking that everything in France was state-controlled.

(6) When you argue that the incarceration of the indigents occurred mainly in the seventeenth and eighteenth centuries, and that of the insane in the nineteenth century – it is true that I know not what to answer any more than I can guess to which passage of my book you refer, since it is entirely concerned with the slow evolution from one form of confinement, intended mainly for the poor, into a confinement involving medical treatment. You content yourself with repeating my general thesis while twisting it into an objection.

(7) Contrary to what you claim, I never compared 'the treatment of the mad' to that of lepers. I pointed out that a certain number of disused leprosaria were employed for other purposes and in particular [for] a confinement which was, in the seventeenth and eigheenth centuries, only very partially therapeutic.

(8) You reproach me with having placed under the same 'conceptual umbrella' the treatment of schoolchildren, the poor, criminals and the insane. And you emphasize the fact that the condition of the indigents has greatly improved in the last two hundred years and that children 'at least up to the 1960s' are increasingly better educated. Now,

(a) I never denied what you put forward in these last two propositions; I never even broached the subject.

(b) I did not, in my book on insanity, ever touch upon the

question of schoolchildren and their education. Can you quote the passage where I am supposed to have done so?

(c) Neither is the presence of criminals (often enjoying a special status) alongside the poor and the insane in the same places of isolation pure invention on my part. It is a fact borne out by documents I quote, more particularly on pages 56–123 and pages 414–21. Are you in a position to deny this fact and to back your denial with convincing documents?

My problem was to understand the logic of a practice which could concern madmen, criminals and the poor. But which in no way concerned children, or the nineteenth and the twentieth centuries, as you would have the reader believe.

(9) Finally, harking back once more to this thesis I never upheld (according to which doctors were 'behind the great confinement of the insane'), you argue that society was anxious to 'pay for incarceration' and that there was, in this respect, an important social demand on the part of the family circle and the entourage; in France, the *lettre de cachet*, which was one of the means of administrative incarceration, was more often than not demanded by the families, and confinement, even at Bicêtre, had to be paid for, in many cases. Besides you must not imagine that it was only the 'well-to-do families' you mention who made such requests and were willing to pay for the subsequent upkeep.

All in all: nine major errors, spread out over two small columns and a bit; that's a lot. I am not in the habit of replying to criticisms as I consider the reader quite capable of putting blatant adulterations right all by himself. However, the regard in which you are held prompts me to submit to you these few answers, which could be far more detailed. Indeed, they provide me with an opportunity to ask you a few questions.

(1) The 'fidelity' you show to my book surprises me. You could have quoted from sources other than those I refer to, mentioned different facts, opened new perspectives. You have done no such thing. Out of the nine reproaches you level at me, four (numbers 3, 4, 5, and 6) consist in repeating what I said while pretending I never said it; three others (1, 2, and 8) consist in turning round, word for word, what I said and ascribing to me the subsequent thesis which has become untenable. As for the ninth reproach, it combines, rhetorically, the two methods used throughout the development.

(2) I fear you have taken a considerable risk. Think of those who have read my book; think of those who will read it and want to collate it with your review of it. Is it of no importance to you that people may believe you to be 'unconcerned with historical detail of time and place, or with rigorous documentation'?

(3) Don't you agree that the probity essential to any scientific work should rule out such procedures? Don't you agree that only by respecting the work and the thought of an author can one prevent criticism from falling prey to the bad habits of hurried journalism?

(4) I first published my book more than twenty years ago. It was, at the time, a little 'solitary' in a field the historians had, perhaps, not fully explored. It is of course necessary that it should be revised, refined, corrected, enlarged upon. Fortunately, since then, the problem has developed, as you justly point out, into a topical question. However, doesn't the fact that, twenty years later, it gives rise to so many obvious adulterations on the part of someone who should have stayed cool-headed signify that the problems it has attempted to deal with are still charged with passion? All the more reason then for one to be, in discussion, as attentive and as scrupulous as possible. Even when madness is restricted to a subject matter, it has something of a blinding effect on the mind.

It is for this reason I suggest we resume, amicably and in all serenity, the debate on these problems, in as agreeable a manner as possible to both sides. But first, I would appreciate a paragraph-by-paragraph collation of what you have written about my book with what I have actually written. The reader is entitled to know where the truth lies.

Do let us try, together, to provide the means to this end.

Michel Foucault

Paris, France

2   Reply of Lawrence Stone

I am sorry that Professor Foucault is disturbed by my criticism of his ideas. Today he enjoys an almost unparalleled position of intellectual dominance over the interpretation of many key aspects of the evolution of Western civilization since the seventeenth century. We are none of us infallible, and Professor Foucault would surely concede that someone in his well-deserved position of pre-eminence must expect his ideas to be subjected to reasoned and temperate critical scrutiny. The historian faces several problems in dealing with the writings of Professor Foucault. One is that he is not at all easy to understand, because of what an unkind critic has called 'his obscure, arrogant, sensationalist, and opaque form of discourse, which by his own admission is a "labyrinth into which I can venture . . . in which I can lose myself." '[14]

A second problem is caused by the tenuous connection of structuralism to history. Even if they can be understood, the systematic structures of discourse that are alleged to underlie major intellectual changes cannot always be made to conform to the intractable realities of historical evolution as revealed in the records: the facts don't always support the theory. Thus Foucault may be superbly insightful in propounding certain brilliant conceptualizations about the eighteenth century, such as 'the great confinement,' or 'the desire to know' about sex, or 'the birth of the clinic,' or the transformation of grammar. But he may also have made mistakes, perhaps not fatal ones, in his chronology, typology, and causal explanations, and may be lacking hard data needed to prove his hypotheses.

For example, on the basis of a small number of quotations, he has postulated a major shift in consciousness in the eighteenth century, from believing that it was cruel to criminals to confine them with madmen to believing that it was cruel to madmen to confine them with criminals. To the historian, such a shift of *mentalité* would require a lot more proof than a bare handful of quotations and the fact that the two groups were indeed separated.[15]

A third problem is that Foucault's generalizations lend themselves so easily to adaptation and extension, and perhaps distortion, by others. Thus his remarks about 'the Doctor as an alienating figure' gave support and encouragement to others, like R. D. Laing in Britain and Thomas Szasz in America, to press their belief that institutional psychiatry is largely a conspiracy for power and prestige by a professional group with very dubious scientific credentials.[16] Foucault certainly never sank to such mundane sociological explanations, but his writings led logically to it. Similarly he has never mentioned schoolchildren among the confined; but a host of American and English critics of the school as a repressive institution have drawn that conclusion from his work. Lastly, the English version of *Madness and Civilization* is a translation of an abridged version made by the author, only one-third of the original 613 pages, which is possibly the cause of some confusion among English readers, and certainly for the sense that many of the ideas are poorly documented.

On reflection, I think I did Professor Foucault an injustice on two counts. First, I did not make sufficiently clear what everyone knows, namely that his true originality lies in his structuralist mode of explanation, concerned not with such mundane matters as how men pursue self-interest, or the way in which professional and bureaucratic groups develop independent interests of their own, or even what it is they think about their work. He is concerned with structural ways of *how* they think, their modes of discourse, which according to him determine everything else.

The second way in which I did Professor Foucault an injustice was that I failed to make it clear that I was dealing with a large international body of thought covering many disciplines, namely Foucaultism. Now it is probable that not all the ramifications of Foucaultism meet with the approval of the master himself, although he has so far done nothing, so far as I know, to repudiate them. It is his followers who have taken up his denial of humanitarian or Enlightenment motives behind the evolution of the moral care of the mad, or a medical approach to disease, to put forward a more sociological conspiracy theory about psychiatrists and doctors; and it is they who have taken up his concept of the great confinement in prisons, asylums, and hospitals, and added schools to the list.

One can, I think, debate the extent to which an original thinker is responsible for the ramifications, or extensions, or perversions, of his work by others. Can Marx be held responsible for Marxism? Can Foucault's pessimistic evaluation of lunatic asylums be held to have been a factor in the recent discharge of thousands of helpless psychiatric patients onto the pitiless streets of New York? Dr Gerald Weissmann of the New York University School of Medicine believes that these tragic cases are indeed a remote by-product of Foucault's negative evaluation of the philanthropic dream of Pinel, coupled with the fashionable claims by the English revisionist psychiatrist R. D. Laing that schizophrenia is not a disease.[17]

This leads directly to the central criticism I made of Professor Foucault's ideas, but one to which he has not responded. Although he claims moral neutrality, in practice he denies any philanthropic motive to the great reformers of mental treatment in the late nineteenth century. In *Madness and Civilization* he denigrates Tuke, since 'the religious and moral atmosphere was imposed from without, in such a way that madness was controlled, not cured' (p. 244) in a place 'where any manifestation of madness will be linked to punishment' (p. 246). The key principles of Tuke are defined as 'surveillance and judgment' (p. 251). Foucault firmly links the new reformed asylum to patriarchy and the bourgeois family.

Nor does Pinel fare any better at Foucault's hands: with him the asylum becomes 'an instrument of moral uniformity and of social denunciation' (p. 259). Foucault describes it as one of 'the paradoxes of Pinel's "philanthropic" and "liberating" enterprise, this conversion of medicine into justice, of therapeutics into repression' (p. 266). In consequence 'Madness will be punished in the asylum, even if it is innocent outside it' (p. 269). He writes that 'our philanthropy recognizes the signs of benevolence towards sickness where there is only a condemnation of idleness' (p. 46).

This stress on control, repression, and punishment has been combined by Foucault with emphasis on the growing power of 'the medical personage . . .' (p. 269) 'whose powers borrowed from science only their disguise, or at most their justification' (p. 271). 'In the patient's eyes, the doctor becomes a thaumaturge . . .' (p. 275). 'The doctor, as an alienating figure, remains the key to psychoanalysis' (p. 278). (Why alienating?) Foucault's final words on the late eighteenth-century transformation of the treatment of mental illness describe it as 'that gigantic moral imprisonment which we are in the habit of calling, doubtless by antiphrasis, the liberation of the insane by Pinel and Tuke' (p. 278). Small wonder that the sociologists of professionalization were stimulated by him to look for an explanation in a struggle for turf and dominance by doctors and psychiatrists.

Exactly the same pessimistic evaluation has been applied by Foucault to the concurrent evolution of clinical medicine, which he summarizes in the following way: 'The abyss beneath illness, which was the illness itself, has emerged into the light of language – the same light, no doubt, that illuminates the 120 *Journées de Sodome, Juliette*, and the *Désastres de Soya*.'[18] Here again we find a denial of the Enlightenment as an advance in human under-

standing and sensibility, and a causal linkage of it to the sexual
fantasies of domination, violation, and torture which obsessed the
mind of Sade. As for the charitable investment of money by the
rich in building hospitals for the poor, in *Birth of the Clinic*
Foucault ascribes this act to a self-interested desire to obtain
subjects for human medical experimentation: 'what is benevolence
towards the poor is transformed into knowledge that is applicable
to the rich . . .' (p. 84). 'The doctor's gaze is a very small saving
in the calculated exchanges of a liberal world' (p. 85). 'Like civilization, the hospital is an artificial locus in which the transplanted
disease runs the risk of losing its essential identity' (p. 17). Small
wonder that such language has led to a host of conspiracy theories
about both the medical profession and the rise of the hospital.

The main objection to this 'dominance and control' model of
human relationships is that is is based on an obscure structuralist
theory of discourse, which may or may not be well founded. It is
a model so all-embracing as to be virtually meaningless. It can
include anything from using forced labor in the Gulag Archipelago
to teaching children to brush their teeth. Since man is a social
animal, and since all of social life involves some form of influence,
molding, direction, or compulsion, the reduction of all social
relationships to issues of power renders it almost impossible to
make the fine intellectual, moral, and material distinctions necessary
for any serious evaluation of change in history.

For example, when does social control end and socialization
begin? One definition of the latter is 'a neutral concept concerned
with the objective needs of society to guide, restrain and control
the members so that they generally observe accepted conventions
in thought and behaviour.'[19] No society has ever existed, or can
exist, without socialization. Moreover, the iron law of oligarchy
usually causes attempts at some degree or other of the imposition,
if necessary by force, of the views of one group upon another. For
historians, it is precisely these fine distinctions which make one
society at one time different from another, but Foucault's blanket
structuralist affirmation of dominance and control severely limits
any discussion of such refinements.

The second weakness of Foucault's model is that it totally
neglects the near-certainty of serious differences in beliefs and aims
among the so-called controllers, as well as in the methods they use.
Third; it ignores the gap between intentions and results. As often

as not in history, the movers and shakers either fail in their objectives, or the consequences turn out very differently from what they
expected, due partly to the perverse recalcitrance of human nature
among the controlled. Fourth, the model reduces the actors in
history to two, the controllers and the controlled, ignoring the
pluralism extant in all social systems, and the wide variety of
influences of state, church, family, and peer groups, which are at
work to mold men's minds.

Fifth, Foucault's model assumes not only that all controllers seek
power for the same end, but also that all the controlled, given a
free choice, would reject the mold imposed upon them. The idea,
for example, that many of the poor might be positively anxious,
of their own free will, to adopt bourgeois values and behavior for
themselves and their children in order to get on in the world, or
the sick to be cured, or the mad to be treated and protected in
an asylum, is all but eliminated in Foucault's dominance model.
Curiously enough, this is where liberal historians link up with
Marxists, for the latter also dislike the control model since it appears
to be incompatible with their class-conflict concept of society.[20]

The 'dominance and control' model, therefore, tends to oversim-
plify the historical process, reduce society to two polarized groups,
distort the psychology and values of the controllers, make unwar-
ranted assumptions about their success in imposing their will,
underestimate the strength and independence of the culture of the
supposedly controlled, and eliminate any possibility that the
society, including the controlling elite, is pluralistic and divided in
its objectives.[21]

Finally, the Foucault model ignores the moral dilemmas of
society past and present. It is of no help to us in tackling the real
and difficult task of today, which is to decide which kinds of state
intervention in personal life are justified by the social benefits
accruing, and which are not. Foucault's model is useless in solving
the real dilemmas we face in dealing with such delicate moral issues
as the right of the individual to on-demand divorce, pornography,
abortion, a minimum standard of living, equal access to financially
limitless health care and to as many finite resources – whether oil
or rhinoceros horn – as he can pay for, and so on.

After this statement of retractions and general objections, let
me now turn briefly to the points of detail raised by Professor
Foucault.

1. (a) Madness as shameful and so to be hidden: 'the shameful promiscuity of madness' (*Madness and Civilization*, p. 225); '*L'internement cache la déraison et trahit la honte qu'elle suscite*' (*Folie*, pp. 162–3).

(b) Dating. 'the first moments of the "Confinement" . . ., that royal edict of April 27, 1656 that led to the creation of the *Hopital Général*' (*Madness and Civilization*, pp. 46–7); 'From the creation of the *Hopital Général* . . . until the end of the eighteenth century, the age of reason confined' (*Madness and Civilization*, p. 65); '*Le classicisme a inventé l'internement*' (*Folie*, p. 64); '. . . *aussi soudain que le grand Renfermement du XVII siècle* . . .' (*Folie*, p. 404).

There is one page of random accounts of confinement of the poor in sixteenth-century England, but little is drawn from it (*Folie*, p. 65).

2. 'A conspiracy of professionals.' This is admittedly not Professor Foucault's motive of change, but I have shown how his writings can lead, and have led, others to this conclusion.

3. Confinement of the mad in the Middle Ages: there is only one page (p. 10) about this in the English abridged edition, although more in the French. But I cannot see that even there it plays any part in Foucault's argument. I fail to understand how one can be 'hidden away and at the same time exposed.' To my mind this is an unintelligible contradiction in terms.

4. Differences between France and England: not discussed in the English edition, and only discussed in passing in the French on pp. 67–74; pp. 483–96 concern Tuke and Pinel. I can find no serious discussion of the proliferation in eighteenth-century England of private madhouses, as opposed to French state-supported ones (it is possible that I am defeated by the absence of indexes).

5. Exactly: but the evidence does not fully support the thesis, in my opinion.

6. Treatment of lepers and madmen: In *Madness and Civilization*, 'The leper was removed from the world, and from the community of the Church visible . . .' (p. 6). Then leprosy disappeared, and after an interval (filled in the French version [pp. 16–18] by the victims of veneral disease), the mad were placed in some of the old leprosaria. Here 'the formulas of exclusion would be repeated, strangely similar two or three centuries later. Poor vagabonds, criminals, and "deranged minds" would take the part played

by the leper' (p. 7). 'The asylum was substituted for the lazar house. . . . The old rites of excommunication were revived, but in the world of production and commerce' (p. 57).

7. Correct: the school as a place of confinement is part of Foucaultism, especially in America. Foucault has never, to my knowledge, mentioned schools as a part of the era of repression, but it is a typical, almost inevitable extension of his ideas.

8. We both agree that people – relatives or the parish – paid to have their mad relatives put away. In England in the eighteenth century this was the normal method of incarceration, very different from the Foucault model in which the doctor was the decision maker. The main motive was demonstrably shame.

In brief, I do not believe I have distorted Professor Foucault's thoughts in any way, except the two which I have freely admitted, and for which I apologize. He, however, has not directed himself to the central issue of my criticism, namely his pessimistic evaluation of Enlightenment thought, and the institutions and professions that grew out of it. It is his recurrent emphasis on control, domination, and punishment as the only mediating qualities possible in personal and social relationships that I find one-sided.

CHAPTER 16 · Homicide and violence

Historians are not yet agreed about the facts, causes, or consequences of changes in the level of violence in society from the
Middle Ages until the present. In both the lengthy introduction
and the lengthy conclusion of a recent book about the activities of
a gang of robbers in remote Westmorland in the late seventeenth
century, Dr Alan Macfarlane has advanced the thesis that by
present-day standards, and perhaps those of other countries at the
time, early modern England was an exceptionally peaceful and
violence-free society.[1] Those numerous scholars from Macaulay
onwards who have taken the contrary view, that the early modern
Englishman was far more violence-prone than those of today, have
been charged with making a wholly false dichotomy in English
history. There is therefore a clear division of opinion among
historians about an aspect of social life which profoundly affects
our vision of ourselves in relation to our past. Were our forefathers
in the medieval and early modern period very much more prone
to violence than ourselves, or were they not?

The first objection to Dr Macfarlane's data, of which his own
book is an example, is that a single village does not offer a population large enough to allow any meaningful statistical deductions
to be drawn from it about the one crime about which the evidence
is most reliable, namely homicide. Homicide rates are estimated as
so many per year per 100,000 population, which in England since
the thirteenth century has varied from twenty to one. In a large
pre-modern village of five hundred souls, one would therefore not
expect to find more than one homicide every ten to two hundred
years! Clearly nothing useful can therefore be derived from such
evidence as is available about homicide in one small English village
in the sixteenth and seventeenth centuries.[2] No population smaller
than that of a county or a substantial town is large enough to
produce meaningful results. Nor is anything gained by examining
how many people in the past went about with weapons, for the

simple reason that most homicides were committed with bare hands; or with a stick or club; or with a knife, which everyone, however poor, carried with him for cutting his food; or with a sword, which was carried by all gentlemen at all times as a badge of status. All these weapons involve face-to-face violence, which guns do not.

If we assume that the best-recorded crime of violence is homicide, and that homicide in the nature of things represents the most extreme example of violent assault in general, the most promising line of inquiry would seem to be a concerted effort to draw together the available data on homicide in England from the thirteenth to the twentieth century. This is precisely what has recently been done by Professor T. R. Gurr, in an intriguing article tucked away in a periodical which few historians are likely to read. Although he is studying homicide in the West, his historical data before the nineteenth century are drawn entirely from England.[3]

Gurr freely admits all the problems about the reliability and significance of crime statistics, with which we are now all too familiar from other sources. He also admits that the difficulties facing attempts to calculate rates of crime per capita per year in the remote past are compounded by uncertainties about the size of population at risk. On the other hand, he argues that homicide is the most difficult of crimes to conceal, and the most likely to be recorded. Between 1200 and 1400 there occurred important changes in the definitions of manslaughter and murder, but there is no evidence that they adversely affected records of death by violence, either in coroners' inquests or in trials at the assizes. Indeed, the progressive shift of the burden of prosecution from the relatives of the deceased to some public authority, and the nineteenth-century development of an organized police force, have tended to increase the reliability of the evidence by reducing to insignificance those acts of homicide which were concealed, compounded behind the scenes by money payments, or settled out of court by the violent code of the vendetta, as was so often the case in the Middle Ages.[4]

Three possible arguments have been put forward to suggest that the efficiency of record-keeping of homicides might have declined over time, but none of them are convincing.[5] The first is that in the later seventeenth and eighteenth centuries coroners acted arbitrarily and inefficiently. No doubt they did, but there is no evidence whatever that their actions were any more slipshod than those of their medieval predecessors. The statute of 1487 (3 Henry VII, cap. 1) complained that because of their inefficiency 'great boldness is given to slayers and murderers.' If it was enforced, the statute should have considerably improved the quality of reporting of homicides. Second, it is argued that in the late seventeenth and eighteenth centuries coroners' juries were more likely than before to return a suicide as accidental death, in order to relieve the family from economic destitution by the seizure of all its property. But this last is a hypothesis which is wholly unproven, and on the face of it unlikely. Juries were certainly more anxious to save the property of the family of a suicide, but the available evidence indicates that they achieved this end by eventually returning almost all cases of suicide as performed while *non compos mentis*, a verdict which would not alter the homicide statistics. Third, the decision by modern quantitative historians of crime to include or exclude infanticide will affect their statistics. But it would only alter the general trend if all those working in one period (say the sixteenth century) made one choice, and all those working in another (say the eighteenth century) made another. Of that there is not the slightest evidence. There is, however, evidence to suggest that in the late seventeenth century very weak indictments were being returned by the Grand Jury, which were not returned later. This would certainly lessen the apparent size of the decline, but not undermine it.[6]

The only other way in which homicide rates may have been artificially changed by factors not related to actual violence is as a result of an improvement in medical care, so that an increasing number of the wounded recovered. However, no one seriously suggests that medicine had much impact on death from gangrene or infected wounds before the discovery and acceptance of the importance of sterilization towards the end of the nineteenth century. This factor therefore can only affect the trend of the homicide graph long after the great decline had occurred.

Gurr also puts forward the argument that public tolerance of manslaughter had tended to decline in the eighteenth, nineteenth and twentieth centuries, due to a progressive 'sensitization to violence' which has slowly reduced the amount of physical force employed in English daily life. The reason for this growth in 'sensitization' is left obscure. Much of the physical violence in the early modern period seems to be associated with drunkenness, but there is no evidence that alcohol consumption per capita was declining (except for gin after it was heavily taxed) before the prohibition movement of the nineteenth century.

If there were such a growth of sensitization, whatever its cause, one would expect an increase in the number of recorded prosecutions for manslaughter over time rather than a decline, even if the real level of these crimes remained constant. Consequently, any upward trend in official data about homicide would be highly suspect. But, as Gurr rightly says, 'evidence for a long-term statistical decline in the incidence of assault has a *prima facie* plausibility, because it runs counter to increased public sensitization and official attention.' If evidence indicating such a decline is found, the odds are that it underestimates the true scale of the shift, since record-keeping has improved rather than decayed over the centuries.

A further argument about the relative reliability of homicide data is based on the theory of convergence. If different types of legal evidence all point to a similar trend, then the reality of that trend becomes more plausible. If, for example, coroners' rolls records of homicide and court records of private prosecutions for assault both move in roughly the same direction, they reinforce each other's credibility, since homicide is only an aggravated, and often accidental, type of assault. Moreover, if the apparent downward trend is sufficiently pronounced, the change is large enough to override all but the most extreme cases of uncertainty about the size of the population at risk or the comprehensiveness of the records.

The data for England between 1250 and 1800 are admittedly rather skimpy, with only some twenty-odd sets of evidence over five and a half centuries. Some are for individual towns over short periods, but some are for whole counties over two hundred years. Long-run nationwide statistics do not exist, and are never likely to be available, but what we have is now sufficient to make it possible to advance a plausible argument.

Taken together, these data reveal an unmistakable general trend (see Fig. 1). It looks as if the homicide rates in thirteenth-century England were about twice as high as those in the sixteenth and seventeenth centuries and that those of the sixteenth and early seventeenth centuries were some five times higher than those today. Gurr concludes that 'these early estimates of homicide rates . . .

Figure 1 Historical trends in violent crime in England

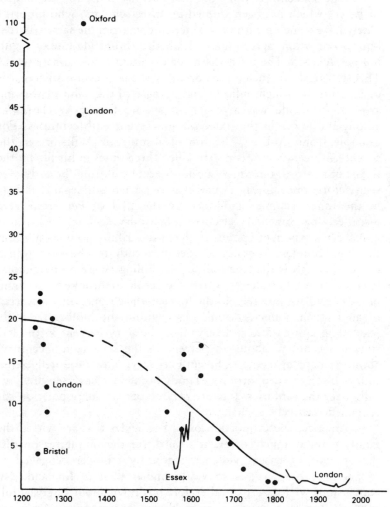

Note and source: T. R. Gurr, 'Historical Trends in Violent Crime: A Critical Review of the Evidence,' *Crime and Justice: An Annual Review of Research*, 3, (1981), p. 313, fig. 1: 'Indicators of Homicides per 1000,000 population in England, thirteenth to twentieth centuries. Each dot represents the estimated homicide rate for a city or county for periods ranging from several years to decades . . .'.

sketch a portrait of a society in which men [but rarely women] were easily provoked to violent anger, and were unrestrained in the brutality with which they attacked their opponents. Interpersonal violence was a recurring fact of rural and urban life.[7]

For the sixteenth century the best data are those for the county of Essex, which has been studied by three scholars, who unfortunately have come up with very different data from the same records, but two of whom agree on an Elizabethan homicide rate of 6.7 to 6.8 per 100,000. The third has made no attempt to estimate rates.[8] This statistical evidence is supported by the impressionistic records of individuals, which indicate that because of the habit of wearing swords, homicide was as common among the upper classes as among the lower in the sixteenth and seventeenth centuries. For example, John Aubrey, the son of a squire in Wiltshire in the seventeenth century, was nearly killed three times in his life by the thrust of a sword: once in a London street by a drunk he had never seen before; once during a quarrel among friends in legal chambers in the Inner Temple; and once by the Earl of Pembroke at a disorderly parliamentary election at Salisbury.[9]

Aubrey's experience points to the most striking peculiarity about the high homicide period of the thirteenth to the seventeenth century, which is that the bulk of the killings were by neighbors, friends, or total strangers, often the result of drunken bar-room brawls or village quarrels. In the fourteenth century, only 8 percent of all English homicides took place within the biological family (excluding apprentices and servants), about 15 percent in the late sixteenth century, about 20 percent in the seventeenth century, about 35 percent in the eighteenth century, and about 50 percent today. But if the proportion of family homicides has risen dramatically over the centuries, the rate per 100,000 of the population has remained relatively unchanged.[10]

In America, the proportion of all homicides that are within the family is today much lower, at a third, for the simple reason that the amount of casual violence there, by strangers engaged in mugging or burglary, is so vastly higher than in England. No conclusions whatsoever can therefore be drawn about English violence or domestic relations from these contemporary American statistics.[11]

There are so many possible factors in play here, however, that it is difficult to draw any useful conclusions about the nature of family relations from these data. It is certainly noticeable how large a proportion of victims within the family in the seventeenth century were children (and in the household were servants and apprentices) whereas today the victims of most family homicides are spouses or lovers. This suggests that family homicide due to casual brutality has declined, while family homicide due to sexual passion has increased. As for later developments, improved forensic science must have reduced the allegedly large number of undetected murders by poison of husbands by wives; on the other hand the rise in the ease of divorce must nowadays be splitting up many couples before tensions reach the homicide point. Thus the evidence about family homicide does not point clearly in any single direction, and certainly not to cast doubt on the growth of affective individualism in the family.[12]

If most early modern homicides were outside the family, this pattern is repeated in litigation, which also shows a very high level of personal animosity between non-family members. Thus in New England in the seventeenth century there were relatively few cases in the courts of conflict within a particular family, but 'an enormous quantity of actions between neighbors.' It is this extreme litigiousness that has caused historians like Professor John Demos to describe the seventeenth century village as characterized by 'an atmosphere of contention, of chronic and sometimes bitter enmity,' or Professor Michael MacDonald to declare that 'seventeenth century villages bore no relation to the peaceable kingdoms anxious urbanites imagine made up "the world we have lost" . . .; hatred, fear and violence were endemic in rural England before the Industrial Revolution.' Drs Wrightson and Levine concur that 'to imagine the tone of village life as an idyll of rustic harmony would be to err grievously. The village was riddled with petty conflicts.' A reviewer of Professor Demos's recent study of witchcraft in seventeenth-century New England, *Entertaining Satan*, was driven to observe that 'one emerges . . . sighing with relief that one did not have to live in these gossip-ridden, mean-spirited, endlessly litigious and generally rather nasty villages.'[13]

The only hard data in print about homicide during the late seventeenth and eighteenth centuries are for Surrey, Sussex, and Essex. In Surrey Professor Beattie found a homicide rate beginning at about six per 100,000 in the 1660s, falling to two in the 1720s, and then to under one after 1780. The fall in Sussex was also to a fifth of the earlier level. The Essex data of Dr Sharpe can be used to show the same high rate for the early seventeenth century, and a falling off thereafter. If we make a conservative estimate of the population of Essex at about 80,000 for the first half of the century and 90,000 for the second, this gives a homicide rate per 100,000 of 4.3 in the first half of the century but only 2.8 in the second, as compared with the nearly seven recorded for the late sixteenth.[14] This fall is shown in both the Beattie and the Sharpe data to have occurred between 1660 and 1780, and is the most dramatic between the fourteenth and the twentieth century. By the third quarter of the eighteenth century the convicted murder rate (while is by no means the same as the homicide rate) for London and Middlesex, that is for the whole of the metropolis north of the river, was already extremely low, a mere four a year on average. This supports the comments of contemporary foreign travelers that violent crime in England was by then also low.[15] Although assault indictments tend to come and go in waves, they do indeed show a generally downward trend similar to that for homicides. Thereafter the evidence is much firmer, and points unmistakably to a continued but slower fall in homicide per 100,000 throughout the eighteenth, nineteenth, and early twentieth centuries.

If this data on homicide is at all reliable, as it seems to be, its assembly by Professor Gurr in the graph (Fig. 1) shows fairly conclusively that from the fourteenth to the twentieth century the trend in England has been unmistakably downward. Why? There are two possible explanations, one cultural and one social, the two being supportive of one another rather than alternatives. Professor Gurr suggests that the prime cause was a complex cultural shift, what Norbert Elias has called 'the civilizing process' slowly seeping down from the upper classes to the violence-prone poor. Thus Yves Castan has shown with great brilliance the operation of the concept of '*honnêteté*' in the eighteenth century, how the stress on civility, politeness, and propriety spread down from intellectual aristocratic salons to wider sectors of society.[16] The taming of upper-class violence by the code of the duel after the late sixteenth century was followed by the transformation of manners in the late seventeenth century, and then by the humanitarian ideology of the Enlightenment. The theory is that, first launched by intellectuals, lawyers, nobles, and bourgeois, these new attitudes slowly penetrated all sectors of society, with the result that interpersonal physical violence has been on the decline in all areas of life. Some scrappy evidence about the prevalence of wife-beating and better data about child-abuse in working-class families in the nineteenth century tend to support this theory of a slow downward drift of less violent cultural norms, assuming that one can be sure that more civilized domestic habits by now prevailed in genteel and bourgeois circles.[17]

Even when dealing with the last half of the nineteenth century, after the introduction of the police force, the closest student of the subject, V. A. C. Gatrell, has concluded that when it comes to crimes of violence 'we are forced . . . to explain the decline in terms of heavy generalizations about the "civilizing" effects of religion, education and environmental reform.'[18] Structural/functional explanations of historical change today need to be supplemented and enriched by cultural and intellectual factors, and any historian who continues to ignore the latter is falling behind modern scholarship.

The most convincing evidence to demonstrate a major shift of societal values from feudal honor to bourgeois money, and so from violence to litigation, is the change after 1680 in the response of an upper- or middle-class husband to his wife's adultery. Before, he was likely to assault the seducer or challenge him to a duel. After 1680 he sued the seducer in the civil courts for trespass upon his property, and claimed – and received – substantial pecuniary damages.[19] Price-tags had now been set on masculine honor and female shame. This commercialization of values was accompanied by a slow revulsion of public opinion against overt physical cruelty. Evidence for this comes from the cessation of the burning alive of heretics, witches, and women who poisoned their husbands; the decline of highway robbery, brutal violence in the streets of London, and the murder by mobs of unpopular individuals; the rising hostility to such things as cruelty to animals, the slave trade, public executions and whippings; and the rise of affective individualism in the family and of a hardening of judicial attitudes to marital cruelty and child-abuse.[20] Professor Beattie has also detected this very striking decline in the practice and acceptance of cruelty and violence in public and private life in the eighteenth century, a development he also ascribes to an underlying shift of manners and *mentalité*. Thus everything points to a transformation of attitudes to cruelty and violence during the eighteenth century, the causes of which must lie partly in social and economic changes and partly in changes of public attitudes inspired by ideas taken from a wide variety of cultural sources, including the Enlightenment, Romanticism, and Evangelical religion. Writing in the early nineteenth century, that shrewd and knowledgeable observer Francis Place had no doubts about the direction and reality of the trend in the previous half century: 'the progress made in refinment of manners and morals. . . . We are a much better people than we were then, better instructed, more sincere and kind-hearted, less gross and brutal, and have fewer of the concomitant vices of a less civilized state.'[21]

A similar but more sociologically based explanation for the decline of crimes of violence over the past five centuries would link it to a shift from a feudal to a bourgeois society. In the former, honor and status are the most prized attributes, and crimes are therefore directed against the person; in the latter, money and market relationships form the basis of social organization, and crimes are therefore directed against property: hence the progressive shift over the centuries from the one to the other as society modernizes. This plausible hypothesis has been used in France to explain the different rates of violence in the more advanced north and the more backward south of the St Malo–Geneva line.[22] As a very broad generalization this is probably correct, but it has been found that regional differences make the story far more complicated than such a simple model would predict. Local cultural, social, political, and legal factors need to be taken into account if a fully plausible explanation is to be developed which is consistent with the evidence.

One explanation which will not hold, however, is that which would ascribe the decline to 'the outcome, among other things, of English society being more policed than before.'[23] The fact that the great decline of homicide and violence occurred between 1660 and 1800, and so occurred before the introduction of a police force, and that it was accompanied by so wide a variety of humanitarian movements, renders this explanation wholly unacceptable.

There are indications that the generally downward trend of homicide rates from the thirteenth century onward may have been interrupted at least twice. It looks as if there may have been a sudden upswing of urban violence in the early fourteenth century just before the Black Death.[24] As a result, the highest homicide rate so far recorded anywhere in the West at any period appears to be that of Oxford at that time (not entirely caused by rowdy undergraduates). We do not know the cause of this first wave, but it seems likely that it was associated with the stresses of overpopulation.

The evidence for Essex suggests that there may have been a second wave of violent crime, including homicide, in Elizabethan and Jacobean England. This may perhaps most plausibly be explained by growing conflict and anomie in both villages and towns, exemplified in a variety of significant ways. For one thing litigation was exploding, presumably as conflict between neighbors increased and as traditional means of arbitration collapsed. Cases brought before the courts all increased at this period far faster than the demographic growth. Taking the village of Terling in Essex, the amount of interpersonal litigation in local courts, both secular and ecclesiastical, shows 'a dramatic upsurge' in the late sixteenth and early seventeenth centuries, followed by a decline. 'Both the numbers of cases and the numbers of persons prosecuted rose much faster than did the population of the village. Something was happening.'[25] That 'something' was affecting not merely this single village but the society as a whole, as is shown by evidence of criminal prosecutions for all the counties in the Home Circuit.[26] Other indicators of social disintegration and anomie in late sixteenth- and early seventeenth-century England are a high bastardy rate;[27] a high level of witchcraft accusations between villagers;[28] a staggeringly high rate of denunciations of neighbors for sexual deviance;[29] and a high rate of suits for slander of all kinds by neighbors (mostly women).[30] What all this suggests is that between 1560 and 1620 there was an abrupt rise in a wide variety of indicators of social anomie, and of a breakdown of consensual community methods of dealing with conflict. Both ethical and economic fissures were opening up within the village and exacerbating conflict between neighbors. Until checked by the vigorous enforcement of Puritan ideology and morals and by the institution of a regular poor-relief system in the seventeenth century, there were all the signs of a socio-cultural crisis in the village in the late sixteenth and early seventeenth centuries.[31]

This crisis was probably brought on by a combination of socially unmanageable demographic growth, a collapse of cultural norms and controls in the wake of the Reformation, the spread of a profit-oriented ideology, and a growing economic fissure between rich and poor. Professor Gurr has tentatively ascribed one of the causes of these crime waves partly to the temporarily brutalizing effects of war, especially the sudden demobilization of large numbers of penniless and unemployed soldiers, a fact that Professor Hay has recently and most convincingly shown to govern indictments for theft in eighteenth-century England.[32] Partly also, these crime waves may be caused by a rise, due to sudden demographic growth, in the proportion of the population who are males in the violence-prone age range of fifteen to twenty-five. This may, for example, partly explain the 1560–1640 rise in England generally, as well as the upsurge of indictments for crimes of violence in the great conurbation of London in the decades after 1690.[33] It may also help to explain the rise of violent crime all over the West in the 1960s and 1970s. It has to be admitted, however, that no one really knows why, for example, the homicide rate in America is not only vastly higher than in other Western countries, but also has risen by an alarming 60 percent since 1960 and is now leveling off.[34]

The most interesting and difficult question of all is the social and psychological meaning of a decline in the homicide rate to a fifth of its former level between the late sixteenth century and the end of the eighteenth. What difference did this fall make to contemporary perceptions about the quality of life? Fear of violence did not predominate in sixteenth- and early seventeenth-century Puritan sermon literature,[35] but Puritan preachers then, like evangelical preachers today, were primarily concerned with more interesting personal sins – lust, greed, and pride. One does not hear much from Billy Graham today about crime in the streets. But as Cockburn has observed, Shakespeare's 'degree' speech in *Troilus and Cressida* 'stands in eloquent testimony to an entire generation of *bons bourgeois* haunted by the spectre of crime and violent disorder.' The huge literature on the violent and thievish ways of the Elizabethan underworld of gangs of sturdy beggars reflects the same fears, and in 1575 the Privy Council responded to these fears by trying to ban the use of handguns in the committing of crime.[36] It is also noteworthy that in the sixteenth century the lay and clerical governing elite were seriously concerned about aristocratic gang violence, so much so that they had brought it more or less under control by 1600.[37]

In the early eighteenth century there was a new wave of fear of violent crime, reflected in the (largely unused) draconian extensions of the death penalty, including the Black Act of 1723. Daniel Defoe, Bernard de Mandeville, Henry Fielding, and Sir John Fielding expressed their anxiety about an increase of riot, armed burglary, street mugging, and highway robbery. In London in the early eighteenth century, people were said to be afraid to go out after dark for fear of being 'blinded, knocked down, cut or stabbed.' In 1749 Horace Walpole observed that 'one is forced to travel, even at noon, as if one were going to battle.' These perceptions certainly do not match the rapid decline in homicide, although they do appear to reflect the reality of a temporary rise in violent crimes against property and person in London in the 1720s to 1740s, which declined again in the latter half of the century.[38]

If one asks what difference a very high homicide rate made to contemporary perceptions of the quality of life in the early modern period, the answer is much more problematic. At that period, death was a constant and overt part of life, striking at all ages and not hidden away as it is today. Nor should we forget how easily we have accustomed ourselves to a level of carnage on the roads that matches or surpasses the high homicide rates of the past. Thus the rate of traffic deaths in Houston, the highest in America, is twenty per 100,000, while the second highest is in Los Angeles at fourteen.[39] But there is no sign whatever that these ominous statistics have had the slightest effect on slowing down the massive immigration into those two cities.

The argument that life was not very pleasant in English villages between about 1560 and 1660 rests largely on other criteria than that of the rate of homicide. Obviously all social groups, from the family to the village to the nation, operate simultaneously at the two levels of consensus and conflict, and which of the two is taken to be predominant is in the eye of the observer. It is also true that legal records reveal societies at their atypical worst. But it is difficult to read the records of civil and ecclesiastical litigation in that period without coming away depressed by the exceptionally oppressive atmosphere of neighborly hostility and espionage. It seems as if everyone was constantly spying on everybody else, and backbiting, slander, defamation and delation of neighbors to the authorities appear to have been favorite occupations at that time.

Finally, the universal practice up to the 1680s of close neighborly surveillance, gossip, mediation, and warning, was a powerful instrument for social control and the preservation of social order. The system applied enormous pressure upon sexual and other deviants to make them conform to village norms, under the threat of obtaining a bad reputation.[40] Those convicted of petty larceny at the assizes were shamed by a public whipping through the streets. Others reported to the ecclesiastical authorities had to endure the shame punishment of public penance in church on a Sunday, standing before the congregation barefoot, clad only in a white sheet, and holding a candle. These shame punishments sometimes drove those condemned to them to contemplate flight or suicide in order to avoid such humiliation.[41] On the other hand much of this gossip had a malicious or jealous tinge to it, was often fueled by personal animosities, and was often false, as frequent defamation suits in the late sixteenth and early seventeenth centuries suggest. Moreover, a good reputation tended to be associated with the 'better sort' in the village, those with greater social status and economic resources, so that the whole system of delation and gossip was geared to the maintenance of the existing hierarchy. Delinquents of good reputation from the better sort tended to be protected by their status from criticism and delation by the 'poorer sort.' A good reputation was often an effective defense against an accusation, just as a bad reputation tended to be accepted as evidence of guilt. Amidst the rising tide of defamation litigation, the prominence of evidence for these hostile attitudes points to an especially fragmented quality about village life from about 1560 to 1660. Sharpe and Macfarlane seem to be alone in their roseate view of social relations at that time.[42] To say this is not to subscribe to any crude *Gemeinschaft/Gesellschaft* dichotomy, for English villagers appear to have become less quarrelsome again in the eighteenth century, or at least they sued one another a great deal less frequently.

The quality of family life at that time is also only a minor part of the 'pessimist' argument. There is no doubt that my earlier assessment of family relationships in the pre-1660 period was excessively over-schematized, based on far too little data. Further research in ecclesiastical court records also shows that the values and attitudes of Elizabethans were very unlike our own, and also significantly different from those of the eighteenth century. The new evidence, and the finding that nearly half the victims of domestic homicide in the seventeenth century were either children or stepchildren,[43] do not support the conclusion that 'normal family relationships in the past were . . . basically similar to those current in twentieth-century England.' As anthropologists are never tired of telling us, other people are indeed other.

Perceptions of a high homicide rate thus play only a small part in the 'pessimist' argument, although its reality should be a sobering thought for the 'optimists.' It is right to suggest that societies often do not place all that much stress upon this matter, even if they are aware of it. But if the homicide rate bears some relation to the level of violence in society at large, then it is an indicator of something to which people are certainly sensitive. Whether or not there is a direct correlation between movement in the homicide rate and the reality and perceptions of violent crime seems to depend on the circumstances. Thus in early eighteenth-century England the long-term homicide rate seems to have been dropping fast, just at a time when the short-term level of violent robbery and burglary in London was rising. Similarly today Englishmen living in cities are worried about the evident rise in street violence and burglary, although there has been no shift in the very low homicide rate. On the other hand Americans today are very frightened of the rising tide of violent urban crime, and talk about it much as did Londoners in the early eighteenth century. In this case the fear correlates with a dramatic rise of homicides, for example in New York City from four per 100,000 population in 1901 to twenty-seven per 100,000 in 1981.[44]

One has to conclude, therefore, that under different conditions, changes in the actual levels and the perceptions of violence some-times are, and sometimes are not, related to changes in homicide rates. One important difference between England and America today is that the English are a generally unarmed population, whereas very many Americans are armed with handguns. As a result, the homicide rate in America is vastly higher than that in England, and the proportion of homicides carried out by strangers in the course of crime or a dispute, rather than as a result of domestic family quarrels, is also vastly higher. Another difference is that in America there is a large underclass, defined by race,

deprived of family or community socialization, and without hope
of escape from indigence and unemployment because of drug abuse
and lack of education. A disproportionate number of both homicides and violence are committed by young males from this underclass. Consequently there is not necessarily a direct or simple
correlation between changing long-term homicide rates – however
dramatic – and the changing short-term perceptions of violence
expressed at different times by contemporaries.[45] But it would be
a serious mistake to underestimate the significance in the long run
of the massive decline in homicide rates over time in its effect on
the quality of life, and on the levels not only of real but also of
perceived violence.

Professor Gurr's paper, and my own comments on and additions
to it, are obviously highly speculative in their causal models, but
it is hard to see how it is possible to challenge the weight of
evidence for a great secular decline of homicide, the most serious
of all crimes of violence, which occurred in England over five
centuries, but was especially rapid between about 1660 and 1800.
What is now needed is an intensive search for more data, on a
county-wide basis not village by village, and more sophisticated
testing of causal correlations. It already seems clear, however, that
medieval English society was twice as violence-prone as early
modern English society, and early modern English society at least
five times as violence-prone as nineteenth-century English society.
It also seems clear that in pre-modern times most of this violence
took place outside the family, whereas today it occurs within it.
The notion that there was once upon a time a peace-loving, conflict-
free, Golden Age of the village, whether located in the Middle
Ages or the early modern period, is shown to be a myth. It is one
whose unexpected resurrection in the late twentieth century owes
more to nostalgic romantics yearning for 'the world we have lost,'
or to social scientists with polemical axes to grind about the moral
superiority of the English since the thirteenth century, than it does
to historical reality. All the evidence accumulated by historians
argues against it. We are today infinitely more destructive in war
than our ancestors, but in our daily lives the English at least are
also, for some reason, far less prone to casual violence. The social
and psychological meaning of such statistical facts, however,
remains open to argument and interpretation.

CHAPTER 17 · Children and the family

Although three-quarters of a century have passed since Freud first drew attention to the crucial effect of childhood events in determining adult character and behavior patterns, it was not until the 1950s that there appeared the first general history of childhood in the West. Of the four significant studies of this phenomenon, all have been written by non-historians, persons who, with respect to the profession, are marginal men.

In 1955 J. H. van den Berg, a Dutch psychologist, published *Metabletica, of Leer der veranderingen (The Changing Nature of Man)*, a bold, overarching, psychohistorical study of parental relations to children, based mainly on philosophical sources like Rousseau.[1] In 1960 Philippe Ariès, a French director of publications at the Institute for Applied Research for Tropical and Subtropical Fruits, published his now famous *Centuries of Childhood*.[2] In 1970 David Hunt, an American historian who has also worked as a psychologist with disturbed children, reinterpreted some of Ariès's French seventeenth-century material in *Parents and Children in History*, using a modified Eriksonian model of ego-development.[3] And in 1974 Lloyd deMause, an American academic dropout, a successful businessman and self-taught psychohistorian, produced a collective volume, *The History of Childhood*, the key essay in which was his own lengthy general survey of 'The Evolution of Childhood' ranging from the Greeks and Romans to the present day.[4]

The first problem in studying the history of childhood is how to choose the appropriate psychological model. Nothing in the historical record disproves Freud's theory about how at different stages of infantile development different erogenous zones become the foci of sexual stimulation, thus providing a logical explanation of the later relationship between oral, anal, and genital pleasure. Nor does the historical record do anything to belittle the importance of sublimation, or of the unconscious operating with a secret dynamic of its own. What it does do, however, is to cast very great doubt upon the assumption that the particular kinds of infantile traumas upon which Freud laid so much stress have been suffered by the whole of the human race at all times and in all places. It is now fairly clear that four of the main traumas Freud looked for and found among his patients, and therefore assumed to be universal, are dependent on particular experiences which did not happen to the vast majority of people in most of the recorded past, but which were peculiar to middle-class urban culture of late Victorian Europe. Provided that it was carried out slowly, as it apparently was in many cases, the oral trauma of weaning can hardly have been a serious one when it occurred as late as fifteen to eighteen months after birth. The anal trauma of toilet training is unlikely to have existed in a population which lived amid its own excrement, which hardly ever washed, and whose women and children wore no underpants.

The only detailed historical example of toilet training in the past that we have is, unfortunately, that of a less than typical person, a future king, the young Louis XIII in the early years of the seventeenth century. His training apparently did not begin until he was sixteen months or so, and was not internalized before about three years. He, at any rate, cannot have been traumatized by pressure to control his sphincters at an early age. We just do not know about how other children were toilet trained, but there is the strong negative evidence that contemporary child-rearing manuals do not even discuss the matter.

Although children in the past, as we shall see, had to endure far worse things, the passage through the oral and anal stages of childhood, in the purely technical sense, does not seem to have been particularly traumatic. As for the genital stage, the one example we have – again that of Louis XIII – suggests that no one was bothered by infantile and childhood sexual autoeroticism, sexual display, or sexual curiosity. Louis could get courtiers to kiss his penis, and was allowed to poke his little fist up the vaginas of several ladies-in-waiting. We also know that most families slept in one room, while even if they did not, houses were poorly constructed with thin board partitions through which it was easy to see or hear – as Fanny Hill soon found out. Consequently, from a very early age most children must have witnessed their parents and others – to say nothing of animals – engaged in sexual intercourse.

There is also the negative evidence that childhood and adolescent masturbation was not regarded as a mortal sin in the eighteenth-century Catholic confession manuals (although it was in the Middle Ages), and that although the paranoid drives to suppress all hints of autoeroticism began in 1710, it did not catch on before the early nineteenth century. Finally, we know that half of all children would have lost one parent before completing adolescence, and that in England a majority of them left home anyway between the ages of seven and fourteen, to act as servants in other people's houses, to serve apprenticeships, or to go to boarding school. Under such circumstances the conflict of wills between parents and their adolescent children, which rips apart so many modern homes today, can have had little opportunity to develop. The identity crisis of puberty was normally passed away from home.

It is now possible to provide alternatives to these historically inappropriate traumas advanced by Freud as self-sufficient explanations of adult personality problems. As David Riesman has put it,

> There has been a tendency in current social research, influenced as it is by psychoanalysis, to over-emphasize and overgeneralize the importance of very early childhood in character formation. Even within this early period, an almost technological attention has sometimes been focused on what might be called the tricks of the child-rearing trade: feeding and toilet training schedules.

This 'assumes that once the child has reached, say, the weaning stage, its character structure is so formed that, barring intensive psychiatric intervention, not much that happens afterward will do more than bring out tendencies already set.'[5]

No one doubts that child-rearing practices affect the adult personality, but acceptance of the theories of more recent ego-psychologists like Erikson and Hartmann opens up a new range of possibilities for the historian.[6] These theories involve hypotheses about the continued plasticity of the ego far into adulthood as it responds, through a series of crises, to the twin challenges of maturation and the influences of the family, the culture, and the environment. Not only do these theories have a strong ring of truth about them in the light of common experience, but they have the enormous advantage to the historian that they admit ego-development into periods of the life cycle when historical data become more readily available.

Second, since these developmental theories admit the influence of the social and cultural environment in affecting the nature, timing, and resolution of the recurring crises, they allow the historian to view the problem of ego-development in a broad historical frame. Clear evidence of distinctive features of national character, and fundamental shifts in character over time, for example from the other-directed to the inner-directed personality, can be explained in broader terms than those internal to the family itself.

This does not mean, however, that childhood experience in the past was without its effects on the adult personality. On the contrary, the experiences of the average child were so damaging that I believe that a large number of adults, at any rate of the gentry class in the period with which I am most familiar, namely, the sixteenth and seventeenth centuries, were emotionally stunted and found it extremely dificult to establish warm personal relationships with other people.

This was probably caused by four factors. The first was the frequency with which infants at that period were deprived of a single mothering and nurturing figure to whom they could relate during the first three or four years of life. Upper-class babies were mostly taken from their real mothers and put out to wet-nurse. These nurses were often cruel or neglectful, and they often ran out of milk, as a result of which the baby had to be passed from nipple to nipple, from one unloving mother-substitute to another. Even if it stayed with one nurse, to whom it became attached, the weaning process at about eighteen months inflicted the terrible psychological trauma of final separation from the substitute mother-figure and return to the alien world of the natural mother. This kind of experience is known to be psychologically and even physically damaging, leading to 'deprivation dwarfism' and emotional atrophy in later life.

The second factor was the very high death rate. The constant threat and reality of the sudden loss of a parent, nurse, brother, sister, or friend soon taught the child to be wary of sinking too much emotional capital in any human being. Third, the practice of tight swaddling in the first months or even year of life is believed to isolate the infant from its surroundings and to give it a sense of both frustrated rage and yet helpless acceptance of the cruelty and duplicity of the world. Thus there could be, and often was, a combination of sensory deprivation, motor deprivation, and emotional deprivation – to say nothing of oral deprivation – in the first critical months of life, of which the consequences upon the adult personality are now known to be very serious and long-lasting in reducing the capacity for warm social relationships.

Finally, there was the deliberate breaking of the young child's will, first by the harshest physical beating and later by overwhelming psychological pressures, which were thought to be the key to successful child-rearing in the sixteenth and seventeenth centuries. These four factors all contributed to a 'psychic numbing' which created an adult world of emotional cripples, whose primary responses to others were at best a calculating indifference and at worst a mixture of suspicion and hostility, tyranny and submission, alienation and rage.

Given the validity of 'psycho-history' as a legitimate enterprise, which is the most profitable field in which this research can be pursued? In my opinion, it will not be in the application of this or that psychological theory to the analysis of some particular person in history – Luther or Leonardo da Vinci or Woodrow Wilson or Hitler or Gandhi. What can more fruitfully be done is to study changes in family patterns and structures of specific classes or status groups in particular places. These changes will include relations of the nuclear core to the kin and the community, and economic and social power and affective relations between both husbands and wives and parents and children.

In that sense van den Berg, Ariès, and deMause are pursuing a far more promising line of historical inquiry than those who have tried to use psychology to interpret the behavior of individual figures in the past. I just do not think that such things as the extermination of six million Jews can be explained by the alleged fact that Hitler's mother was killed by treatment given her by a Jewish doctor in an attempt to cure her cancer of the breast; or that Luther's defiance of the Roman church can be explained by the brutal way he was treated by his father or by his chronic constipation.

These things may perhaps be necessary causes, but they certainly are not sufficient, and the result of such work to date has been disappointing, partly because of the flimsiness of the evidence of childhood experience, partly because of the speculative nature of the causal links with adult behavior, partly because of the neglect of the influence of the great processes of historical change in religion, economics, politics, society, and so on. As Malinowski pointed out in 1927, 'Man disposes of a body of material possessions, lives within a type of social organization, communicates by language, and is moved by systems of spiritual values.'[7] Any explanation of his history which ignores these cultural facts is not likely to be very convincing.

The first general model of childhood development in the West was that of Philippe Ariès. It is a pessimistic one of degeneration from an era of freedom and sociability to an era of oppression and isolation. According to him the Middle Ages and the sixteenth century were a period of happy social polymorphism, in which there were no divisions of ranks or ages, no separation of the child from the adult, no privacy, no external pressures from the state or the needs of an industrial economy, no internalized work ethic. Children and adults mixed together easily and naturally, wearing the same clothes, playing the same games, and working together on the same jobs. They also shared from the beginning a common knowledge of both sex and death. This easy egalitarian familiarity was one in which child abuse could not occur. It all sounds too good to be true – as indeed it is.

In the seventeenth century, as a result of the spread of new kinds of Christianity into both Protestant and Catholic regions, a new attitude toward children developed, an event he describes as 'the discovery of childhood.' This was not the work of Renaissance humanists but of seventeenth-century clergy. There was a rising concern for the child, which took two forms. First, there was a tightening of family bonds, along with the isolation of the family from external influences and a growing concern by the parents for their children; and second, there was a growing fear of the inherent corruptibility of the child by sin, leading to severity toward him in the home and to his isolation in schools regimented by age groups and disciplined to suppress all signs of moral backsliding. Medieval sociability was replaced not by Enlightenment individualism but by the isolated child-centered family and by the school, in both of which the prime concern was the taming of the will.

The rise of the repressive boarding school is the significant feature of this development, involving as it did a progressive extension of the period of childhood into adolescence and even beyond: 'The central event is quite obvious: the extension of school education.'

This transformation of attitudes toward childhood preceded demographic change, and indeed became itself the cause of demographic change when in the late eighteenth and nineteenth centuries it inspired a deliberate policy of contraception.

Ariès's book has had a dazzling success and has been the *primum mobile* of Western family history in the last two decades. As a pioneer work, erudite, imaginative, and inventive, it deserves all the praise and attention it has received. It is the kind of pathbreaking book no traditional historian could have written, and without it our culture would be the poorer. But for all its seminal brilliance, there remain unanswered certain basic questions. Is its methodology sound? Are its data reliable? Is its causal hypothesis valid? Are the alleged facts and alleged consequences true? In short, is the model correct, and if so, for what areas and for what classes?

In the first place, Ariès omits to point out the undeniable fact that between the Middle Ages and the nineteenth century the institution of the family lost many of its older functions to a series of impersonal institutions, such as poorhouses for the indigent, alms houses for the old, hospitals for the sick, schools for the children, banks for credit, and insurance companies for protection against catastrophe. Its legal, political, and economic functions declined before the ever-encroaching march of the institutions of the modern state. This functional erosion enhanced the prominence of the last area of family concern, the nurturance and socialization of the infant and young child.

Furthermore, the power of the state undermined the influence of the kin, and thus increased the isolation and privacy of the nuclear family. This process can hardly be called the rise of the family, but rather its reorientation to serve a narrower, more specialized function. The rise of the school is best seen not as part of the same process as the growth of the child-oriented family, but as its very antithesis, the transfer to an impersonal institution of a socializing function previously performed by the family. Moreover, although the repressive school was based on the theory of original sin, it was only in its first stage, in the seventeenth century, that the more child-centered family was also repressive and there is clear evidence that by the eighteenth century among the English upper classes it was loving, affectionate, and nurturant.

Thus Ariès's model is broken-backed, for his two agents of

change, the child-centered family and the repressive school, were pulling in different directions and were caused by different ideas and influences. It thus lacks explanatory cohesion, as both Hunt and deMause point out. Moreover, its use of evidence, particularly iconographic evidence from art, to prove that the 'discovery of childhood' actually happened, is not very convincing. For example, we now know for certain that although the Florentine bourgeoisie of the fifteenth and sixteenth centuries decorated their houses with painted and sculptured putti, they emptied them of flesh and blood babies, who were all sent out to wet-nurses in the countryside. Putti, which Ariès uses as evidence of the discovery of childhood, are therefore really not evidence at all.

In addition, the thesis has a unilinear view of historical evolution which is contrary to the known facts. Children were more harshly treated in the sixteenth and seventeenth centuries and again in the nineteenth century at the two peaks of religious zeal for moral reform than they were in the eighteenth or twentieth centuries, and perhaps also than in the fifteenth century. Ariès's chronology is very vague. One can never be quite sure whether one is dealing with the sixteenth or the seventeenth or the eighteenth century, and the book dodges about from century to century in a most confusing and indeed ahistorical way.

It is as vague in its geography as it is in its chronology, ranging casually from Italy to France to England for its evidence. For example, the presence of effigies of long-dead babies on tombs was relatively rare in France, but extremely common in England in the late sixteenth and early seventeenth centuries – a distinction whose significance Ariès completely ignores. Flogging died out in French schools in the eighteenth century but persisted in English schools into the twentieth. Wet-nursing died out in eighteenth-century England but persisted well into the nineteenth century in France on a very large scale. Geography clearly matters.

There is also too little attention paid to the particular class which is being dealt with. Ariès deduces the attitude to infantile sexuality of the society as a whole from that of the entourage of the future Louis XIII. The development of the boarding school teaching the classics, which affected only a tiny minority of the population, becomes a key event in early modern history. And finally, the powerful historical forces that affected the family so profoundly, changes in religion, political power, industrialization, urbanization, and poverty, are virtually ignored. Ariès's book is in fact a history of French schools, and of upper-class and middle-class parents and children, that lacks the necessary historical context of time, place, class, and culture. A fascinating pioneering book, it is now recognized to be badly flawed in both its methodology and its conclusions.

David Hunt's book is a psychological gloss on that by Ariès. It begins with a brilliant critique of Eriksonian ego-psychology, pointing out that the latter's optimism is ill-founded, for generativity is a fragile cultural artifact, not an instinctive human response. Consequently, in reality children have often been neglected and abused. Hunt also criticizes Ariès's historical model for its nostalgic, even reactionary, *Gemeinschaft-Gesellschaft* Durkheimian view of change, and for its exaggerated stress on the school.

He then settles down to a detailed analysis of Dr Héroard's account of the upbringing of the infant Louis XIII. He stresses the child's very close relation to his father, the all-powerful and virile Henry IV, and his very distant relations with his mother; and the way the child's will was deliberately broken from the age of two by frequent whippings in order to instill the basic principle of obedience. He points to Louis's later life as an unhappy, semi-impotent husband and, by a great leap of the imagination, attributes this to the experiences of his upbringing: knowing the physical facts of sex but not their psychological meaning, confused by contradictory signals about what was permitted and what was not, cowed by frequent whippings, and more or less isolated from his mother. Hunt further stresses the traumatic nature of the break at the age of seven, when he put on adult clothes, and was transferred from the control of women to that of men. His conclusion is that not sex, not anality, but 'infantile autonomy was the major child-rearing problem in seventeenth century society,' and that this was linked to anxieties about status in a hierarchical law-and-order society.

Hunt is correct to stress that the breaking of the will was the key element in child-rearing in the sixteenth and seventeenth centuries, but it has to be pointed out that his evidence is in many respects less than satisfactory. In the first place (as I have mentioned), he is dealing with the son and heir of a king, and it is probably not legitimate to extrapolate the education of such an exalted person to that of, say, the middle-class child at the same period. Second, he has worked exclusively from the printed record of Dr Héroard's diary, which was published in the mid-nineteenth century, and which contains only a relatively small part of the whole text. It appears that in the manuscript the doctor's main preoccupation was neither sexuality nor discipline, but the child's health, and that much of it is therefore a detailed record of the daily input-output flow of food and excreta respectively. Until the total diary has been published, any conclusions based upon the published Victorian extract must remain suspect. Finally, the link between the adult personality traits and the infantile experience remains no more than an interesting speculation.

DeMause's model of historical change is the exact opposite of that of Ariès's, for it is optimistic. It is based on the following five propositions: (1) Parent-child relations are an independent variable in history. (2) There are only three possible adult reactions to children: projective, reversal, and empathic; the first two resulting in hatred and cruelty, and the third in love and affection. (3) Changes in parent-child relations are not affected by religious, social, political, economic, or any other factors, but operate by 'psychogenesis,' a process by which the parents' capacity to regress to the psychic age of the child has improved slowly over the centuries. Thus from generation to generation parents do a little better each time, until we reach the present when the perfect child is just around the corner. It is apparently as inevitable and self-contained a process as Darwinian evolution, 'a powerful private force for change in historical personality,' operating 'wholly independent of public events, economic, social, whatever.' (4) There has been an upward linear progression in the history of childhood for the last two thousand years, from the Infanticide Mode of classical antiquity to the Abandonment Mode of the early Middle Ages to the Ambivalent Mode of the late Middle Ages and early modern period to the Intrusive Mode of the eighteenth century – the great watershed – to the Socialization Mode of 1800-1950 to the Helping Mode of 1950 onward. (5) Child-rearing practices provide the key to the transmission of all other cultural traits visible in the adult.

Prodded by critics, deMause asserts that his model is not unilinear but multilinear, and involves 'methodological individualism' – whatever that means – not 'psychological reductionism.'

These disclaimers do nothing to solve the problem of how to regard so bold, so challenging, so dogmatic, so enthusiastic, so perverse, and yet so heavily documented a model. For deMause child-rearing has replaced Marx's control of the means of production and the class war as the key element around which the whole of history has to be conceived: our task as historians is to construct 'a scientific history of human nature.' Are we dealing here with what Clifford Geertz has described as 'the natural tendency to excess of seminal minds' or with a hopelessly unscholarly aberration, hanging loosely in the void between history and psychology, and lacking the methodological rigor of either discipline?

DeMause's essay undoubtedly makes enthralling, if horrifying, reading. One learns about the way the writers of antiquity treated infanticide as a normal and sensible way to dispose of unwanted children; of how they amused themselves by using little children for fellatio or anal intercourse; of how the bones of child sacrifices are to be found in the foundations of buildings ranging from 7000 BC to 1843 AD; of how seventeenth-century nurses played catch-ball with the tightly swaddled infants and sometimes dropped them, with lethal consequences; of how infants were dipped in ice-cold baths, in order to harden them, or perhaps merely to baptize them, but in practice sometimes killing them; about how the doorsteps and dunghills of eighteenth-century European towns were littered with bodies of infants, dead, dying, or just abandoned; how some wet-nurses systematically starved their charges to death to save money or simply because they had accepted too many babies for their milk supply; of how children were ferociously beaten, shut up in the dark, deprived of food, terrified by bogeymen, taken to see hangings and corpses, sold into prostitution, blinded and otherwise mutilated to attract alms, castrated to supply testicles for magic, had their teeth ripped out to supply dentures, and in the nineteenth century suffered clitoridectomy, the attachment of toothed penile rings, and even nightly imprisonment in straitjackets to prevent masturbation – and so on, and so on, and so on.

What is one to make of this catalogue of atrocities? One obvious problem is the extent to which deMause is generalizing from the particular in constructing his linear model of child care. He clearly has a special taste for the macabre, and often grossly exaggerates, but in general it looks as if some of his basic conclusions are probably well founded. Antiquity undoubtedly regarded infanticide as casually as many of us regard abortion today, and certainly Christianity changed attitudes on this subject. There can also be no doubt that children were often neglected and exploited in the past, and there is growing evidence that the critical change to a more affectionate parent-child relationship took place in the eighteenth century.

The first question is whether this adds up to a linear theory of progress. The eighteenth-century change occurred mainly in England and America, and was largely confined to the professional and gentry classes. But middle and upper-class parent-child relations worsened again significantly in the nineteenth century, before improving in the twentieth. The middle-class Victorian father was a terrifying, and often cruel, authority figure. As for the children of the poor, their condition probably deteriorated during the demographic, urban, and industrial explosion of the late eighteenth and early nineteenth centuries. But during the nineteenth century, contraception, humanitarian legislation, slowly improving economic conditions, welfare services, and schools probably improved the lot of the children of the poor, just at the time when that of the rich was worsening. The theory of linear progress is thus clearly a false one, and the story of change will have to be traced country by country and class by class, since each has its own individual life history.

Second, the 'psychogenic' causal theory of change in parental attitudes is mere mystical nonsense. The reaction of parents to children is far from being limited to the projective, reversal, and empathic, as proposed by deMause. Everything suggests that in the past most parents have treated their children as inevitable by-products of sexual pleasure, sometimes bitterly unwelcome, sometimes barely tolerated, sometimes useful to be exploited economically, and sometimes cherished and loved. Most frequently, however, the response seems to have been one of relative indifference. The cruel truth – crueller, perhaps, than anything deMause has suggested – may be that most parents in history have not been much involved with their children, and have not cared much about them. Hence the staggering infant mortality rates – between a quarter and a third were dead before the age of one – were caused not by deliberate parental hostility, as he suggests, but rather by ignorance, poverty, and indifference. Most children in history have not been loved or hated, or both, by their parents; they have been neglected or ignored by them.

For all its brilliance, deMause's model is thus defective in certain critical respects. There is no unilinear upward progression of childhood felicity, different stages apply to different classes in different countries, while there are huge time lags between different countries at the same period; the psychogenic theory of parental evolution is an unproven and implausible hypothesis; parent-child relations have altered in response to cultural determinants such as religious beliefs, economic pressures, customary practices, state power, etc.; parents have not normally had intense relations with their children but rather have regarded them with some indifference; and finally, it is an oversimplification to argue that 'the child is father to the man' and that brutalized children automatically result in brutalized adults, who then take out their frustrations in war, violence, and murder. Unfortunately, neither modern ego-psychology nor modern genetics nor modern anthropology suggests so simplistic a chain of causation.

The other essays in deMause's book do something to flesh out, or sometimes to contradict, his model, but many of them are a little disappointing. One reason for this is that the source materials for such a study are very unsatisfactory, and that they get thinner and thinner the farther back one goes in time. They consist either of advice on child-rearing by doctors, theologians, and moralists, which are often totally contradictory and may or may not bear any relation to behavior in practice; or else a number of individual well-documented examples, which may or may not be representative of a class or nation or period. The gathering of such materials often results in no firm conclusions at all, but merely in a series of contradictory and ambiguous impressions.

Taken chronologically, the first successful essays are those by Professor Marvick on Louis XIII, based at last on the manuscript record, and by Professor Illick on seventeenth-century England and America, in which the reader is brought face to face with the hard demographic facts of high infant and child mortality. Under these conditions, no parent could retain his or her sanity if he or she became too emotionally involved with such ephemeral creatures as young children. Aloofness, or the acceptance of God's will or

sending one's children away from home were three natural solutions to this problem of how to deal with their deaths.

Professor Illick also makes the very interesting point that American practice preceded Lockean theory of child-rearing, a suggestion
further developed by Professor Walzer in his essay on eighteenth-
century American childhood, where again the evidence suggests
closer relationships between parents and children in America than
was the case in England, owing partly to the shortage of servants to
look after the children, and partly to the lower death rate. There is a
dramatic contrast between this fairly humane picture of family life
in eighteenth-century America and the brutality and indifference
which Professor Dunn shows was still the norm in nineteenth-
century Russia. Could it be that the child-centered family started
first in America, moved then to England, and slowly traveled east,
not reaching Russia until the twentieth century? If so, it is a purely
cultural artifact which has been slowly diffused from class to class
and from country to country, but without any clear line of
progress.

In view of the weaknesses as well as the brilliant insights of the
models presented by Ariès and deMause, what are we to put in their
place? One of the many problems of studying childhood in isolation
is that it lends itself to passionate polemics – all the authors have an
obvious axe to grind. Another more serious objection is that it is
impossible to study children in isolation from those who killed
them off or fed them, neglected them or nurtured them, beat them
or fondled them, namely, their parents. The history of childhood is
in fact the history of how parents treated children. (A similar
objection can be made against the current flood of books about the
history of women, an even more emotion-laden subject, which also
cannot properly be studied in isolation from those who dominated
them economically and sexually, exploited them, beat them, denied
them education and opportunities for professional advancement,
and who also pampered them, petted them, supported them in
comfortable leisure, put them on pedestals, sexually fulfilled them,
and sometimes even loved them – namely, men.) The proper unit of
historical studies in this area is thus neither children nor women nor
men, but the family, the institution within which all these personal
interactions take place.

It should be stressed that major changes took place first in

America and England, then later spread to France, and later still further east, and also that they were at first exclusively confined to the propertied classes, gentry, professional men, and higher bourgeoisie – families which were not so grand as to be able to maintain a small army of nursery staff to take care of the children for them, but rich enough to indulge in the luxury of sentiment. There are plenty of examples of truly loving parents in the eighteenth century, and the first peak of permissiveness in gentry class child-rearing was reached toward the end of that century, only to decline thereafter. These new attitudes spread very slowly, by a process of stratified diffusion, upward into the high aristocracy and downward into the lower middle class and then to the poor, encouraged and supported by the humanitarian impulses first set in motion by the eighteenth-century Enlightenment, and transformed into legislative action during the course of the nineteenth century.

It should also be stressed that this stage theory of family evolution does not imply any value judgment about the march of progress, or any assumption that the nuclear, individualistic, emotionally bonded family type which has emerged must necessarily always be better, in some social and moral sense, than the family types which preceded it. It is arguable that possessive individualism is an ideal which has no demonstrable basis in psychological or social reality, and has brought with it some evil consequences as well as many benefits.

As Philip Slater has pointed out in his recent book *The Earth Walk*, 'The notion that people begin as separate individuals, who then march out and connect themselves with others, is one of the most dazzling bits of self-mystification in the history of the species.' The result is not only the Bill of Rights but also the undermining of community organizations, the consequent enhancement of the power of the centralized state, and a narcissistic obsession by the individual with self-fulfillment which is so often inevitably self-defeating. Since affective ties are limited to the nuclear family, both husband and wife tend to develop exaggerated expectations of sexual and emotional satisfaction, which encourage the rocketing figures of divorce. This concentration also often leads to over-intense parent-child relationships, which result in children who are obsessive over-achievers and who experience great difficulty in cutting the umbilical cord at the period of adolescence and emergence into the world: they find themselves still tied to their parents by strings of love and/or hate.

Despite its many virtues, the rise in the West of the individualistic, nuclear, child-orientated family which is the sole outlet of both sexual and affective bonding is by no means always an unmixed blessing. Nor is it at all clear that it will necessarily survive the twentieth century, in view of the impossible demands which are so often made upon it, and the many signs of a reaction against it by men, women, and children. It is a final ironic thought that just as deMause is heralding the advent of the perfect parent-child relationship based on the permissive theories of A.S. Neill, many American young are losing interest in children, and are choosing not to have any at all. When they do have them, they are also, it seems, either turning away from treating them with permissiveness in the home or are dumping them in day-care centers at the earliest opportunity. The cycle of history is revolving once more: 'progressive' parents, 'progressive' schools, and 'progressive' colleges are all on the decline, just at the moment when deMause sees the promise of the arrival of the 'free' child-rearing millennium.

CHAPTER 18 · Love

Central to the argument of this paper is a proposition put forward by my colleague Robert Darnton:

One thing seems clear to everyone who returns from field work: other people are other. They do not think the way we do.

And if we want to understand their way of thinking, we should set out with the idea of capturing otherness.[1]

What this means for our present purposes is that we cannot assume that people in the past – even in our own Western Judeo-Christian world – felt, let alone thought, about love the way we do.

The two most common types of love are between two adolescents or adults of different sexes, and between mothers (and to a lesser degree fathers) and children. Of course there are other types – between two homosexuals, siblings, and closely bonded friends of the same gender – but they are not of such central importance as the first two. Before examining the very complex issue of love in history, it is therefore first necessary to make a fundamental distinction between attachment between two sexually mature persons, usually of the opposite gender, and attachment to the child of one's body.

The real mystery about both these kinds of love is that they have a history at all. One would assume that something so basic to nature's single-minded stress on reproduction as the mating instinct between men and women and the maternal instinct to protect and nurture infants would be constants throughout the time of man on earth. This is almost certainly the case, but what is so remarkable is the way in which, in lower as well as higher civilizations, these instincts have frequently – even normally – been overridden by custom, socialization, economic calculation, and the needs and wishes of the family and the kin. The mating and nurturing instincts are never destroyed, but are often effectively controlled or even suppressed. A striking example of mating control is the way that in the West in the sixteenth and seventeenth centuries men and women delayed marriage some ten years after puberty, but exercised sufficient sexual self-restraint to keep the pre-nuptial conception and bastardy rates remarkably low.[2] An equally striking example of control of the natural instinct is the way more and more French women from the towns and cities in the late eighteenth and early nineteenth centuries were sending their infants out into the country to wet-nurse for nine months to a year, instead of feeding and caring for them themselves at home, although the known result was a significantly higher mortality rate.[3]

In examining the history of love between the sexes, it is necessary to distinguish between three related but distinct psychological phenomena. Romantic love, the intense but ephemeral experience of 'falling in love,' has to be separated, at least for analytical purposes, from two other states of mind which are historically far more common and more generally accepted as natural and morally appropriate. The first is a passion for immediate sexual access to a particular person. Under the spell of this emotion, the libido becomes exclusively focused upon a specific body of flesh, rather than taking the form of a general state of sexual excitement capable of satisfaction by any promiscuous coupling. This passion is complicated, however, by the observed fact that it tends to be soon slaked by free access to the desired body, so that sexual passion is proverbially ephemeral. On the other hand prolonged refusal of consummation may keep the passion at boiling point for a while, but will sooner or later create so much frustration, especially in the male, that the object of the passion will be transferred to some other target.

Romantic love also has to be distinguished from a second condition – a state of mind and not a passion – which is one of settled and well-tried mutual affection. This develops between two people who have known each other for a long time and have come to trust each other's judgment and have full confidence in each other's loyalty. This condition of caring may or may not be accompanied by exciting sexual bonding, and may or may not have begun with falling in love. Indeed, it may well develop after marriage rather than before it.

Historians and anthropologists are in general agreement that

sexual attraction is a universal instinct, but that romantic love –
this usually brief but intensely felt and all-consuming passion for
another person – is culturally conditioned, and therefore common
only in certain societies at certain times, or even in certain social
groups within those societies, usually the elite with the leisure to
cultivate such feelings. They are, however, less certain whether or
not romantic love is merely a culture-induced sublimated psychological overlay on top of the biological drive for sex, or whether it
has biochemical roots which operate quite independently from the
libido. Would anyone in fact 'fall in love' if they had not read
about it or heard it talked about? Did poetry invent romantic love;
or love, poetry?

Some things can be said with certainty about the history of the
phenomenon.[4] One is that cases of a mixture of sexual and romantic
love can be found at all times and places and have often been the
subject of powerful poetic expression, from the Song of Solomon
to Shakespeare. On the other hand, it is certain that social approbation of romantic love is historically not at all common. The
reason for this is very simple. In most societies relatively little
weight is given to the concerns or wishes of the individual relative
to those of the group, and until recently the most important of all
groups was the family or the kin. It was the interests of the latter
which were normally and naturally given priority over the feelings
of individuals, even supposing they existed in so custom-bound
and patriarchal a society. Consequently the passion of love has
normally been regarded by theologians, moralists, social commen-
tators, and adult society at large as a dangerous and ephemeral
emotion which can seriously disrupt the essential business of
arranging marriage by parents and kin with the purpose of creating
new and advantageous property or political relationships.[5]

There is empirical evidence to support the theory that in family
formation love is an alternative motive to kinship obligation in a
zero-sum game, so that as the one increases in importance, so the
other must decrease proportionately. The sociological function of
love is to form a bond between two individuals that is stronger
than the ties still binding them to their respective families of origin.
All societies can therefore be plotted on a continuum ranging from
one like that of our own today, which gives almost untrammeled
priority to spontaneous romantic love between individuals, to the

one prevalent in most areas of the world in the past, which gave almost untrammeled priority to the kin.

Another fact that seems indisputable is that not only the forms of expression used within romantic love, but the situations which generate such emotions, as well as their duration and intensity, are all dictated in large measure by the processes of socialization and the customs and conventions of the society. On the other hand it is equally clear that any typology of families according to the respect accorded to love would have very clearly to distinguish one social class or status group from another. It would also have to allow room for sports, for individual families within a single class or status group which do not conform to the modal type. This is what makes argument by example rather than by statistics so extremely hazardous when it comes to establishing change over time. A backward family within a given group may differ completely in its behavior and attitudes from a progressive one, so that visible change may be strung out over a period of a century or so.

The evidence for romantic love before the age of printing is largely confined to elite groups, which of course does not mean that it may not have occurred lower down the social scale among illiterates. As a socially approved cultural artifact it was first seen in Europe in the southern French aristocratic courts of the twelfth century, made fashionable by a group of poets, the troubadours. This was a society with a large surplus of bachelor knights, hanging around noble courts and seeking fame, fortune, and sexual satisfaction wherever they could find them. The culture dictated that this love should usually occur between an unmarried knight and a married lady, and that it should either go sexually unconsummated or should be adulterous. This cultural ideal certainly penetrated into wider circles in the Middle Ages – witness the love affairs of Abelard and Heloise or Aucassin and Nicolette – but it should be noted that none of these stories ended happily.[6]

By the sixteenth and seventeenth centuries, the evidence at last begins to become quite extensive, thanks to the spread of literacy and the printing press. We begin to have love letters written by the individuals rather than a scribe, love poems like Shakespeare's Sonnets, and autobiographies by women primarily concerned with their love life. All the courts of Europe were evidently hotbeds of passionate intrigues and liaisons, some romantic, some sexual. The printing press began to spread pornography to a wider public, thus stimulating the libido, while the plays of Shakespeare indicate that romantic love was a familiar concept to his audience, which was drawn from London society at large. An interesting reflection of the occasional presence of romantic love is the way psychiatric patients in the seventeenth century were sometimes driven to distraction and melancholia by the blocking of love matches by unsympathetic parents.[7] The rise of the novel in the eighteenth century, concerned as it was almost exclusively with the conflict between love and interest as motives for marriage, marks the coming of age of romantic love.

Whether these appearances of romantic love were officially sanctioned, however, is another question. We simply do not know how Shakespearian audiences reacted to Romeo and Juliet. Did they, like us, and as Shakespeare clearly intended, fully identify with the young lovers? And if they did, after they had left the theatre did they wipe their eyes and continue to act like the lovers' parents, who were trying to stop these irresponsible adolescents from allowing an ephemeral and irrational passion from interfering with the serious business of politics and patronage? What is certain is that every advice book, every medical treatise, every sermon and religious homily of the sixteenth, seventeenth, and early eighteenth centuries firmly rejected as suitable bases for marriage both romantic passion and lust – which by the eighteenth century were beginning to be seen as separate categories. Romantic love, involving uncontrollable and all-consuming passion, and a wholly unrealistic idealization of the object of desire as flawless in all respects, was regarded as a form of temporary mental derangement, which made rational decision-making about the choice of a mate for life entirely impossible. It was almost universally thought that marriage was best arranged by parents, who could be relied upon to choose socially and economically suitable partners, who would enhance the prestige, power, and wealth of the kin group as a whole. It was believed that after marriage, sexual relations and daily economic and social cooperation would automatically create the necessary bonding between the two strangers, and so maintain the harmony and stability of the new family unit. It seems that this was a not at all unreasonable assumption, since recent investigations in Japan have shown that there is no difference in the rate of divorce between couples whose marriages were arranged by their parents and couples whose marriages were made by individual choice based on romantic love. It would seem from this data that the arranged and the romantic marriage have an equal chance of turning out well, or of breaking up.[8]

The freedom of choice of a spouse allowed to the individuals concerned varied in inverse proportion to the amount of property and political influence at stake. For all classes who possessed property, that is the top two-thirds in purely economic terms, marriage before the seventeenth century was arranged by the parents, and the motives were the economic and political benefit of the kin group not the emotional satisfaction of the individuals. In England in the seventeenth and eighteenth centuries it slowly became accepted that the prime object was 'holy matrimony,' a sanctified state of monogamous married contentment. After the middle of the sixteenth century, the English prayerbook defined one of the purposes of a Christian marriage as 'mutual society, help and comfort that one ought to have of the other, both in prosperity and adversity.' Eventually it came to be realized that this was best achieved by allowing the couple to make their own choice, provided that both sets of parents agreed that the social and economic gap was not too wide, and that marriage was preceded by a long period of courtship. But this was a change of attitude that occurred only slowly over several centuries.

Among the upper and middling propertied classes it was not until the late seventeenth or early eighteenth century that there was a clear shift of orthodox opinion about marriage away from giving priority to the interests of the kin and the parents and towards the liberation of the individual will; and away from economic or political considerations towards those of well-tried personal affection. By the late seventeenth century the individuals were normally granted a right of veto over candidates in marriage selected by parents or kin. By the eighteenth century marriage was preceded by three to six months of intensive courting, between a couple from families roughly equal in social status and economic wealth. In the upper propertied classes courtship only took place with the prior consent of parents on both sides. It was a process carefully controlled at all stages by parents, whose prime concerns were both the happiness of the child and the benefit, financial or otherwise, of the family or kin as a whole. The crux of the business was the bargaining for portion and jointure, and here the parents or kin still retained the right of veto.

More enigmatic is the role of romantic love in courtship and marriage among the very small property holders and the property-less poor, who comprised about two-thirds of the population.[9] Among this majority of the population, the average age of marriage in England from the late Middle Ages to the nineteenth century oscillated between about twenty-four and twenty-eight, which was long after full sexual maturity. By that time most adolescent males and females had been separated for up to a decade from their parents, many of whom would anyway be dead. Males had been sent off at about the age of fourteen to sixteen to apprenticeship to a trade, or as living-in 'servants in husbandry,' meaning agricultural laborers for a farmer. Very many females had also been sent away at the same age into domestic service with their social superiors, about one family in three possessing at least one maidservant. Both sexes among the poor and those well above the poverty line were therefore surprisingly free to make their own choice of a potential spouse, although convention and moral pressure led most couples to seek at least the formal consent of their 'friends' – that is, any living parent, close relative, or patron. Only at the very lowest economic level of near destitution, where no money or property whatever was at stake, was full freedom of choice the norm, for the simple reason that no one else cared.

The motives for choice were based on a complex mixture of personal attraction, financial calculation, and factors like status and health. Passionate love, however, was almost universally deplored as a sound basis for marriage, even in these lowly circles, although there is no doubt whatever that it sometimes occurred among adolescents. By the sixteenth century, and probably before, court records make it clear that individuals from the lower social groups often married for affection, combined with a confused set of motives, including lust, a desire to avoid loneliness, and the eco-nomic necessity to have a strong and healthy assistant to run the farm or the shop. It was generally expected in the village community that married couples would behave 'lovingly' towards each other, but of course this did not always happen. In many a peasant marriage, the husband seems to have valued his cow more than his wife. Attachments – not passionate but deep – certainly developed among the poor, but the extent to which they took priority over material interests or sexual desire varied very widely indeed. Most marriages seem to have been based on a mixture of hard-headed calculation and personal preference. What is clear is that among the poor the individuals made their own choice of persons to be courted, and first met in church, at the alehouse, or at the many village feasts or hiring fairs.

There is no suggestion of any chaperonage system among the poor in sixteenth-, seventeenth-, or eighteenth-century England. Once paired off, the couple began an elaborate courting ritual that lasted anything from six months to several years, during which each sized the other up as a possible partner for life. This courting procedure was astonishingly free in England, and often involved all-night sessions alone together in the dark in a room with a bed, usually with the knowledge and consent of the parents or masters. In the seventeenth century only relatively rarely, and then only at a late stage after a verbal engagement to marry, did full sexual intercourse commonly take place during these nights, but it is certain that conversation and discussion of the possibilities of marriage were accompanied by much embracing and kissing, and probably also by what today is euphemistically called 'heavy petting.'[10] It was also accompanied by the exchange of 'tokens' or small presents. Among the poor, this prolonged period of courtship often culminated in a contract, a solemn verbal engagement, often conditional on the approval of the 'friends' of each party, meaning the parents, close relatives, and other influential older persons from whom there were financial expectations or upon whom there was some dependence. The contract was often accompanied by symbolic gestures like an exchange of rings, or the breaking in two of a silver coin, each party keeping a half.

It was only at this late stage that 'friends' and parents were informed and the financial negotiations were begun, to decide how much the bride would bring to the marriage in the form of a portion or household goods, what was the capacity of the husband to support a family, what assurance the couple had of independent housing, and so on. Not infrequently these negotiations broke down, with consequent acute distress to one or both individuals concerned, who had possibly spent two years of emotional capital on the courtship.

At all levels of society, therefore, there was a complex admixture of emotion and interest, affection and calculation, and a complex

interaction between the wishes of the individuals and those of their
'friends.' The higher the social level, the more parents and friends
dominated the situation and controlled the outcome; the lower in
the social and economic scale the families were, the more free were
the individuals to make their own choices, although that choice
was itself not infrequently based as much on economic calculations
as emotional commitment.

Only in the late seventeenth and early eighteenth centuries did
patriarchal ideas of parental power, even at the highest levels of
society, begin to give way to a new ideal of affective individualism,
so that the companionate marriage emerged first to compete with,
and finally to take full priority over, calculations of interest and
economic advantage.[11] By the late eighteenth century the ideal of
the companionate marriage had spread to the upper classes of
England, the American colonies, and France. If the poor were still
the freest to choose their marriage partners, they may by then
have been the group most strongly motivated by calculations of
economic advantage.

Thus if an early modern peasant said, 'I love a woman with forty
acres of land,' just what did he mean? Did he lust after the body
of the woman? Did he admire her good health, administrative
and intellectual talents, and strength of character as a potential
housekeeper, income producer, and mother of his children? Was
he romantically head over heels in love with her? Or did he above
all prize her for her forty acres? Deconstruct the text as we wish,
there is no way of getting a clear answer to that question; and in
any case, if we could put that peasant on the couch today and
interrogate him, it would probably turn out that he merely felt that
he liked the woman more because of her forty acres.

Only a little less ambiguous is the common situation where a
man, after earnestly courting a woman for many months or even
years, finally declared, 'I love her dearly and will marry her if her
brother gives her £200.' In this case the emotional bond was there,
but the willingness to forge a marriage bond still depended in the
end upon money not love.

Three conclusions seem clear from the historical record. The first
is that there has throughout history been a direct correlation
between high rank and income and strict parental and/or kin
control of marriage and the choice of a spouse. The greater the
status and the property involved in a marital union, the smaller the

role of personal choice permitted. Lower down the social and economic system, however, the degree of freedom of choice has been much greater. But whenever some money or property, however small, changed hands, parents or 'friends' always exercised some influence, even if only a power of veto. That power varied greatly in its exercise from family to family, depending on personalities and circumstances. Only the totally propertyless were left entirely free to make their own choices, but often their extreme poverty made marriage impossible anyway.

Second, the need for affection as a necessary bonding for a durable marriage was generally recognized from the time of the Roman Empire or earlier, but it was long regarded as something that could be left to grow automatically out of the marital sexual and business relationship. It was therefore thought that in arranging a marriage, love could safely be subordinated to considerations of property, money, and political influence. This was a prediction which in fact turned out to be correct, provided that both parties were of a reasonably flexible and accommodating disposition, and that neither had a strong aversion to the other – a situation that usually led to the collapse of the negotiations. Thus affection has usually been considered desirable in marriage, and the principal change over time has been the increased prominence given to it as a factor influencing personal choice. This change, defined as the rise of affective individualism, can be seen taking place in England from the late seventeenth century to the late eighteenth.

Finally the idealization of romantic love and its elevation to being the key factor in the choice of a spouse is a highly specific cultural construct limited, in both time and space. It first became prominent in the mid-eighteenth century, under the influence of Rousseau, and as a result even the propertied classes began permitting their children greater freedom of choice. The idea that romantic or sexual passion should be the prime factor in determining choice, however, was for a long time only a very minority view. It only became part of the conventional wisdom in the West in the twentieth century, largely as a result of the explosion of romantic novels, plays, and films.

The degree to which this romantic love culture has permeated the modern world makes it very difficult to tell whether or not it should be taken too seriously. Everyone is now expected at some point or other to 'fall in love,' and is thought to be missing an important life experience if no such thunderbolt strikes. It is therefore likely that large numbers will successfully persuade themselves that it has happened to them, or will pretend to themselves that it has happened. In fact, however, it is more than likely that their motives are still the traditional ones of the avoidance of the unendurable pangs of loneliness, the desire for economic assistance and social stability, and the convenience of having sexual access to a familiar partner whenever it is wanted. The wish, at some point, to have children is also an ultimate ambition, coupled since the eighteenth century with a fear of financial hardship if there are too many of them. More typically of the past (and certainly sometimes of the present beneath the rhetoric of romantic love) there often lie only modest expectations of what can be hoped for from marriage. This was well expressed by Lady Harriet Spencer in 1780, when she observed about the man she proposed to marry, 'I think I have a better chance of being reasonably happy with him than with most people I know.'[12] A century later an aristocratic woman like Lady Harriet would have been in hot pursuit of romantic love, and her description of her proposed husband would have been expressed in wholly different language, but her real attitude might well have been much the same.

A second problem in evaluating the role of romantic love between adults in our society is that it is now obscured by a new development, the saturation of the whole culture through every medium of communication with sexuality as the predominant and overriding human drive, a doctrine whose theoretical foundations were provided by Freud. In no society in the known past has sex been given so prominent a role in the culture at large, or has sexual fulfillment been elevated to such pre-eminence in the list of human aspirations – in a vain attempt to relieve civilization of its discontents. Under these conditions, it is almost impossible today to distinguish the psychological passion of romantic love from the physical passion of lust. But the enormous success today of pulp fiction concerned almost exclusively with romantic rather than physical love shows that women still hanker after the experience of falling in love. Whether the same applies to men, however, is more doubtful, so that there may exist a wide gender gap on this subject, which justifies this distinction between love and lust.

One result of basing marriage on such ephemeral passions as love and lust has been a rocketing divorce rate. It should be pointed out, however, that if the American underclass is excluded from this generalization, the present-day family is not, as is generally supposed, disintegrating because of a divorce rate of up to 50 percent. In fact the median duration of marriage today is almost exactly the same as it was three hundred years ago. Divorce, in short, now acts as a functional substitute for death: both are means of terminating marriage at a premature stage. It may well be, however, that the psychological effects on the survivor are very different, although in most cases women suffer much the same catastrophic economic consequences. But broken marriages, step-children, and single-parent households were certainly as common in the past as they are today, the only difference being the mechanism which has brought about this situation: before, it was the accident of disease; today it is the human will – a product of the ceaseless quest for romantic love and sexual fulfillment.

On the other hand there is no evidence that this romanticization and sexualization of the motives for engaging in long-term and very intimate day-to-day association with another individual has turned out to be a success. It could plausibly be argued that the rising tide of separation and divorce is at least in part a product of frustrated hopes of a totally unrealistic level of mutual happiness and concord. An abandonment of marriage based on those ephemeral passions, lust and romance, and a return to a more hard-headed and realistic assessment of the basic strengths and weaknesses of the character of the proposed spouse, might well produce much more stable marital relationships, and even perhaps more contented marriages.

The second type of love is that which develops between the parent, especially the mother, and the child. Here again we are, as historians, faced with the intractable problem of nature versus nurture, of the respective roles of biology and culture. The survival of the species demands that the female adult should take optimum care of the child over a long period, to ensure its survival. This is particularly necessary among humans since the child is born prematurely compared with all other primates, because of its exaggerated cranial size, and so is peculiarly helpless for an exceptionally long period of time. Moreover experiments with primates have shown that it is close body contact in the first weeks of life which creates the strong bond between mother and child. A passionate attachment of the mother for its child therefore seems to be both a biological necessity for survival and a proven fact.

On the other hand recorded human behavior indicates that cultural traditions and economic necessity may often override this biological drive. For over 90 percent of human history man has been a hunter-gatherer, and it is usually impossible for a woman carrying two babies to perform her vital daily task of gathering nuts and fruit and berries. Barring sexual abstention, which seems unlikely, some form of infanticide must therefore have been a necessity for early man, imposed upon him by the need to collect food for survival.

Other factors came into play in more recent times. From at least classical antiquity to the eighteenth century it was normal in Europe to swaddle all babies at birth – that is, to tie them up head to foot in bandages, taken off only to remove the urine and faeces. This automatically reduced body contact with mother, and therefore presumably eliminated most of the crucial bonding effect between mother and child. Secondly, all women who could afford to do so were in the habit of putting their infants out to wet-nurse from the moment of birth until they were about one and a half or two years old. Wet-nursing was particularly prevalent in urban France, for reasons which are obscure, and in 1780 the chief of police in Paris estimated that only 1,000 of the 21,000 babies born in the city each year were breast-fed by their mothers.[13] The prime reason for this practice among the more well-to-do was undoubtedly the accepted belief that sexual excitement spoils the milk. Few husbands were willing to do without the sexual services of their wives for a year or more, so all who could afford to do so sent the child out to wet-nurse. But this meant that for all except the tiny minority who could afford to take the nurse into the house, the child was removed within a few days of birth and put in the care of a village woman some distance from the home. Under these conditions, affection between parents and children could not begin to grow until the child returned to the home at about the age of eighteen months or two years, and the relationship of the child to its wet-nurse might well be closer than to its natural mother – as was the case with Shakespeare's Juliet.

In any case, the child's return to its mother would only take place if it did not die at wet-nurse. There is overwhelming evidence that the mortality rate of children out at wet-nurse was very much higher than that of children breast-fed by their mothers, and contemporaries were well aware of this. It is difficult to avoid the suspicion that one reason for the practice, particularly for its enormous expansion in France in the nineteenth century, was that it served as an indirect but calculated method of infanticide, out of sight and out of mind. This suspicion is reinforced by the huge numbers of children in the eighteenth and nineteenth centuries who were abandoned and deposited in workhouses or foundling hospitals, only a small fraction of whom survived the experience. Whatever the intentions of the founders, in practice the foundling hospitals acted as socially acceptable means of family limitation after birth. Few women other than those who gave birth to bastard children practiced infanticide themselves, if only because the risks were too great. But overlaying and stifling by accident while in the same bed during the night, putting out to wet-nurse, abandoning in the street or to public authorities, or depositing in foundling hospitals served the same purpose. Unwanted children of the poor and not so poor were somehow or other got rid of after birth in all these socially acceptable ways.[14]

These common practices in the eighteenth and even nineteenth centuries raise questions about the degree of maternal love in this society. This is not an easy question to answer, and historians are deeply divided on this issue. Some point to evidence of mothers who were devoted to their children and seriously disturbed by their premature deaths. Others point to the bleak statistics of infant mortality, about 25 percent or more dead before the age of two, a figure deliberately increased by wet-nursing, abandonment, and infanticide by neglect – practices which have been described as 'post-natal family planning.' A mid-nineteenth-century Bavarian woman summed up in a nutshell the strong practical causes and limited emotional consequences of so high a rate of infant mortality: 'The parents are glad to see the first and second child, especially if there is a boy amongst them. But all that come after aren't so heartily welcome. Anyway not many of these children live. Four out of a dozen at most, I suppose. The others very soon get to heaven. When little children die, it's not often that you have a lot of grief. They're little angels in heaven.'[15]

Another question is how kindly children were treated if they did survive. I have suggested that sixteenth- and early seventeenth-century societies were cold and harsh, relatively indifferent to children, and resorting to frequent and brutal whippings from an early age as the only reliable method of discipline. Calvinism, with its grim insistence on original sin, encouraged parents and schoolmasters to whip children, in order, quite literally, to beat the Hell out of them. I have argued that only in the eighteenth century did there develop a more optimistic view of the infant as a plain sheet of paper upon which good or evil could be written by the process of cultural socialization. The more extreme view of Rousseau, that the child is born good, in a state of innocence, was widely read, but not, so far as can be seen, very widely accepted – for the rather obvious reason that it is contradicted by the direct experience of all observant parents.

It is also the case that by the eighteenth century mothers and children in upper-class society saw more of one another than they had before, when the latter were largely left in the care of servants. This sharing of leisure activities and excursions created another new bond of affection, but once again a bond confined to those who had the leisure, namely the propertied classes.

To sum up, first there is ample evidence for the widespread practice of calculated selective neglect accompanied by maternal detachment in poor societies ignorant of contraception. This was a practice and state of mind which lasted well into the nineteenth century in Europe, although disguised in socially acceptable forms, and one which still exists in the Third World today. There is also evidence that children, even of the rich, were often treated with calculated brutality in the sixteenth and seventeenth centuries, and again in the nineteenth, in order to eradicate original sin; the eighteenth and the twentieth century are two rare periods of educational permissiveness. As for the poor, they have always tended to regard children very largely as potential economic assets and treated them accordingly. Their prime functions have been to help in the house, the workshop, and the field, to add to the family income, and to support their parents in sickness or old age. How much room was left over from these economic considerations for love, even between the child and its mother, remains an open question. There is certainly literary evidence in early modern times of mothers and fathers who were shattered emotionally by the death of a child; but there are also stories of others who were relatively indifferent. The very high infantile mortality rate before the late nineteenth century certainly made it risky to get too emotionally involved with a child under the age of two. More than that it is difficult to say.

Elizabeth Badinter drew the following conclusions from all this evidence as applied to early modern and modern France:

> The history of motherhood among French women over the last four centuries is not especially comforting. It reveals great variations in behavior and in the quality of love expressed. . . . Contrary to many assumptions, maternal love is not a deeply rooted given in women's natures.[16]

An anthropologist who has been studying maternal detachment and infant survival in a Brazilian shanty town today has come to the same conclusion:

> Maternal thinking and practices are socially produced, rather than determined by a psycho-biological script of innate or universal emotions, such as has been suggested in biomedical literature on 'maternal bonding', and, more recently, in the new feminist literature on maternal sentiments.[17]

We can safely conclude, first, that passionate attachments between young people can and do happen in any society as a by-product of biological sexual attraction, but the diffusion and social acceptability of romantic love have varied enormously over time and class and space, and are determined primarily by cultural norms and property arrangements. Historically, romantic love has been highly concentrated in the leisured propertied class, has generally been disapproved of, and first won grudging acceptance in the eighteenth century, and full acceptance only in the twentieth century. Second, there is certainly a strong instinctive biological component in the passionate attachment of mothers to children, but it too has often been overlaid by the economic necessity for very high infant mortality, by religious views about the nature of the child, and by cultural practices such as wet-nursing which removed the child from the mother in the critical first weeks and months of life.

We are in a unique position today, in that society, through institutions of public welfare, has taken over the economic respon-sibilities previously fulfilled by children to take care of their aged parents; contraception is normal and efficient; our children almost all live to adulthood; our marriages are rarely broken by the death of a spouse until old age; our culture is dominated by romantic notions of passionate love as the only socially admissible reason for marriage; sexual fulfillment is regarded as a natural right for both sexes; and divorce is easy, common, and carries no stigma. Behind all this there lies a frenetic individualism, a restless search for the sexual and emotional ideal in human relationships, and a demand for instant ego gratification. Carried to extremes, this demand is inevitably self-defeating and ultimately destructive.

Most of this is new, a unique product of our Western culture and technology. It is, therefore, quite impossible to extrapolate from values and behavior in the present to those in the past. Historical others – even our own forefathers and mothers – were indeed other; they lived by different codes than we do, and approached birth, marriage, and death with very different attitudes. Not even love – sexual love between adults, and love between parents and children – has been a constant. On the one hand, it should never be forgotten that changes in rhetoric do not necessarily mean changes in underlying attitudes, and that changes in expectations bear little necessary relation to changes in experience. On the other hand, we must face the fact that the evidence strongly suggests that culture and economic necessity have often had more influence on behavior than instinct. Love has not been an unchanging constant in history.[18]

CHAPTER 19 · Sexuality

Biologists have taught us that the principal purpose of nature is to reproduce the species, most commonly by sexual specialization. Human reproduction, however, is peculiar and indeed unique in a number of ways. The first is that the enlarged size of the cranium makes it necessary for the human foetus to be born prematurely, relative to those of other primates, in order to pass through the birth canal. The infant is consequently especially helpless and unformed at birth, and remains almost entirely dependent on its parents or some adult for at least seven or eight years, and is not fully self-sufficient and sexually mature until about fourteen years after birth. In order to survive, it needs the combined attention of both parents for an exceptionally long time, and the mother consequently needs to keep the father in the family. To do so she rewards him with on-demand sexual favors all the year round, having at some period in the distant past lost the periodic oestrus of other mammals. This biological functionalism explains satisfactorily the evolution of the monogamous and fairly durable nuclear family. Other important aspects of human sexuality, however, have no such functional utility. One is the capacity of the female to continue sexual activity decades after her reproductive capability has ceased. Another is her capacity for multiple orgasms, which not only serves no reproductive purpose but also far outmatches that of the male, whose equipment is designed for only a fairly low level of sexual activity.[1] In this last respect women are to men as an AK-47 automatic rifle is to a sixteenth-century musket.

Given this situation, it might be conjectured that human beings live lives of uninhibited sexual pleasure, limited only by physical capacity, and therefore that sexuality has no history. This seems to be the view of a sociobiologist, Robin Fox, who has gone so far as to claim that 'a great deal that can be said about human sexuality can be disposed of as the sexual behavior to be expected of a large-bodied, large-brained, slow-breeding, omnivorous mammal.'[2] But things, alas, are far more complicated than that. Human beings are thinking animals: they are guided by moral codes and fear of God's wrath, and consumed with emotions of guilt and shame, to say nothing of an anxiety about mental and physical health in the present and an apprehensive comprehension of death in the future. In consequence, they have managed to erect around the simple physiological arrangements for perpetuating the species some of the most bizarre, complex, and glittering edifices of moral, religious, and medical prescriptions and taboos in the whole history of mankind. They are triumphs of man's ingenuity and almost limitless capacity for pseudo-scientific investigation, imaginative deduction and unverifiable speculation. The end result is the formulation of wildly different codes of behavior.

Men and women have always added elaborate refinements to the simple act of penetration and ejaculation that fertilizes the egg, as required by nature. But it is a curious anomaly of modern life that the extraordinary history of the twists and turns of this acculturation process is almost unknown to the most sophisticated and widely read in this sex-obsessed society of ours. We have a vague idea, derived from Freud, that because of the weight of our Judeo-Christian traditions we are especially liable to sexual dysfunctions and anxieties. But just what these traditions were, and when they developed, and what came before them, we mostly do not know. There is something very illogical about the way we scrutinize with so much attention our individual sexual history on the psychoanalyst's couch, but inquire so little about our collective sexual history as heirs – and prisoners – of an ancient sexual culture. As a result, the long and weighty history of sexuality that still presses so heavily upon us is largely ignored by sociologists, psychologists, psychoanalysts, and sexologists, who saturate the public with their advice on this absorbing topic. A prime reason for this neglect of the past is that only in the last decade or so have historians begun to excavate that past, delving into both the values propounded by philosophers, theologians, and moralists, and the actual reality of human behavior in so far as it can be reconstructed.

The libido has always been subjected to the conflicting influences of ascetic repression and erotic stimulation. Both have coexisted in competition with each other in all cultures, but their relative strength and influence have varied enormously from period to period, and within the same period from class to class. On the one hand, sexual libertinism, until recently largely confined to a wealthy and indolent elite, often concentrated around a court, has invented a remarkable panoply of tricks and devices, including masturbation, fellatio, cunnilingus, and even physical aids and sexual toys from vibrators to ben wa balls to dildoes. Erotic art, handbooks, and pornographic literature have been produced by every higher civilization from ancient Egypt, China, classical Greece and Rome down to Japan, India, and the early modern and modern West.[3]

But having provided itself with all these artificial stimuli, the human species has then proceeded to enmesh the simple act of sexual reproduction in a massive array of moral and aesthetic injunctions, ascetic codes of conduct, and theological laws and prescriptions of the most extraordinary complexity, variety, and severity. Even the most primitive of tribes in the jungles of the Amazon turn out to have ambivalent feelings about these 'Anxious Pleasures.'[4] For long periods of time, the full moral, administrative, and judicial powers of Church and State have been directed towards controlling the libido and directing it into strictly delimited channels. It is hardly surprising, therefore, that sexuality has a long and complicated history, deeply affected by public policy, law, morality, religion, community attitudes, and customs. These in turn have been influenced by such diverse factors as viral changes caused by travel contacts between previously isolated communities, such as the introduction of syphilis into Europe in the early sixteenth century or of AIDS to the West in the late twentieth; or technological changes such as the first primitive condoms made of gut introduced in the seventeenth century, to be replaced in the nineteenth century by ones made of galvanized rubber. An example of the interaction between technological change and changes in attitudes is reflected in the fact that the first condoms served primarily as prophylactics against venereal disease and have only in the last hundred years come to be used as contraceptives, within as well as outside marriage, along with other late twentieth-century technological inventions such as coils and birth control pills.

The distance we have traveled in our attitudes towards sexuality in the West over the last 2,500 years can be illustrated by some stark comparisons. First, to a young upper-class male citizen of Athens in the fifth and fourth centuries B.C., it was perfectly proper and moral to use the body of a male or female slave for whatever sexual pleasure took his fancy, whether it be sodomy or fellatio but today almost the only taboo in the modern sexologists' book is the sexual use of another without allowing the latter any pleasure or profit, and without the latter's free consent.

Second, to the ancient world of Greece and Rome, men – and it was above all a masculine society – were regarded as naturally bisexual and no distinction was made between the love of boys and the love of women. It was simply a matter of taste, about as significant as preferring coffee or tea for breakfast. The crucial distinction in law and morality was between those who took the active and those who took the passive role – the penetrators as opposed to the penetrated. This concept effectively degraded submissive boys, women, and slaves of both sexes, and elevated active men, regardless of their gender preference. To us, gender preference is all-important, and the distinction between the active and the passive role of only minor significance.

Third, in the late eighteenth, nineteenth and early twentieth centuries, doctors were unanimous in telling their contemporaries that masturbation was extremely dangerous to their health, while theologians were equally insistent that it was a mortal sin. Today sexologists tell us that masturbation is not only harmless, both physically and morally, but even an essential step towards the 'orgasmic imperative' which now dominates our society. One modern sexologist has made the implausible claim that 'masturbation . . . makes it possible to have satisfactory sexual relationships later on. It provides an apprenticeship that logically precedes the training for the real relationship.'[15]

Fourth, from the Stoic Seneca in the second century AD to St Jerome in the fourth to the Spanish theologian Thomas Sanchez in the sixteenth to the English propagandist and novelist Daniel Defoe in the eighteenth, it was generally held that passionate sexual love between spouses within marriage was not only indecent but positively sinful. St Jerome, quoting Seneca, claimed that 'nothing is more impure than to love one's wife as if she were a mistress; . . . men should appear before their wives not as lovers but as husbands'; he called married sexual passion adultery, while Defoe denounced it as 'matrimonial whoredom.' The reason for this was that Christian ascetics viewed all sex as immoral, except for the single purpose of procreation.[6] It should not be indulged in for the gratification of pleasure or even to cement marital affection. And yet today we regard sexual love as essential to a good marriage, and its absence as grounds for divorce.

It should perhaps be pointed out that these modern sexologists with their apparently liberating doctrines are in fact erecting a new dichotomy of mind and body to replace the ancient ones of the Platonic pagan world and Christianity. It has been observed that 'present day norms tend to provoke a conflict between immediate surrender to the demands of the sense, and an increased conscious mastery of the organic processes. . . . One must . . . abandon oneself to sensation, without ceasing to submit one's actions to a rational calculation of "sexual expedience." ' The gloomy conclusion is that we are witnessing 'the surreptitious re-entry of this antithesis, and all that flows from it, chiefly asceticism and intellectualism.'[7] If this is true, which I think it is, then we are still as hog-tied to the dualism of the spirit and the flesh, the mind and the body, as any Early Father in the Syrian desert seventeen hundred years ago. After all this effort to create a culture of pure sensuality, the body is still, in the 1980s, a prisoner of the mind. Thus the history of sexuality is not the history of what people actually did, which inevitably is a somewhat boring topic, since the options are limited by the structure of the human body. It is concerned with something much more interesting, which is the ideas that have attempted, with varying success, to dominate and control this activity, and the social systems that have resulted from the adoption of these ideas and patterns of behavior.

It is clear from the historical record that sexuality has always been problematic, to widely varying degrees, for every unit in the social system from the individual to the State. For a woman it has been problematic, partly because of the cultural pressures for pre-marital virginity and marital fidelity to which she has usually been subjected, and partly because of the severe social and economic consequences of an illegitimate pregnancy. For a man, sexuality has been problematic, since it is a perpetual challenge either to his virility or to his powers of self-control. For the family it has been problematic since it is through legalized sexual union in marriage that family property, prestige, and power are transmitted, accumulated, or diminished. Since a woman's virginity has in most societies been her strong card in the marriage market, along with her face and her fortune, in many societies wealthy families have virtually imprisoned their womenfolk in the home, and married them off as soon as they reached sexual maturity. For the neighborhood, sexuality is problematic since any adulterous connection or any rape or seduction of young boys or girls is liable to lead to violence and civil disorder.

For the local community, the strict confinement of the sexual drive within legalized channels is also of prime importance, both to avoid social conflict and to limit the number of deserted wives and illegitimate children who of necessity will become an economic burden upon the public funds. To the Church – especially the Christian and Muslim churches – sexuality and its control serve as a paradigm for other moral and spiritual qualities, and are frequently monitored with the most extreme care, both to reduce the total level of sexual passion and sensual worldly pleasure, and to channel sexuality into the legitimate reproduction of the species. For the State sexuality is problematic since it has the responsibility of transforming the injunctions of religion into enacted law; of enforcing that law; and also of ensuring that the population reproduces itself and provides a constant supply of young males for war. Thus there is no social unit, political institution, or moral code which is not in some way deeply involved in the simple act of sexual congress.

The literature on the history of sexuality falls into five groups: those which deal with sexuality in the West in general; those which are concerned with the ancient world and with the great transition in the late antique period to the new ethic of sexual austerity; those which trace the story through the Christian Middle Ages; those which deal with the new transformation of the early modern period from the Renaissance through the Reformation and Counter-Reformation to the eighteenth-century Enlightenment; and finally those which struggle with the nineteenth-century combination of intense prudery and an equally intense scientific investigation driven by 'the desire to know,' as Foucault has aptly called it.[8] Only the astonishing sexual revolution of the middle to late twentieth century is missing from the literature under review.

DATA AND METHODOLOGY

Before discussing what these writings tell us, it is first necessary to enter certain caveats. If anything is certain about the history of sexuality it is that in no society has a single cultural norm been universally observed, or even been paid lip-service. In any complex society there have always been a variety of subcultures of sexual behavior. There is always a licit sexual culture side by side with an illicit one liable to persecution and punishment, and in between the two a grey area, often a very large one, in which the two come together. For example, attitudes to fornication and adultery are directly related to attitudes to the idea of marital sexual monopoly: rape has sometimes led to marriage. Moreover, at every epoch there has been a dialogue between the competing cultures of eroticism and asceticism. Sometimes one and sometimes the other has for a while obtained the upper hand, but perhaps more frequently each has exercised moral hegemony over certain sectors of the population, while competing for influence over all the others.

In early modern and modern Western societies, there appear to have been at least three major class cultures of sex. The working class has had a culture of direct and crude male-dominated sexuality, without much foreplay or erotic sophistication. Since no property is involved at this marginal social level, there has always been much casual concubinage or so-called marriages based on vague promises. The middling classes, when we can glimpse them, have tended to be provident and inhibited, an attitude consonant with their thrifty and calculating economic behavior. The elite, especially at courts, have tended to be promiscuous and have sometimes practiced a highly sophisticated and variegated sexual libertinism. In most societies, there has been a distinct homosexual subculture and in one – classical Athens – a special kind of idealized homosexuality may actually have predominated over heterosexuality among the elite in terms of moral esteem if not of practice. As will be seen, the degree to which homosexuality has been admired, ignored, tolerated, or viciously suppressed has varied enormously over the ages.

A more serious problem is that of evidence. At all times there has been a large – sometimes a gigantic – gap between, on the one hand, the prescriptions of theologians, philosophers, and moralists, supported in part by the enacted laws, and, on the other, actual sexual behavior. Things may be proclaimed as immoral and prohibited by law, which in practice everyone is doing with a clear conscience, rather like exceeding the speed limit today. This difficulty can only be overcome – if at all – by studying the wide variety of evidence available, in full recognition that each has its own limitations.

For example, Aristotle in his *Nichomachian Ethics* classifies adultery – by men as well as women – as a clearly wicked action, like theft or murder. But at the same period, Athenian law put domestic slaves of both genders at the sexual disposal of their masters, *hetaerae* (semi-permanent and public mistresses) flourished as a well-recognized institution, and prostitutes were readily available. There is no evidence whatever that an upper-class fifth-century Greek male regarded his own adultery as at all wicked, or even scandalous, although adultery by married women was strictly forbidden.

Similarly, the Christian Church has always placed great stress on the importance of monogamous marriage and has denounced the evil of adultery. On the other hand, a penitential handbook for guidance of priests hearing confession, datable somewhere between the seventh and eleventh centuries, advises asking the question of a husband: 'Have you taken your wife or your maid servant from the rear?' The punishment for such a sin was forty days' fasting, regardless of whether it was committed with wife or maidservant. It should be noted, first, that there is no extra penalty for adultery in this clause of the penitential; and second, that it evidently regards sex by a man with a maidservant as a perfectly normal event. Only the sexual position was sinful (because used by animals) and needed to be expiated.[9] The writings of theologians, philosophers, and moralists thus tend to display the world in unrealistically stark tones of black and white, divinely ordained sexuality or Sodom and Gomorrah, and to be remote from actual practice. On the other hand, moral codes, usually derived from religion, have often in the long run had a massive impact on both internalized culture and external repression.

In addition to these theological injunctions, medical ideas – usually false ones – have had a great effect upon behavior. One enduring medical belief has been the gross physical harm done by an excessive expenditure of semen by males. This has resulted in diverse practices: in the ancient world, the emphasis laid upon sexual moderation; in China, the careful cultivation of special techniques of intercourse without ejaculation for the conservation of Yang; and in the West, the anti-masturbation panic of the eighteenth and nineteenth centuries.[10] Another medical belief prevalent in the West at all times except the nineteenth century has been the belief in the almost limitless lubricity of women. Such medical theories have dominated whole civilizations and the private lives of many who lived in them.

Diaries and letters are very illuminating, but those which deal with sexual matters are few in number, almost entirely the work of men, almost entirely drawn from elite society, and almost certainly atypical even of their sex or class in their obsessive concern with such matters. The historian would be foolish to avoid using them, but he must always be aware of the dangers of generalizing from what may well be an atypical particular.

Perhaps the most useful evidence of all is that of prosecutions for sexual deviance in the courts of law, since this links the enacted law, the moral attitudes of the judges or jury, and actual behavior. Sir Kenneth Dover's subtle study of Greek homosexuality relies heavily on a speech for the prosecution in a trial concerning homosexual acts in 346 BC.[11] Since the prosecutor was trying to influence a jury, the assumption is that the values he put forward reflected those of his audience. In his path-breaking book about sexuality in Renaissance Florence, Guido Ruggiero has drawn a careful and convincing picture of changing behavior and changing attitudes among different social groups by the use of records of law enforcement against sexual deviants. From a study of the illicit, it is possible to draw the boundaries of the licit. Prosecution, he argues, does not *create* boundaries, but it 'helps to reify the perception of boundaries.' These boundaries are usually internalized, determined more by custom and tradition than by the power of repression.[12] The successful use of legal records by Dover and Ruggiero should provide models for future scholarship in this area. Similarly the records of divorce court cases, if they are described in sufficient detail, throw a vivid light upon the values and attitudes of protagonists, witnesses, and judges.[13] If especial care is taken to study the rhetoric used in court to persuade judges and jurors, reliable conclusions can be drawn about sexual *mentalités* in the past.

There is also erotic art and literature. These may be more revealing about eccentric and illicit sexuality than the common and licit; they may be part of a religious cult, such as the cult of the phallus in Greece, of the Tantra in India or Taoism in China, and they may be subject to stylistic and even technical conventions: for example it is much easier for an artist explicitly to depict a couple in the rear entry position than the missionary, which may account for the heavy preponderance of the former in the erotic art of most times and places – the Orient being an exception to this generalization. And lastly, the writings and artifacts were usually made for an exclusive and possibly secretive elite, and may well bear no relation to the views or behavior of the population at large – witness for example the exotic undergrowth of English elitist pornographic literature of the highest sexual sophistication and obscenity at the height of mid-Victorian sexual prudery.[14] In one case – that of classical Greece – an embarrassingly large amount of the surviving evidence comes either from erotic vase paintings or from pornographic jokes by writers of stage comedy such as Aristophanes.

Finally, virtually all this evidence, except for some litigation, was produced by men. Our direct evidence for women's views about sexuality in the past is almost entirely lacking, and we are left to assume – perhaps wrongly – that they conformed to the stereotypes ascribed to them by men. That stereotype was for a long while a pejorative one, since the woman is the passive partner in the sexual act. This led St Augustine to the astonishing observation that 'the body of a man is as superior to that of a woman as the soul is to the body.'[15] In the light of the manifest defects of all these kinds of evidence, Ariès rightly concluded that 'it is hard for the historian to penetrate the silence that reigns over vast areas of human life.'[16]

If the records are inadequate, the modern models of historical interpretation are hardly more helpful. The pressure-cooker model of modern sex investigators such as Alfred Kinsey treats sexuality as a matter of 'outlets,' or orgasms, and not at all as the end-product of a complex web of cultural, religious, and legal prescriptions whose origins go far back in historic time. Freudian theory hypothesizes that sex is so powerful a drive that it dominates our unconsciousness, and is only with the greatest difficulty kept within bounds by the restraints of civilization. These restraints, however, are said to be often the cause of serious psychological disturbances. This may perhaps be true of certain classes and cultures, although it posits the stark alternatives of uninhibited sexual freedom or civilization, which historically do not seem to have been the only options available. Clinical Freudianism, with its stress on penis-envy, early incentuous experiences (real or imagined), and the Oedipus complex looks increasingly like the product of a Victorian, central European, middle-class, male chauvinist society. Some of the major hypotheses may well not apply to other times and other places.

The most ambitious attempt to write a total history of sexuality is that of the late Michel Foucault, of which three volumes have already been published and a fourth is yet to come.[17] Like all his work it is primarily a highly sophisticated philosophical discourse based upon prescriptive texts. It deliberately omits sexual practice and behavior, and ignores the historical background of the texts even more than do his earlier writings. Volumes II and III, which are concerned with Greece and Rome, provide a one-sided analysis of philosophical discourses, based entirely on works available in translation, and treated entirely out of cultural or historical context. Foucault does not even bother to tell his readers who were the authors of the texts he dissects with such skill, what were their formative experiences, sometimes even what century they lived in or where they came from in the far-flung Roman Empire from Scotland to the Euphrates. The texts of one he makes great use of – Hippocrates – are in fact works by various men spanning several centuries. There is no hint of the size or nature of their readership, nor any attempt to discriminate between enormously influential texts such as those as Plato, Galen, or St Augustine, and those of obscure writers such as Artemidorus or Musonius Rufus.[18]

The reader is offered no hint of the causes of the great revolution in attitudes in the late antique period, except a half-hearted repetition of the tentative hypotheses of Paul Veyne.[19] The weakness of such a purely textual analysis of philosophical ideas, especially when confined to works in translation taken out of cultural or social context, has been set out by both Paul Veyne and John Boswell: 'It is almost fatally tempting for the historian, like the moral theologian, to pick out those factors and doctrines which eventually gained universal acceptance as orthodox. . . . The historian is apt to accept the notion that a particular opinion triumphed because this or that influential thinker espoused it, disregarding the fact that many equally prominent theologians . . . may have held contrary views.' For example, 'there is little reason to assume that the specific objections of influential theologians played any major role in the development of anti-homosexual feelings in Christian Europe.' History simply cannot be written exclusively from these materials, because of the vast gulf between academic theory and popular belief, to say nothing of popular practice. Thus Boswell correctly observes of St Augustine's sexual ethic that 'Christian society has in the main ignored it and at many points rejected it openly.' Veyne raises a similar objection to Foucault's methodology: 'It goes without saying that a philosophy by itself can never be the sole cause of an evolution [in behavior], for then it is necessary to explain why this philosophy was adopted and obeyed to the letter.'[20]

There is a clear consensus in all the books under review that sexuality has had a long and astonishingly complicated history, intimately linked to family structure, social systems, religious beliefs, clerical controls, and civic and state power. The Moral Majority are quite right to see the radical changes in attitudes to, and the practice of, sexuality in America in the last quarter of this century as symbolic of much wider and more fundamental changes in our society, culture, and polity. It is symptomatic of a general permissiveness that some find intolerable and dangerous.

THE ANCIENT WORLD

A great deal is now known about sexuality in the classical Greek world of the sixth, fifth, and fourth centuries BC. Like ourselves in the late twentieth century, the Greeks saw sexual pleasure as a positive good; just as war was presided over by the god Mars, so sex was the area of life taken care of by the goddess Aphrodite. Close inspection makes it clear, however, that all the key concepts concerning the moral economy of sexuality in classical Greece were entirely different from our own. In addition to dividing the species into those who played the active role in sex and those who played the passive, the Greeks saw a second great division between those who controlled their appetites and practiced sex in moderation, and those who were incontinent or orgiastic. This rule was based on considerations of good health, moral virtue, and military fortitude. Our modern division between those men who are faithful to their wives and those who are not certainly existed in theory in classical Greece – it was used by Aristotle – and that between heterosexuals and bisexuals or homosexuals was in some circles recognized. But neither played the crucial role they have done in later Christian societies.[21]

The sexual culture of Greek male citizens of the fifth and fourth centuries BC was unusual since, in addition to the acceptance of bisexuality as the norm – the word *aphrodisia* was applied to both heterosexual and homosexual intercourse – it also made much of an idealized form of pederasty. The bond between an older free man and a pubescent free boy was regarded, in elite intellectual circles, as the highest and purest form of love. This may have been a relatively new development, since there is no explicit hint of it in Homer, who is in general very discreet about sex. Not even in the relationship on and off the battlefield between Achilles and Patroclus does Homer suggest a sexual component. On the other hand, this omission can perhaps be explained by the fact that Homer and his audience simply took the sexual bond for granted.

The classical Greek idealization of elite pederasty was hedged about by all sorts of quite rigid taboos. Anal and oral intercourse were regarded as crude and vulgar, and sexual contact took place face to face between the thighs of the boy, thus obliging the man to crouch in a most awkward position (which looks guaranteed to bring on a backache). If the boy allowed himself to be penetrated anally, he supposedly forfeited his rights to citizenship. Second, the boy was expected to obtain no sexual pleasure from the encounter. Third, it was shameful for a boy of good family to take money for his services, although he certainly expected rich presents. Fourth, the boy should only surrender his body to a worthy suitor, whom he admired and who would provide him with intellectual conversation and education and moral support. Not surprisingly, therefore, a number of vase paintings depict a handsome boy rudely rejecting the none too delicate advances of a bearded man, who is usually portrayed stroking the boy's beardless face with one hand and his nude limp genitals with the other.[22]

This was certainly not an exclusively homosexual society but a bisexual one, in which the lovers married and had children in the normal way. But the women were strictly confined to the home, while the idle men and boys strutted about half naked in the sunlit streets, directing their love and enthusiasm to pederastic flirtations in the gymnasium. It was a fragile cultural construct, limited to upper-class male free-born citizens and hedged around by strict conventions. Exactly when this artificial culture fell into decay is very hard to establish, because of the inadequacy and ambiguity of the evidence. The vase paintings, which all date from *c.* 570 BC to *c.* 470 BC, present graphic and often brilliant illustrations of the physical details of pederastic courtship and copulation, sometimes accompanied by unmistakable evidence of love and affection. There follows a disturbing fifty-year gap from *c.* 470 BC, when the vase paintings stop, to *c.* 420 BC, when philosophical, legal, and literary evidence begins. The philosophers, especially Plato, were very uncertain about homosexuality and wavered in their opinion of its ethical propriety. Plato is responsible for the concept of sublimated homosexual love, epitomized by the episode in which the elderly Socrates successfully resisted the temptation to sleep with the beautiful Alcibiades, to the latter's astonishment. Aristotle is more cautious, and very wary about stating whether or not homosexual activity is or is not against nature because non-procreative.

At exactly the same time as these elitist writings appeared, Aristophanes was producing his comedies for a lower-middle-class audience of poor freemen. His work is marked not only by the 'reduction of homosexual eros to the coarsest physical terms but also by its displacement from the centre to the periphery of Athenian sexual life; for comedy is fundamentally heterosexual.' Thus the plot of *Lysistrata* only works because there were assumed to be no alternative sexual outlets for the soldiers except for the striking women. Moreover, Aristophanes totally ignores the elaborate rituals and taboos that in fact surrounded upper-class pederasty, and assumes that the only homosexual contact is sodomy, coupled with masturbation of the penetrated by the penetrator. One can only conclude that already by the late fifth century (and perhaps always) the Athenian ethic and practice of pederasty was restricted to the upper classes and did not affect the lower classes, who regarded the whole business as disgusting. By the late fourth century, coarse jokes about homosexuality die away and by the third century there is evidence of a 'general inhibiting respectability' in the literature and plays, which is perhaps a foretaste of the pagan and Christian asceticism which was later to sweep across the Mediterranean world.[23] The dichotomy between the soul and the body, elaborated by Plato and other Greeks, has rightly been described by E. R. Dodds as 'the most far-reaching and perhaps the most questionable . . . of all [Greece's] gifts to human culture.'[24]. But it was an idea so powerful that it is still alive and well in the West over 2,300 years later.

But what of the women of Athens, the neglected wives, favored *hetaerae* (or mistresses), and sexually exploited female slaves? There is no doubt that there was something very odd about classical Greek sexuality. In art, there is a repetitious emphasis on the erect phallus which is obsessive by the standards of any other advanced society. This is shown not only by the extremely numerous vase paintings, but also by the two huge stone phalli, parts of which still stand on their original short pillars in the sacred enclosure at Delos – today passed daily by hordes of unobservant tourists.[25]

We have been taught to regard Periclean Athens as the cradle of much that is most admirable about Western civilization: the alphabet, classical art and architecture, philosophy and tragic drama of the highest quality, and courageous victory by a tiny democracy over the mighty oriental tyranny of Persia. Professor Keuls sees it quite differently, as the despotic rule of male chauvinist sex-crazed 'phallocrats,' who created a mythology of rape, exploited slaves of both sexes for sexual purposes, sequestered and neglected their wives, and only treated their boyfriends and mistresses – the *hetaerae* – with any degree of affection.[26] According to Keuls, the Athenians' ruthless and exploitative treatment of boys, slaves, women, and other city-states was not only similar in nature but causally linked. Drunk with male power and with the imperial aggression that accompanies such a system of values, the Athenian phallocrats first committed deliberate genocide on the helpless Greek inhabitants of Melos, who merely asked to stay neutral in the Peloponnesian war, and then brought about the ruin of Athens by a reckless military adventure, the ill-fated expedition to Sicily. The argument is supported by 343 illustrations, mostly of erect phalli. They make an impressive spectacle, and a fairly convincing case is put forward for the existence of a crudely male-oriented society which treated its women and slaves peculiarly abominably and then foundered in military adventurism.

But Keuls fails to demonstrate a direct linkage between the macho sexuality of the Athenian male citizens and the militarism and imperial expansion of Athens. Still less does she prove her far-fetched theory that the sensational scandal of the mutilation of the herms (stone pillars with a head of Hermes and a projecting phallus which stood outside most Athenian front doors) was the work of a group of feminist and pacifist women, protesting against both sexism and militarism.[27] She describes Zeus as 'the master rapist,' sees Greek temples as box-like vaginae surrounded by phallic pillars, and even a purse full of money as an 'economic phallus.' The purchase of a woman's favors she describes as 'rape by money.' She positively hates Athenian men, and greets the final defeat of Athens by Sparta in 404 BC with the sardonic comment: 'the Attic genius had lost its penis.' After a while, it becomes evident that there is an obsessive, even manic, quality about an interpretation of Greek culture exclusively in phallic terms, which renders implausible the alleged tight linkage between the undoubted Athenian fixation upon the phallus and exploitative oppression of women and slaves on the one hand, and ruthless imperial military aggression on the other. This is a deeply flawed book, but despite its excesses and absurdities no one after reading it and examining the illustrations can ever feel quite the same again about Periclean Athens.

Sexuality in ancient Rome followed at least some of the same basic rules as it had in Athens four centuries before. Among the upper classes, bisexuality was taken as normal and the main divisions were between the active and passive role-players, and between a man's self-controlled use or his intemperate abuse of his sexual powers. But the Greek idealization of pederasty with free upper-class boys had vanished, and with it the elaborate conventions and taboos. Homosexual relations were now confined to slave boys and presumably took the form of sodomy. Such liaisons were apparently extremely common, and Gibbon claimed that during the first two most flourishing centuries of the great Roman Empire, only one emperor (Claudius) was not either bisexual or homosexual.[28] No one objected when Hadrian had statues of his boy lover Antinous erected all over the Empire after his premature death. Marital fidelity was the ideal, but among the elite multiple divorces and remarriages, often for political reasons, were common, slaves continued to be kept and used for sexual purposes, many men kept mistresses, and to judge from fragments of literature and the frescoes at Pompeii, brothels abounded. If we are to believe Petronius' satiric story of Trimalchio's feast in *The Satyricon*, a certain amount of polymorphous perversity was practiced not only by the court and the landed elite but also by the rich commercial classes.[29]

LATE ANTIQUITY AND EARLY CHRISTIANITY

By the second century AD there appeared the first rumblings of a major revolution in sexuality, among both pagan philosophers and the Christian Fathers. The Stoics and the neo-Platonists were the first to urge not merely moderation and self-control, but sexual asceticism. Plato and other Greeks had long ago claimed the superiority of the soul over the body. Embroidering on that fatal dichotomy, Seneca argued that 'Pleasure is a vulgar thing, petty and unworthy of respect, common to dumb animals,' and some Christian Fathers, among them St Jerome, preached that *all* sexual pleasure was sinful and to be avoided. This extreme stress on the struggle to purify the body in this world is hardly surprising for a religion which believed in the complete physical resurrection of flesh and body in the next, an idea which the pagans found absurd. 'Flesh is the axis of salvation,' observed Tertullian. But even this was not enough. The early Christians 'vied with each other in heaping abuse upon the body, describing it as "clay and gore", "a filthy bag of excrement and urine" . . . St Anthony blushed every time he had to eat or satisfy any bodily function. Because the body's life was the soul's death, salvation lay in mortifying it.' This was a feeling which somehow was combined with a belief in the future resurrection of that hated body.[30]

What better way was there to mortify the body than to deny it all sexual pleasure? Many early Christians regarded marriage as 'a competition in continence,' themselves abstained from sexual relations all their lives, and preached that all sexual pleasure was sinful, as did SS Ambrose and Jerome. Some even went so far as to castrate themselves, as did Origen. 'A contempt for the human condition and a hatred of the body was a disease endemic in the entire culture of the period.' Man had to learn to control not only his bodily lusts, but his very thoughts, so that both body and soul were free from sin. There was thus a major shift from an aesthetic of sexual pleasure to a purification of desire.[31]

Stoics and Christians not only advocated a new sexual austerity, but also combined to erect a new dichotomy, this time between attitudes to a wife and attitudes to other women. St Jerome copied Seneca in arguing that the duties of a wife were to be a fertile breeder, a good mother, and a prudent housekeeper, but that sexual passion should play no part in the relationship with her husband.

This is hardly surprising, since until fairly recent times the purpose of marriage has had nothing to do with romantic love, sexual passion, or even necessarily friendship. It was a business arrangement between two propertied families for the production of legitimate children to inherit their property; for the extension of both families' political connections; for the social placement and status enhancement of women; and for capital transfers between families through the dowry. Among the lower classes, where there was no dowry to give or property to inherit, Veyne claims that it was hardly worth the trouble to go through so formal a ceremony, although the true extent of concubinage in the Roman world is obscure and disputed.[32]

This new sexual asceticism greatly narrowed the boundaries dividing the licit from the illicit, denigrated the role of sex in human life, and limited so far as possible its use even within marriage to the purposes of procreation. These were ideas which seem to have owed little or nothing to the Jewish tradition, which always regarded licit sexual activity as a sacred duty and a supreme pleasure, remained tolerant of homosexuality as expressed in the story of David and Jonathan, and only drew the usual harsh line against female adultery.[33]

The new asceticism began with the Stoics, but was taken up and developed much further by the Christians. As is well known, St Paul put marriage far below virginity on the scale of morality, a mere reluctant compromise to deal with the problem of concupiscence. Along with this went the development, borrowed from the Stoics, of the idea of the indissolubility of the marriage bond, a doctrine which lasted until the nineteenth century. The Christians also insisted on marital fidelity by the husband as well as the wife, a moral imperative which from that day to this has been honored as much in the breach as the observance. In the early years of the Church, these ideas led to some strange consequences. Thus the early Christian bishops married and begot children who would carry on their priestly functions, and then at about forty adopted 'virginity' and thereafter lived lives of abstemious chastity.[34]

Boswell rightly sums up these major moral and spiritual changes in ways of thinking about sexuality, sexual pleasure, and marriages as 'this crucial transition in Western history,' and Ariès as 'one of the great turning points in the history of our civilization.'[35] The causes of the social diffusion of this revolution in Western thought, however, remain obscure. This is not a subject that interested Foucault, who as a philosopher was only concerned with the texts. Paul Veyne has made the very interesting suggestion that it should be associated with the transformation of the senatorial class into a disciplined and obedient imperial bureaucracy. If so, it would be a psychological reaction to a new social situation. The same quest for disciplined social and sexual respectability was, he suggests, as attractive to third-century Roman aristocratic bureaucrats as it was to nineteenth-century bourgeois businessmen.

Veyne explains the attraction of sexual asceticism to the free poor as an escape mechanism, caused by reaction to their oppressed and despised condition. Instead of rebelling, they adopted a policy of sexual self-repression. Their gains from this strategy were symbolic, not real: self-respect, dignity in the eyes of their masters, and the approbation of God. Veyne believes that 'this popular reaction, which led to a plebeian conservatism, is the principal reason for sexual repression in all centuries.' He suggests that the Christian leaders, following the Stoics, skillfully exploited these two convergent subterranean shifts of *mentalité* among the senatorial bureaucracy and the free poor, and thereby achieved their remarkable success in proselytizing despite persecution.[36]

A rather different sociological explanation is offered by Boswell, who suggests that what happened was the overthrow by the countryside of the more tolerant and hedonistic values associated with city life, a change reinforced by the rise to power of emperors and theologians whose origins and ideas were those of the distant provinces in the now enormous Empire. For Boswell, the new asceticism thus grew out of the collapse of the urban economy and culture in the late Roman period, and their replacement by the austere beliefs of conservative provincial country dwellers.[37] Neither of these explanations is entirely convincing, but each is at least not implausible. Either is preferable to no explanation at all, except that somehow a wholly new ascetic sexual morality preached by pagan Stoics and Christian Fathers swept across the Mediterranean, replacing the older tradition of tolerant hedonism.

Whatever the cause of this great moral mutation, the result was the start of a shift from a world of bisexuals divided between the penetrators and the penetrated, to one divided between reproductive heterosexuality and sterile homosexuality: from marriage as a relatively rare legal condition undertaken for purposes of property disposal and inheritance, to marriage as a normal condition of that great majority of mankind unable to live a life of total chastity; from sex as pleasure to sex as a means of procreation; from a tolerance of male bisexual promiscuity in marriage to an ideal of male and female pre-marital chastity and marital fidelity; from easy divorce and remarriage to indissoluble marriage and strong discouragement of remarriages; from the moral acceptability of the use of slaves against their own will as sexual playthings to a new universal code of sexual behavior no longer dependent upon the status of the parties involved; and finally from incest as merely a sin to incest as against nature. 'The ascetic', concludes Veyne, 'is a dandy of morality.'[38]

THE MIDDLE AGES

Naturally it took many centuries for the working out and implementation of the various aspects of this new ascetic morality. Above all else, the Church strove during the early Middle Ages forcefully, but in the end vainly, to impose upon the laity some extraordinary restrictions upon the licit times for married sexual activity. The evidence of penitentials from the sixth to the eleventh century – which were intended to be used as guidance to priests in the confessional – show the most intense efforts to restrict the legitimate period of sexual relations to a very small number of days. The principal forbidden times for religious reasons were all Saturdays, Sundays, Wednesdays, and Fridays, and the three forty-day fast periods before Easter and Christmas and after Whitsuntide. In addition, some penitentials added major feast days of the Church and the days of the Apostles. Forbidden times for reasons of female impurity included periods of pregnancy, the period after birth and before churching, and during menstruation. Some penitentials also included periods of breast-feeding, which might last a year or more.

If most of these injunctions were taken seriously and enforced – something which of course we have no means of knowing – they would have reduced the number of days available for sexual relations by an average fertile couple to between twenty-one and forty-four a year.[39] Flandrin argues that these severe restrictions may be the explanation for the demographic stagnation at a low level throughout Western Europe from the sixth to the eleventh century. This is a large and speculative suggestion, which jumps without a shred of evidence from prescription to behavior, but what is more certain is that in the eleventh century the penitentials changed their tone and relaxed their restrictions. In particular, the prohibitions on Wednesdays, Fridays, and Saturdays were abandoned, the duration of the three great fast periods was halved from forty days to twenty, and the forbidden time of pregnancy was reduced to the last three months.[40] This suggests a belated recognition by the church authorities that they were making impossible demands upon the strength of will of the laity.

Apart from conformity to the concept of female impurity, the idea behind these restrictions had been to reduce sexual activity to the minimum necessary to reproduce the species, rather than allow it to be used for mutual pleasure all the year round. They were also a means of providing time for preparing the soul for God and for expiating sins, and a device for expelling the Devil. Behind them lay a magical conception of time which is to be found in many cultures. But these particular demands upon spouses required feats of sexual continence which appear to be almost without parallel in any other known society. The only close example is the advice offered in Chinese tracts, which recommended only about a hundred days annually as magically or morally auspicious for sexual relations.[41] The partial abandonment of these demands in the eleventh century marked a triumph of reason over fanaticism, and a shift of attention by the Church to more practical objectives that might actually be achieved.

It was not until the twelfth century that the Church finally managed to bring under some control the widespread practice of concubinage;[42] to assert the principle that priests could not marry, since they were supposed to emphasize their sacred character by practicing chastity;[43] to insist that marriage was finally declared indissoluble; and, most surprising of all, to claim that in canon law the test of a legally binding marriage was not the blessing of the Church or the will of the parents, but the free consent of both spouses. This last was a doctrine which ran directly counter to the practice of the elite laity, who had used – and went on using – the arranged marriage to accumulate property and extend political connections. The result was a five-hundred-year tussle between canon law theory and secular elite practice. Similarly the Christian injunction that marriage involved sexual fidelity by the husband as well as the wife also ran directly counter to secular practice and was as often violated as observed.

Boswell argues that throughout the first twelve hundred years of Christianity there was no clearcut theological condemnation, and certainly no energetic legal repression, of male homosexuality. It had not yet become *the* 'unnatural' vice. This may be true in general, but Flandrin has found some penitentials which rank sodomy along with incest among the most serious of all sexual crimes.[44] More certain is Boswell's discovery in the twelfth century, not only of courtly love which we already knew about, but of a major explosion of overtly homosexual literature. He claims that homo-eroticism, whether sublimated or physical, was for a while 'the animating force of most Christian life-styles.'[45] This may be an exaggerated statement, but sublimated homo-eroticism certainly affected some of the most famous bishops and saints of the period, such as St Anselm or St Aelred of Rievaulx. At a more popular and more openly physical level, there is evidence that specialized male brothels were available in north-central France in Paris, Chartres, Orleans, and Sens, while a common philosophical *topos* was a debate between Ganymede and Helen about the relative sexual attractiveness to men of boys and women.[46] The sexual values and practices of the ancient world clearly took a very long time to die out.

This short flowering of sexual tolerance in the twelfth century came to a shattering halt in the thirteenth, when a new and far more ferocious wave of repression of all forms of deviance descended upon Europe. There was vigorous official repression by Church and State of all forms of religious, moral, and sexual deviants, including Albigensians, heretics, Templars, Jews, usurers, witches, adulterers, and homosexuals.

There was, however, a striking exception to this tidal wave of repression. One variety of what is usually regarded if not as deviant then at least as sinful sex, namely the use of prostitutes, was not merely tolerated in the late Middle Ages, but was positively encouraged by the organization of municipally licensed brothels in formally designated red light districts. The facts are now beyond dispute, since many scholars have all independently come to the same conclusions.[47] The prime reason for this exception would appear to have been the danger to social peace created by the fact that the average male age of marriage among the well-to-do had risen to the late twenties or even early thirties, some ten or fifteen years after puberty. All towns were faced with the problem of calming roving bands of sexually frustrated single men, and brothels were regarded as useful, indeed necessary, tranquilizers for bachelors. They relieved sexual frustrations and so both avoided public riots and saved respectable matrons from the threat of gang-rape in the streets. As St Augustine had long ago remarked, 'remove prostitutes from human affairs, and you will destroy everything with lust.'[48]

These municipal brothels had an additional attraction for married men. A visit to one of them, unlike one to an unlicensed brothel, gave immunity to the client from a charge of adultery in ecclesiastical law, and the consequent obligation of penance, and also from prosecution in a royal court. Finally, the City Fathers made money out of the business. The only limitations placed upon the practice of the profession was that the brothels were forbidden to do business during church services on Sundays and during Holy Week. By the fifteenth century, almost every town in southern France or Italy seems to have had a licensed brothel, while villages were taken care of once a week by scheduled visits by a licensed prostitute from a nearby town. As for the prostitutes themselves, they were treated as respectable members of society, like any other guild, and were allowed to take a formal part in civic processions and festivities.[49]

THE EARLY MODERN AND MODERN PERIODS

In the sixteenth century, everything changed once more. All over Europe, the towns shut down their licensed brothels and embarked on a vigorous drive to suppress all forms of extra-marital sex. By 1562 one-fifth of all the criminal cases coming before the courts in Calvinist Geneva dealt with fornication, while the Counter-Reformation was not far behind in its puritanical zeal. In Spain, brothels were declared illegal in 1623, and prostitution was made a penal offense in 1661, despite lingering doubts whether such action might not increase the temptations to the far worse sin and crime of sodomy.[50] Town and village authorities were empowered to break into and search houses where they suspected that fornication might be taking place. Convicted prostitutes were whipped half-naked through the streets until the blood ran down their backs. Their clients were shamed by being made to stand in church on Sunday on a platform in front of the whole congregation, dressed in a white sheet and holding a candle, a public shame punishment many would willingly have paid large sums of money to avoid. In seventeenth-century England and New England, the same shame punishments were inflicted upon couples proven guilty of pre-nuptial conception by the birth of a baby within eight months of marriage. It should be pointed out that in the early modern period, unlike today, the word 'whore' had a double meaning. Today it is confined to a woman who sells her body promiscuously for money. In the sixteenth to eighteenth centuries it also meant a woman who had sexual relations with someone not her legal husband, whether for romantic love or sexual passion or mere goodwill or curiosity.

All these efforts and linguistic habits are the products of a society anxious to enforce sexual abstinence upon the unmarried and to reduce the amount of consensual unions, concubinage, and pre-nuptial cohabitation. Children of the middle and upper classes, after the age of fourteen or so, were safely shut away behind the walls of boarding schools and colleges under the watchful eyes of bachelor clerics. By the late sixteenth century, this new wave of repression was fully functioning, in both Protestant and Catholic countries. It enlisted the combined repressive efforts of State and Church, and was directed by political, religious, municipal, and village leaders.

At the same time as all the rival state churches were closing brothels, punishing adulterers, forbidding concubinage, and making sodomy a capital offense, some of them were also shifting to encourage sexuality within marriage in certain significant ways. The Protestants recognized that sexual passion within 'Holy Matrimony' was desirable for pleasure, to help to bind the spouses to one another, as well as for procreation, and their clergy were positively encouraged to marry. Moreover, in all Protestant countries except England marriage was no longer regarded as an indissoluble sacrament but as a solemn contract. It was therefore breakable, with full divorce and permission to remarry, on grounds of desertion, female adultery, or life-threatening male cruelty. Whereas in the fifteenth century the State and the Church had combined to control and license sexual morals for the sake of public order, in the sixteenth they combined to suppress extra-marital sexuality, and (within strict limits) to accept sexual pleasure in marriage, for the sake of public decency. Even Fanny Hill ends up by marrying her beloved Charles, in doing so combining in marriage both romantic love and sexual passion.

What caused this remarkable shift in public opinion and policy against extra-marital sexuality? No one really knows. A minority movement for the suppression of prostitution was evident in the late fifteenth century, so that the emotional fury engendered by the Reformation merely built on an existing trend of opinion, just as the sexual asceticism of the early Church Fathers had built on the writings of the pagan Stoics. What was new was the theological emphasis that sexuality should henceforward be strictly confined within marriage, which now consequently became the prime focus of heterosexual love. In Protestant Europe, 'Holy Matrimony' replaced chastity as the Christian ideal. The new stress on marriage appears as early as 1450 in Venice, where fornicating couples were encouraged by the courts to get married. Even in case of rape, the courts pressed for a settlement of the matter by marriage. Thus the protection and encouragement of marriage and the family had become a central concern of the Venetian state at least by 1450.[51]

Similarly by 1400 the Venetian courts were becoming increasingly concerned about sodomy, which they began to treat as one of the most serious of all crimes, along with treason and heresy. It was now regarded as a crime against nature as well as a threat to the safety of the city, which was thought to be liable to suffer the fate of Sodom and Gomorrah. Two points stand out in this story. One is that the traditional view that the most vile and despicable of the two actors is the passive one had come to an end. Legal opinion had shifted sharply to the more modern attitude of blaming the sexual aggressor rather than his victim or accomplice. The second is the steady and startling rise of sodomy cases before the Venetian courts, from five to nearly two hundred every twenty-five years from the mid-fourteenth to the late fifteenth century. The more zealously the court investigated and prosecuted homosexuality, the more cases of sodomy it discovered.[52] It can plausibly be suggested that homosexuality and the repression of homosexuality go in waves, periods of indifference creating greater public exposure, and greater public exposure eventually generating a backlash of fear and repression.

The motor force behind the repression of the sixteenth century seems to have been new concepts of virtue and honor, now closely identified with marriage and the family. There was a powerful desire to repress, which cannot merely be attributed to the growing power of the Renaissance state to control the lives of its subjects. In any case, states, however powerful, usually have more important things to do than attempt to stamp out fornication and adultery. The sixteenth century was a period of destructive civil wars, declining real wages, rising population, and increased unemployment and vagrancy. All states attempted to cope with these problems by harsher measures to enforce law and order. But this hardly explains why the drive to order should have been so fiercely concentrated on deviant sexuality, not only on sodomy, which almost everywhere was made a penal offense punishable by death, but also on all forms of extra-marital sex, fornication, concubinage, and adultery. One reason for the emphasis on sexual repression may well be a moral panic generated by the explosive spread of a most virulent form of syphilis in the early sixteenth century, supposedly an import from the New World. The disease, with its horrible tertiary symptoms, rapidly reached epidemic proportions before it could be checked by the introduction of treatment by mercury, and perhaps by a mutation of the virus so as not to destroy its host too rapidly.

At exactly the same time there appeared a directly opposite trend of thought, a semi-submerged undercurrent of eroticism, especially in Italy, which ran directly counter to the general drift to sexual asceticism and repression. For example, Aretino in the mid-sixteenth century wrote defiantly: 'a good pair of buttocks is possessed of greater power than all that has ever proceeded from philosophers, astrologers, alchemists and necromancers.'[53] Aretino's writings and Julio Romano's drawings and engravings of sexual postures were almost the first works of pure eroticism or pornography in the West for over a thousand years. From Petronius and Martial to Aretino there was virtually nothing.[54]

This Italian eroticism of the sixteenth century suggests that the repression was far from fully effective in confining the sexual drive to the narrow pathway of marriage. And yet, despite the late age of marriage, bastardy rates and pre-nuptial conception rates in the seventeenth century were surprisingly low, and homosexuality was largely confined, so far as the records go, to the nobility and courtiers in the major cities, who were largely immune from the law. But where did the libido go? Was it sublimated in religious zeal, or diverted into masturbation or the various forms of non-procreative sexual activity? We do not know and probably never will. All that can be said with certainty is that in England, New England, and parts of France, there is clear evidence that among the lower classes the courting procedure included what was known in England and America as 'bundling.' This consisted of all-night sessions in which a courting couple were alone in the dark in a room with a bed, a practice carried out with at least the tacit consent and complicity of the adults. In the seventeenth century these all-night encounters do not seem to have resulted in a great deal of pre-marital pregnancy, to judge by the low rates of bastardy and pre-nuptial pregnancy.[55]

In the eighteenth century, the sexual life of the West took yet another turn. Most Protestant churches relaxed their previous tight grip on the sexual behavior of their congregations, although in Catholic areas the confessional box remained an effective control device. In England, for example, official tracking down and pros-ecution of fornication by the church courts had ceased by the 1730s. On the other hand, between 1680 and 1800 the age of marriage for women fell by three years, from twenty-six and a half to twenty-three and a half, and for men by two, from twenty-seven and a half to twenty-five and a half. At the same time the proportion of adults of both sexes who never married fell from 18 percent to 6 percent. One would have expected that both these trends would have reduced the number of extra-marital concep-tions, but in fact the reverse occurred. In a sample of villages and small towns, the proportion of all first births conceived out of wedlock, including pre-nuptial conceptions of children of future married couples and conceptions of future bastards, rose from 12 percent in the late seventeenth century to an astonishing 50 percent in the late eighteenth.[56] Since if London were to be included in the sample the figure would certainly be much higher, in late eigh-teenth-century England, pregnancy clearly preceded and often caused marriage, rather than vice versa. On the other hand many of these conceptions were caused by the *expectation* of future marriage, which in a growing number of cases was not fulfilled. The resultant proliferation of bastards whom no one wanted caused the rise of institutions to deal expeditiously with the situation: 'killing wet-nurses' whose function it was to dispose of the infants in as short a time as possible, and foundling hospitals or work-houses which in practice served the same purpose. As a result the average expectation of life for an illegitimate baby of the poor in the eighteenth century was more a matter of weeks or months than of years.

The eighteenth century also saw the first large-scale production and consumption of high-quality pornography, such as *Fanny Hill*, which was based on the new conventions of the novel, creates a guilt-free paradise of heterosexual promiscuous and polymorphous perversity, and then ends by subsuming both love and sex within the bonds of a happy marriage.[57] Homosexuality not only continued to flourish with impunity among the elite, but also began once more to come out into the open among the lower classes, at any rate in the great conurbation of London where homosexual clubs and alehouses sprang up. But public opinion in the eighteenth century was perhaps even more ferociously hostile than ever before to those of the lower classes who thus flaunted their sexual prefer-ence, and they therefore ran the risk of severe punishment and even hanging. In 1726 there was discovered in London a flourishing homosexual subculture centered around the equivalent of present-day bath-houses, where up to fifty men would assemble of an evening for sexual purposes. This resulted in a wave of pros-ecutions, leading to a few hangings and many sentences to the pillory. Because of the intense hostility to homosexuality among the London poor – especially women – thoughout the eighteenth and nineteenth centuries, exposure in the pillory was the equivalent of prolonged torture, and occasionally even death. In 1762, for example, a convicted sixty-year-old homosexual was put in the pillory in Cheapside: 'the populace fell upon the wretch, tore off his coat, waistcoat, shirt, hat, wig and breeches, and then pelted and whipped him till he had scarcely any signs of life left.'[58] On the other hand, it is remarkable that very few were condemned to death, and that quite a number were acquitted. Juries and judges still were more influenced by the law than by moral panic. More-over, a homosexual brought to trial in 1726 defiantly staked out a new claim to individual freedom: 'I think there's no crime in making what use I please of my own body.'[59] It was to take another 250 years for so radical a notion to become generally accepted.

The suggested explanations – xenophobia and the activities of the Society for the Reformation of Manners – seem inadequate to explain the strength of hostility among the English poor. Their extreme reaction to homosexuality seems to indicate a major shift of attitudes, by which the sodomite was no longer regarded as a bisexual, but as someone acting a role which violated gender defini- tions by exclusive preference for the male sex, effeminacy, and pederasty. On the other hand, in some intellectual circles in late eighteenth-century England homosexuality was regarded as ethi- cally neutral, the chief evidence being some five hundred pages of unpublished notes, essays, and plans for a book on adult homo- sexuality and pederasty made by the Utilitarian jurist and philos- opher Jeremy Bentham, written between 1774 and 1825.[60]

At the same time as these signs of more open acceptance of sexual passion for its own sake in marriage, and even some tolerance for homosexuality, a strong counter-current is also visible, shown by the extraordinary popularity throughout the eighteenth century of books denouncing the appalling moral and medical dangers of masturbation, a revival in a new form of the age-old belief that semen was a precious fluid to be husbanded with care. This anti- masturbation panic, first led by the clergy but then taken up and driven to extremes by the medical profession, appears as something of an anomaly within the eighteenth-century sexual code. It was a panic which grew to hysterical proportions in the Victorian period, only to die away again in the twentieth century.[61] There were also other ways in which the eighteenth century displayed a continued modesty and even prudery in its sexual conduct. It is clear, for example, that couples almost never stripped naked in the eighteenth century in order to make love. Even honeymoon couples went to bed at night and got up again next morning dressed in a shirt and a smock, and there is evidence that they kept them on all night. Nor in the hundreds of cases of sexual intercourse and foreplay recorded in detail in divorce court proceedings is there more than the very occasional hint of the practice of oral sex.[62] Even in the male fantasy world of pornography it does not occur very frequently in the eighteenth century.

On the other hand, this relative absence of oral-genital contacts may perhaps be explained by the fact that even in the eighteenth century very few men and women, even among the elite, regularly washed themselves. The Roman practice of bathing had at last died out in the late Middle Ages, and from the fifteenth to the seven- teenth century men and women changed their linen regularly but rarely washed anything but their faces and hands. Washing the body only began slowly to become common again among the high aristocracy in the eighteenth century, especially in France where the first bidet is recorded in 1726.[63] Poor hygiene alone is thus sufficient to explain the lack of interest shown in oral sex in the eighteenth century, even on the part of people long accustomed to the noisome nature of their surroundings and their own bodies.[64]

Despite intensive research, sexuality in the nineteenth century is still much of a mystery. On the one hand, it displayed what seems like the all-time pinnacle of hypocritical prudery and sexual asceticism. As an example of the growing prudery, as early as 1770 Wedgwood was obliged to add fig-leaves to all the nude classical gods on his china intended for a middle-class market. But 'fig-leaves are not always enough,' and some figures had to be entirely re-draped. Only the most expensive items, for sale to the aristocracy, could still find a market in their classical nudity.[65]

Another sign of the times was the partial replacement of the ancient and durable idea of women as more lubricious than men by a novel and fairly widespread concept of women as sexless, domesticated child-bearing machines.[66] The prevalence of this idea in Victorian society has recently been challenged, but the evidence to support such a view is not convincing.[67] Peter Gay makes much of the diary of one highly orgasmic (and adulterous) middle-class New England woman, but it would be strange indeed if there was *no* orgasmic bourgeois woman in the nineteenth century.[68] Her abnormality is emphasized by the fact that she lived for years in a *ménage à trois*, hardly a normal experience for a Victorian lady. Our only statistical evidence concerns a mere forty-five respondent wives of members of the Stanford University faculty in the late nineteenth century. The results are ambiguous. Only a little more than half the sample thought that sex was a pleasure for both parties; a fifth said they never had any sexual desire; two-thirds thought that the prime purpose of the sexual act was procreation; and only a third claimed that they 'usually' or 'always' achieved orgasm. This data certainly somewhat qualifies and moderates the assertion of the popular Dr Acton, writing in the middle of the century, that 'the majority of women (happily for them) are not much troubled with sexual feelings. . . . She submits to her husband, but only to please him, and but for the desire for maternity, would rather be relieved from his attentions.' Acton was

only speaking of 'the majority of women' – a point often forgotten –
and the Stanford evidence suggests that towards the end of the
century about half the sample more or less held his opinions, but
that the other half did not.[69]

Perhaps the most bizarre manifestation of the Victorian attitude
to sexuality was the raising of the fear of masturbation, already
growing in the eighteenth century, to a dominant obsession of both
doctors and moralists. It was widely asserted as a scientific fact,
and was widely believed, that the practice led to insanity and a
host of physical ailments. It was a phobia which reached its apogee
towards the end of the nineteenth century, and has today almost
entirely disappeared.[70] It remains a mystery why the medical
profession adopted the novel position in the early eighteenth
century, after centuries of toleration based on the concept of the
need for occasional ejaculation to maintain the balance of bodily
fluids, and why they stuck to it, without a shred of evidence, for
over 150 years. At the same time as masturbation was being actively
repressed, male homosexuality, pederasty, and female adultery
were also vigorously condemned and punished. Of this there can
be little doubt. It is evident that the object was to confine all forms
of sexual release within the bounds of the marital bed, the one
exception – a tacit toleration for casual male adulteries – being
explained by the need to give rein to the irrepressible animal nature
of males. A case could therefore be made that all this repression
and redefinition of the illicit was merely designed to protect and
support the Victorian family. This conclusion would find support
from many of the more moderate writers of the age, but it still
would not explain the hysterical quality of the rhetoric used in
much of the literature on the subject.

If the facts of a massive attempt in the nineteenth century to
redefine and narrow the boundaries of licit sexuality and to confine
it within the family are clear enough, the causes remain obscure.
There was clearly a moral panic among the upper classes of Europe
in the face of the threat posed to their status and position by the
ideas of equality emerging from the French Revolution in the 1790s.
There was a fear among the hereditary governing classes that unless
they set an example of family respectability to their inferiors in
terms of sexual morality and religious piety, they too might suffer
the fate of the French nobility. There was also a strong moral
asceticism, associated with late eighteenth-century evangelical

religion in England and German Pietism on the Continent, at work as early as 1770, if Wedgwood's middle-class market is anything to go by. Both religious movements were the inspiration for moral crusades against all forms of deviant sexuality. In England, this led to active lobbying for a new legislation and more active law enforcement against prostitution, pornography, homosexuality, and the like. Romanticism added to the stew by supplying an unrealistic ideal of the female gender as naturally pure and unsullied by sexual desires. Middle-class women consequently found themselves both elevated on a pedestal and confined to house and home. An ideology of female sexual purity, gender inequality, and patriarchy was thus an accidental by-product of the Romantic movement. At the same time, 'natural' sex became equated with national strength; and 'unnatural' sex with military, political, and economic decay, the decline of Rome being cited as a prime example of the latter. Thus nineteenth-century nationalism further reinforced the drive for an external show of prudery and sexual restraint. Finally, it has been suggested that a 'spermatic economy' was a sexual ethic peculiarly appropriate to the acquisitive and retentive bourgeoisie of the Victorian era. But these are all very vague hypotheses which are extremely difficult to prove or disprove.[71]

In practice, however, things did not altogether follow this repressive scenario, especially among the very rich and the very poor, so that there is another side to Victorian sexuality. It is known that large numbers of the urban proletariat were living in casual concubinage;[72] that a vast army of urban prostitutes and highly specialized brothels serviced all classes of men; that venereal disease was a serious social scourge and a threat to the armed forces;[73] and that some of the most elaborate and obscene pornography ever produced was circulating among a tiny handful of elite connoisseurs.[74] Among the elite, homosexual relations, whether emotional or physical, were almost the norm for adolescents in some of the sexually segregated public schools, even if the standard educational fare of the classics from Plato to Juvenal was carefully bowdlerized to exclude all mention of the subject.[75] At the same time as attitudes and behavior were moving in these contradictory directions, the first major inquiries into the medical and psychological aspects of sex were being launched in scientific circles. This 'desire to know' was a central characteristic of nineteenth-century sexuality, culminating in the works of men as diverse as Havelock Ellis and Freud, as Foucault was perhaps the first to point out.

What is certain is that the ferocious hostility to homosexuality among the poor which had existed in the early eighteenth century now spread to the upper and middling classes who operated the courts of law as judges and juries. Whereas in the early eighteenth century very few convicted homosexuals were hanged, and exposure in the pillory, although a horrible experience, was rarely fatal, things were strikingly different a century later. In the first thirty years of the nineteenth century some sixty homosexuals were convicted and hanged in civil courts, and another twenty under naval regulations. There was thus a striking escalation in the ferocity of punishment and scale of persecution from the early eighteenth to the early nineteenth century. 'Homophobia' clearly reached a perhaps unprecedented peak among the poor in the nine-teenth century, lasting as late as 1895, when Oscar Wilde had to be protected from an angry mob.[76] This is all the more extraodinary since 'an England which in many ways was the most liberal country in Europe could condemn homosexuals to the rope and the pillory at a time when on the continent the medieval laws which made sodomy a capital offence had been totally repudiated.'[77]

Today, in the late twentieth century, the wheel of sexual morality has once more turned, and we are living in a period of quite unprecedented sexual toleration, and of a sexualization of all aspects of everyday life from sea-bathing to the selling of automobiles. Ariès rightly complained that 'we see sex in everything. Every cylinder is a phallus.' Up till now sexual libertinism has been confined to narrow elite circles, often around a court. Today, however, popular books with huge circulations, such as Masters and Johnson's *Human Sexual Response* and Alex Comfort's *The Joy of Sex*, have disseminated among all classes of the population a hedonistic philosophy of sexuality which previously was confined to an elite few.[78] The current widespread diffusion of these ideas is a phenomenon unique in the history of developed societies. It was undoubtedly facilitated by two major technological changes: the development of cheap, reliable, and more or less safe contracep-tive devices, and the discovery of antibiotics which could rapidly cure venereal diseases. But the spread of sexual toleration to homo-sexual activity, which is unaffected by contraception, proves that the ideas are more important than the technology.

There are two central concepts underlying the modern sexual morality. The first is that each consenting adult has total freedom to seek pleasure by doing what he or she pleases with his or her body, with due respect only for rapidly eroding standards of public decency. The second is an extension to its ultimate limit of the concept of individualism, an ideology which has been growing in the West since the late seventeenth century. Modern sexologists such as Masters no longer view sexual intercourse as a method of procreation, nor even as a means of pair-bonding for married couples, but as two quite independent sexual experiences. He declares that every orgasm is 'an entirely egocentric affair.' As a result, Béjin concludes that for the modern sexologist 'the partner is the helpful parasite in a fundamentally autoerotic act.'[79]

This new and unique sexual culture may well not last much longer, in view of the deepening moral tangle about abortion, as medical technology makes the problem of what is and what is not a viable foetus a more and more unanswerable question; the rising tide of feminist hostility to the exploitative and humiliating aspects of some pornography; and the steady expansion of 'moral majoritarian' prudery and demands for sexual control. There is also growing public anxiety about the social consequences of the apparent disintegration of the traditional family, now that the divorce rate in America has reached 50 percent and the illegitimacy rate is creeping up close to 20 percent. The figures for Western Europe are lower, but the trend is steadily upward towards the American model. Larger and larger numbers of households are today composed of single persons, or pairs of diverse genders, living together outside formal marriage. This is not a new phenomenon, but the scale on which it is now occurring and its spread to all social levels are certainly unprecedented. Finally the appearance or spread of so far incurable new venereal diseases such as herpes, chlamydia, and AIDS – the last of which is fast threatening to become as terrible a scourge as was syphilis in the sixteenth century – has made it impossible any longer to regard promiscuous sex as a cost-free and victimless form of entertainment. For the first time in decades society has been obliged to prohibit – on grounds of public health not morality – certain sexual practices between consenting adults.

Whether the trend towards near total freedom for adults is temporary or permanent has yet to be seen, and the degree to which it is the cause of social instability and of maladjusted children is still unproven. What is certain is that it does not seem to be increasing the sum of human happiness, as was anticipated when the sexual revolution began in the 1960s. Sexual liberation is forging its own new chains, psychological, social, and medical, and the growing and well-founded fear of AIDS may well bring the so-called sexual revolution to a grinding halt, barely a generation after it all began.

CONCLUSION

The work of a pioneer band of distinguished historians has slowly and painstakingly revealed the outlines of the extraordinary and erratic history of changing attitudes to sexuality in the West since the sixth century BC, and has described the philosophical and religious systems of ideas which lay behind those changes. What is disappointing, however, is the poverty of the explanations offered for the success of the great moral revolutions they have uncovered. As a philosopher, Foucault was not interested in historical caus-ation. For the major revolution of late antiquity, Veyne advanced a dual theory. First, it filled the psychological needs of a new self-disciplined imperial bureaucracy which transformed the Roman senatorial class from machismo warlords into sexually ascetic clerks. This would account for the appeal of the new ascetic morality to this senatorial class, which supplied the early Church with bishops. Second, the popularity of the new religion among the lower classes was a reactive response of the free poor to a deepening sense of oppression and lack of self-respect. The adoption of the new ascetic Christian sexual morality was thus in both cases a psychological response to a social situation.[80]

It is indeed plausible that when things begin to go badly wrong, as was happening during the decline and fall of the Roman Empire, men and women take to ascetic morality and mystical religion in order to provide an explanation of, and salvation from, their growing misfortunes, and to assuage their feelings of guilt. The trouble is the *ex post facto* nature of this type of argument. When-ever something puzzling occurs, historians tend to fall back on vague sociological generalizations such as the rise of the bour-geoisie, or the growth of a sense of anxiety and anomie. But just as the bourgeoisie have constantly been rising since the twelfth century, so there has almost never been an age without anxiety. Let us take a concrete example. Most people would agree that the decades since 1945 have been ones of exceptional and widespread anxiety, generated by fears of a collapse of civilization through a nuclear holocaust, the population explosion, or the destruction of the environment by pollution. If this had been a period characterized by the rise of religious fanaticism and an eager acceptance of the most rigid and repressive sexual codes there would have been no difficulty in explaining the popularity of such trends by the high level of anxiety. As it is, however, the period has until very recently been characterized in the West by a progressive secularization of belief and an unprecendented outburst of sexual permissiveness. This suggests that the anxiety theory of sexual repression should be treated with the greatest care, and used only when the documentation is very clear indeed. It has yet to be demonstrated that a sense of the world falling apart can be shown to have been particularly pervasive among the free poor of the Mediterranean world in late antiquity.

E. R. Dodds, who wrestled twenty years ago with the same phenomenon (and found it entirely repulsive), argued that symptoms of milder forms of asceticism can certainly be traced back to the Greeks, but that in its extreme third-century form it was something new. He saw 'the whole development less as an infection from an extraneous source than as an endogenous neurosis, an index of intense and wide-spread guilt feelings. The material distresses of the third century certainly encouraged it, but they did not occasion it, since its beginnings . . . lie further back.' He noted that Porphyry had remarked that only sick souls stand in need of Christianity, and had added that 'sick souls were numerous in our period.' Above all, Christianity offered a sense of community and sociability in a collapsing world, and a shared moral asceticism was a powerful bonding force to hold the group together.[81]

Boswell offers a rather different but equally socio-psychological explanation of the same phenomenon, which he attributes to the capture of the failing empire by provincials and villagers bringing with them their rural values intolerant of all forms of sexual deviance. This is quite plausible with regard to homosexuality which, apart from special cases of adult males isolated from females in ships and prisons, has always seemed to flourish best in an urban setting. The trouble is, however, that sexual asceticism is hardly a standard feature of rural life, and there is no evidence whatever that it was so in late antiquity. Moreover, Boswell himself abandons this argument when he has to explain the second, even greater repression of deviants that occurred in the thirteenth century. Since this period saw the apogee of the medieval urban economy and culture, it is impossible to explain the repression by a new triumph of rural values or even an economic crisis. Instead Boswell falls back on the rise of a bureaucratic and legalistic state, coupled with mounting xenophobia generated by the Crusades. But bureaucratic formalism and crusading zeal hardly seem adequate to explain so major a transformation in moral attitudes and official action.[82]

The same problem arises with the third wave of intolerant repression of all forms of deviation in the sixteenth century. Vigorous attacks were made upon sodomy, prostitution, fornication, and all forms of non-procreative marital sex, as well as Judaism and witchcraft. After 1520 the religious crisis of the Reformation and Counter-Reformation was clearly a vitally important factor, as also was the epidemic spread of a particularly virulent form of syphilis. But the drive against witchcraft began long before, in about 1480,[83] as did the drive against prostitution and sodomy.[84] Moreover, the rise of the Renaissance state hardly explains the obsessive concern with sexual morality. The social and economic upheavals of the sixteenth and seventeenth centuries obviously called for increased measures of social control, but not for hunting down and exterminating Jews, sodomites, or witches. The Reformation and Counter-Reformation can explain the persecution of religious heretics but hardly the drive for sexual austerity.

The fourth and last wave of sexual intolerance, beginning in the 1790s, can perhaps be attributed to fear of social upheaval caused by the French Revolution, evangelical religion, the Romantic ideal of woman as unsullied by sexual desire, the austere values of the new industrial and commercial bourgeoisie, and modern nationalism with its association of national weakness with sexual libertinism. These are quite plausible causes, but even taken together they are hardly fully convincing, especially since popular prudery was rising as early as the 1770s before most of these ideologies had taken root. As for the alternating waves of toleration and indifference, there is as yet not even the suggestion of a causal model.

It should be noted that historians of sexual *mores* in other societies have done no better in developing plausible causal models. Van Gulik believed that in China a major shift from permissiveness to a sexual puritanism – one which still continues to this day – occurred in the thirteenth century, and became very much more severe in the seventeenth. He suggested that it all began because of a specific historial event, the hiding by Chinese householders of their women from the Mongols who were billeted amomg them in the mid-thirteenth century. Bodde rejects this implausible hypothesis, and attributes the change to a longer and slower process of social and intellectual transformation caused by the rise of neo-Confucian prudery and Buddhist asceticism in reaction to the communal sex practices of Taoism. He traces the growth of asceticism back much earlier, and believes that during the greater part of imperial history 'the prevailing Chinese attitude towards sex . . . was repressive, puritanical and masculine,' involving female foot-binding, the withholding of male ejaculation, very limited auspicious times for sexual intercourse, and no public nudity or dancing between the sexes. As for the artistic and literary erotica of the Ming period, it was restricted to a very small wealthy urban elite. About the reasons for the popular acceptance of so long-lived an ascetic sexual culture in China, Bodde remains ambiguous and baffled.

Turning from causes to consequences, Bodde points to the equally unsatisfactory conclusion that, if the origins of repression or libertinism remain obscure, their results are equally so. Sexual libertinism does not always lead to the collapse of civilizations, and sexual puritanism is not always a stimulus to cultural greatness, scientific innovation, and imperial conquest. He concludes: 'it almost seems as if sex, despite its overwhelming importance for the individual, after all may not be such a decisive factor in the development of societies.'[85] If this is true, a huge amount of philosophical, moral, religious, and medical thinking, and of political and administrative energy devoted to repression and persecution of what at different times has been deemed illicit sexual activity, may all have been a total waste of human brain-power, time, and effort.

The intermittent ebbs and flows in the long history of the West of a passion for redefining the boundaries of the licit and the illicit in sexual life remain one of the most baffling phenomena facing the social historian, the historian of ideas, and the historian of *mentalité*. Thanks to the meticulous research of many scholars, we now know the broad outlines of the facts, but the causal mechanisms and the resulting social consequences still elude us. The characteristics that all these episodes of repression have in common is that they have usually included attacks on most forms of deviance, whether racial/religious (Jews or Arabs), or exclusively religious (heretics), or magical (witches), or occupational (usurers), or political (traitors), or sexual (homosexuals or fornicators). All are driven by moral panic, a great fear, but just what it is that triggers off this group hysteria and what it is that calms it remains as obscure as are the results of such repressions and relaxations. All that can be said for certain is that over the long history of Western civilization, there has been no such thing as 'normal sexuality.' Sexuality is a cultural artifact which has undergone constant and sometimes dramatic changes over time, and there is every reason to suppose that there are still more surprising transformations in store in the not too distant future.[86]

CHAPTER 20 · Old age

It is a truism that historians tend to ask questions about the past that are of direct concern to the societies in which they live. In the nineteenth century, the central issues were nation-building and constitutional law; in the early twentieth century, they were economic development and class relationships; today it is *mentalité*, that untranslatable French word meaning the way people regard the cosmos, themselves, and one another, and the values according to which they model their behavior toward each other.

The subject of the attitudes adopted toward old age in the past has hitherto been wholly neglected. The reason for this neglect lies in the current association of old age with death, although in fact the connection is a very recent one since in the past most people died young rather than old. This association has blocked research, since for nearly half a century we have been living in a society which thinks and speaks and writes more and more explicitly about sex, but thinks and speaks and writes less and less explicitly about death. We have lived through a period of 'the pornography of death,' when it has been a taboo subject for polite conversation. In the last decade this taboo has collapsed, and historians, like the rest of us, have rushed to fill the vacuum. There is now a special branch of learning called 'Thanatology,' and historians of death, like Philippe Ariès or Michel Vovelle, have suddenly appeared on the scene.[1]

It is hardly surprising, therefore, that this revival of interest in death has, in its turn, brought about a growing interest in old age. Previously preoccupied, because of Freudian stress on the significance of this period for later development, with infancy and childhood (where Philippe Ariès was once again the pioneer), historians have now suddenly turned their attention to the aged. It was time to do so, for the vacuum that earlier historians left was filled by false images of a Golden Age. An English sociologist, Bryan Wilson, recently assured his readers that in pre-industrial, traditional societies 'an individual might anticipate old age with pleasure, as a time when declining physical energy would be compensated by social esteem for experience.' He had obviously never heard of King Lear. The chairman of the American branch of the International Association of Gerontology had earlier taken the same line, asserting that 'before the Industrial Revolution, almost without exception the aging enjoyed a favorable position. Their economic security and their social status were assured by their role and place in the extended family ... '[2]

What are the facts, as recently examined by Professor Fischer, Mr Thomas and Mr Laslett?[3] In the first place, as anthropologists have known all along, traditional societies are very ambivalent in their attitudes toward the old. So long as an elderly person retains his faculties, he serves as the Nestor of the community, the venerated fount of ancient wisdom and folklore, the living substitute for history books in a preliterate society. But once those faculties fail, he tends to be despised and ridiculed, and is often either deliberately killed or allowed to die of neglect and malnutrition. Early modern, pre-industrial Western societies had much the same ambivalence, if less crudely and harshly expressed. Of the traditional seven ages of man, the last two, from fifty onward, were hardly described in terms of respect and veneration. As Shakespeare put it in *As You Like It*, the sixth age 'shifts into the lean and slippered pantaloon,' while the seventh 'is second childishness and mere oblivion, sans teeth, sans eyes, sans taste, sans everything.'

Along with the physical decay, which set in early in those days, went psychological deterioration. The old were thought of as characteristically 'peevish, forgetful, covetous, garrulous and dirty,' and not infrequently impotently lustful as well, as illustrated by the popular legend of the venerable Aristotle being ridden naked around his garden on all fours by the youthful Phyllis, armed with a whip. Nor were the old accorded the respect which they thought to be their due, and Shakespeare's shepherd in *The Winter's Tale* merely echoed centuries of complaints when he asserted that between the ages of sixteen and twenty-three, young men think of nothing but 'getting wenches with child, wronging the ancientry, stealing, fighting.'

If the ideal of a premodern society did not include respect for old age, it showed equally little respect for youth. 'Until a man grow unto the age of twenty-four years, he is wild, without judgment and not of sufficient experience to govern himself!' It was regarded as 'a

slippery age, full of passion, rashness, wilfulness.' The prevailing
attitude, as I read the literature, was hostile to both youth and age,
and strongly supportive of the mature, 'grave and sad men who are
above the levities of youth and beneath the dotages of old age.' Such
a society cannot reasonably be described as gerontophilic, since it
distrusted the old as much as it distrusted the young. On the other
hand, high fertility and high mortality meant that it was demographically a youthful society. As a result, despite the stress on
maturity, the membership of the House of Commons, to give but
one example, consistently comprised about 45 per cent of men
under forty in the seventeenth and eighteenth centuries. Moreover,
the use of patronage gave immense opportunities to a privileged
few. Not only did some very young men often inherit vast fortunes
and power through the early death of their fathers; others were
catapulted into high office by the patronage of an influential friend,
who was often their father. Thus it came about that in 1667 a debate
in the House of Commons was opened by a son of George Monck,
the architect of the Restoration of Charles II: he was fourteen years
old.

A central feature that distinguished a premodern society from our
own is that there were huge numbers of young people, all eager for
power and property, and not many old people, to be either
respected or despised, taken care of or neglected. In seventeenth-
century England, persons over sixty comprised at most 8 per cent of
the population, compared with 19 per cent today. Seniority was
certainly the principle around which society organized its institutions – churches, guilds, corporations, or universities – and mandatory retirement was unknown. In practice, however, the paucity of
the old meant that, then as now, positions of authority were mainly
held by men in their forties and fifties. The few who lived into their
sixties often achieved positions of eminence by mere virtue of
longevity: thus two-thirds of those recorded in *Who's Who in
History 1603–1714* had reached the age of sixty or more.[4]

As the physical powers of these few old men waned, the only way
they could assure themselves respect and sustenance was by clinging
tenaciously to office, property, and power. Relatively few old
persons lived alone, partly because there were not many of them,
partly because many contrived to keep an unmarried daughter at
home to look after them. Relatively few households, however, were
composed of three generations, and these were usually bound

together not by affection but by economic necessity and legal obligation. For conventional wisdom, enshrined in the bible, recommended that 'As long as thou livest and hast breath in thee, give not thyself over to any. For better it is that thy children should seek to thee, than that thou shouldst stand to their courtesy.'

If a peasant turned his holding over to his son when his physical powers failed, he usually took great care to ensure, in legal deed, that the obligations of the latter to provide for him were stipulated in minute detail, down to the number of candles to be supplied, and free access to the kitchen fire. Any failure to comply with any single provision caused the automatic revocation of the deed. Seventeenth-century parents had no illusions about how children might treat them if given the chance: 'No prison can be more irksome to a parent than a son's or daughter's house.'

The conclusion is inescapable: in premodern England (and America) the old were respected only as long as they retained control of property, and thus the power to make their children obey them. The lot of those without property was grim indeed, for they were reduced to semi-starvation and beggary, at the mercy of institutionalized poor relief in England, or the inadequate and uncertain chances of private charity elsewhere. Those sociologists who still believe in a pre-industrial Golden Age for the old should take a look at Olwen Hufton's recent horrifying description of the conditions of the life of the poor in eighteenth-century France.[5]

The great change between the early modern period and the present is the growing age stratification of society. Youthful precocity is now suppressed by the lock step of the age-cohort as it marches inexorably through an increasingly extended educational system. At the other end of the age spectrum, mandatory retirement and public and private pension schemes have left a growing body of old people in a state of redundancy, extruded from the full citizenship conferred by participation in the workforce, but most of them at last in tolerable economic circumstances.

Professor Fischer is the first scholar to embark on a sweeping survey of attitudes toward the aged from the seventeenth to the twentieth centuries (even taking a tentative look into the future). His book is elegant in both its prose and its use of concepts, and ingenious in the use of a wide variety of data. It has a surface brilliance that is most attractive, and it is a work of erudition, inventiveness, and passion, an almost irresistible combination.

His thesis is briefly as follows. Up to 1780 Americans were indeed gerontophilic in theory, just as the sociologists claim they were in practice. He points out that the very names for persons in authority, like 'senator' or 'alderman,' derive from words meaning old. He quotes Cotton Mather to the effect that 'the two qualities go together, the ancient and the honorable.' His chief evidence that theory was translated into practice is the seating of the population in Massachusetts meeting houses by age, rather than by wealth or status. He admits, however, that this respect was highest for property-holding healthy males, and was slight to nonexistent for the propertyless poor and for old women.

The great watershed, the shift from a gerontophilic to a geron-tophobic society, took place, Professor Fischer believes, in the fifty years between 1770 and 1820, a period of 'deep change' in every aspect of American life, including politics, economics, demography, society, religion, and values. If true, this proposition would put a final nail in the coffin of modernization theory, since it would make all these fundamental transformations precede instead of follow industrialization and urbanization. The chain of causation would be stood on its head.

The range of evidence chosen by Professor Fischer to prove his point well illustrates both the extraordinary ingenuity demanded of a historian of *mentalité*, and his capacity to pick the significant item out from a vast and diverse array of facts. First of all, Professor Fischer shows that the basis of seating in Massachusetts meeting houses shifted from age to wealth, the seats now being put up to auction to the highest bidder. Second, he points to the introduction of a mandatory retiring age for officials, beginning with some judges in 1777. This was an innovation that infuriated the eighty-nine-year-old John Adams: 'I can never forgive New York, Connecticut or Maine for turning out venerable men,' he wrote angrily to the unsympathetic Jefferson.

Next he turns to a clever exercise in cliometrics, scrutinizing census returns to extract statistical evidence that men tended to overstate their age in the eighteenth century, but to understate it in the nineteenth. The conclusion he draws is that the cult of age was replaced by the cult of youth. Fourth, he points out that in the eighteenth century men looked older than their years, by wearing powdered wigs and long coats, while in the nineteenth century they looked younger, by wearing natural hair or toupees and tight-fitting waistcoats and trousers. Fifth, he argues that there developed a new language of abuse and ridicule for the old. Former neutral words became pejorative, new words of abuse were introduced, and old words of respect disappeared. Sixth, in eighteenth-century family portraits the paterfamilias towered over his wife and children, in a vertical composition; in the nineteenth century he was on the same plane, in a horizontal composition. Seventh, partible or divided inheritance replaced primogeniture in the legal codes of the new republic. Eighth, there was a decline in the proportion of children named after their grandparents.

Awed by this battery of evidence, the reader is at first stunned into submission. How can he resist so brilliantly presented, so various, so comprehensive, so wide-ranging a body of evidence? Surely after all this, he thinks, Professor Fischer has triumphantly proved his theory, and in doing so given a masterly display of historical virtuosity in the manipulation of data to reveal states of mind.

The answer, alas, is that he has not. Under careful scrutiny, each piece of evidence used to prove the case turns out to be ambiguous, or unfounded, or inadequately based, or, if valid, open to another explanation. The strongest argument is the first, the change in seating arrangements in twenty-one Massachusetts meeting houses between 1765 and 1836. But this could just as well be explained by an ideological shift from deference to democracy, and a recognition of the fact of growing economic inequality. The retirement of judges at seventy seems to be no more than a very modest attempt to remove senile members from the bench before they did too much damage to the practice of justice. The retention of judges up to the age of sixty-nine can hardly be regarded as a triumph of youth over age!

As for the age-heaping in census returns, the four cases offered for the years between 1636 and 1787 are highly ambiguous. Not one of the four shows a uniform trend to exaggerate age, and the huge bunching – up to 40 per cent – in each tenth year, thirty, forty, fifty, etc., in any case makes it imprudent to draw any conclusions from this evidence. The changes in hairstyle and costume did take place, but it has to be remembered that powdered wigs only came into fashion in the late seventeenth century, while in the sixteenth and early seventeenth centuries natural flowing hair and elegantly youthful clothes went comfortably together with alleged gerontophilia.

In pointing to a shift in language, Professor Fischer has misread his evidence. His source, and mine, is the OED. 'Gaffer' never became pejorative, lasting well into the late nineteenth century in its old neutral or positive meanings. 'Graybeard' stayed neutral throughout. 'Old-timer' is a late nineteenth-century American word, entirely neutral in meaning. Among pejorative words, 'bald-head' dates from 1535, 'codger' from 1756, 'geezer' from 1885, which is not much help. Positive words that are alleged to have disappeared, like 'grandsire' or 'forefather,' run from the fourteenth century to the late nineteenth. 'Grandad' or 'grandaddy' became more common in the nineteenth century. The verb 'to grandfather up,' meaning to flatter, is so rare that it was only used once, in 1748. One is forced to conclude that nothing useful can be derived from this exercise in semantics.

As for naming patterns (based on one town in Massachusetts), the naming of boys after grandparents shows a random zigzag pattern, and the decline is only unmistakable for girls. This evidence, if it means anything at all, can be better explained by the changing relationship of the nuclear family and the kin than by any change in attitude toward old age.

Professor Fischer may be right about the arrangement of family portraits, but one would like more than a mere thirty pictures, covering the 140 years from 1729 to 1871, on which to base a conclusion. In any case the explanation is more likely to be that individualism and egalitarianism which de Tocqueville thought to be distinguishing characteristics of the early nineteenth-century American family, rather than any shift to gerontophobia. Since in practice partible inheritances were already the norm, the abolition of primogeniture was a largely meaningless gesture made by Jefferson and others toward the ideal of egalitarianism.[6] If Professor Fischer thinks it had something to do with the decline of respect for the aged, the onus is on him to produce some quotations to show that this was what Jefferson had in mind.

This lengthy examination of the evidence for 'deep change' between 1770 and 1820, for a profound shift in attitude toward age and youth, appears to undermine the foundations of the hypothesis. But where does it leave us? The most important change is demographic, the remarkable rise of the aged as a proportion of the adult population. In seventeenth-century America only about 25 per cent to 40 per cent of twenty-year-olds could expect to reach the age of sixty; among those born in 1840 the proportion was 60 per cent; and among those born in 1960 it is 90 per cent.

The effect of such a change on prospects of early promotion can easily be imagined. Mandatory retirement became a necessity in order to prevent this rapidly growing mass of the elderly from clogging up the channels of advancement. Even so, almost every profession grew older in the nineteenth century, and the proportion of men under forty in the House of Commons was halved. Private and then national pension schemes were developed in the early twentieth century to deal with the growing economic hardships of the retired, in the same way that the state was taking responsibility for many other social problems, from unemployment to housing to health. As a result, the really severe economic problems of the old have been more or less dealt with (unless or until Social Security goes bankrupt). Many studies have shown, moreover, that the car, the plane, and the telephone have maintained or even increased the contacts between grandparents and their children and grandchildren. So the situation for the old is serious, but not desperate. It is certainly far less desperate for the poor than it was in the pre-industrial 'Golden Age.'

There remains, however, a particularly acute source of anxiety for many of the old, arising from the demographic, ideological, and institutional changes in the twentieth century. This is the psychological sense of redundancy among the retired because they are living in a society still wedded to the Puritan work-ethic. They feel that they have been thrown on the scrapheap as useless to the community, and they are not satisfied just to sit in the sun and watch the world go by. It may well be, however, that the work-ethic is now on the decline in late twentieth-century America, and is being replaced by a new ethic of hedonism, the pursuit of pleasure and leisure. If this is so, it will have profound consequences for our society, many of them bad. But one good thing may be that the elderly retired will feel much more positive about their idle lot. It may also perhaps be that their flight to Florida and California is itself helping to stimulate this shift in attitudes toward work and leisure throughout the society.

American (and English) society, therefore, never was gerontophilic, even in theory, and it is certainly not gerontophobic now.

If the latter were true, we would be pushing the old into gas ovens, or letting them die in squalor, instead of spending staggering sums of money on pensions, medical care, and nursing in order to prolong the expensive lives of these productively useless and increasingly numerous creatures. No doubt the care and nursing are sometimes callous and inadequate; but no society in world history has devoted more of its gross national product on providing for the aged.

In fact, everything suggests that our attitudes toward the old are not so very different today from those of Shakespeare, and that such difference as there is takes the form of greater kindness – most of us still stand up for them in buses to let them sit down – and greater willingness to pay heavily (through taxes) for their welfare. As for intimacy and affection, there never were many three-generation households, any more than there are now. We are no more, and no less, anxious to have grandparents under foot than were our forefathers.

When Charles Colson wished to impress the American public with the degree of his servile devotion to Richard Nixon, he proclaimed that he would cheerfully walk over his grandmother to serve him. The use by Colson of this particular imagery suggests that he recognized that late twentieth-century Americans still regard walking over grandmothers as a serious act of sacrilegious impiety, just as did the Greeks in the days of Homer. Nor should it be forgotten that only a few years ago all the democracies of the Western world were content to entrust their fate to aged grandfatherly figures: Eisenhower, Churchill, de Gaulle, Adenauer ('*der Alte*'), and de Gasperi. There is not much sign of any decline in respect for the old in that recent trend in political behavior.

What, then, has happened? In the last twenty years there has taken place a (possibly temporary) shift of attitudes toward the relative merits of youth and middle age. The victims of the change are not the old but those 'sad,' mature, sober men who were so admired in premodern times. If thrown out of work after the age of forty-five, they now find themselves virtually unemployable. Nobody wants to hire a middle-aged man or woman. The more grotesque aspects of the cult of youth of the 1960s have all but disappeared, but what has survived is an unwillingness to recognize and reward the wisdom and experience of maturity. Youthful vigor and virility are now sought after, in college presidents, in top business executives, and in senators and congressmen. Thus the real change, which has only taken place in the last twenty years, long after, not before, the industrial revolution reached maturity, has been the demotion of the middle-aged and the elevation of the adolescent and the youth.

CHAPTER 21 · Death

Judging by the archeological evidence, it seems clear that in one respect at least, Freud was wrong. The discontents of civilization seem to have been focused, not on the suppression of the id, but rather on apprehensions about the prospects and nature of life after death. Some of the most gigantic constructions, some of the most splendid and extravagant works of art, some of the most complex rituals have all been devoted to the interment, housing and equipping of the dead, in preparation for the journey of the soul beyond the grave. By 50,000 B.C., Neanderthal man was burying his dead with flowers, and by 7000 B.C. sophisticated ancestor worship was flourishing at Jericho. We still stand amazed at the pyramids of the Pharaohs at Giza, at the gigantic burial mound of Silbury Hill – the largest man-made structure in Europe – at the towering pyramid tomb of the High Priest deep in the Yucatan forest at Palenque, at the bee-hive tombs at Mycenae, at the great multi-chambered megalithic tombs in the long barrows of north-west Europe. The museums of the world are crammed with the funerary equipment of dead kings and nobles. In Cairo is desplayed the golden furniture of Tutankhamun; in London, the jewellery, silver plates and ornamented shield from the ship burial cenotaph of the Anglo-Saxon king at Sutton Hoo; in Athens, the golden mask of a Mycenaean king; in Châteaudun, the gigantic classical Greek bronze krater, carted half across Europe and then buried with an unknown Celtic princess at Vix. The examples are endless, but the conclusion is obvious: men could, they believed, take it all with them, and it had to be nothing but the best.

Of course these gargantuan treasure-filled monuments served a social as well as a ritual purpose. Even the hidden grave-goods were far grander than was strictly necessary for the functional dispatch of the soul on its posthumous journey. The superstructures were the product of an edifice-complex, vain-glorious displays of the social status of both the dead and the living survivors, who could afford not only to bury for ever underground such fabulous riches, but also to waste so much scarce manpower on the erection of eye-catching symbols of immortality. Moreover, the sheer opulence of the furnishings, and the not infrequent inclusion of slaughtered concubines and slaves, show that the grave goods were also intended to bring pleasure to the deceased. They were meant to allow him to enjoy the same luxuries, the same sensual indulgences, the same sumptuous life style, in the next world as he did in this. In stark contrast to Christ's belief that it is more difficult for a rich man to get into Heaven than for a camel to pass through the eye of a needle, the kings and nobles of pagan antiquity expected to have it good in both worlds. That the servicing of the soul was the critical function, however, is proven by the success of the great monotheist religions, Judaism, Christianity and Islam, in putting an end to this practice of equipping the dead with material goods for a journey. Wives, concubines, slaves, horses, ships, chariots, armor, weapons, furniture and jewellery no longer accompanied their owner into the grave, since they no longer served the dead in the after-life. Of course this did not happen overnight, and as late as the 8th century the Merovingian kings were still burying their dead with elaborate grave goods, despite their Christian piety. Because of its belief in the ultimate resurrection of the body, Christianity also placed limits on the nature of the interment: cremation ceased to be a viable option. At the same time, the size of funerary monuments also shrank. On the other hand, Christianity did nothing to stop the elaboration of the ritual surrounding the act of dying, the subsequent ritual of mourning, the ritual of the funeral, and rituals to appease or assist the souls of the dead.

This persistent and universal belief in an after-life is a very odd phenomenon. It is as if the rational part of the brain makes man unique in his awareness that the one inevitable event in his life is death. And yet at a deeper level of consciousness, the more intuitive part of the brain cannot reconcile itself to the fact of the inescapable extinction of oneself and those to whom one is attached. The individual therefore postulates the existence of the soul, as an entity which will live on after his physical decay. It almost looks as if for half a million years the two parts of the brain have been irreconcilably at war with each other, each refusing to accept the conclusions of the other. As Erwin Panofsky pointed out, 'there is hardly any sphere of human experience where rationally incompatible beliefs so easily coexist, and where pre-logical, one might almost say metalogical feelings so stubbornly survive in periods of advanced civilization as in our attitudes towards the dead.'[1] A final twist to the paradox is that the concept of rationality developed in the West in the eighteenth century concurrently with the concept of individualism. In consequence, the probability of personal extinction became at the same time more logically compelling and more emotionally unacceptable. In consequence, the intellectual and psychological tension has actually intensified in the last 200 years.

Which brings us back to Freud, who postulated an eternal conflict between Eros and Thanatos. This theme was given an historical dimension in that most brilliant work of the neo-Marxist school, Norman O. Brown's *Life Against Death*, and is reflected in current popular slogans of the young, such as 'Make Love, not War.' In biological fact, however, sex and death are causally linked. Nature sees to it that any species which reproduces the genes by sexual union of two individuals has built-in mechanisms which ensure the elimination of the parents, so as to allow space for the new genetic material to grow and to reproduce in its turn. In other words, death is essential to genetic diversification by sexual union.

There is incontrovertible evidence that preoccupation with death has absorbed a significant amount of both psychic energy and economic output in the West from the first to the twentieth centuries, that the elaboration of a vision of Heaven and Hell has been the theme of the greatest poets from Dante to Milton, and that most of the greatest sculptors of the West, like Michelangelo, have devoted much of their time and talents to funerary monuments. Despite all this, until very recently death has been a subject barely touched upon by the historians. Art historians have long been compelled to pay more attention, distinguished examples being the books of A. Tenenti and Erwin Panofsky.[2] Panofsky was the first to offer the key distinction between 'prospective' art and ritual, designed magically to manipulate the future, either to make the souls of the dead happy in their after-life or to prevent them from bothering the living, and 'retrospective' art and ritual designed merely to commemorate the past achievements of the dead. He also pointed out how the Pauline doctrine of salvation by faith alone, which later became so central to Protestant theology, eliminated in theory the retrospective element and focused funerary art upon deliverance from the dangers of the after-life.

It was not until the Renaissance that stress on retrospective personal glory increased, and with it the size and opulence of the visible monument over the grave: witness Brou, Innsbrück, Henry VII's chapel in Westminster Abbey or the royal tombs at Saint Denis. Admittedly these are displays of family pride rather than protection against the malevolent actions of ghosts or comfort for the soul in the after-life. Nevertheless, even in the sixteenth and seventeenth centuries, the ancient underlying motive remains: *timor mortis conturbat me*, a fear demonstrated by the persistence of the *transi*, the image of the naked corpse either in *rigor mortis*, slit open and sewn up by the embalmer, or in full decomposition and being devoured by worms.

Before we examine Philippe Ariès's massive book, it is helpful to know something about the author.[3] M. Ariès is not a professional historian, but a man who earns his living as the head of an information center in a research institute on tropical fruit. Although he studied history in the usual way at the Sorbonne, he failed his *agrégation* in 1943, and abandoned a career as a professional historian. He is also unusual in Paris intellectual circles, since he is a pious Catholic and since he comes out of, and has remained loyal to, a milieu strongly attached to right-wing nationalism, ultraroyalism, and nostalgic traditionalism, and since he was for some considerable time an active member of the *Action Française*. As will be seen, this personal background is essential to an understanding of the author's work. It also explains why M. Ariès is the odd man out in French historiography. Although his interest in *mentalités* is now suddenly fashionable in the great and dominant *Annales* school of historians in Paris, although its mixture of anti-Enlightenment philosophy and historical ethnography is very close indeed to that of the current Parisian guru, Michel Foucault, he is nevertheless a prophet without much honor in his own country. In England and America, however, his book *Centuries of Childhood*[4] has had a stunning impact, partly because of its sheer originality and boldness, partly because of good timing, coinciding as it did with Erikson's work on childhood and intensive public rethinking about modes of upbringing. It has been one of the most influential works of history of the 1960s, stimulating an outburst of research into family history which is now in full flood in America and England. For an amateur and a foreigner, this is a remarkable, indeed a unique achievement. And now he has done it again, providing a sweeping model of change in attitudes towards death over a thousand years, which is likely to have the same ripple effect as did *Centuries of Childhood.*

Ariès postulates five main stages in the slow, erratic, overlapping evolution of attitudes towards death from the ninth to the twentieth centuries, each stage being identified by what in fact appear to be different definitions of the nature of man in relation to death. The first is not really a stage but a condition, based on a structure of belief which runs unaltered among the masses right up to the nineteenth century, and which he calls 'We All Die.' The key ritual is the deathbed scene: a public display of repentance and calm acceptance of the end. Death is not particularly frightening, and the fate of the individual is quietly subordinated to the future of the collectivity, the society, the status group and the family. Life after death is no more than a kind of sleep, for an indeterminate period.

The second stage, labelled 'Death of Self,' emerged in the eleventh to thirteenth centuries, and only affected the intellectual and social elite. It is characterized by the concept of the Last Judgment, when God will determine the fate of each soul on the basis of personal behavior during life; by the transformation of the mass for the dead from an occasional collective ritual to a frequent instrument for the salvation of a particular soul; and by a shift in emphasis from the deathbed to the funeral, performed as an ostentatious theatrical display; all of which would explain the increased use of the written will to make provision for the funeral, burial and masses for the soul. These changes were caused by a shift in the balance of emphasis from the collectivity to the individual, expressed by a fierce love of life and all the material goods of this world. Moreover, the immortal soul is clearly separated from the rotting flesh. In northern Europe the face of the deceased was covered up, while at the same time the art of the macabre was displaying the unseen corpse in full corrupt decay. Ariès sees this macabre art not as a reflection of human despair, generated by the Black Death and the atrocities of the Hundred Years' War, as Huizinga believed, but as the counterpart of a passionate lust for life and material possessions.

The third stage, labelled 'Protracted and Imminent Death' (taken from a somewhat obscure phrase of Madame de La Fayette, '*la mort longue et proche*') deals with a collapse of the defences against nature. Both sex and death resume their savage untamed power, expressed most strikingly in the work of the Marquis de Sade, The agony and the orgasm are reunited in a single sensation, symbolized by the erection allegedly experienced by men as they are hanged.

The fourth stage, labelled 'Thy Death,' is the product of the rise of familial attachment to lover, child, spouse or parent. This new phenomenon, which is linked to the growth of privacy and of the close emotional bonding of the nuclear family, I have elsewhere defined as 'affective individualism.'[5] In the eighteenth century it certainly becomes, for the first time, the predominant psychological driving force of the elite in north-west Europe. Pathetic grief at the loss of a loved one, now unrestrained by traditional ritual, consequently becomes the normal response to death, and the center of attention shifts from the dying to the bereaved. Emphasis again moves towards the individual, this time to the survivor rather than the dying man. At the same time, romanticism transforms death from a thing of fear to a thing of beauty. It is now almost eagerly anticipated, especially by those millions dying slowly and gracefully of tuberculosis, while alarm about the prospect of eternal torment in Hell subsides. The belief in the connection between sin, suffering and death, has been decisively altered. As a result, death becomes merely a staging point, a preparation for the reunion of loved ones in the next world.

Finally the twentieth century develops such a phobia of death that it is banished altogether. This fifth stage, labelled rather obscurely 'Inverted Death' (rather than 'Forbidden Death,' which would have been much better) flourishes most strongly in England and America. As sex emerges from the closet, death is pushed back into it, not to be spoken of in polite society. Dying is left to medical technology and takes place no longer in the home but in a hospital. Funerals are abbreviated and simplified, cremation becomes normal, mourning is thought of as a form of mental sickness. Man is defined as the doctors see him, a mere assemblage of obsolescent organs. These latest developments are the product of a sharp decline in belief in survival after death, and a further evolution of individualism, as the dying man has become so enveloped by familial solicitude that the truth about his disease and even his imminent death are carefully concealed from him, for fear of making him miserable. This is the last hurrah of the Jeffersonian Enlightenment ideal of the Pursuit of Happiness: since death is obviously a threat to happiness, it is not only banished from human sight and conversation, it is even concealed from its victim. In America, reaching its apogee at Forest Lawn, the reality of death is hidden also from the survivor, thanks to the art of the embalmer. Cheeks are plumped up with injected waxes and the face and hands are given elaborate cosmetic treatment. The corpse is exposed in its coffin for public inspection, but now made to look younger, handsomer, happier than in real life. No one worries that homeless ghosts or evil spirits may occupy this all too carefully preserved flesh. There is also a sixth and newest phase, which began in about 1970 and is characterized by a growing revulsion against the mechanical, spare-parts view of man, a reassertion of his right to decide how and when and where he will die.

Death, like madness and magic, is now out in the open again, which is what makes this book so timely. It is curious how much the right-wing traditionalist Philippe Ariès has in common with the left-wing radical Michel Foucault, not only in their historical methodology of the ethnographic packrat, but also in their basic interests and their conclusions about the nature of our society and the diseases that afflict it. Both authors share a common distaste for some of the characteristic institutions of our optimistic, rationalist, post-Enlightenment world of social engineers – the prison, the insane asylum, the hospital. Over forty years ago, Lucien Febvre complained that 'we have no history of love, death, pity, cruelty, joy.' Now, thanks in large part to the labors of one gifted, isolated amateur, some of these lacunae are being filled. On the other hand, there can equally be no doubt that the book has serious weaknesses. In the first place, unlike *Centuries of Childhood*, it is very difficult to read. Some of this obscurity arises from a failure to distinguish clearly between the various elements which constitute the whole complicated death syndrome. The deathbed ritual may take place in the home, or in the poorhouse, or in the prison (common in the eighteenth century), or in the hospital (also common in the eighteenth century and normal now). It may take place in public, with or without a priest in attendance, or in isolation in a hospital.

The mourning is usually highly ritualized, with the wearing of black clothes, exposure of the body, watching, the wake, etc. In the eighteenth century it became expressive and emotional, and more recently it has been publicly suppressed altogether.

The funeral may be expensive and solemn, or cheap and hurried, as occasion or pocket dictates. It may or may not be accompanied by relatives or mourners. The place of burial in antiquity was always outside the city walls. Only the Christians put the dead in among the living, clustered around the tombs of the saints, right inside the church for the elite, and nearby in the church-yard for the masses. This practice lasted until the nineteenth century, when sheer pressure of numbers got too great, the stench of rotting bodies too intolerable, and burials were once more banned altogether from church interiors and cemeteries were removed into the distant suburbs.

The body itself may be embalmed, or incinerated, or put into a family vault, or it may first be buried and then dug up and the bones moved to an ossuary. The body may be regarded with loathing, as in the ancient world or today; or with respect, as in the Middle Ages, when it was washed, prepared and laid out in public view for the wake and even the funeral.

The monument erected over the grave may be anonymous or familial or individual in its identification. It may be prospective, concerned with the future, with imagery of the soul being lofted into Heaven by angels, or retrospective, an account and illustration of the achievements of a life-time. It may be religious, with a stress on the Christian piety of the deceased and the hope of salvation by faith or good works, or it may be purely secular, the most striking examples of which are equestrian statues of men in armor prancing about inside churches, like that of Bartolomeo Colleoni at Bergamo. It may stress the personality or the social status or the occupation of the deceased. The judgment of God may be thought to be collective, offering eternal salvation for all believing Christians, or personal, dependent upon divine grace, the intercession of saints, the prayers of priests, or the faith or good works of the deceased. There may be two judgments, the first at death and the second at the Last Judgment, or only one. There may be two destinations, Heaven or Hell, or three, Heaven or Hell or Purgatory. Souls may spend the interval between death and the Last Judgment, when they are once more reunited with their bodies, as ghosts unhappily prowling around the living, or stashed away securely and fairly comfortably in Purgatory.

The living may regard the souls of the dead with fear and hatred as threatening spirits, to be either propitiated by kindness and generosity or exorcized with magic; or as objects of pity, to be helped by the lavish provision of goods for the journey, or by the hire of expensive specialists to pray for their swift passage to Heaven. The dying may have sufficient confidence in their families to leave these arrangements to them, or they may have sufficient doubts to spell them out in legally attested wills.

Given this large number of semi-autonomous rituals and concepts in the process from dying to the final disposal of body and soul, given the wide range of options, given the extreme slowness of shifts of opinion, especially below the intellectual and social elite, given the mental ambiguity and confusion with which most of us regard the problem of death, it is hardly surprising that historians have considerable difficulty in identifying trends and that only by heroic over-simplification can broad stages be detected.

Even when one does find apparently overwhelming statistical evidence of change, the causes are not entirely clear. For example, Professors Vovelle and Chaunu have made exhaustive quantitative studies of wills, and have proved beyond doubt that reference to the disposal of the soul (and body) tend to disappear after 1740 and are virtually gone by 1780, at any rate in Catholic Provence and Paris.[6] Wills thereafter are exclusively devoted to the disposition of worldly goods. One is tempted to conclude, with Professor Vovelle, that a great tide of secularization swept over France, blotting out the intense baroque piety of the late seventeenth and early eighteenth centuries. But can we be sure? Baroque retables in the area, also studied by Professor and Madame Vovelle, show no such trend, continuing to be popular, if stereotyped in content, well into the late nineteenth century.[7] It could be that the nature of piety changed into other, more spiritual, forms which do not show up in wills. In other words the statistical evidence for the rise of baroque piety seems clear enough, but the apparent decline might, in part at least, be evidence of anti-clericalism – for the clergy had been the main beneficiaries of that piety – rather than of Enlightenment secularism.

A second possibility is that the new, affectively-bonded, family structure of the eighteenth century relieved the dying man of the need to make legal provision for his body and soul, since he was now sure that he could rely on his loving relatives to carry out his wishes and do the right thing by him. This is an intriguing suggestion, but a purely speculative one. On the other hand, there is no sign of any diminution in the size and expense of funerary monuments in churches and churchyards in the late eighteenth and early nineteenth centuries, despite the lack of legal provision for their erection. Here we have a classic example in which years of patient quantification have produced results which are clear enough in themselves, but whose interpretation remains uncertain and not susceptible to a scientific solution.[8]

But Ariès's own methodology also is not altogether satisfactory. He gathers up data like a jackdaw from here, there and everywhere in the great rubbish-heap of historical evidence, and scrambles it all together across time, space, religious divisions and cultural watersheds. Many of the sources are those slippery items, romances and novels, the *Chanson de Roland*, Charlotte Brontë, Tolstoy and Solzhenitsyn. There is a certain amount of liturgical data and some study of wills, but of course not a hint of quantification – there is not a statistic in the whole 642 pages. Funerary inscriptions are put to good use, as is iconographic evidence from tomb sculpture, some of it compiled by art historians, but much assembled by Ariès himself in some 40 years of travel throughout Western Europe and the Mediterranean. (One of the principal difficulties in evaluating all this evidence is the failure of the publisher to provide the book with even a single plate.) Finally, there is a rag-bag of information culled from folk-lore, descriptions of rituals, moralistic deathbed literature, family correspondence, discussions of the location and sanitation of interment in churches and cemeteries, and so on.

His treatment of time and space is even more disturbing as he takes his reader on a dizzy roller-coaster up and down the centuries and in and out of countries. Page 16 swings from a comment of Chateaubriand in the early nineteenth century to an Italian text of 1490, to a story of the early eighteenth century, to a fable by La Fontaine. Page 306 includes the *Chanson de Roland*, La Fontaine and Tolstoy in a single sentence, followed by references to a Chancellor of Florence in 1379 and an Italian lady of the late eighteenth century. It requires a strong head to swallow down so potent a mixture without intoxication.

Given all these reservations about his methodology, how does Ariès's chronological framework stand up? His postulate of a more or less timeless popular belief, over the last thousand years, in a kind of sleep after death, regarded as an existential fact to be dealt with in traditional ritualistic ways, makes very good sense. His last, late twentieth-century, stage, involving destruction of this ancient belief-system thanks to the erosion of faith in an after-life, the popularity of the medical view of man as a bundle of physical parts, and the irresistible invasion of privacy by medical technology, seems incontrovertible. But the dating of the emergence of 'Death of Self,' a personalized concept of death among the elite, to the eleventh and twelfth centuries is not so convincing. There are very few spheres of human activity in which the concept of individualism can be seen emerging in the twelfth century. The alleged growing obsession with the sensual pleasures of life and with material goods is hard to document, while the personalized fear of the Last Judgment was soon mitigated by the growth of belief in Purgatory and in the power of prayers to the Virgin and the Saints and of masses for the dead to spring the soul from this transit camp. He is, however, right to point out that salvation had become less collective, less assured to all Christian believers, and more individual, dependent on good works and intercession for the remission of personal sins.

The concept of 'Death of Self' is a useful one, but it should be transferred to its rightful place in the sixteenth century and ascribed primarily to the Renaissance and the Reformation. The former has always, and rightly, been associated with the exaltation of the individual, whether shown in Machiavelli's *Prince* and Marlowe's *Tamburlaine*, or in the personalized portraits and busts of *cinquecento* art. The latter, which stressed Predestination and salvation by faith alone, had the paradoxical effect, as Max Weber long ago pointed out, of increasing psychic anxiety and stimulating moral introspection, individualism and the acquisitive instinct for worldly goods. Shifted to the sixteenth century, therefore, the 'Death of Self' stage can be preserved and indeed strengthened.

The third stage of 'Thy Death' in the late eighteenth century is fully proven, although I would tend, on the basis of English evidence, to push its beginning back into the early part of the century. But it is certainly to be associated with the rise of family love, both between parents and children and between spouses or lovers.

The 'Protracted and Imminent Death' stage is the least comprehensible and convincing of all. In so far as I understand it (and I am not at all sure that I do), the only point of it seems to be to stress the malign effects of the Enlightenment, rationalism and science in stripping away the ancient controls over sex and death. De Sade admittedly needs explaining, but it is easy to exaggerate his cultural significance, and surely unnecessary to create a special stage in the mental structure of Western civilization in order to accommodate him.

To conclude, by dropping this one stage, and shifting up the date of another by three centuries and changing its causation, the Ariès framework can be made to work in a plausible manner, and to tie in with the major shifts in the evolution of European culture.

When one asks *why* these changes occurred, Ariès does not offer a very clear answer. In his conclusion, he suggests that attitudes towards death are affected by changes in the relative strength and weakness of four 'parameters.' The first is individualism, the relative weight attached to the self and the group. The second is the defences erected against the erratic and uncontrollable forces of nature which constantly threaten to dissolve the social order. Of these forces, the two most dangerous, and therefore most heavily controlled, are sex and death. The third is the belief in survival after death. The final parameter is the belief in the close linkage of sin, suffering and death, all of them bad and all of them tied together in the myth of the 'Fall.' Ariès apparently regards these four parameters as independent variables, and makes no attempt to explore the underlying factors which cause them to change. Another difficulty is that they are so broad and so vague that it is almost impossible to prove that any specific change, say a shift in burial customs, is linked to any one of them.

If one ignores this argument, which appears in the conclusion almost as an afterthought, and looks instead at the body of the text, it is apparent that the intellectual concept of individualism and the social organism of the family bulk very large in his interpretation, and one has to assume that he regards them as critical. But what he leaves out is far more surprising than what he puts in. For one thing, he tells us virtually nothing about the underlying biological and demographic facts. For a proper appreciation of the ubiquitous presence of death in premodern Europe, one is obliged to look elsewhere, for example to François Lebrun's unforgettable picture of death in Anjou in the eighteenth century.[9] Ariès never explains to his readers that the association of death with old age, which we today regard as so natural, is in fact a late nineteenth and twentieth-century development, and that in earlier times death struck at all ages, especially during infancy but also young adulthood. It was therefore an infinitely more familiar presence than it is with us, for whom death before the age of 55 is a relative rarety. Ariès's story sweeps serenely over this great watershed in human experience of death without even mentioning it.

The reason for this omission is, presumably, because he does not think it is important. He quite rightly rejects any simplistic notion that there is a mechanical relationship between biology and behavior. He would be properly skeptical of Pierre Chaunu's suggestion that the pessimism of the fifteenth century, the optimism of the sixteenth, the pessimism of the seventeenth and the optimism of the eighteenth are related to changes in the mortality rates and expectations of life.[10] Even the recent suppression of death is at least as much due to medical technology and a waning belief in life after death as it is to the demographic transition.

But if demography is not the key for Ariès, then what is? He has never told us, either in his book about children or in this book about death, what causes attitudes towards such fundamental matters to alter. He barely mentions changes in either economic structure or in the modes of production. He pays far too little attention to social factors, especially aspirations for status, the desire to make a show, to maintain respectability, or to dazzle the community. For all of recorded time, men have got the funerals, the monuments and the prayers they or their relatives have been willing to afford, and their motives for this expenditure, which in all classes has often been very heavy indeed, have been dictated as much by considerations of prestige and status as by a desire to facilitate the passage of the soul to Heaven. This is something almost entirely ignored by Ariès. Nor can he see much difference between Catholic and Protestant attitudes to death. This eliminates for him the role of Protestant and Counter-Reformation theology, which is why he misses the rise of Baroque death ritual which Vovelle and Chaunu have discovered in the wills. How he can ignore a change which led a half of all Christians to reject Purgatory and masses for the dead remains a mystery.

He also misses the taboo, so powerful and popular in the late seventeenth, eighteenth and nineteenth centuries, against any tampering with the body of the dead. This is something which explains the decline of embalming of the rich, who now rejected this interference with their physical remains. Hence the horror felt at the ritual violation of the taboo as a punishment, by the practice of hanging the corpse of some felons in chains, left to twist slowly,

slowly in the wind, while decomposing in full public view. Hence also the great pitched battles fought in the eighteenth century around the gallows for possession of the body of ordinary hanged felons, claimed by the law and the students to be carried off as subject for an anatomy lesson by the surgeons, and claimed by relatives and the mob for a decent burial. Deeply felt popular superstitions, whether about ghosts or corpses, should never be ignored by the historian.

Worse still, Ariès virtually ignores such massive intellectual currents as the Renaissance and the Enlightenment. The first leads Ariès to mis-date the rise of the 'Death of Self' stage by several centuries. The second leads him to underestimate the growth of anti-clericalism among the elite, and the decline of belief in the after-life among an even smaller, but very important minority. The Deists in the late eighteenth century were very active in France in destroying the traditional Catholic death-bed rituals of priestly confession and absolution. In *La Nouvelle Héloïse*, Rousseau shows Julie making her personal unaided peace with her Maker, surrounded by no one but her intimate family. Professor McManners has rightly called this 'an intense, introverted family affair, the supreme crisis of domestic affection.' The clergy are now wholly excluded. Voltaire, on the other hand, had no familial affections, and staged a stunning theatrical show, a carefully contrived and highly public display of philosophic ambiguity which kept everybody guessing till the end. Even more radical, and difficult to fit into the model, are the open atheists: David Hume, who so frightened Boswell by his calm acceptance of imminent personal annihilation; or the Comte de Caylus, who announced to the bishop and relatives assembled around his death-bed, hoping to bring the errant sinner to salvation, 'I can see you want to talk to me for the good of my soul ... But I am going to let you into my secret: I haven't got one.'[11]

On the other hand Ariès must be given credit for treating culture as an independent variable in its own right. He would never talk, as Chaunu does, about 'l'assault récent du quantitatif au troisième niveau,'[12] partly because he is dubious about the value of quantification anyway, but still more because he refuses to treat culture, *mentalité*, or systems of value as a third storey superstructure, perched on the more solid foundations of economic and demographic facts and social structure. He realizes that the effects of economic and social change are great but never direct, being always mediated through the screens of culture, religion and political power. His weakness, however, is his tendency to treat culture as the *only* variable, instead of one of many, which gives his explanatory model a curiously one-dimensional quality, by contrast with the extraordinary richness and variety of his evidence, and his remarkable gift for extracting significance from such diverse and contradictory materials. As a result, all that tends to be left as the moving force in history, apart from the rise of individualism and the nuclear, affection-bonded, family (whose origins are obscure), is a kind of Jungian collective consciousness. Given his conservative views it is hardly surprising that this collective consciousness should show a sad declension from the sixteenth to the twentieth centuries, a slippage away from a quasi-mystical golden age when death came easily, naturally, and publicly.[13]

Despite these reservations, it would be wholly false to end on a negative note. Ariès has written a work which contains many brilliant insights and flights of imagination, as well as a mass of esoteric and fascinating information. He has given us a chronological framework of attitudes toward death over the last thousand years which makes very good sense. It is in some ways an odd, cranky, perverse and muddled book, but there can be little doubt that it will prove to be a seminal work of historical scholarship, a major landmark in the historiography of the late twentieth century.

Professor Stannard has gone about his business in quite a different way, taking a single, clearly defined provincial culture, that of the Puritans of New England, and looking at changes in their attitude toward death over a limited period of 300 years from the seventeenth to the nineteenth centuries.[14] Working within this much narrower perspective, he can be much more precise and convincing in his analysis, and in doing so he brings valuable support to the Ariès model.

The central beliefs of the seventeenth-century Puritans were the Calling, the obligation to be actively engaged in this world; Predestination, the idea that salvation of the soul is pre-ordained by God and not a reward for good works, and that only very few are destined to be saved; and millenarianism, a belief that Christ's second coming is imminent, a prospect which tempered the pessimistic forecast of predestination.

To the Puritans, death was a fearful and uncertain ordeal. They died hard, loaded with guilt, with doubts about salvation and certain only about the awful reality of the torments of Hell. Few cultures have been more afraid of death, and have provided fewer means of assuaging those fears. Puritans did not believe in Purgatory, nor in the possibility that the prayers or rituals performed by the living could aid the dead. Consequently funerary rites were reduced to a minimum, funeral sermons were occasions for theological encouragement of the living rather than individualized eulogies of the dead, and grave monuments were no more than plain headstones, in conformity with Puritan hostility to graven images. Simplicity and anonymity were the rule.

But this could not, and did not last. Belief in Predestination eventually resulted in anomie and cognitive dissonance, an intolerable tension between the doctrine of salvation by faith alone, and the compulsion to do good works as the only means of convincing oneself that one is among the saved. This basic internal contradiction in Puritan ideology was in the long run unendurable, and led in the eighteenth century to a liberalization of belief in order to relieve the tension. As New England society became more complex, more dense, and more wealthy, social distinctions reasserted themselves in the form of elaborate funerals for the elite, accompanied by embalming of the corpse to allow the family time to plan the ceremony and assemble the guests and food. The rise of individualism caused funeral sermons to turn into personal eulogies, and tombstones to become more iconographically elaborate. In New England, as in England and later France, the eighteenth century saw a rise of the isolated affection-bonded nuclear family. This isolation increased the stress on the bereaved by depriving them of community support at the same time that emotional attachment to the deceased increased. By the mid-eighteenth century New Englanders were romanticizing death. They now accepted it easily, in a burst of confidence in salvation, or at least in peace in the afterlife. The overpowering seventeenth-century fear of death and Hell had evaporated, and in consequence the grinning skulls on the tombstones gave way to winged cherubs' heads. The cemetery was now described as a 'dormitory.' Finally, in the twentieth century, there took place the familiar concealment of death, its dominance by medical technology, and its occurrence in isolation and drugged insensibility in hospital. These processes were a response to the end of belief in an afterlife and to fear of the empty void to come.

One may, however, question the common assumption that death today is more terrible than ever. Admittedly one is likely to die alone in the sterile ward of a hospital, surrounded by machines and tubes and machine-like attendants. Admittedly this isolation and loss of individual control deprive the dying of the challenge to put on a show, to make a 'good death' before relatives, friends and neighbors (which was the reason why Dr Johnson objected so strongly to the abolition of public hangings). But how many ever achieved this ideal in practice? The poet Crabbe, who in his capacity as a country doctor had attended many deathbeds, had his doubts on this score. How many were so physically ravaged by pain or by disease that they were either beyond caring or a foul-smelling embarrassment to the onlookers? Is it better to die in agony or stupefied by pain-killers? Is it better to face the certainty of annihilation or the possible torments of Hell? The current criticism of modern 'medicalized' death seems to be based not only on a resentment of the tyranny of doctors, but also on a good deal of false romanticism about a lost golden age of death in the bosom of the family. It is also based on a failure to appreciate that it is our greatly increased capacity to prolong life, not the ambitions of doctors, which has created the current situation. Moral indignation is entirely out of place in dealing with technological innovation, which marches on with a life of its own.

Stannard explains the changes he has observed by the use of two main variables. The first is religion, apparently because he believes, along with Hobbes and Malinowski, that fear of things unknown, and particularly of ghosts and life after death, is the ultimate cause of religious beliefs. The second is the relationship of the individual to the collectivity, especially as expressed in the family. The rise and then fall of belief in Original Sin, Predestination, and Hell, and the rise in affective individualism and romanticism within the family, are sufficient in themselves to explain with elegance and parsimony the changing attitudes towards death over three centuries in New England.

Although there are still many loose ends to be tidied up, and many problems and ambiguities still to be resolved, it is remarkable how well the recent works on death all tend to point in the same general direction. As a result we can begin dimly to see a pattern emerging. The history of death is at last being formally linked to religious, family and intellectual history, although it has still to be fully tied in to economic, social, technological and medical history. In the last ten years historical demographers have proved statistically how recently and how dramatically the prospects of dying have changed, now that the expectation of life at birth has risen from about 30 to about 70 years. Historians of epidemiology have demonstrated the shattering effect of bubonic plague, syphilis, measles, smallpox, malaria, tuberculosis, cholera, influenza, etc. Social historians have shown in vivid detail just what all this meant in human terms, how every aspect of human life and aspirations was governed by the ever-present fear of death.

Ariès, Stannard and others have formulated a plausible and reasonably coherent account of the chronological stages in the evolution of attitudes toward death. The painstaking analysis of wills by Vovelle and Chaunu and their students have demonstrated both the upsurge of baroque piety in late seventeenth-century France, focused particularly on Purgatory and masses of the dead, and its subsequent decline after 1740. Taken together, the works of these scholars add up to the most original and important historical advance of the 1970s. Moreover, if the authors are right in thinking that ideas about death provide a good indicator of the character of a whole civilization, then this new field of inquiry is central to the understanding of the evolution of Western man.

NOTES

I HISTORY AND THE SOCIAL SCIENCES

1 Footnote references have been limited to direct quotations or to further developments of the argument. The authors and their works mentioned in the text are too well known to need documentation. I am very grateful to the students and faculty members of the seminar at Princeton conducted by myself and Professor Arno J. Mayer, in discussion with whom the arguments of the essay have been modified and refined over the years. I am also extremely grateful for some trenchant and pertinent comments on a penultimate draft by my colleague and friend, Professor Robert Darnton, who saved me from many excesses and errors. For those that remain I am solely responsible.

2 Edward G. W. Bill, *University Reform in Nineteenth-Century Oxford: A Study of Henry Halford Vaughan, 1811-1885*, Oxford, 1973, pp. 69-72.

3 Walter Bagehot, *The English Constitution*, London, 1867.

4 Elias H. Tuma, 'New Approaches in Economic History and Related Social Sciences,' *Journal of European Economic History*, 3, no. 1, Spring 1974, p. 175.

5 Liam Hudson, *The Cult of the Fact: A Psychologist's Autobiographical Critique of his Discipline*, New York 1972, p. 12.

6 Carl Bridenbaugh in *New York Times Book Review Section*, 24 January 1965.

7 For a brilliant analysis of the development of *Annales* and the historical school it represents, see J. H. Hexter, 'Fernand Braudel and the *Monde Braudelien* ... ,' *Journal of Modern History*, 44, no.4, December 1972, pp. 480-541.

8 Lucien Febvre, *Combats pour l'histoire*, second edn Paris 1965.

9 Gabriel A. Almond in *American Sociological Review*, 29, no.3, June 1964, pp. 418-19.

10 For an insight into the current approaches of this school, see Jacques Le Goff and Pierre Nora, *Faire de l'histoire*, Paris 1974.

11 London, *Times Literary Supplement*, 28 July 1966, p. 647.

12 Hudson, *The Cult of the Fact*, p. 13.

13 James Boswell, *The Life of Samuel Johnson*, 2 vols, Everyman's Library, London, 1949, Vol. 2, p. 451.

14 E. J. Hobsbawm, 'From Social History to the History of Society,' *Daedalus: Journal of the American Academy of Arts and Sciences*, Winter 1971, pp. 20-45.

15 Edward A. Wrigley, *Population and History*, London 1969; and David V. Glass and D. E. C. Eversley, eds, *Population in History: Essays in Historical Demography*, London 1965.

16 For some examples of this eclectic approach, see Stephan Thernstrom and R. Sennett, eds, *Nineteenth-Century Cities: Essays in the New Urban History*, New Haven, 1969; Harold J. Dyos and Michael Wolff, eds, *The Victorian City: Images and Realities*, London, 1973; and Leo F. Schnore, *The New Urban History: Quantitative Explorations by American Historians*, Princeton, 1974.

17 W. S. Robinson, 'Ecological Correlations and the Behavior of Individuals,' *American Sociological Review*, 15, no. 3, June 1950, pp. 351-7.

18 For some discussion of psychohistory, see Cushing Strout, 'Ego Psychology and the Historian,' *History and Theory: Studies in the Philosophy of History*, 7, no. 3(1968), pp. 281-97; Alain Besançon, 'Vers une histoire psychoanalytique,' *Annales, Économies, Sociétés, Civilisations*, 24, no. 3, May–June 1969, pp. 594-616, and 24, no. 4, July-August 1969, pp. 1011-33; Bruce Mazlish, 'What Is Psychohistory?' *Transactions of the Royal Historical Society* (London), 5th ser., 21, 1971; and Frank Manuel, 'The Use and Abuse of Psychology in History,' in *Historical Studies Today*, ed. Felix Gilbert and Stephen R. Graubard, New York: W.W. Norton, 1972. Other examples of the genre are to be found in Bruce Mazlish, ed., *Psychoanalysis and History*, rev. edn, New York, 1971; and Robert Jay Lifton, ed., *Explorations in Psychohistory: The Wellfleet Papers*, New York, 1974.

19 For two collections of representative work by this new school, see Robert W. Fogel and Stanley L. Engerman, eds, *The Reinterpretation of American Economic History*, New York, 1971; and Peter Temin, ed., *The New Economic History: Selected Readings*, Harmondsworth, 1973.

20 E. J. Hobsbawm, 'Labor History and Ideology,' *Journal of Social History*, 7, 1974, p. 376.

21 For assessments of the virtue of the 'new economic history,' see Thomas C. Cochran, 'Economic History, Old and New,' *American Historical Review*, 74, no. 5, June 1969, pp. 1561-72; M. Levy-Leboyer, 'La new economic history,' *Annales, Économies, Sociétés, Civilisations*, 24, no. 5, September–October 1969, pp. 1035-69; H. J. Habakkuk, 'Economic History and Economic Theory,' in *Historical Studies Today*, ed. F. Gilbert and S. R. Graubard, pp. 27-44; and Albert Fishlow, 'The New Economic History Revisited,' *Journal of European Economic History*, 3, no. 2, Fall 1974, pp. 453-67.

22 Lawrence Stone, 'Prosopography,' *Daedalus*, Winter 1971, pp. 46-79.

23 Pierre Goubert, 'Local History,' *Daedalus*, Winter 1971, pp. 113-27; and Lawrence Stone, 'English and United States Local History,' *Daedalus*, Winter 1971, pp. 128-32.

24 Hudson, *The Cult of the Fact*, p. 64, n. 11

25 Review of Keith V. Thomas, *Religion and the Decline of Magic*, by E. P. Thompson, in *Midland History*, 1, no. 3, Spring 1972, pp. 41-55.

26 Michael Drake, ed., *Applied Historical Studies: An Introductory Reader*, London, 1973, p. 1. For a powerful, witty, and well-argued

statement of the more traditional view of history as a profession, see J. H. Hexter, *The History Primer*, New York 1971.

27 For a good, well-documented summary of the most recent work in and claims for this methodology, see Robert W. Fogel, 'The Limits of Quantitative Methods in History,' *American Historical Review*, 80, no. 2, April 1975, pp. 329–50. It is not easy from this article to see what the limits are.

28 For three of many devastating reviews of this work, see H. Gutman, 'The World Two Cliometricians Made,' *Journal of Negro History*, 60, no. 1, January 1975, pp. 53–227; P. A. David and P. Temin, 'Slavery: The Progressive Institution,' *The Journal of Economic History*, 34, Fall 1974; and T. L. Haskell, 'The True and Tragical History of *Time on the Cross*,' *New York Review of Books*, 22, no. 15, 2 October, 1975.

29 Historical Data Archives, collected by the Inter-University Consortium for Political Research at the University of Michigan.

30 George Selement, 'Perry Miller: A Note on his Sources in *The New England Mind: The Seventeenth Century*,' *William and Mary Quarterly*, third ser., 31, July 1974, pp. 453–64.

31 J. -P. Aron, P. Dumont, and E. Le Roy Ladurie, *Anthropologie du conscrit français*, Paris, 1974; and Peter Laslett, ed., *Household and Family in Past Time: Comparative Studies in the Size and Structure of the Domestic Group over the Last Three Centuries in England, France, Serbia, Japan, and Colonial North America, with Further Materials from Western Europe*, Cambridge 1972.

32 E. A. Wrigley, ed. *Identifying People in the Past*, London 1973.

33 François Billacois, 'Pour une enquête sur la criminalité dans la France d'Ancien Régime,' *Annales, Économies, Sociétés, Civilisations* 22, no. 2, March–April 1967, pp. 340–7; and J. M. Beattie, 'The Pattern of Crime in England, 1660–1800,' *Past and Present*, no. 62, February 1974, pp. 47–95.

34 E. P. Thompson, 'The Moral Economy of the English Crowd in the Eighteenth Century,' *Past and Present*, no. 50, February 1971, pp. 76–136.

35 Robert W. Fogel, 'The Limits of Quantitative Methods in History,' *American Historical Review* 80, no. 2, April 1975, pp. 346–8.

36 Hudson, *The Cult of the Fact*, pp. 74–6. Dr Hudson's book is a brilliant but alarming critique of the state of modern psychology.

37 Carl E. Schorske, 'Politics and the Psyche in *fin de siècle* Vienna: Schnitzler and Hofmannsthal,' *American Historical Review*, 66, no. 4, July 1961, pp. 930–46; his 'The Transformation of the Garden: Ideal and Society in Austrian Literature,' ibid., 72, no. 4, July 1967, pp. 1283–320; his 'Politics in a New Key: An Austrian Triptych,' *Journal of Modern History*, 39, no. 4, December 1967, pp. 343–86; and his 'Politics and Patricide in Freud's *Interpretation of Dreams*,' *American Historical Review*, 78, no. 2, April 1973, pp. 328–47.

38 Quoted by Hudson, *The Cult of the Fact*, p. 155.

39 Ibid., p. 155.

40 Gertrude Himmelfarb, 'The "New History,"' *Commentary*, 59, no. 1, January 1975, pp. 72–8; Jacques Barzun, *Clio and the Doctors: Psycho-history, Quanto-history and History*, Chicago, 1974. See also Jacques Barzun, 'History: The Muse and Her Doctors,'*American Historical Review*, 77, no. 1, February 1972, pp. 36–64 and rejoinders ibid., 77, no. 4, October, 1972, pp. 1194–7; and Elie Kedourie, 'New Histories for Old,' London *Times Literary Supplement*, 7 March 1975, p. 238.

2   PROSOPOGRAPHY

Research for this paper was supported by grant GS 1559X from the National Science Foundation.

1 The word prosopography goes back to the Renaissance, but first came into prominent use among scholars in 1743. C. Nicolet, 'Prosopographie et histoire sociale: Rome et Italie à l'époque republicaine,' *Annales, économies, sociétés, civilisations*, no. 3, 1970, n. 3. It provides a concise and accurate term for an increasingly common historical method, and is already in standard use by one group in the profession. It therefore seems very desirable that it should pass into everyday use among modern historians.

2 H. D. Lasswell and D. Lerner, *World Revolutionary Elites: Studies in Coercive Ideological Movements*, Cambridge, Mass., 1965.

3 D. A. Rustow, 'The Study of Elites,' *World Politics* 18, 1966.

4 Nicolet, 'Prosopographie et histoire sociale.'

5 Joshua Wilson, *Biographical Index to the Present House of Commons*, London, 1806; A. Collins, *The Peerage of England*, London, 1714; A. Collins, *The Baronetage of England*, London, 1720; J. Burke, *The Commoners of Great Britain and Ireland*, London, 1833–8; W. F. Hook, *Lives of the Archbishops of Canterbury*, London, 1860–76; G. Hennessy, *Repertorium Ecclesiasticum Parochiale Londinense*, London, 1898; J. Campbell, *Lives of the Lord Chancellors*, London, 1845–7; J. Campbell, *Lives of the Chief Justices*, London, 1849; E. Foss, *Biographia Juridica, A Biographical Dictionary of the Judges of England ... 1066–1870*, London, 1870; H. W. Woolrych, *Lives of Eminent Sergeants-at-Law*, London, 1869; C. Dalton, *English Army Lists, 1661–1714*, London, 1892–1904; C. Dalton, *George the First's Army, 1716–1727*, London, 1910; J. Campbell, *Lives of the Admirals*, London, 1742–4; J. Charnock, *Biographia Navalis*, London, 1794–8; W. Munk, *Roll of the Royal College of Physicians of London*, 1861; A. B. Beaven, *Aldermen of the City of London*, London, 1908–13; J. Gillow, *Bibliographical Dictionary of English Catholics, 1534–1902*, 1885–1902; D. C. A. Agnew, *Protestant Exiles from France in the Reign of Louis XIV*, Edinburgh, 1886; J. and J. A. Venn, *Alumni Cantabrigienses*, Cambridge, 1922–54; J. Foster, *Alumni Oxonienses*, Oxford, 1891–2.

6 Charles A. Beard, *An Economic Interpretation of the Constitution of the United States*, New York, 1913.

7 *Ibid.*, 1935, pp. 73, 324, xii-xiv.
8 A. P. Newton, *The Colonising Activities of the English Puritans*, New Haven, 1914.
9 It was not followed up until the publication of J. H. Hexter, *The Reign of King Pym*, Cambridge, Mass., 1941.
10 M. Gelzer, *Die Nobilität der römischen Republik*, Leipzig-Berlin, 1912; F. Münzer, *Römische Adelsparteien und Adelsfamilien*, Stuttgart, 1920.
11 John Raymond, *New Statesman*, 19 October 1957, pp. 499-500.
12 Some examples are published in D. K. Rowney and J. Q. Graham, *Quantitative History*, Homewood, Ill. 1969, part VI.
13 The leaders of this intellectual revolution were the French, Marc Bloch and Lucien Febvre.
14 Beard, *Economic Interpretation of the Constitution*, p. xiv; R. Syme, *The Roman Revolution*, Oxford 1939, p. vii. For a description of this historiographical sea-change in Roman history, see Nicolet, 'Prosopographie et histoire sociale,' n.4.
15 L. B. Namier, *England in the Age of the American Revolution*, second edn, London 1961, p. 229.
16 J. C. Holt, *The Northerners*, Oxford, 1961; J. E. Neale, *The Elizabethan House of Commons*, London, 1949; M. F. Keeler, *The Long Parliament, 1640-1641*, Philadelphia, 1954; L. B. Namier and J. Brooke, *The House of Commons, 1754-1790*, London, 1964; E. J. Hobsbawm and G. Rudé, *Captain Swing*, London, 1969; G. E. Aylmer, *The King's Servants: The Civil Service of Charles I, 1625-1642*, London, 1961; W. L. Guttsman, *The British Political Elite*, London, 1963.
17 For a suggestive, if highly speculative, survey of the possibilities of genetic influence see C. D. Darlington, 'The Genetics of Society,' *Past and Present*, 43, 1969.
18 Beard, *Economic Interpretation of the Constitution*, pp. 17-18.
19 Syme, *Roman Revolution*, p. viii; D. A. Winstanley, reviewing Namier in *English Historical Review*, 44, 1929, 660.
20 A. Momigliano reviewing Syme in *Journal of Roman Studies*, 30, 1940, 75.
21 As quoted in D. A. Rustow, 'Study of Elites,' p. 713.
22 L. R. Taylor, *Party Politics in the Age of Caesar*, Berkeley, 1949, p. 23; E. Badian, *Foreign Clientelae*, Oxford, 1958, p. 1.
23 K. B. McFarlane, 'Bastard Feudalism,' *Bulletin of the Institute for Historical Research*, 21, 1945; Neale, *Elizabethan House of Commons*, pp. 24, 27.
24 Namier, *England in the Age of the American Revolution*, p. 19. See also Syme, *Roman Revolution*, p. vii; Holt, *The Northerners*; Neale, *Elizabethan House of Commons*; N. Annan, 'The Intellectual Aristocracy,' in J. H. Plumb, ed., *Studies in Social History*, London, 1955.
25 For example, W. O. Aydelotte, 'The Country Gentlemen and the Repeal of the Corn Laws,' *English Historical Review*, 82, 1967; 'Voting Patterns in the British House of Commons in the 1840's,' in Rowney and Graham, *Quantitative History*.
26 D. Brunton and D. H. Pennington, *Members of the Long Parliament*,

London, 1954. For a convincing refutation of the theory 'that genealogical and political links would normally concide' in the early eighteenth century, see G. Holmes, *British Politics in the Age of Anne*, London 1967, pp. 327–34. C. Meier, *Res Publica Amissa*, Wiesbaden 1966, and a review of it by P. A. Brunt in *Journal of Roman Studies*, 58, 1968, 229–32.

27 For an example which has been criticized on these grounds, see L. Stone, *The Crisis of the Aristocracy: 1558–1641*, Oxford 1965. D. C. Coleman, 'The "Gentry" Controversy and the Aristocracy in Crisis, 1558–1641,' *History*, 51, 1966; E. L. Petersen, 'The Elizabethan Aristocracy Anatomized, Atomized and Reassessed,' *Scandinavian Economic History Review*, 16, 1968; S. J. Woolf, 'La Transformazione dell'Aristocrazia et la Revoluzione Inglese,' *Studi Storici*, December 1968; J. H. Hexter, 'The English Aristocracy, Its Crises, and the English Revolution, 1558–1660,' *Journal of British Studies*, 8, 1968. The failure to work out sufficiently detailed subcategories seriously reduced the usefulness of Brunton and Pennington's study of the Long Parliament.

28 J.-Y. Tirat, 'Problèmes de méthode en histoire sociale,' *Revue d'Histoire Moderne et Contemporaine*, 10, 1963, p. 217.

29 T. K. Rabb, *Enterprise and Empire: Merchant and Gentry Investment in The Expansion of England, 1575–1630*, Cambridge, Mass., 1967. For a review that makes this and other points, see J. J. McCusker in *Historical Methods Newsletter*, 2, June 1969, pp. 16–17. Another example of this problem is David Pottinger's claim that the writers of Old Regime France were drawn predominantly from the *noblesse d'épée* and the high bourgeoisie – a conclusion reached after the elimination of 48.5 per cent of all writers because their social background could not be discovered. D. Pottinger, *The French Book Trade in the Ancien Regime, 1500–1791*, Cambridge, Mass., 1958. I owe this criticism to Professor Robert Darnton.

30 D. Greer, *The Incidence of the Terror During the French Revolution: A Statistical Interpretation*, third edn, Cambridge, Mass., 1964, pp. 385–7. A slightly different example of the same fallacy is D. Lerner's attempt to show that the Nazi leaders were 'marginal men,' when his definition of marginality clearly comprised over half the population (Rustow, 'Study of Elites,' p. 702).

31 H. R. Trevor-Roper, *The Gentry, 1540–1640 Economic History Review*, Supplement I, 1953; W. G. Hoskins, 'The Estates of the Caroline Gentry,' in W. G. Hoskins and H. P. R. Finberg, eds, *Devonshire Studies*, London, 1952; J. T. Cliffe, *The Yorkshire Gentry*, London, 1969, chap. 15; A. Everitt, *The Community of Kent and the Great Rebellion, 1640–1660*, Leicester, 1966, pp. 143–4, 243–4. For another example of the same error, see D. Donald, 'Towards a Reconsideration of Abolitionists,' in his *Lincoln Reconsidered*, New York, 1956; R. A. Skotheim, 'A Note on Historical Method: David Donald's Towards a Reconsideration of Abolitionists,' *Journal of Southern History*, 25, 1959.

32 Syme, *Roman Revolution*, p. 7.
33 See P. A. Brunt's remarks in *Journal of Roman History*, 58, 1968, pp. 230–1.
34 Namier, *England in the Age of the American Revolution*, p. 18; Beard, *Economic Interpretation of the Constitution*, p. 13.
35 Momigliano reviewing Syme in *Journal of Roman Studies*, 30, 1940, p. 76; H. Butterfield, *George III and the Historians*, London, 1957, p. 211.
36 R. Walcott, *English Politics in the Early Eighteenth Century*, Oxford, 1956; J. H. Plumb, *The Origins of Political Stability: England, 1675–1725*, Boston, 1967, pp. xiv, 44–6, 135–8; Holmes, *British Politics in the Age of Anne*, pp. 2–4, 327–34.
37 H. R. Trevor-Roper, 'Oliver Cromwell and His Parliament,' in his *Religion, the Reformation and Social Change*, London, 1967.
38 Butterfield, *George III and the Historians*, pp. 208–9.
39 L. J. Edinger and D. S. Searing, 'Social Background in Elite Analysis: A Methodological Enquiry,' *American Political Science Review*, 61, 1967.
40 Peter Heath, *The English Parish Clergy on the Eve of the Reformation*, London, 1960, pp. 187–96; M. Bowker, *The Secular Clergy in the Diocese of Lincoln, 1495–1520*, Cambridge, 1968.
41 G. A. J. Hodgett, 'The Unpensioned Ex-Religious in Tudor England,' *Journal of Ecclesiastical History*, 13, 1962.
42 G. Baskerville, *English Monks and the Suppression of the Monasteries*, London, 1937; Hodgett, 'The Unpensioned Ex-Religious in Tudor England.'
43 L. B. Smith, *Tudor Prelates and Politics*, Princeton, 1953.
44 M. Aston, 'Lollardy and the Reformation: Survival or Revival?' *History*, 49, 1964; J. F. Davis, 'Lollard Survival and the Textile Industry in the South-East of England,' *Studies in Church History*, 3, 1966; W. Clebsch, *England's Earliest Protestants, 1520–1535*, New Haven, 1964.
45 C. H. Garrett, *The Marian Exiles*, Cambridge, 1938; M. Walzer, *The Revolution of the Saints*, Cambridge, Mass., 1965, pp. 92–113; J. E. Neale, *Elizabeth I and Her Parliaments, 1559–1581*, London: Cape, 1953, part I.
46 W. G. Hoskins, 'The Leicestershire Country Parson in the Sixteenth Century,' *Essays in Leicestershire History*, Liverpool 1950; F. W. Brooks, 'The Social Position of the Parson in the Sixteenth Century,' *British Archæological Society Journal*, 3rd ser., 10, 1948; D. M. Barrett, 'The Condition of the Parish Clergy Between the Reformation and 1660,' Ph.D. diss., Oxford, 1949; P. Tyler, 'The Status of the Elizabethan Parochial Clergy,' *Studies in Church History*, 4, 1957.
47 There is a good deal of incidental prosopographical material in P. Collinson's great book, *The Elizabethan Puritan Movement*, London, 1967. P. S. Seaver, *The Puritan Lectureships*, Stanford, 1970, chaps. 5, 6.
48 A. G. Dickens, 'The First Stages of Romanist Recusancy in Yorkshire,

1560–1590,' *Yorkshire Archaeological Journal*, 35, 1941. See also J. Bossy, 'The Character of Elizabethan Catholicism,' *Past and Present*, 21, 1962; B. Magee, *The English Recusants*, London, 1938.

49 For a summary of the controversy see L. Stone, *Social Change and Revolution in England, 1540–1640*, London, 1965, pp. xi–xxvi; M. E. Finch, *The Wealth of Five Northamptonshire Families, 1540–1640*, Oxford, 1956; Cliffe, *The Yorkshire Gentry*; H. A. Lloyd, *The Gentry of South-West Wales, 1540–1640*, Cardiff, 1968; Stone, *The Crisis of the Aristocracy*. In the last few years some twenty doctoral theses have been or are being written on groups of gentry in various counties.

50 Cliffe, *The Yorkshire Gentry*, p. 354. These percentages and the conclusions drawn from them are mine, not Dr Cliffe's.

51 Prosopography has also undermined another hypothesis about the causes of the Civil War, namely H. R. Trevor-Roper's claims about the role of the bureaucracy. G. E. Aylmer, 'Office-holding as a Factor in English History, 1625–42,' *History*, 44, 1959.

52 Unpublished theses by pupils of Sir John Neale, a brilliant synthesis and interpretation of whose findings is set out in his *Elizabethan House of Commons*. T. L. Moir, *The Addled Parliament of 1614*, Oxford, 1958; Keeler, *The Long Parliament*; Brunton and Pennington, *Members of the Long Parliament*; P. J. Pinkney, 'The Cromwellian Parliament of 1656,' Ph.D. diss., Vanderbilt, 1962; M. E. W. Helms, 'The Convention Parliament of 1660,' Ph.D. diss., Bryn Mawr, 1963.

53 Everitt, *The Community of Kent*, p. 143; V. Pearl, *London and the Outbreak of the Puritan Revolution*, London 1961, p. 160; R. G. Howell, *Newcastle upon Tyne and the Puritan Revolution*, Oxford, 1967, pp. 171–3. The old elite held on in Suffolk. See A. Everitt, *Suffolk and the Great Rebellion, 1640–1660*, Suffolk Record Society, 3, 1960.

54 Distinguished elite studies by American scholars in American history include: J. T. Main, *The Upper House in Revolutionary America, 1763–1788*, Madison, 1967; D. J. Rothman, *Politics and Power: The United States Senate, 1869–1901*, Cambridge, Mass., 1966; S. H. Aronson, *Status and Kinship in the Higher Civil Service*, Cambridge, Mass., 1964; B. Bailyn, *New England Merchants in the Seventeenth Century*, Cambridge, Mass., 1955; C. W. Mills, *The Power Elite*, New York, 1956; P. M. G. Harris, 'The Social Origins of American Leaders: The Demographic Foundations,' *Perspectives in American History*, 3, 1969, pp. 159–346. For bibliographies of the mass school, see n. 12 above.

55 See M. Clubb, 'The Inter-University Consortium for Political Research: Progress and Prospects,' *Historical Methods Newsletter* 2, 1969.

56 The first abortive attempt to launch this project was in 1929, when an official committee was set up by the House of Commons to investigate 'the materials available for a record of the personnel and politics of past members of the House of Commons from 1264 to 1832, and the cost of desirability of their publication.' The committee reported favorably and in the 1930s Colonel Wedgwood produced two volumes on MPs

between 1439 and 1509. Unfortunately he failed to publish the third volume of synthesis and in any case his methods were so criticized that further work along these lines was abandoned. J. C. Wedgwood, *History of Parliament, Biographies of Members of the Commons' House, 1439–1509*, London, 1936–8. Review by M. McKisack in *English Historical Review*, 53, 1938, pp. 503–6.

57 E. Le Roy Ladurie, N. Bernageau, and Y. Pasquet, 'Le conscrit et l'ordinateur: perspectives de recherches,' *Studi Storici*, 10, 1969. Recent French studies of elites include: F. Bluche, *Les magistrats du Parlement de Paris au XVIIIe siècle*, Paris, 1960; A. Corvisier, *L'armée française de la fin du XVIIe siècle au ministère de Choiseul*, Paris, 1964; L. Girard, A. Prost, R. Gossez, *Les Conseillers Généraux en 1870*, Paris, 1967.

58 See J. E. Neale, 'The Biographical Approach to History,' in his *Essays in Elizabethan History*, New York, 1958, pp. 229–34.

3 THE REVIVAL OF NARRATIVE: REFLECTIONS ON A NEW OLD HISTORY

I am much indebted to my wife, and my colleagues, Professors Robert Darnton, Natalie Davis, Felix Gilbert, Charles Gillispie, Theodore Rabb, Carl Schorske and many others for valuable criticism of an early draft of this paper. Most of the suggestions I have accepted, but the blame for the final product rests on me alone.

1 These recent 'new historians' should not be confused with the American 'new historians' of an earlier generation, like Charles Beard and James Harvey Robinson.

2 For the history of narrative, see L. Gossman, 'Augustin Thierry and Liberal Historiography,' *History and Theory*, Beiheft 15, 1979, and H. White, *Metahistory: the Historical Imagination in the Nineteenth Century*, Baltimore, 1973. (I am indebted to Professor R. Starn for directing my attention to the latter.)

3 E. Le Roy Ladurie, *The Territory of the Historian*, New York, 1979, p. 15 and Part I, passim.

4 An unpublished paper by R. W. Fogel, 'Scientific History and Traditional History' (1979) offers the most persuasive case that can be mustered for regarding this as the one and only truly 'scientific' history. But I remain unconvinced.

5 F. Braudel, *La Mediterranée au Temps de Philippe II*, Paris, 1949; P. Goubert, *Beauvais et le Beauvaisis de 1600 à 1730*, Paris, 1966; E. Le Roy Ladurie, *Les Paysans du Languedoc*, Paris, 1966.

6 E. Le Roy Ladurie, 'L'histoire immobile,' in his *Le Territoire de l'Historien*, II, Paris, 1978 (written in 1973).

7 R. Darnton, 'Intellectual and Cultural History,' *History in our Time*, ed. M. Kammen, Ithaca, 1980.

8 M. Zuckerman, 'Dreams that Men dare to dream: the Role of Ideas in Western Modernization,' *Social Science History*, vol. 2, 3, 1978.

9 F. Furet and J. Ozouf, *Lire et Ecrire*, Paris, 1977. See also K. Lockridge, *Literacy in Colonial New England*, New York, 1974.

10 I refer to the debate triggered off by R. P. Brenner, 'Agrarian Class Structure and Economic Development in Pre-Industrial Europe,' *Past and Present*, 70, 1976.

11 R. W. Fogel and S. Engerman, *Time on the Cross*, Boston, 1974; P. A. David *et al.*, *Reckoning with Slavery*, New York, 1976; H. Gutman, *Slavery and the Numbers Game*, Urbana, 1975.

12 E. Le Roy Ladurie, *Le Territoire de l'Historien*, vol. I, Paris, 1973, p. 14 (my translation).

13 C. Geertz, 'Deep Play: Notes on the Balinese Cock-fight' in his *The Interpretation of Cultures*, New York, 1973.

14 D. P. Jordan, *The King's Trial: Louis XVI v. the French Revolution*, Berkeley, 1979. Reviewed in *Publishers' Weekly*, 13 August, 1979.

15 N. Elias, *The Civilising Process*, New York, 1978.

16 T. Zeldin, *France 1848-1945*, vols I, II, Oxford, 1973, 1979 (translated as *Histoire des Passions Françaises*, Paris, 1978). See also R. Mandrou, *Introduction à la France Moderne* (1500-1640), Paris, 1961.

17 P. Ariès, *L'Homme devant La Mort*, Paris, 1977.

18 J. Delumeau, *L'alun de Rome*, Paris, 1962; *La Vie économique et sociale de Rome dans la seconde moitié du XVI siècle*, Paris, 1969; *Le Catholicisme entre Luther et Voltaire*, Paris, 1971; *La Mort des Pays de Cocagne: Comportments Collectifs de la Renaissance à l'Age Classique*, Paris, 1976; *L'Histoire de la Peur*, Paris, 1979.

19 P. R. L. Brown, *The Making of Late Antiquity*, Cambridge, Mass., 1978.

20 G. Duby, *Le Dimanche de Bouvines: 27 Juillet 1214*, Paris, 1973.

21 C. Ginzburg, *The Cheese and the Worms*, Baltimore, 1980.

22 E. Le Roy Ladurie, *Montaillou, Village occitan de 1294 à 1324*, Paris, 1975; *Le Carnaval de Romans*, Paris, 1979.

23 C. M. Cipolla, *Faith, Reason and the Plague in Seventeenth Century Tuscany*, Ithaca, 1979.

24 E. J. Hobsbawm, *Primitive Rebels*, Manchester, 1959; *Bandits*, New York, 1969; *Captain Swing*, New York, 1969.

25 E. P. Thompson, *Whigs and Hunters*, New York, 1975.

26 R. Darnton, *The Business of the Enlightenment*, Cambridge, Mass., 1979.

27 N. Z. Davis, 'Charivari, Honneur et Communauté à Lyon et à Genève au XVII⁰ Siècle,' in *Le Charivari*, ed. J. Le Goff and J. C. Schmitt (forthcoming).

28 K. V. Thomas, *Religion and the Decline of Magic*, New York, 1971.

29 L. Stone, *Family, Sex and Marriage in England 1500-1800*, New York, 1978.

30 S. Schama, *Patriots and Liberators: Revolution in the Netherlands*, New York, 1977.

31 G. R. Elton, *Star Chamber Stories*, London, 1958.

32 H. R. Trevor-Roper, *The Last Days of Hitler*, London, 1947.

33 H. R. Trevor-Roper, *The Hermit of Peking*, New York, 1977; A. J. A. Symons, *Quest for Corvo*, London, 1934.

34 R. Cobb, *The Police and the People*, Oxford, 1970; R. Cobb, *Death in Paris*, New York, 1978.

35 C. Russell, *Parliament and English Politics 1621–29*, Oxford, 1979, J. P. Kenyon, *Stuart England*, London, 1978; see also articles in the *Journal of Modern History*, vol. 49 (4), 1977.

36 E. Le Roy Ladurie, *The Territory of the Historian*, p. 285; H. R. Trevor-Roper, *History, professional and lay*, Oxford, 1957, p. 21.

37 C. Ginzburg, 'Roots of a Scientific Paradigm,' *Theory and Society*, 7, 1979, p. 276.

38 E. Le Roy Ladurie, *The Territory of the Historian*, p. 111.

39 R. Darnton, 'Intellectual and Cultural History,' appendix.

4   THE REFORMATION

1 G. H. Williams, *The Radical Reformation*, Philadelphia, 1962.

2 A. G. Dickens, *Reformation and Society in Sixteenth Century Europe*, New York, 1966.

3 G. R. Elton, *Reformation Europe 1517–1559*, New York, 1966.

4 G. R. Elton, *The Tudor Revolution in Government Administrative Changes in the Reign of Henry VIII*, Cambridge, 1953.

5 G. R. Elton, *Policy and Police: the Enforcement of the Reformation in the Age of Thomas Cromwell*, Cambridge, 1972.

6 *Letters and Papers of Henry VIII*, VII, no. 420.

7 R. C. Cobb, *The Police and the People: French Popular Protests 1789–1820*, Oxford, 1970.

8 A. G. Dickens, *Lollards and Protestants in the Diocese of York 1509–1558*, Oxford, 1959.

9 K. Samuelson, *Religion and Economic Action*, New York, 1964.

10 *The Apologia of Robert Keayne*, ed. B. Bailyn, New York, 1965.

5   TERRIBLE TIMES

1 *The Lisle Letters*, I–VI, ed. M. St Clare Byrne, Chicago, 1981.

6   REVOLUTION AND REACTION

1 Barrington Moore, Jr, *Social Origins of Dictatorship and Democracy: Lord and Peasant in the Making of the Modern World*, Boston, 1967.

2 C. B. McPherson, *Political Theory of Possessive Individualism*, Oxford, 1962.

7   THE CRISIS OF THE SEVENTEENTH CENTURY

1 T. H. Aston, *Century of Crisis 1560–1660*, New York, 1966.
2 J. Elliot, *The Revolt of the Catalans; A Study of the Decline of Spain (1598–1640)*, Cambridge, 1964.
3 P. Geyl, *The Nethelands Divided*, London, 1936; P. Geyl, *The Netherlands in the Seventeenth Century*, London, 1961–4; P. Geyl, *History of the Low Countries: Episodes and Problems*, London, 1964.

8   PURITANISM

1 R. Mandrou, *Introduction à la France Moderne (1500–1640): Essai de psychologie Historique*, Paris, 1961.
2 E. P. Thompson, *The Making of the English Working Class*, London 1963.
3 Thomas, *Religion and the Decline of Magic*, London, 1971.

9   CATHOLICISM

1 H. Belloc, *Europe and the Faith*, London, 1921, H. Belloc, *A History of England*, London, 1925–32. G. K. Chesterton, *A Short History of England*, London, 1917. E. Waugh, *Brideshead Revisited*.
2 H. Aveling, *The Northern Catholics 1558–1790*, London, 1966. H. Aveling, *The Handle and the Axe: the Catholic Recusants in England From Reformation to Emancipation*, London, 1976.
3 J. Bossy, *The English Catholic Community 1570–1850*, New York 1976.

10   PURITANISM

1 P Collinson, *The Elizabethan Puritan Movement*, London, 1967.
2 C. Hill, *Economic Problems of the Church from Archbishop Whitgift to the Long Parliament*, London, 1956.
3 P. Seaver, *The Puritan Lecutreships: The Politics of Religious Dissent*, Stamford, 1970.
4 C. Hill, *Society and Puritanism in Pre-Revolutionary England*, London, 1964.
5 M. Walzer, *The Revolutionary of the Saints*, Cambridge, mass., 1965.

11   COURT AND COUNTRY

1 H. R. Trevor-Roper, *The Gentry, Economic History Review*, Supplement I, 1953; P. Zagorin, *The Court and the Country: the Beginnings of the English Revolution*, London, 1969.

12 THE NEW EIGHTEENTH CENTURY

1 L. B. Namier, *The Structure of Politics at the Accession of George III*, London, 1929; and *Personalities and Powers*, London, 1955.

2 J. P. Kenyon, 'The Revolution of 1688,' in *Historical Perspectives: Studies in English Thought and Society*, ed. Neil McKendrick, London, 1974; and *Revolution Principles: The Politics of Party, 1689–1720*, Cambridge, 1977.

3 E. P. Thompson, 'The Moral Economy of the English Crowd in the Eighteenth Century,' *Past and Present*, 50, 1971; E. P. Thompson, 'Patrician Society, Plebian Culture,' *Journal of Social History*, 7, 1974; E. P. Thompson, 'Eighteenth-Century English Society: Class Struggle without Class?' *Social History*, 3, 1978.

4 A. McInnes, 'When Was the English Revolution?' *History*, 67, 1982; C. Roberts, 'The Constitutional Significance of the Financial Settlement of 1690,' *Historical Journal*, 20, 1977; and P. G. Dickson, *The Financial Revolution in England, 1688–1756*, New York, 1967.

5 G. S. Holmes, *British Politics in the Reign of Queene Anne*, New York, 1967; G. S. Holmes and W. A. Speck, *The Divided Society: Parties and Politics in England 1694–1716*, New York, 1968.

6 J. H. Plumb, *The Origins of Political Stability in England, 1675–1725*, New York, 1967.

7 L. Colley, *In Defiance of Oligarchy: The Tory Party 1714–60*, Cambridge, 1982.

8 Q. Skinner, 'The Principles and Practice of Opposition: The Case of Bolingbroke versus Walpole,' in *Historical Perspectives*, ed. Neil McKendrick.

9 J. Brewer, *Party Ideology and Popular Politics at the Accession of George III*, London, 1976; and 'Commercialization and Politics,' in *The Birth of a Consumer Society: The Commercialization of Eighteenth-Century England*, ed. N. McKendrick, J. Brewer, and J. H. Plumb, Bloomington, Ind., 1982.

10 D. Hay, 'Property, Authority, and the Criminal Law,' in *Albion's Fatal Tree: Crime and Society in Eighteenth-Century England*, ed. D. Hay, P. Linebaugh, J. C. Rule, E. P. Thompson, and C. Winslow, London, 1975; J. L. Langbein, 'Albion's Fatal Flaws,' *Past and Present*, 98, 1983; C. Herrup, 'Law and Morality in Seventeenth-Century England,' *Past and Present*, 106, 1985.

11 J. A. Phillips, *Electoral Behavior in Unreformed England: Plumpers, Splitters and Straights*, Princeton, 1982.

12 J. G. A. Pocock, *The Machiavellian Moment: Florentine Political Thought and the Atlantic Republican Tradition*, Princeton, 1975; J. G. A. Pocock, 'Machiavelli, Harrington and English Political Ideologies in the Eighteenth Century,' *William and Mary Quarterly*, 3rd ser., XXII, 1965; B. Bailyn, *The Intellectual Origins of the American Revolution*, Cambridge, Mass., 1967.

13 J. Cannon, *Aristocratic Century: The Peerage of Eighteenth-Century England*, Cambridge, 1984; J. Cannon, 'The Isthmus Repaired: The

Resurgence of the English Aristocracy 1660–1760,' *Proceedings of the British Academy*, LXVIII, 1982; L. and J. C. Stone, *An Open Elite? England 1540–1880*, Oxford, 1984.

14 For a glimpse of the contents of these houses, see *The Treasure Houses of Britain*, ed. G. Jackson–Stops, National Gallery of Art, Washington, 1985.

15 G. Holmes, *Augustan England: Professions, State and Society, 1680–1730*, London, 1982; G. Holmes, 'The Professions and Social Change in England 1680–1730,' *Proceedings of the British Academy*, LXV, 1979.

16 L. Stone, 'A Rejoinder,' *Past and Present*, 108, 1985, p. 220; N. T. Phillipson, 'The Social Structure of the Faculty of Advocates in Scotland 1661–1840,' in *Law-Making and Law-Makers in British History*, ed. A. Harding, London, 1980.

17 J. H. Pruett, *The Parish Clergy Under the Later Stuarts: The Leicestershire Experience*, Champaign, Ill., 1978, p. 53.

18 P. J. Corfield, *The Impact of English Towns 1700–1800*, Oxford, 1982; P. J. Corfield, *The Transformation of English Provincial Towns 1600–1800*, ed. P. Clark, London, 1984, chs 5–10.

19 E. A. Wrigley, 'A Simple Model of England's Importance in Changing English Society and Economy 1650–1750,' *Past and Present*, 37, 1967; E. A. Wrigley, 'Urban Growth and Agricultural Change: England and the Continent in the Early Modern Period,' *Journal of Interdisciplinary History*, XV, 1985, pp. 684–95.

20 J. R. Wordie, 'The Chronology of English Enclosure 1500–1914,' *Economic History Review*, 2nd ser., XXXVI, 1983.

21 P. Borsay, 'The English Urban Renaissance: The Development of English Provincial Urban Culture,' *Social History*, 2, 1977; M. Reed, *The Georgian Triumph 1700–1830*, London, 1983.

22 R. S. Neale, *Bath 1680–1850: A Social History*, London, 1981.

23 *The Birth of a Consumer Society*, ed. N. McKendrick, J. Brewer, and J. H. Plumb.

24 F. Mendels, 'Proto-Industrialization: The First Phase of the Industralization Process,' *Journal of Economic History*, XXXII, 1972; *Industrialization Before Industrialization*, ed. P. Kriedte, H. Medick, and J. Schlumbohm, Cambridge, 1982.

25 D. C. Coleman, 'Proto-Industrialization: A Concept too Many,' *Economic History Review*, 2nd ser., XXXVI, 1983.

26 E. A. Wrigley, 'The Process of Modernization and the Industrial Revolution in England,' *Journal of Interdisciplinary History*, 3, 1972.

27 M. D. George, *London Life in the Eighteenth Century*, London, 1925 (reprinted 1966).

28 E. P. Thompson, 'The Moral Economy of the English Crowd,'; J. Rule, *The Experience of Labour in Eighteenth-Century English Industry*, London, 1981.

29 Those supporting a growing cultural rift include K. Wrightson, *English Society 1580–1680*, London, 1982, p. 220; D. Rollison, 'Property, Ideology, and Popular Culture in a Gloucestershire Village 1660–1740,'

Past and Present, 93, 1981. Skeptics include M. Ingram, 'Ridings, Rough Music and the "Reform of Popular Culture" in Early Modern England,' *Past and Present*, 105, 1984.

30 E. P. Thompson, 'Patrician Society, Plebeian Culture.'

31 R. W. Malcolmson, *Popular Recreations in English Society*, Cambridge, 1973, chs 6, 7.

32 *The Birth of a Consumer Society*, p. 113.

33 E. A. Wrigley and R. S. Schofield, *The Population History of England 1541–1871*, London, 1981; 'The Growth of Population in Eighteenth-Century England,' *Past and Present*, 98, 1983.

34 E. A. Wrigley, 'Family Limitation in Pre-Industrial England,' *Economic History Review*, 2nd ser., XIX, 1966; C. Wilson, 'Natural Fertility in Pre-Industrial England 1600–1799,' *Population Studies*, XXXVIII, 1984.

35 P. Lindert, 'English Living Standards, Population Growth, and Wrigley–Schofield,' *Explorations in Economic History*, 20, 1983.

36 L. and J. C. Fawtier Stone, *An Open Elite? England 1540–1880*, pp. 87–100.

37 A. Perrenoud, 'Le Biologie et l'Humain dans le Déclin séculaire de la mortalité,' *Annales E. S. C.*, 40 (1), 1985.

38 Wrigley and Schofield, *op. cit.*, pp. 528–9.

39 P. Razzell, *The Conquest of Smallpox: The Impact of Inoculation on Smallpox in Eighteenth-Century Britain*, Firle, 1977.

40 Perrenoud, *op. cit.*, pp. 131–3; E. Le Roy Ladurie, 'Un Concept: L'unification microbienne du monde XIVᵉ–XVIIᵉ Siècles,' *Revue Suisse d'Histoire*, 4, 1973.

41 R. Porter, *English Society in the Eighteenth Century*, London, 1982.

42 H. Fielding, *Amelia* (Everyman Edition), 2, p. 228.

43 Anon., *The Laws Respecting Women*, London, 1777, p. iii.

13 THE LAW

1 E. Le Roy Ladurie, *Montalillou, Village occitan de 1924 à 3124*, Paris, 1975.

2 J. S. Cockburn, 'The Nature and Incidence of Crime in England 1559–1625,' in J. S. Cockburn (ed.), *Crime in England 1550–1800*; J. Beattie, 'The Patterns of Crime in England 1660–1800,' *Past and Present*, 62, 1974.

3 E. P. Thompson, *Whigs and Hunters: the Origins of the Black Act*, New York, 1975; Douglas Hay, Peter Linebaugh, John G. Rule, E. P. Thomspon and Cal Winslow, *Albion's Fatal Tree: Crime and Society in Eighteenth Century England*, New York, 1965; E. P. Thompson, 'Eighteenth Century Crime, Popular Movements and Social Control,' *Bulletin of the Society for the Study of Labour History*, 25, 1972; E. P. Thompson, 'Patrician Society, Plebeian Culture,' *Journal of Social History*, 7, 1973–4. E. P. Thompson, 'Eighteenth Century English Society: Class Struggle Without Class', *Social History*, 3, 1978.

4 Apart from Thompson's writings, see E. J. Hobsbawm, 'Social Criminality,' *Bulletin of the Society for the Study of Labour History*, 25, 1972.
5 *An Ungovernable People: The English and Their Law in the Seventeenth and Eighteenth Centuries*, ed. John Brewer and John Styles, New Brunswick, J. J., 1980, p. 400.

14   THE UNIVERSITY

1 H. F. Kearney, *Scholars and Gentlemen: Universities and Society in Pre-Industrial Britain, 1500–1700*, Ithaca, 1970.
2 R. L. Greaves, *The Puritan Revolution and Educational Thought*, New Brunswick, NJ., 1969.

15   MADNESS

1 E. A. Wrigley and R. Schofield, *The Population History of England 1541–1871*, Cambridge, Mass., 1982, p. 484 n. 60. I confess I find this argument dubious, as is explained.
2 M. Foucault, *Madness and Civilization: A History of Insanity in the Age of Reason*, New York, 1965.
3 P. Alleridge, 'Management and Mismanagement at Bedlam, 1547–1633,' in *Health, Medicine and Mortality in the Sixteenth Century*, ed. C. Webster, Cambridge, 1979, p. 144.
4 *London Chronicle*, 1788, p. 294.
5 J. Shklar, 'Putting Cruelty First,' *Daedalus*, Summer 1982.
6 Many of these objections have been raised by H. C. E. Middlefort, 'Madness and Civilization in Early Modern Europe,' in *After the Reformation: Essays in Honor of J. H. Hexter*, ed. Barbara Malament, Philadelphia, 1980. See also A. Scull, 'The Domestication of Madness,' *Medical History*, XXVII, 1983; A. Digby, 'Changes in the Asylum: The Case of York, 1777–1815,' *Economic History Review*, 2nd ser., XXXVI, 1983.
7 D. P. Walker, *Unclean Spirits: Possession and Exorcism in France and England in the Late Sixteenth and Early Seventeenth Centuries*, Philadelphia, 1982.
8 M. Pelling and C. Webster, 'Medical Practitioners,' in *Health, Medicine and Mortality in the Sixteenth Century*.
9 M. MacDonald, *Mystical Bedlam: Madness, Anxiety, and Healing in Seventeenth-Century England*, New York, 1982.
10 A. L. Rowse, *Sex and Society in Shakespeare's Age: Simon Forman the Astrologer*, New York, 1976, p. 167.
11 M. Heyd, 'The Reaction to Enthusiasm in the Seventeenth Century,' *Journal of Modern History*, no. 53, 1981.
12 M. MacDonald, 'The Inner Side of Wisdom: Suicide in Early Modern England,' *Psychological Medicine*, no. 7, 1977.

13 *Madhouses, Mad-Doctors, and Madmen: The Social History of Psychiatry in the Victorian Era*, ed. A. Scull, Philadelphia, 1982. See also Andrew Scull, *Museums of Madness: The Social Organization of Insanity in Nineteenth Century England*, New York, 1979.

14 H. C. Erik Midelfort, 'Madness and Civilization in Early Modern Europe: A Reappraisal of Michel Foucault,' in *After the Reformation, Essays in Honor of J. H. Hexter*, ed. Barbara C. Malament, Philadelphia, 1980, p. 249.

15 Michel Foucault, *Histoire de la folie à l'âge classique*, Paris, 1972; original publication, 1961, pp. 417–18. Consultation of this huge work is not helped by the total absence of an index, also lacking in the abridged English edition: *Madness and Civilization*, New York, 1965.

16 R. D. Laing and A. Esterson, *Sanity, Madness and the Family*, New York, 1965. Thomas S. Szasz, *The Manufacture of Madness: A Comparative Study of the Inquisition and Mental Health Movement*, New York, 1970.

17 G. Weissmann, 'Foucault and the Bag Lady,' *Hospital Practice*, August 1982.

18 Michel Foucault, *The Birth of the Clinic: An Archaeology of Medical Perception*, New York, 1973, p. 195. For another lyrical reference to Sade, see *Madness*, pp. 282–5.

19 F. M. L. Thompson, 'Social Control in Victorian Britain,' *Economic History Review*, no. 34, 1981, p. 191. This article is a devastating critique of how young English historians have recently latched onto the concept, with very unfortunate consequences.

20 G. Stedman-Jones, 'Class Expressions vs Social Control,' *History Workshop Journal*, no. 4, 1978.

21 For evidence of the slow growth of humanitarianism in the eighteenth century, as opposed to Foucault's model of a swift shift to repression and incarceration, see: N. Fiering 'Irresistible Compassion: An Aspect of Eighteenth Century Sympathy and Humanitarianism,' *Journal of the History of Ideas*, 37, 1976; R. McGowen, 'A Powerful Sympathy: Terror, the Prison and Humanitarian Reform in Early Nineteenth Century Britain,' *Journal of British Studies*, 25, 1986; P. Spierenburg, *The Spectacle of Suffering*, Cambridge, 1984, ch. 6.

16   HOMICIDE AND VIOLENCE

1 A. Macfarlane, *The Justice and the Mare's Ale: Law and Disorder in Seventeenth-Century England*, Cambridge, 1981, pp. 1–26, 173–98. K. Wrightson and D. Levine, *Poverty and Piety in an English Village: Terling 1525–1700*, London, 1979, p. 116.

2 D. H. Hay, *An English Rural Community: Myddle Under the Tudors and Stuarts*, Leicester, 1974. A. Macfarlane, *Reconstructing Historical Communities*, Cambridge, 1977.

3 T. R. Gurr, 'Historical Trends in Violent Crime: A Critical Review of the Evidence,' *Crime and Justice: An Annual Review of Research*, 3,

1981, pp. 295–343. I am grateful to Professor Gurr for several helpful criticisms of a first draft, and for permission to reproduce his graph, which is derived from the following sources: C. I. Hammer, Jr., 'Patterns of Homicide in a Medieval University Town: Fourteenth-Century Oxford,' *Past and Present*, 78, 1978; G. B. Given, *Society and Homicide in Thirteenth Century England*, Stanford, 1977; B. A. Hanawalt, *Crime and Conflict in English Communities 1300–1348*, Cambridge, Mass., 1979; B. A. Hanawalt, 'Violent Death in Fourteenth- and Early Fifteenth-Century England,' *Comparative Studies in Society and History*, 18, 1976; P. E. H. Hair, 'Deaths from Violence in Britain: A Tentative Secular Survey,' *Population Studies*, 29, 1971; J. M. Beattie, 'The Pattern of Crime in England 1660–1800,' *Past and Present*, 62, 1974; J. S. Cockburn, *Crime in England 1550–1800*, Princeton, 1977; J. Samaha, *Law and Order in Historical Perspective: The Case of Elizabethan Essex*, New York, 1974; V. A. C. Gatrell, 'The Decline of Theft and Violence in Victorian and Edwardian England,' *Crime and Law Since 1850*, ed. V. A. C. Gatrell *et al.*, London, 1980; David Pierce *et al.*, 'London: The Politics of Crime and Conflict, 1800 to the 1970s,' in *Politics of Crime and Conflict*, ed. T. R. Gurr *et al.*, Beverly Hills, 1977. J. A. Sharpe, *Crime in Seventeenth Century England: A County Study*, Cambridge, 1983, appeared too late to be used by Professor Gurr. J. M. Beattie, *Crime and the Courts in England 1660–1800*, Princeton, 1986, ch. 3, also appeared too late, but its statistical conclusions had already been published. For the eighteenth century, J. M. Beattie, 'Judicial Records and the Measurement of Crime in Eighteenth Century England,' in *Crime and Justice in Europe and Canada*, ed. L. A. Knafla, Montreal, 1980. For the nineteenth century, see V. A. C. Gatrell and T. B. Hadden, 'Criminal Statistics and Their Interpretation,' in *Nineteenth Century Society*, ed. E. A. Wrigley, London, 1972.

4 T. A. Green, 'Societal Concepts of Criminal Liability for Homicide in Medieval England,' *Speculum*, XLVII, 1972; T. A. Green, 'The Jury and the English Law of Homicide, 1200–1600,' *Michigan Law Review*, 74, 1976; J. D. J. Havard, *The Detection of Secret Homicide*, London, 1960; J. M. Kaye, 'Early History of Murder and Manslaughter,' *Law Quarterly Review*, 83, 1967.

5 J. A. Sharpe, 'The History of Violence in England: Some Observations,' *Past and Present*, 108, 1985, pp. 218–19.

6 J. M. Beattie, *Crime and the Courts*, pp. 110–12. I owe the information about suicide verdicts to Professor Michael MacDonald.

7 Gurr, *op. cit.*, p. 307.

8 Cockburn, *op. cit.*, p. 55; Samaha, *op. cit.*, p. 20; Sharpe, *Crime in Seventeenth Century England*, p. 34.

9 *Aubrey's Brief Lives*, ed. O. L. Dick, London, 1962, p. xviii.

10 B. H. Westman, 'The Peasant Family and Crime in Fourteenth Century England,' *Journal of British Studies*, XIII, 1974, p. 16; B. A. Hanawalt, 'Violent Death in Fourteenth and Fifteenth Century England,'

Comparative Studies in Society and History, XVII, 1976; Beattie, *Crime and the Courts*, Table 3.3.

11 Sharpe, *Crime in Seventeenth Century England*, pp. 34–5 (for these reasons, I find his comparisons between England and America invalid); M. A. Zahn, 'Homicide in the Twentieth Century United States,' in *History and Crime: Implications for Criminal Justice Policy*, ed. J. A. Inciardi and C. E. Faupel, Beverly Hills, 1980; J. Q. Wilson and R. J. Herrnstein, *Crime and Human Nature*, Boston, 1985; E. Currie, *Confronting Crime: An American Challenge*, New York, 1985; T. Morris and L. Blom-Cooper *A Calendar of Murder: Criminal Homicide in England since 1957*, London, 1964, p. 279.

12 It should be noted that there have now appeared no fewer than six books demonstrating the rise of affective individualism in the late eighteenth century among the middle and upper classes up and down the American seaboard, which tends to strengthen the hypothesis of a similar rise among the same classes in England half a century before. See M. B. Norton, *Liberty's Daughters: The Revolutionary Experience of American Women 1750–1800*, Boston, 1980; C. Degler, *At Odds: Women and the Family in America 1776 to the Present*, New York, 1980; D. Blake Smith, *Inside the Great House: Planter Family Life in Eighteenth Century Chesapeake Society*, Ithaca, 1980; J. Fliegelman, *Prodigals and Pilgrims: The American Revolution against Patriarchal Authority, 1750–1800*, Cambridge, Mass., 1982, ch. 5; J. Lewis, *The Pursuit of Happiness: Family and Values in Jefferson's Virginia*, Cambridge, Mass., 1983; L. Kerber, *Women of the Republic: Intellect and Ideology in Revolutionary America*, Chapel Hill, NC, 1980. For the seventeenth century, see L. Koehler, *A Search for Power: The Weaker Sex in Seventeenth Century New England*, Urbana, Ill., 1980. The evidence for the English upper and middle classes is also now supported by the following independent studies: R. Trumbach, *The Rise of the Egalitarian Family: Aristocratic Kinship and Domestic Relations in Eighteenth Century England*, New York, 1978; J. S. Lewis, *In the Family Way: Childbearing in the British Aristocracy 1760–1860*, New Brunswick, NJ. 1986, ch. 1; S. Staves, *Players' Scepters*, Lincoln, Nebr., 1979, ch. 3; K. M. Rodgers, *Feminism in Eighteenth Century England*, Urbana, Ill., 1982. None of this, of course, casts any light on the changing *mentalité* of the poor.

13 J. Demos, *A Little Commonwealth*, New York, 1970, pp. 49, 136; M. MacDonald, *Mystical Bedlam*, Cambridge, 1981, p. 109; Wrightson and Levine, *op. cit.*, p. 110; P. Boyer in *The New Republic*, 10 and 17 January 1983, p. 46.

14 Beattie, *Crime and the Courts*, Table 3.4; Sharpe, *Crime in Seventeenth Century England*, p. 34; Samaha, *op. cit.*, p. 20; W. Hunt, *The Puritan Moment: The Coming of Revolution to an English County*, Cambridge, Mass., 1983, chs 2, 3, 6; F. G. Emmison, *Elizabethan Life: Disorder*, Chelmsford, 1970.

15 J. H. Langbein, 'Shaping the Eighteenth-Century Criminal Trial: A

View from the Ryder Sources,' *University of Chicago Law Review*, 50, Winter 1983, pp. 44–5.

16 N. Elias, *The Civilizing Process: The History of Manners*, New York, 1978; Y. Castan, *Honnêteté et relations sociales en Languedoc au XVIII^c siècle*, Paris, 1974, pp. 56–7.

17 For duelling, see L. Stone, *The Crisis of the Aristocracy 1558–1641*, Oxford, 1965, pp. 242–9. The last death in a duel in England took place in 1852 (D. T. Andrew, 'The Code of Honor and its Critics: The Opposition to Duelling in England 1799–1850,' *Social History*, 5, 1980). For nineteenth-century working-class violence, see M. May, 'Violence in the Family: An Historical Perspective,' in *Violence and the Family*, ed. J. P. Martin, London, 1979; N. Tomes, 'A "Torrent of Abuse": Crimes of Violence between Working Class Men and Women in London 1840–1875,' *Journal of Social History*, XI, 1978; G. Behlner, *Child Abuse and Moral Reform in England 1870–1908*, Stanford, 1982.

18 *Crime and the Law: The Social History of Crime in Western Europe since 1500*, ed. V. A. C. Gatrell, B. Lenman and G. Parker, London, 1980, p. 300.

19 S. Staves, 'Money for Honor: Damages for Criminal Conversation,' *Studies in Eighteenth-Century Culture*, XI, 1982.

20 This last conclusion is drawn from cases for marital separation on grounds of cruelty brought before the Court of Arches between 1660 and 1820. It should be observed that a similar shift of societal values against physical cruelty was in progress in Amsterdam in the same period and for much the same reasons: P. Spierenburg, *The Spectacle of Suffering*, Cambridge, 1984, ch. 6.

21 Beattie, *Crime and the Courts*, pp. 111–12, 124, 132–9; F. Place, *Autobiography*, ed. M. Thale, Cambridge, 1972, p. 87.

22 P. Deyon, *Le temps des prisons: essai sur l'histoire de la délinquance et les origines du système pénitentiaire*, Paris, 1975, pp. 77–8; S. G. Reinhardt, 'Crime and Royal Justice in Ancien Regime France: Modes of Analysis,' *Journal of Interdisciplinary History*, XIII, 1983, pp. 437–9.

23 Sharpe, *Crime in Seventeenth Century England*, p. 47.

24 Hammer, *op. cit.*, p. 13.

25 Wrightson and Levine, *op. cit.*, pp. 114–15.

26 J. S. Cockburn, *The History of English Assizes, 1558–1714*, Cambridge, 1972, p. 102; F. G. Emmison, *Elizabethan Life: Morals and the Church Courts*, Chelmsford, 1973, p. x; Samaha, *op. cit.*, p. 19.

27 P. Laslett et al., *Bastardy and Its Comparative History*, Cambridge, Mass, 1980, pp. 95, 123; P. Laslett, *Family Life and Illicit Love in Earlier Generations*, Cambridge, 1977, pp. 119, 153.

28 MacDonald, *op. cit.*, p. 199. About one in five of those mentally distressed who consulted the Rev. Richard Napier thought they were bewitched.

29 Emmison, *op. cit.*, p. 1. The proportion of the population accused has been estimated at about one in seven.

30 J. A. Sharpe, *Defamation and Sexual Slander in Early Modern England: The Church Courts at York*, Borthwick Papers, 58, pp. 4, 9; J. A. Sharpe, 'Litigation and Human Relations in Early Modern England: Ecclesiastical Defamation Suits at York,' in *Disputes and Settlements*, ed. J. Bossy, Cambridge, 1983. Dr Sharpe interprets this rise of litigation as first steps towards an out-of-court settlement, 'towards bringing neighbourly tensions to a close', that is as attempts by other means to return to communal harmony through traditional village arbitration. Faced with a similar rise of private litigation about defamation (and physical violence) in southern France between 1770 and 1790 Professor Reinhardt has concluded that 'their goal was not so much the peaceful resolution of disputes . . ., but the traditional goal of humiliating and ruining their opponents' (Reinhardt, *op. cit.*, p. 458). The evidence seems ambiguous on this point.

31 Wrightson and Levine, *op. cit.*, 5, 7; Hunt, *op. cit.*, 3, 5, 6.

32 D. Hay, 'War, Death and Theft in the Eighteenth Century,' *Past and Present*, 95, 1982, pp. 139–46.

33 Beattie, *Crime and the Courts*, p. 11.

34 See Wilson and Herrnstein, *op. cit.*, Zahn, *op. cit.*, and Currie, *op. cit.*

35 This point is raised by J. A. Sharpe, 'The History of Violence in England: Some Observations,' *Past and Present*, 108, 1985, pp. 211–15.

36 J. S. Cockburn, *Crime in England 1550–1800*, pp. 49, 58; *The Elizabethan Underworld*, ed. A. V. Judges, London, 1930; F. Aydelotte, *Elizabethan Rogues and Vagabonds*, Oxford, 1913.

37 Stone, *op. cit.*, ch. 5.

38 Beattie, 'The Pattern of Crime in England, 1660–1800', pp. 47–8, 61, 68, 72–3; J. M. Beattie, *Crime and the Courts*, p. 141; E. P. Thompson, *Whigs and Hunters: The Origin of the Black Act*, London, 1975; Daniel Defoe, *Street Robberies Considered*, London, 1728; Bernard de Mandeville, *An Enquiry into the Causes of the Frequent Executions at Tyburn*, London, 1725; Henry Fielding, *An Enquiry into the Causes of the Late Increase of Robbers*, London, 1751. For studies of violent crime in eighteenth-century England, see. D. Hay *et al.*, *Albion's Fatal Tree: Crime and Society in Eighteenth Century England*, London, 1975; *An Ungovernable People: The English and Their Laws in the Seventeenth and Eighteenth Centuries*, London, 1980, ed. J. Brewer and J. Styles; *Walpole Correspondence* ed. W. S. Lewis *et al.*, IV, New Haven, Conn., 1939, p. 111.

39 *New York Times*, 26 November 1984, A, p. 12; it should be noted that the vast increase in traffic in the last 150 years, and the shift from the slow horse to the fast internal combustion engine, has not greatly increased traffic mortality per capita, which in England in 1840 seems to have been about 6 per 100,000 (population from E. A. Wrigley and R. S. Schofield *The Population History of England 1541–1871*, London, 1981, Fig. 7.8, and traffic deaths from Beattie, *Crime and the Courts*, p. 86 n. 30.

40 S. D. Amussen, 'Féminin/Masculin: Le genre dans l'Angleterre de l'époque moderne', *Annales E.S.C.*, March–April 1985.
41 See, for example, Visitation Articles and responses to them by church-wardens up to the 1660s; *Buckinghamshire Record Society*, 7, 1947; *Sussex Record Society*, 49, 50, 1947–9. For the collapse of the system of control in the late seventeenth and early eighteenth centuries, as churchwardens ceased to report delinquents and penance was either dropped or commuted to a money payment, see *Lincolnshire Record Society*, 4, 1912; *Yorkshire Archaeological Society*, Record Series 71, 1928; and M. G. Smith, *Pastoral Discipline and the Church Courts*, Borthwick Papers, 62, 1982.
42 Sharpe, 'Litigation and Human Relations in Early Modern England'; Macfarlane, *op. cit.*
43 J. A. Sharpe, 'Domestic Homicide in Early Modern England,' *Historical Journal*, XXIV, 1981, pp. 37, 48.
44 *New York Times*, magazine section, 27 January 1985, p. 24.
45 Dr David Harris Sacks has pointed out to me that this relationship is also especially problematic in the Middle Ages, when so many homicides appear to have been the result of a series of group confrontations or 'affrays,' involving many persons and varying degrees of violence and mayhem (letter of 5 December 1983).

17   CHILDREN AND THE FAMILY

1 J. H. van den Berg, *The Changing Nature of Man: Introduction to a Historical Psychology (Mebabletica)*, trans. H. F. Croes, New York, 1975.
2 Phillippe Ariès, *Centuries of Childhood: A Social History of Family Life*, trans. Robert Baldick, New York, 1965.
3 David Hunt, *Parents and Children in History: The Psychology of Family Life in Early Modern France*, New York, 1970.
4 Lloyd deMause, ded., *The History of Childhood*, New York, 1974.
5 David Riesman, *The Lonely Crowd*, New Haven, Conn., 1950.
6 Erik Erikson, *Childhood and Society*, New York, 1963; Erik Erikson, *Identity and the Life Cycle: Selected Papers*, New York, 1959; Heintz Hartmann, *Ego Psychology and the Problem of Adaption*, New York, 1964.
7 B. Malinowski, *Sex and Repression in Savage Society*, London, 1927, p. 18.

18   LOVE

1 R. Darnton, *The Great Cat Massacre and Other Episodes in French Cultural History*, New York, 1984, p. 4.
2 E. A. Wrigley, 'English Population History from Family Reconstitution: Summary Results 1600–1799,' *Population Studies*, 37, 1983.

3 G. D. Sussman, *Selling Mother's Milk: The Wetnursing Business in France, 1715–1914*, Champaign, Ill., 1982.

4 For further discussion of these issues as applied to English history, and for references, see L. Stone, *The Family, Sex and Marriage in England 1500–1914*, New York, 1977.

5 W. J. Goode, 'The Theoretical Importance of Love,' *American Sociological Review*, 24, 1959. See also J. Sarsby, *Romantic Love and Society: Its Place in the Modern World*, London, 1983, ch. 1.

6 G. Duby, *The Knight, the Lady and the Priest: The Making of Modern Marriage in Medieval France*, New York, 1983; D. De Rougemont, *Passion and Society*, London, 1940.

7 M. MacDonald, *Mystical Bedlam*, Cambridge, 1981.

8 *Journal of Family History*, 8, 1983, p. 100; R. Blood, *The Love Match and the Arranged Marriage in Japan*, Toronto, 1967.

9 R. Houlbrooke, *The English Family 1450–1700*, London, 1984; K. Wrightson, *English Society 1580–1680*, London, 1982, ch. 3; R. Houlbrooke, 'The Making of Marriage in Mid-Tudor England,' *Journal of Family History*, 10, 1985; M. M. Sheehan, 'Choice of Marriage Partner in the Middle Ages,' *Studies in Medieval and Renaissance History*, new series, 1978; J.-L. Flandrin, *Les Amours paysannes* (XVIe – XIXᵉ siècles), Paris, 1970. Research into ecclesiastical court records in England from 1660 to 1820 confirm and extend these findings.

10 Lambeth Palace, Court of Arches MSS. The current view, that bundling was confined to the Celtic fringe of Wales and Scotland, and also New England, is incorrect. It was normal all over southern England, and presumably also in the north.

11 Stone, *op. cit.*, ch. 6.

12 J. S. Lewis, *In the Family Way*, New Brunswick, N. J, 1986, p. 19.

13 E. Badinter, *Mother Love: Myth and Reality*, New York, 1981, p. xix.

14 The literature on infanticide (rare), infant abandonment, and early death by deliberate neglect or wet-nursing in Western Europe up to the nineteenth century is now enormous. See, for example: L. de Mause, *History of Childhood*, New York, 1974; C. Delasselle, 'Les enfants abandonnés à Paris au XVIIIᵉ siècle,' *Annales E. C. S.*, 30, January-February 1975; J.-L. Flandrin, 'L'Attitude devant le petit enfant . . . dans la civilisation occidentale,' in *Annales de Demographie Historique*, 1973; Sussman, *op. cit.*; K. Wrightson, 'Infanticide in Seventeenth Century England,' *Local Population Studies*, 15, 1975. What is particularly striking is that although infanticide was a penal offense carrying the death penalty, eighteenth-century juries almost invariably acquitted the accused, even in clear contradiction to the evidence (*Old Bailey Sessions Papers*, 1720–60, *passim*)

15 *Interest and Emotion*, ed. H. Medick and D. W. Sabean, New York, 1984, p. 91.

16 Badinter, *op. cit.*, p. xxiii.

17 Nancy Scheper-Hughes, 'Culture, Scarcity and Maternal Thinking: Maternal Detachment and Infant Survival in a Brazilian Shantytown,' *Ethos*, 1986, p. 292.

18 For the very different view by an 'historical anthropologist' that love did not change very much in England from 1300 to 1840, see A. Macfarlane, *Marriage and Love in England: Modes of Reproduction 1300–1840*, Oxford, 1986, reviewed by L. Stone in the *Times Literary Supplement*, 16 May 1986.

19   SEXUALITY

1 The male has small testes and sperm reserve, so that both semen quantity and sperm count fall if he ejaculates more than once every two days (P. Anderson, 'The Reproduction Role of the Human Breast,' *Current Anthropology*, 24, 1983, pp. 25–6). For other views about female primates see *Female Primates: Studies by Female Primatologists*, ed. M. Small, New York, 1984.

2 R. Fox, 'The Condition of Sexual Evolution,' in *Western Sexuality: Practice and Precepts in Past and Present Times*, ed. P. Ariès and A. Béjin, New York, 1985, p. 2.

3 P. and E. Kronhausen, *The Complete Book of Erotic Art*, New York, 1978.

4 T. Gregor, *Anxious Pleasures*, Chicago, 1985.

5 A. Béjin, 'The Influence of Sexologists,' in Ariès and Béjin, *op. cit.*, pp. 204, 213.

6 Jerome quoted by P. Ariès, 'Love in Married Life,' in Ariès and Béjin, *op. cit.*, p. 134; J. Boswell, *Christianity, Social Tolerance and Homosexuality*, Chicago, 1980, pp. 147–8, 164; D. Defoe, *Conjugal Lewdness, or Matrimonial Whoredom*, London, 1727.

7 Béjin, *op. cit.*, p. 211.

8 M. Foucault, *The History of Sexuality, vol. I: The Desire to Know*, New York, 1978.

9 J.-L. Flandrin, *Un Temps pour embrasser: aux origines de la morale sexuelle occidentale (VIe–XIe siècles)*, Paris, 1983, p. 116.

10 R. van Gulik, *La Vie sexuelle dans la Chine ancienne*, Paris, 1971, pp. 177–9, 188–91, 200; D. Bodde, 'Sex in Chinese Civilization,' *American Philosophical Society Proceedings*, 129, 1985, p. 162; M. Beurdeley, *Chinese Erotic Art*, Fribourg, 1969.

11 K. J. Dover, *Greek Homosexuality*, New York, 1978, pp. 19–109.

12 G. Ruggiero, *The Boundaries of Eros: Sex Crimes and Sexuality in Renaissance Venice*, New York, 1985, p. 147.

13 I am working on a history of marital breakdown in England from 1660 to 1820, based on the extensive records of litigation for separation and divorce.

14 S. Marcus, *The Other Victorians: A Study of Sexuality and Pornography in Mid-Nineteenth Century England*, New York, 1966.

15 Boswell, *op. cit.*, p. 157 n. 87.

16 Ariès, *op. cit.*, p. 136.

17 M. Foucault, *Histoire de la sexualité: vol. I, La Volonté de savoir; vol. II, L'Usage des plaisirs; vol. III, Le Souci de soi*, Paris, 1984.

18 *Ibid.*, III, pp. 16, 196.
19 P. Veyne, 'La Famille et l'amour sous le Haut-Empire Romain,' *Annales E. S. C.*, 33, 1978. This is perhaps the most brilliant article in the whole history of sexuality.
20 Boswell, *op. cit.*, pp. 163–5; Veyne, *op. cit.*, p. 39.
21 K. J. Dover, 'Classical Greek Attitudes to Sexual Behaviour,' *Arethusa*, 6, 1973.
22 K. J. Dover, *Greek Homosexuality*, illustrations from B114, 486, 634; R520 for sexual intercourse; and from B65, 76, 271, 342, 598; R196, 295 for courting.
23 *Ibid.*, pp. 148, 151.
24 E. R. Dodds, *Christian and Pagan in an Age of Anxiety*, New York, 1970, p. 29.
25 D. Mountfield, *Greek and Roman Erotica*, New York, 1982, p. 6.
26 E. C. Keuls, *The Reign of the Phallus: Sexual Politics in Ancient Athens*, New York, 1985. For a more balanced view of Athenian women see S. Pomeroy, *Goddesses, Whores, Wives and Slaves*, New York, 1975, ch. V.
27 Keuls, *op. cit.*, pp. 385–403.
28 Boswell, *op. cit.*, p. 61; P. Veyne, 'Homosexuality in Ancient Rome,' in Ariès and Béjin, *op. cit.*, pp. 26–34.
29 For Pompei, see Mountfield, *op. cit.*, pp. 5, 7, 32–9, 50–1, 61–4, 72, 74, 81; Petronius Arbiter, *The Satyricon*, tr. W. Arrowsmith, New York, 1959, pp. 86–9, 93, 95.
30 Boswell, *op. cit.*, p. 154; Dodds, *op. cit.*, p. 29.
31 M. Foucault, 'The Battle for Chastity,' in Ariès and Béjin, *op. cit.*, pp. 21–5; Dodds, *op. cit.*, pp. 30–6; A. Rouselle, *Porneia, De la maitrise du corps à la privation sensorielle (IIᵉ – IVᵉ siècles de l'ère chrétienne)*, Paris, 1983; J. Bugge, *Virginitas: An Essay in the History of a Medieval Ideal*, The Hague, 1975; J. Le Goff, 'Le Refus du plaisir,' in his *L'Imaginaire médiéval*, Paris, 1985.
32 P. Veyne, 'La Famille et l'amour,', pp. 40, 43, 48; B. Rawson, 'Roman Concubinage and other *de facto* Marriages,' *Transactions of the American Philological Association*, 104, 1978.
33 R. Patai, *Sex and Family Life in the Bible and the Middle East*, New York, 1959, pp. 158–78.
34 P. Brown, 'Sexuality and Society in the 5th Century A.D.: Augustine and Julian Eclanum,' *Tria corda: Scritti in Honore di Arnoldo Momigliano*, ed. E. Gabba, *Biblioteca di Athenaeum*, 1, Como, 1983, pp. 54–5.
35 Boswell, *op. cit.*, p. 91; Veyne, 'La Famille et l'amour', pp. 48–9; Ariès, *op. cit.*, p. 141.
36 Veyne, 'La Famille et l'amour,' pp. 37–8.
37 Boswell, *op. cit.*, pp. 31–6.
38 Veyne, 'L Famille et l'amour,' p. 49; P. Ariès, 'St Paul and the Flesh,' in Ariès and Béjin, *op. cit.*
39 Flandrin, *op. cit.*, p. 48.
40 *Ibid.*, p. 159; Bodde, *op. cit.*, p. 170 n. 19.

41 Flandrin, *op. cit.*, pp. 106, 115.
42 M. C. Ross, 'Concubinage in Anglo-Saxon England,' *Past and Present*, 108, 1985.
43 C. H. Lea, *The History of Sacerdotal Celibacy in the Christian Church*, Boston, 1884.
44 Flandrin, *op. cit.*, p. 129.
45 Boswell, *op. cit.*, p. 240.
46 *Ibid.*, ch. 9 and p. 262.
47 Ruggiero, *op. cit.*; L. L. Otis, *Prostitution in Medieval Society*, Chicago, 1985; J. Rossiaud, 'Prostitution, Sex, and Society in French Towns in the Fifteenth Century,' in Ariès and Béjin, *op. cit.*; M. E. Perry, 'Deviant Insiders: Legalized Prostitution and a Consciousness of Women in Early Modern Seville,' *Comparative Studies in Society and History*, 27, 1985. In London in the fourteenth century there was a 'marshal of prostitutes' attached to the royal household (J. Bellamy, *Crime and Public Order in England in the Later Middle Ages*, London, 1973, p. 60).
48 Boswell, *op. cit.*, p. 149 n. 50.
49 Otis, *op. cit.*, pp. 30–8, 56; Ruggiero, *op. cit.*, pp. 13, 41; Rossiaud, *op. cit.*, pp. 76–7, 82–7, 94.
50 N. Harrison, 'Nuns and Prostitutes in Eighteenth Century Spain,' *British Journal of Eighteenth Century Studies*, 9, 1986, p. 56.
51 Ruggiero, *op. cit.*, pp. 41–3.
52 *Ibid.*, ch. VI.
53 A. Olivieri, 'Eroticism and Social Groups in Sixteenth-Century Venice,' in Ariès and Béjin, *op. cit.*
54 *L'Erotisme au moyen-âge*, ed. B. Roy, Quebec, 1977.
55 P. Laslett, 'Long-Term Trends in Bastardy in England,' in his *Family Life and Illicit Love in Earlier Generations*, Cambridge, 1977, Tables 3.2 and 3.3; J. Meyer, 'Illegitimates and Foundlings in Pre-Industrial France,' in *Bastardy and Its Comparative History*, ed. P. Laslett *et al.*, Cambridge, Mass., 1980.
56 E. A. Wrigley, 'Marriage, Fertility and Population Growth in Eighteenth Century England,' in *Marriage and Society*, ed. R. B. Outhwaite, London, 1981, p. 162.
57 J. Cleland, *Memoirs of a Woman of Pleasure*, London, 1749. See also D. Foxon, *Libertine Literature in England 1660–1745*, London, 1965, and R. Thompson, *Unfit for Modest Ears*, London, 1979.
58 Quoted in J. M. Beattie, *Crime and the Courts in England 1660–1800*, Princeton, 1986, p. 467.
59 Old Bailey Sessions Papers, December 1718, p. 3, and July 1726, p. 8; A. Bray, *Homosexuality in Renaissance England*, London, 1982, p. 114; R. Trumbach, 'London Sodomites: Homosexual Behavior and Western Culture in the Eighteenth Century,' *Journal of Social History*, 11, 1977; *The Pursuit of Sodomy in Early Modern Europe*, ed. K. Gerard and G. Hekma, New York, 1986.
60 L. Crompton, *Byron and Greek Love: Homophobia in Nineteenth-Century England*, Berkeley, 1985. Bentham remained, however,

strongly opposed to masturbation. For a thoughtful and learned review of a mass of recent literature on the facts of homosexuality and attitudes towards it in early modern Europe, see R. Trumbach, 'Sodomitical Subcultures, Sodomitical Roles, and the Gender Revolution of the Eighteenth Century: The Recent Historiography,' in *Unauthorized Sexual Behavior during the Enlightenment*, ed. R. P. Maccubin, New York, 1986.

61 P. G. Boucé, 'Some Sexual Beliefs and Myths in Eighteenth-Century England,' in his *Sexuality in Eighteenth-Century England*, Manchester, 1982; P. G. Boucé, 'Aspects of Sexual Tolerance and Intolerance in Eighteenth Century England,' *British Journal for Eighteenth Century Studies*, 3–4, 1980–1, pp. 175–80; L. Stone, *Family, Sex and Marriage in England 1500–1800*, London, 1977, pp. 513–16; T. Tarczylo, *Sexe et liberté au siècle des lumières*, Paris, 1983.

62 This evidence comes from the testimony of witnesses in separation and divorce trials in eighteenth-century England, in the Court of Arches and King's Bench. In a list of London prostitutes in 1788, only one boasted of her skill at fellatio (*Harris's List of Covent Garden Ladies for the year 1788*, p. 88). One specifically states that 'she will permit you to . . . examine her whole naked figure,' as if this were a rare attraction (p. 40), and another that 'she is willing to appear in the dress of pure nature' (p. 71).

63 G. Vigarello, *Le Propre et le sale: L'hygiène du corps depuis le moyen âge*, Paris, 1985, p. 118 and *passim*.

64 E. Shorter, *A History of Women's Bodies*, New York, 1983. There is little doubt that Shorter greatly exaggerates the horrors of childbirth and the prevalence of gynaecological diseases in the pre-modern period.

65 N. McKendrick, 'Josiah Wedgwood and the Commercialization of the Potteries,' in *The Birth of a Consumer Society*, ed. N. McKendrick, J. Brewer and J. H. Plumb, Bloomington, Ind., 1982, p. 113.

66 W. Acton, *Functions and Disorders of the Reproductive System*, London, 1857; for the repressive interpretation of Victorian England, see Stone, *op. cit.*, pp. 666–79; B. Barker-Benfield, 'The Spermatic Economy: A Nineteenth Century View of Sexuality,' *Feminist Studies*, I, 1972; *Suffer and Be Still*, ed. M. Vicinus, Bloomington Ind., 1972; A. Comfort, *The Anxiety-Makers*, London, 1967; W. Young, *Eros Denied*, London, 1964; P. T. Cominos, 'Late Victorian Sexual Respectability and the Social System,' *International Review of Social History*, VIII, 1963.

67 For the more liberal interpretation of Victorian sexuality, see F. B. Smith, 'Sexuality in Britain, 1800–1900: Some Suggested Revisions,' in *The Widening Sphere: Changing Roles of Victorian Women*, ed. M. Vicinus, New York, 1977; P. Branca, *Silent Sisterhood*, London, 1975, pp. 126–9; P. Gay, *The Bourgeois Experience, Victoria to Freud*, Vol. I, *Education of the Senses*, Oxford, 1984. For America, there is an admirably balanced overview in C. N. Degler, *At Odds: Women and the Family in America 1776 to the Present*, New York, 1980, chs 11, 12.

68 Gay, *op. cit.*, pp. 71–108.

69 Acton, *op. cit.* (1865 edn) pp. 112–13; C. N. Degler, 'What Ought to Be and What Was: Women's Sexuality in the Nineteenth Century,' *American Historical Review*, LXXIX, 1974.

70 E. H. Hare, 'Masturbatory Insanity: The History of an Idea,' *Journal of Mental Science*, CVIII, 1962; R. P. Neuman, 'Masturbation, Madness and the Modern Concepts of Childhood and Adolescence,' *Journal of Social History*, 1975; R. H. Macdonald, 'The Frightful Consequences of Onanism: Notes on the History of a Delusion,' *Journal of the History of Ideas*, XXVIII, 1967; and J. Stengers, and A. Van Neck, *Histoire d'une grande peur: la masturabation*, Brussels, 1984.

71 M. J. Quinlan, *Victorian Prelude*, London, 1940; G. L. Mosse, *Nationalism and Sexuality: Respectability and Abnormal Sexuality in Modern Europe*, New York, 1985; Barker-Benfield, *op. cit.*

72 J. R. Gillis, 'Peasant, Plebeian and Proletarian Marriage in Britain 1600–1900,' in *Proletarianization and Family Life*, ed. D. Levine, New York, 1984.

73 J. R. Walkowitz, *Prostitution and Victorian Society: Women, Class and the State*, New York, 1980.

74 Marcus, *op. cit.*

75 L. Crompton, *Bryon and Greek Love: Homophobia in Nineteenth Century England*, Berkeley, 1985; J. Chandos, *Boys Together: the English Public Schools 1800–1864*, New Haven, 1984, ch. 14.

76 Crompton, *op. cit.*

77 Review of L. Crompton by B. Knox in the *New York Review of Books*, 19 December 1985, p. 6.

78 Ariès, 'Love in Married Life,' p. 68; W. Masters and V. Johnson, *Human Sexual Response*, Boston, 1966; A. Comfort, *The Joy of Sex*, New York, 1972.

79 Béjin, *op. cit.*, p. 212.

80 Veyne, 'La Famille et l'amour,' pp. 37–9.

81 Dodds, *op. cit.*, pp. 36, 136–7.

82 Boswell, *op. cit.*, pp. 31–6.

83 H. R. Trevor-Roper, 'The European Witch-craze of the Sixteenth and Seventeenth Centuries,' in his *The European Witch-craze*, New York, 1956; *Witchcraft in Europe 1100–1700*, ed. A. C. Kors and E. Peters, Philadelphia, 1972, nos 14–20.

84 Ruggiero, *op. cit.*, pp. 41–43.

85 Bodde, *op. cit.*, pp. 166–70.

86 Opinion polls among the young in America are already revealing evidence of more conservative attitudes towards sexuality than in recent decades (*New York Times*, 20 August 1985, pp. C1, C5).

20 OLD AGE

1 P. Ariès, *Western Attitudes Towards Death*, Baltimore, 1974; M. Vovelle, *Mourir Autrefois*, Paris, 1974.
2 B. R. Wilson, *The Youth Culture and the Universities*, London, 1970, p. 219; F. W. Burgess in *Social Welfare of the Aging*, ed. J. Kaplan and G. J. Aldridge, New York, 1962, p. 350.
3 D. H. Fischer, *Growing Old in America*, New York, 1977; K. Thomas, *Age and Authority in Early Modern England*, Proceedings of the British Academy, LXII, 1976; P. Laslett, 'The History of Aging and the Aged' in his *Family Life and Illicit Love in Earlier Generations*, Cambridge, 1977.
4 S. Smith, 'Growing Old in Early Stuart England', *Albion*, 8, 1976, p. 126.
5 O. Hufton, *The Poor in Eighteenth Century France, 1750–1789*, Oxford, 1975.
6 S. N. Katz, 'Thomas Jefferson and the Right to Property in Revolutionary America', *Journal of Law and Economics*, January 1976; C. Ray Keim, 'Primogeniture and Entail in Colonial Virginia', *Wilson and Mary Quarterly*, Third Series, XXV, 1968.

21 DEATH

For the peace and leisure in which to think out this review I am indebted to the hospitality of the Rockefeller Foundation at the Villa Serbelloni at Bellagio. Some helpful suggestions were supplied by my Bellagio co-residents, Professors Dorothy Nelkin and Joseph Berliner.

1 E. Panofsky, *Tomb Sculpture*, New York, 1964, p. 9.
2 Panofsky, *op. cit.*, A. Tenenti, *La Vie et la Mort à travers l'Art du XVième Siècle*, Paris, 1952; A. Tenenti, *Il Senso della morte e l'Amore della Vita nel Rinascimento*, Turin, 1957.
3 P. Ariès, *L'Homme devant la Mort*, Paris, 1977. P. Ariès, *Western Attitudes towards Death from the Middle Ages to the Present*, Baltimore, 1974. See the revealing interview of Philippe Ariès with André Burguière published in *Le Nouvel Observateur*, 20 February 1978.
4 Philippe Ariès, *Centuries of Childhood*, London, 1962.
5 L. Stone, *The Family, Sex and Marriage in England, 1500–1800*, New York, 1977.
6 Michel Vovelle, *Piété Baroque et DéChristianisation: les Attitudes devant la Mort en provence au XVIIIᵉ Siècle*, Paris, 1973; Pierre Chaunu, *Mourir à Paris*, Paris, 1977.
7 Gaby et Michel Vovelle, *Vision de la Mort et de l'Au-delà en Provence d'après les Autels des Ames du purgatoire*, Paris, 1970.
8 For more favorable views of the contribution of statistical studes to the history of attitudes towards death, see P. Chaunu, 'Un nouveau Champ pour l'Histoire sérielle: le Quantitatif au troisième Niveau,'

in *Mélanges Fernand Braudel*, Toulouse, 1973; E. Le Roy Ladurie, 'Chaunu, Lebrun, Vovelle: la nouvelle Histoire de la Mort' in his *le Territoire de l'Historien*, Paris, 1973.

9 F. Lebrun, *Les Hommes et la Mort en Anjou*, Paris, 1971.

10 P. Chaunu, 'Meurir à Paris XVIᵉ–XVIIᵉ–XVIIIᵉ Siècles,' *Annales: Economies, Sociétés, Civilisations*, 31 (1), Jan.–Feb. 1976, pp. 34–5.

11 J. McManners, *Reflections on the Death Bed of Voltaire*, Oxford, 1975, pp. 14, 16, 19–23.

12 P. Chaunu, *op. cit.*, p. 30.

13 For similar criticisms of Ariès, see M. Vovelle, 'Les Attitudes devant la Mort: Problèmes de Méthode, Approches, et Lectures différentes,' *Annales, Economies, Sociétés, Civilisations*, 31 (1), Jan.–Feb. 1976, pp. 128–31.

14 David Stannard, *The Puritan Way of Death: a Study of Religion, Culture and Social Change*, New York, 1977, pp. x and 236.